COSMOPOLITANISM AND PLACE

AMERICAN PHILOSOPHY

John J. Stuhr, *editor*

Editorial Board
Susan Bordo
Vincent Colapietro
John Lachs
Noëlle McAfee
José Medina
Cheyney Ryan
Richard Shusterman

COSMOPOLITANISM AND PLACE

Edited by Jessica Wahman, José M. Medina, and John J. Stuhr

Indiana University Press

This book is a publication of

Indiana University Press
Office of Scholarly Publishing
Herman B Wells Library 350
1320 East 10th Street
Bloomington, Indiana 47405 USA

iupress.indiana.edu

© 2017 by Indiana University Press

All rights reserved

No part of this book may be reproduced or utilized in any form or by any means, electronic or mechanical, including photocopying and recording, or by any information storage and retrieval system, without permission in writing from the publisher.

♾ The paper used in this publication meets the minimum requirements of the American National Standard for Information Sciences—Permanence of Paper for Printed Library Materials, ANSI Z39.48-1992.

Manufactured in the United States of America

Cataloging information is available from the Library of Congress.

ISBN 978-0-253-02939-3 (cloth)
ISBN 978-0-253-03032-0 (paperback)
ISBN 978-0-253-03033-7 (ebook)

1 2 3 4 5   22 21 20 19 18 17

Contents

Introduction — vii

Part I. Reconstructing Cosmopolitan Ideals — 1

Introduction / Jessica Wahman — 3

1. Déjà Vu All Over Again?: The Challenge of Cosmopolitanism / John Lysaker — 9

2. Home, Hospitality, and the Cosmopolitan Address / Noëlle McAfee — 22

3. Cultural Heritages and Universal Principles / Juan Carlos Pereda Failache — 36

4. Not Black or White but Chocolate Brown: Reframing Issues / Jacquelyn Ann K. Kegley — 45

5. Pragmatism and the Challenge of a Cosmopolitan Aesthetics: Framing the Issues / Robert E. Innis — 59

Part II. Taking Place Seriously — 77

Introduction / José Medina — 79

6. Toward a Politics of Cohabitation: "Dwelling" in the Manner of Wayfarers / Vincent Colapietro — 85

7. Cosmopolitan Ignorance and "Not Knowing Your Place" / José Medina — 107

8. America and Cosmopolitan Responsibility: Some Thoughts on an Itinerant Duty / Jeff Edmonds — 123

9. Loss of Place / Megan Craig — 139

10. The Loss of Confidence in the World / Josep E. Corbí — 161

11. Climate Change and Place: Delimiting Cosmopolitanism / Nancy Tuana — 181

Part III. Reimagining Home and World   *197*

    Introduction / John J. Stuhr   *199*

12 Citizen or Guest?: Cosmopolitanism as Homelessness / Jessica Wahman   *207*

13 Cosmopolitan Hope / Jennifer L. Hansen   *222*

14 Hospitality or Generosity?: Cosmopolitan Transactions / Cynthia Gayman   *235*

15 On Cosmopolitan Publics and Online Communities / Erin C. Tarver   *249*

16 A New "International of Decent Feelings"?: Cosmopolitanism and the Erasure of Class / William S. Lewis   *264*

17 Somewhere, Dreaming of Cosmopolitanism / John J. Stuhr   *280*

    Bibliography   *297*

    Index   *315*

Introduction

We live in an increasingly interconnected world. It is a world of global manufacturing and trade, international travel and almost instant communication, shared climate change and epidemics, and far-flung wars and campaigns of terror. And it is a world of different languages, different narratives, different standards of living. Nations and their borders and boundaries mark us differently as citizens or tourists or immigrants or refugees or homeless.

What is the place of a cosmopolitan morality or politics or culture in this world? What is required of us, and what is possible for us, if we adopt a cosmopolitan worldview that holds that human beings are citizens of the cosmos, equally everywhere citizens, and that there is a universal morality that binds us collectively to care for and respect one another? Should we be cosmopolitans in our feeling and thinking? Should we be cosmopolitans in our actions and institutions? If so, why and how?

Moreover, what is the place of cosmopolitanism in a world of different places—a world of different neighborhoods, different tribes, different nations, and different languages, lineages, and cultures? What can be the status of cosmopolitanism in a world of plural places—most of which, for any particular person, are not home? How might it be possible to articulate and adopt a cosmopolitanism that begins with the reality of place, of multiple places?

The chapters in this volume take up these questions. They address and reconstruct the meaning and value of cosmopolitanism and its moral, political, economic, and cultural challenges to us—both individually and collectively. In doing so, they provide critical perspectives on who "we" are. They also address the importance of place and of differences that cannot be universalized, including the experience of home and community, ignorance of one's own place, and threats to and loss of place. Finally, the chapters here strive to reimagine cosmopolitanism in terms of homelessness rather than home, hope rather than knowledge, pluralism rather than universalism, multiple differences and contestations rather than commonalities, and an agenda for practice rather than an antecedent truth.

It is not possible to avoid these questions of cosmopolitanism and place. Even their evasion will not make them vanish. It also is not possible to answer these questions finally and for all. This volume makes no pretense of doing so. It aims simply to critically clarify thinking and its traditions, to expand our imaginations and present new possibilities for understanding ourselves and our societies, and to provide resources for the creation of more intelligent practice and the realization of more expansive ideals. We invite all readers of this volume to join in and improve this endeavor.

Jessica Wahman, José Medina, and John J. Stuhr

COSMOPOLITANISM AND PLACE

PART I
RECONSTRUCTING COSMOPOLITAN IDEALS

Introduction

Jessica Wahman

The chapters in this first part confront key topics to be addressed by a contemporary cosmopolitanism. All suggest that cosmopolitanism is an orientation worth considering, and some argue explicitly in favor of the position. Many of the authors draw our attention to an increasingly globalized world and suggest this is a prominent reason for taking cosmopolitanism seriously. Our growing access to and consistent impact on one another, they argue, increase our awareness of human connectedness, rendering the possibility of entirely localized commitments both rationally untenable and ethically irresponsible. At the same time, each author claims that a feasible cosmopolitanism, despite its broad vision and aspirations, must nonetheless be rooted in specific places and emanate from situated orientations. Each assumes that a straightforward universalism trivializes the broad multiplicity of ways of life and fails to heed the lessons of traditional cosmopolitanism's refusal to address them. As a result, the arguments affirm a "placed" cosmopolitanism as a pluralistic alternative that can, at the same time, account for our ability to dialogue across cultures and empathize with different others.

To support the claim that cosmopolitanism is worth our consideration, the chapters call our attention to two important observable and likely related aspects of human life: (a) the ability for people to build shared understanding from different points of view, and (b) the possibility of and demand for empathy with human suffering. In the first case, many of the authors focus on possibilities for communication based on reasons and on overlapping experiences. John Lysaker, for example, introduces the classical Greek concept of logos to pose a basic challenge to contemporary cosmopolitanism: how are we to affirm and explain the communicative power of rational speech without grounding it in divine cosmic law? Carlos Pereda, in effect, takes up this challenge by suggesting that existing human practices of justification through reasons contain basic assumptions about the possibility of universally shared understanding. This possibility is not merely theoretical: it is grounded in our observed ability to consider arguments from another person's point of view. And Robert Innis, in considering the possibilities of a cosmopolitan aesthetics, argues that the production of a work of art, at least insofar as the artist aims to be appreciated and understood by others, implies an intelligibility that extends beyond the personal and particular.

In the second case, where the appeal of cosmopolitanism is explained in terms of ethical demands, Lysaker, Noëlle McAfee, and Jacquelyn Kegley each make their cases by relying on the intuition that we should not be indifferent to the well-being of others or to their suffering. As Lysaker notes, the cosmopolitan belief that "nothing human is alien to me" articulates a possible moral virtue as much as it does an assumption about the powers of rational communication. McAfee, for her part, addresses the ways in which political demonstrations and acts of resistance around the world make demands on our attention, and she asserts that to turn away from such demands, no matter how distant, is ethically problematic. And, finally, Kegley shows that the communities we belong to are more porous, shifting, and interwoven than nationalist theories would acknowledge, and that therefore our ethical commitments are better understood as operating on a global scale, albeit to varying degrees.

While the authors affirm the importance of concerning ourselves, in some way, with all humanity and believe in the possibility of shared understanding (even among people coming from very different cultural standpoints and environments), they recognize problems with the classic, rationalist and foundational, cosmopolitanism and its traditional notion of the world citizen. As a result, these chapters take epistemological positions that are empiricist, provisional, and contextualized and thus promote cosmopolitanism as a fallibilistic worldly orientation that aims to preserve a sense of place. Against theoretical attempts to identify the essential characteristics of human nature or to ground all reality in a set of rationally derived laws, a situated and experimental cosmopolitanism would be built on empirically based assertions that are perspectival, contingent, and contestable. Lysaker suggests that cosmopolitanism's sense of "totality"—a universally shared and comprehensible world—should be built on social and psychological theories instead of on analytic, or definitional, claims. Kegley similarly notes that cosmopolitanism does not require an overarching theory or set of a priori conditions for who or what will count as belonging. Rather, any account of human characteristics, values, demands, and interests is to be determined empirically and always, in principle, open to challenge. This, as McAfee puts it, "allows for us to be citizens of a certain place as well as citizens of the world." Innis, rejecting an aesthetics of a priori principles, constructed in the abstract and applied to particular cases, presents his cosmopolitan aesthetics as a site of interweaving hermeneutic practices and asserts that such situated inquiry would produce aesthetic theories that grow from and depend on particularities. Even Pereda's three universal principles of rational discussion read more like guidelines for how to engage in reasonable communication than they do transcendental conditions for its very possibility.

Lysaker opens this part of the volume by presenting a challenge to contemporary cosmopolitan theory. In "Déjà Vu All Over Again? The Challenge of Cosmopolitanism," Lysaker notes the political failure of the nation-state to address the dynamics of globalization and suggests that this may at least partially explain the appeal of a theory that treats human beings as world citizens with global rights and responsibilities. Cosmopolitanism, he argues, "presents a vibrant conception of citizenship grounded in a dynamic learning process regarding the good, which renders indifference to one another a personally and communally debilitating vice." However, this, by itself is not enough of an argument in its favor. To make cosmopolitanism a "viable political project" in the present day, a proponent will have to deal with four major topics endemic to the classical version of the theory but not easily assimilated with contemporary philosophical and political realities: (a) logos (rational speech), (b) norms, (c) totality, and (d) character. Choosing to focus on the latter two, Lysaker argues that engagement with all humanity within a communal and comprehensible domain will require rich social and psychological accounts of human behavior and broad literacy regarding the wide variety of existing cultural meanings and values. Because we are unlikely to be convinced, in this day and age, of the divine unity of a rationally ordered universe, some empirical account must be given of how the world could be viewed as anything like a totality, that is, a universally shared cosmos. To build such a shared world, he argues, we will have to cultivate attitudes and practices that render us concerned with and sensitive to one another: capable of mutual recognition in a world of plural interpretations and meanings, capable of learning from one another, and adaptive in our own habits.

McAfee focuses on this very notion of globally involved practices and habits in "Home, Hospitality, and the Cosmopolitan Address." Here, McAfee presents us with the concept of a cosmopolitan imaginary, one that refers us to "all others" or "the whole world" and, in doing so, can help us reconstruct our sense of interrelatedness. The ethicality of this universal construct is rooted, she claims, in empirical evidence that people the world over generally prefer to direct their own lives. That is, she finds an implicit claim about the universality of the desire for self-determination in demands that "the world" recognize a given act of oppression. (It should be noted that McAfee does not use this empirical claim to make assertions about the nature of human desire in an atemporal or absolute sense. It may well be the case that a worldwide desire for autonomy is a historical contingency, even if it is at present widespread and deeply felt.) In addition to its empirical basis, the cosmopolitan imaginary employs the "meaningful fictions" of rights, dignity, and a cosmos through which we are bound, all of which place demands on us to respond when we discover these moral principles have been violated. Public demands for dignity and freedom can be seen as cosmopolitan addresses and ethical global engagements as necessarily democratic. Taken together, the elements of the cosmopolitan imaginary can, she asserts, open us to new ethical engagements on a global scale. Furthermore, as much as it is globally concerned, an equally important aspect of this world-minded fictive construction is its situatedness: "A cosmopolitan address has to issue from some particular place even as it calls for the world to live up to something better than what is the case. . . . The cosmopolitan address is at the same time particular and universal." Instead of a timeless theory grounded in necessary conditions of human existence, McAfee views her cosmopolitan imaginary as a historically contingent result of changing technologies and international forces. It is not that we ought to care because we belong to the same logical category "human being": rather, we find ourselves more broadly concerned because, in fact, we find ourselves to be more widely interconnected.

In "Cultural Heritages and Universal Principles," Pereda takes up the challenge of reinterpreting the logos of classical cosmopolitanism to fit a more pluralistic contemporary reality. He argues that, in the context of a plurality of norms—not only in the global presence of different cultures but as competing norms within individuals—human beings nonetheless have a practice of rationally justifying these multifarious beliefs to one another and to themselves. This, he claims, implies a kind of universality or at least a presumption of being able to transcend one's normative "home" and form an understanding with others. (Note: this is acknowledged to be a possibility, not an inevitability. The alternative method of persuasion by force remains.) Pereda proposes that we cannot help but start with what he calls a "general credulity principle," that is, a starting point of trusting our own norms and beliefs. But once the demand for justification arises and we are willing to meet that demand with reasons instead of violence, these beliefs operate as presumptive starting points—initially trusted but, in principle, open to question. Once dialogue begins, a second presumption is at work: the universality presumption. To be a reason, Pereda demonstrates, a proposition must be comprehensible as such; that is, it should be convincing to everyone who understands it. This does not mean that every proposition given as a reason will actually serve as one: we can disagree over whether a given statement is true or actually supports the conclusion. Such a qualifier implies that, the same time, there needs to be an ability and commitment to taking up the point of view of the other person. That is, the universality presumption is not just about giving reasons for one's own view but listening and giving fair consideration to the reasons given by others. This brings Pereda to the third, "democratic," presumption in which participants in a discussion are given equal status as reasonable interlocutors. Taken together, this set of presumptions is argued to provide a context in which rational discussion can grow out of a normative pluralism instead of having to put such important and meaningful particularities aside.

Kegley presents us with her version of a pluralistic unity by promoting a "rooted cosmopolitanism." In "Not Black or White but Chocolate Brown: Reframing Issues," Kegley argues that cosmopolitanism need not dichotomize particular and universal relations. By investigating and then rejecting the conventional dualism between individual and community in the debate between nationalism and cosmopolitanism, Kegley argues that a rooted cosmopolitanism amounts to a paradoxical "cosmopolitan place" in which family—and other more intimate and localized—loyalties are imaginatively extended to others. These expanded loyalties do not necessarily weaken local bonds; rather, the broader sensibilities can in turn sensitize us to and enrich our more immediate relationships. To make her case, Kegley first analyzes defenses of nationalism made on communitarian, social justice, and democratic grounds and concludes that such arguments needlessly oppose their positions to a cosmopolitan one in making their cases for thick communities with strong political allegiances and defenses against the forces of globalization. Second, Kegley considers the relationship between place and identity formation. Despite the power that geographical location has in shaping us, both as individuals and as members of a group, places can shift, change, and even travel. We are not invariably rooted in a single location that belongs exclusively and indelibly to "us" or "our group." Therefore, she concludes, cosmopolitanism need not be placeless or espouse a universal cosmic "place." Finally, Kegley draws on American pragmatic idealist Josiah Royce and his concept of the great community to argue for a cosmopolitanism that builds outward from family loyalties to integrate with other groups and, ultimately, within a world community that encompasses and is enriched by varying points of view, cultural commitments, and strategies for determining the good. As with McAfee's cosmopolitan imaginary, Kegley argues that the rooted cosmopolitan community would have to be grounded in the values of dignity, autonomy, equality, and basic human rights. Furthermore, and in line with both McAfee and Pereda, Kegley views the bond of this global community to reside not in a shared human essence but in democratic institutions and habits.

Innis completes this part of the volume by considering the possibilities of a cosmopolitan aesthetics. In so doing, many of the geopolitical themes we have already seen addressed are brought to bear on the world of artistic practices, productions, and interpretations. In "Pragmatism and the Challenge of a Cosmopolitan Aesthetics: Framing the Issues," Innis takes Ben-Ami Scharfstein's 2009 book, *Art Without Borders: A Philosophical Exploration of Art and Humanity*, as his inspiration for composing a pluralistic and pragmatic cosmopolitan aesthetics. Such an aesthetics, he claims, will have to involve a set of interpretive processes rather than an overarching theory of what counts as and constitutes art. To accomplish this, Innis envisions a phenomenological and hermeneutic site of different ways of experiencing beauty (or beauties, given Innis's use of

Crispin Sartwell's *Six Names of Beauty* to show how a concept central to a theory of aesthetics refracts into pluralities as much as it unifies). This experiential background becomes a sort of underdetermined totality (reminding us of Lysaker's earlier challenge) within which the multitude of specific aesthetic theories and artistic traditions emerge. As such, cosmopolitan aesthetic praxis will not be placeless but an intertwining of places. It will be rooted (thus resonating with Kegley's cosmopolitan claims) but also, as with Pereda's account of rational communication, should be capable of transcending the provincial and particular. Innis's concern for such universalist possibilities rests on the idea that art makes a demand on our attention. As such, his advocacy for a cosmopolitan aesthetics is an ethical one similar to McAfee's treatment of the cosmopolitan address. As Innis claims, one engaged with a given work is in some sense obligated to attend to what is put forth as art, no matter how unfamiliar, different, or even threatening.

There is a performative element to Innis's chapter that should not be overlooked. He makes his case for a cosmopolitan site of aesthetic encounters by way of a sustained comparative analysis of Dewey's phenomenological account of aesthetic experience and François Jullien's metaphysical interpretation of Chinese literati painting. He does not do so to present them as the theoretical basis for artistic interpretation but to exemplify aesthetics as a practice of interpretive interweaving. As such, he performs the very hermeneutic process he is, at the same time, identifying as a cosmopolitan aesthetics. Ultimately, Innis invites us to understand these practices of aesthetic engagement as extending beyond artistic concerns and applying to broader possibilities for shared meaning. As he notes, "A truly cosmopolitan aesthetics in the pragmatist mode is a variegated set of hermeneutical exercises in learning to attend to the world and to attend to our modes of attending, including becoming aware of both their limits, their heuristic powers, their material supports, and their affinities."

1 Déjà Vu All Over Again?
The Challenge of Cosmopolitanism

John Lysaker

At one time, let's say 1990, it seemed as if relational ontologies marked a significant advance for those trying to think past the limits of liberal political theory and the more general posture of the modern subject. Appreciating the interconnectedness of all things, and thus the dependency of any given thing, was taken to have more or less clear ethical-political implications, the kind that should lead to a less violent, even a more cooperative, world. The thought was that reified ideologies lead liberal automata to operate in ahistorical silos, producing power and accumulating capital without a feel for the karmic havoc they wreaked on others, the planet, future generations, and eventually themselves. While I was and remain a proponent of such ontologies, even then I felt déjà vu all over again. How often will we reinterpret the world in order to change it? Yes, the world is a web of relations, but violence and exploitation and not really giving a shit are all relations, and no less so than a kiss, a loan, or a high five (all of which can go awry, by the way).

Now, I don't think the problem—of how to relate—goes away if we realize that our being-in-the-world is oriented by more than propositional attitudes, that is, if we do not only think about our relations in terms of beliefs and their assertoric content but also acknowledge how affect, the unconscious, cultural semiosis, ecology, what have you impacts those relations. Those sites render our relations more determinate, and thus inquiry into them enriches self-knowledge, but multiplying and deepening the number and manner of our relations, and developing insights into their currents, still requires us to sort, evaluate, and commit to particular ways of being-in-the-relating. Said even less temperately, relate all you want, and in whatever way you want, (a) such insights won't transform us into relational beings since relations already go all the way down, and thus (b) there is no eluding questions concerning which kinds of relations merit our allegiance, which our meliorating power, and which our aversion, even our active resistance.

Not that the character of our relations might not change, thus generating anew the question of how best to empower or meliorate those relations in their specificity. I suppose that at certain times it was meaningful, possibly even prudent, to think of one's politics and economics as outside global orders. House, village, valley, from sea to shining sea, multiple eco-geo-political forces help shape our polities and delimit their horizons, including those that concern us and them, namely, who we mean when we say *we*. But that seems like a long time ago. Global culture is ubiquitous. Markets as well as the rule (and misrule) of law are full of objects and events, even persons, that can easily serve as symbols of how what once was far is now next door and how the shirt on my back has traveled the world. And as most everyone knows who wants to know, the planet, at an ecosystemic level, is caught in (and impacting) the currents of what we might term such eco-political orders, thereby indicating that we always should think about our "houses" (οἶκοι), and production more generally, at the intersection of economies and ecologies.

But how does one order such a web of nested relations? Because lack of charity also should begin at home, "the experiment entrusted to the hands of the American people," namely, the United States (to recall a line from Washington's inaugural address), still struggles to facilitate life, liberty, and the pursuit of happiness, particularly if one sets the United States into a global context. As Habermas has observed, the unilateral invasion of Iraq made it difficult to regard the United States as a "guarantor of international rights" or as a leading proponent of the rule of law in international arenas.[1] One has to wonder, however, whether the invasion of Iraq was the decisive blow. Since World War II, the United States repeatedly underwrote coups of democratically elected governments, including Iran in 1953, the Dominican Republic in 1963, and Chile in 1973, to name relatively uncontroversial examples.

Domestically the United States continues to face intensified objections to a perceived usurpation of civil society and the rule of law by corporate wealth and interests. One didn't need to be a part of the Occupy Movement to appreciate the disparity currently between 99 percent of the nation and the so-called 1 Percent, who, according to research summarized by the Center on Budget and Policy Priorities, took in two-thirds of the "nation's total income gains from 2002 to 2007," and enjoyed a "larger share of income [also in 2007] . . . than at any time since 1928."[2] But *appreciate* is the wrong word. Such concentrations are troubling. For one, concentrations of wealth, particularly when they persist across generations, threaten equality of opportunity given that greater socioeconomic status (which, while not reducible to wealth, is nevertheless heavily influenced by wealth) correlates with greater access to education, medical, and legal resources, as well as greater freedom from crime and pollution. Moreover, profound disparities in wealth allow the 1 Percent to wield enormous political influence. Super PACs, for example (political action committees), can bankroll candidates with potentially unlimited funds, thereby rendering the "one person one vote" conception of democratic law formation a de facto empty slogan in a time of media-driven will formation. In short, if one considers domestic and international arenas, the United States no longer appears to embody the kind of regime that might orient those seeking to create, maintain, or reconstruct democratic legal orders.

These are disorienting times. And one doesn't find much footing if one imagines a political future based on the nation-state, even though, at the level of political structure, the nation-state remains the principal arena where positive law is debated, written, executed, and reviewed. But, while the nation-state remains a legal, economic, and militarized form that influences the fate of billions of persons, concentrations of global capital likewise influence the fate of billions, and in ways that are irreducible to the policies of nation-states even as these concentrations profoundly shape the policies of nation-states. Moreover, global economies generate a host of externalities, such as global warming, that impact far more than contracted partners.[3] To gain a feel for the scope of global capital, consider that there are well over two thousand multinational US corporations, each of which "holds at least a 10% direct ownership stake in at least one foreign business enterprise."[4] There are also numerous other companies that simply set up shop around the world, either directly or through subcontracted labor. Procter & Gamble, for example, the world's largest consumer products maker, has operations in more than 90 countries and sales in more than 150.

Note that global capital does not only flow out of the United States. Foreign corporations now own companies once inseparable from America's global image. InBev, a company formed in 2004 when the Belgian company Interbrew merged with the Brazilian company AmBev, bought Anheuser-Busch in 2008. The current company, Anheuser-Busch InBev, is the home of brands like Budweiser, Stella Artois, Becks, and Bass. Even in so-called first-world countries, one cannot presume, therefore, that the commercial forces constituting a nation's economic infrastructure are thoroughly or even principally beholden to that nation's legal structure or to its prevailing cultural self-understanding.

I underscore the porous, malleable nature of nation-states because our political present is uncertain at levels that exceed de facto political orders. The flow of capital profoundly influences global fates, and its migrations are difficult if not, at least for the present, impossible to fathom. It is not only our political imagination on the ropes, therefore. Those processes by which material needs are met (and often generated) have also fallen into question. It seems plain as day, I think, that we find ourselves lacking a concrete feel for vital political futures.

In such a bewildering context, one can understand the desire to champion cosmopolitanism. The world of nation-states (as well as those peoples and persons without states) is enmeshed in a dynamic economic system that binds the fates of agents who live at great geographical and cultural distances from one another. A basic commitment to democracy (which underwrites the concerns just expressed) should lead one, therefore, to something like the following: all lives that are subjects in and subject to the emerging global order should have some say in the formation of that order. "No globalization without representation!" the pamphlet might begin. If this intuition is sound, it seems that the present needs a workable conception of the "citizen of the world" that articulates rights, duties, and obligations shared by all who are caught up in collective actions that deny representation to so many directly and profoundly affected by those actions.

I feel the intuitive tug of cosmopolitan discourse, but I have my worries as well. I thus want to consider, in a general and preliminary way, some of the challenges that face cosmopolitan efforts to provide something like a conception of global citizenship, if not an outright global political order. Of course, such approaches are multiform. For some, cosmopolitanism entails a commitment to global justice pursuable through manifold means. Believing that the fate of persons hinges in large measure on their place in global relations whose character derives from more than nation-state legislation, and/or sharing the Rawls-inspired belief that "country of origin" is morally irrelevant with regard to principles of distributive justice, many seek principles and institutions that secure global access to primary goods and protections: for example, Anthony Appiah, Charles Beitz, Simon Caney, and Martha Nussbaum. Other cosmopolitans like Jürgen Habermas, inspired by the European Union and Kant's conception of perpetual peace, seek a constitutionally based, international legal order authorized to regulate how nation-states engage one another and other international actors like multinational corporations and NGOs. Convinced that the rule of law never fulfills its aims, others such as Judith Butler and Jacques Derrida seek an interruptive sense of hospitality toward the purportedly strange or alien, one that draws us past legal compliance into a sociality of shared alterity or vulnerability in that very sharing. Finally, a fourth group containing the likes of Jeremy Waldron conceives of cosmopolitanism as an ethos committed to proactive engagements with a wide range of cultural norms in the thought that each may very well enrich lives conceived as ongoing experiments in personal and collective identity.

I am not surprised to encounter a vast range of views under the figure of a citizen of the world. And yet, despite these differences, certain historical sources, phrases, and concepts recur among cosmopolitans: (a) Diogenes the Cynic and his Stoic heirs, each of whom identifies as a "citizen of the cosmos"; (b) Kant and the "right of hospitality"; and (c) Terrence's *The Self-Tormentor*, which sometimes functions, at least rhetorically, to establish continuity among classical and modern cosmopolitanism.

In what follows, I reflect on (a) and (c). Although both derive from classical cosmopolitanism, the Cynic-Stoic roots of cosmopolitanism remain instructive for a politics hoping to address and inform global political phenomena beyond the figure of the nation-state. They are instructive because they bear with them certain topoi of concern that I cannot imagine any version of cosmopolitanism not addressing. And yet, those topoi seem conspicuously absent in much of the discourses of contemporary cosmopolitanism. I wish to recall them, therefore (classical discussions and their topoi), to clarify what I take to be some challenges facing contemporary cosmopolitanism. Whether it can meet those challenges is a matter I do not pursue here, but I go as far as to argue that these challenges cannot be met if cosmopolitanism maintains a Rawlsian disregard for social theory.

In identifying as a *kosmopolitês*, a "citizen of the cosmos," Diogenes and Aurelius situate themselves within a cosmic order that purportedly governs nature in its manifold appearing. On their view, rational laws, divine in origin, regulate nature, and thus each of us is a "citizen" in virtue of living under these laws. (This is why, at least when referring to classical cosmopolitanism, we should speak of the "citizen of the cosmos" and not the "citizen of the world.") Cynic and Stoic cosmopolitans are able, therefore, to conceive of a morally thick, universal human community. The thought runs something like this.[5] Humans are human through their access to the logos, what we might term rational speech or the ability to give an account of oneself and one's world. Importantly, having logos involves more than having learned speech-making techniques. It involves some access to the genuine order of things, including the soul, the city, and a world of cities, as well as a grasp of one's obligation to live in accord with those orders, which is why I offer the phrase *rational speech* as a nonliteral translation for *logos*. But "access" and "grasp" probably say too little. What is really required is the concrete capacity to learn about, articulate, and act on one's obligations, a set of capacities that, at least in classical philosophy, one associates with ethos or character.

Because logos is divine, all beings who access it share in divinity and thereby merit a certain degree and kind of respect and concern that local custom or rule cannot negate. That said, the concrete commitments of cosmic concern may move in multiple directions. But wherever it leads, it runs through the logos and thus through rational speech. And this is nowhere more evident than in Terence's *The Self-Tormentor* (§139–40). Chremes, a noble, comes upon another noble, Menedemus, who is toiling in the latter's own field. Chremes finds this astounding and asks why. Menedemus replies, peevishly: "Have you so much leisure, Chremes, from your own affairs, that you can attend to those of others—those which don't concern you?" Chremes then delivers a thought that has captivated cosmopolitans of many stripes: "I am a man, and nothing that concerns a man do I deem a matter of indifference to me." I have employed the Project Guttenberg translation because it clarifies, I think, what it means to say, "nothing human is alien to me," which is a common gloss.[6] The claim is not simply that one human can recognize another as "human," but that each is bound in a community of mutual concern, that the affairs of another are one's own, and vice versa. But we should not forget that such concern is bound to the logos, which is why Chremes continues: "Suppose that I wish either to advise *you* in this matter, or to be informed *myself*; if *what you do* is right, that I may do the same; if it is not, *then* that I may dissuade you." Chremes's opening question is thus not improper, as one might infer from Menedemus's reply, which effectively says, "Mind your business." In fact, it is the most proper, for it inquires after the good, and thus fulfills an obligation that Chremes has to himself and to Menedemus: to discover what natural law requires of human beings at every turn.[7]

In a way, the manner in which Chremes engages Menedemus embodies the political ethos of classical cosmopolitanism. Divine law operates at each corner of the cosmos, thus offering a sense of the whole—the law-governed cosmos—as well as an anthropology by way of the category "citizen," which locates us in the cosmic order. Humans purportedly share in divine reason and thus stand closer to the gods than do other animals. Moreover, all persons share this location, and thus humans share a certain nature or "humanity," that is, we are *anthropoi*. But the designation is not merely descriptive; the divinity of the logos instantiates a moral psychology (or ethics)—the soul should be governed by logos, by the best *accounts* that can be given for those activities that are voluntary.

This notion of a properly ordered soul (or character), which leads Chremes to ask Menedemus, "Why are you laboring the fields," opens classical cosmopolitanism onto a political terrain. Natural law allows us (and requires us) to discern our obligations to one another and other polities. (In the least, it mandates that we should not be indifferent to one another.) Of course, cosmopolitans might disagree about what these obligations entail. For example, one might follow Diogenes and take the cosmic order to negate civic orders, or, like Hierocles (whom Nussbaum seems to favor), one might find a series of orders—person, family, city, cosmos—organized as concentric circles, and with that vision in tow, labor to draw the outer rings toward those whose demands are more firmly grounded in our affective (and affectionate) center.[8] But even such disagreements are bound to the logos and the demands it places on us, which sets, I think, the notion of a character, capable of rational speech, near the heart of classical cosmopolitanism.

In his book *Cosmopolitanism: Ethics in a World of Strangers*, Anthony Appiah recalls the discussion between Chremes and Menedemus.[9] He takes the famous line, which he translates as "I am human, nothing is alien to me," to express an interest in cultural contamination and cross-pollination. This probably says too much. Chremes is calling his neighbor to task, not proactively seeking out novel or different practices and conceptions of the good. In fact, Chremes may be interrogating Menedemus because laboring in the field strikes him as improper for a noble. That said, Appiah may be right that an openness to any and all paths to the good is latent within the line: "Suppose that I wish either to advise *you* in this matter, or to be informed *myself*: if *what you do* is right, that I may do the same; if it is not, *then* that I may dissuade you." In each encounter, cross-cultural or not, we may find a superior path to the good, and so we should be open to that possibility, as Appiah stresses. Then again, we might not. And if not, we may be obligated to dissuade another if we are fairly certain his or her path strays from the good, which is another way of "not being indifferent" to others—we don't walk away as they fritter away their lives or debase themselves through vices like avarice, to cite a failing still in abundance.

Generalizing from Terrence's text, Appiah suggests that a cosmopolitan bearing "tempers a respect for difference with a respect for actual human beings."[10] This isn't wrong exactly, but it obscures more than it clarifies. In the exchange between Chremes and Menedemus, there is an acknowledgment of difference but not necessarily a principled respect. Whether some habit, action, or way of life merits respect can be determined only through rational speech, through an exercise of the logos. Not that "difference" exiles one from the human community (save, perhaps, an utter incapacity of rational speech); on this classical view, we are citizens of the cosmos and we are obligated to treat one another (and ourselves) as such. But, and this is a second point, rather than leading us to respect actual persons, classical cosmopolitanism leads us to ask of one another every now and then, "What the hell are you doing with your life?"[11] That is, it leads us to interrogate actual difference (and to welcome interrogation by others) when it veers (or we veer) away from what natural law seems to prescribe, as well as to persuade others (and to welcome the persuasion of others) to get right with the gods.

As I find it, classical cosmopolitanism remains of interest because it presents a vibrant conception of citizenship grounded in a dynamic learning process regarding the good, which renders indifference to one another a personally and communally debilitating vice. But this is not to say that classical cosmopolitanism contains a viable political project for a world as confounding as ours. Because it derives its normative bases, its anthropology, and even its conception of citizenship from a divinely rooted natural law, each of its proposals will be hard-pressed to convince anyone writing after Nietzsche (and not just in a temporal sense).

In *The Gay Science*, Nietzsche writes: "After Buddha was dead, his shadow was still shown for centuries in a cave—a tremendous, gruesome shadow. God is dead; but given the way of men, there may still be caves for thousands of years in which his shadow will be shown. And we—we still have to vanquish his shadow, too."[12] As I have demonstrated, such shadows darken more than the corners of classical cosmopolitanism. Whatever energies remain within its conceptions, therefore, must be won from the wreckage of a form of life grown old.[13]

On my view, classical cosmopolitanism is most instructive as a site of seemingly integral topoi, that is, topics on which any viable form of contemporary cosmopolitanism should have a compelling position. In particular, I think that four foci of classical cosmopolitanism—totality, character, norms, and logos (or rational speech)—direct us toward what is more or less essential subject matter for contemporary discussions. This is not to say that these are only topics for cosmopolitan theory. But I cannot imagine a plausible response to our chaotic present falling silent at any of these points.

Here and now, I want to make a case for the vital importance of two of the four foci: totality and character. I elect these two because the relation of norms and logos (or rational speech) lies at the heart of debates involving Arendt, Benhabib, Habermas, Rawls, and others, and thus I doubt many cosmopolitans will find the inclusion of these topics controversial.[14] But character and totality may prove quite controversial, and thus it seems best to devote my energies to them.

Let us begin with *totality*. Classical cosmopolitanism purports to know the world it aims to settle, and it insists that knowing the nature of X is necessary for knowing the nature of X's proper bearing and development. By knowing the cosmos, more or less, it knows the place of humanity in the order things, and by knowing that place, it knows how to order the soul and cultivate character. In other words, it construes the possible (and delimits the rationally desirable) by way of the actual. Many no longer find this approach sound. Like Rawls in *Justice as Fairness*, they opt to be "realistically utopian," that is, they believe that the "limits of the possible are not given by the actual, for we can to a greater or lesser extent change political and social institutions, and much else."[15]

At its heart, the issue concerns the role of social theory and moral psychology in political philosophy. (I say this because "social theory" is the line of inquiry concerning the social whole insofar as it is a whole, and moral psychology concerns the fate and possibilities of persons within that whole. Each thus drifts into the other.) Rawls is clear, even adamant, that a political conception of justice (as opposed to a metaphysical one) need not overly concern itself with "how people actually behave in certain situations, or how institutions actually work."[16] Instead properly political conceptions aim to determine "what principles of justice are most appropriate to specify basic rights and liberties [which includes rights to primary goods], and to regulate social and economic inequalities in citizens' prospects over a complete life."[17] I do not believe that any actors can credibly perform the task Rawls sets for them without access to the ongoing findings and revisions of social theory and moral psychology. According to Rawls, principles of justice emerge out of a process of reflective equilibrium in which agents, under a veil of ignorance, formulate principles and test their adequacy by imagining their consequences: "It is also important to trace out, if only in a rough and ready way, the institutional content of the two principles. . . . We need to do this before we can endorse these principles, even provisionally. This is because the idea of reflective equilibrium involves our accepting the implications of ideals and first principles in particular cases as they arise. We cannot tell solely from the content of a political conception—from its principles and ideals—whether it is reasonable for us."[18] This passage prompts two thoughts. First, on what basis are implications anticipated? I presume that a kind of stored, empirical knowledge funds these thought experiments; that is, these "implications" are not intuitively available to agents independent of experience and learning. But if this is the case, then considerations about how "people actually behave in certain situations, or how institutions actually work" are permissible in the original position. Rawls's refusal to pursue a thoroughgoing social theory and moral psychology is thus less categorical than selective, and in a muddled fashion. Empirical knowledge is fallible and thus subject to revision. With regard to issues of justice, therefore (and this is my second point), no minimally rational agent would rely on commonsense conceptions of how well vast bureaucratic orders, for example, enable (or frustrate) political participation, or whether market economies are prone to crisis or the institution of de facto oligarchies. Moreover, with regard to primary goods, one would want to know with as much predictive power as possible what is "generally necessary to enable citizens adequately to develop and fully exercise . . . moral powers, and to pursue their determinate conceptions of the good." For example, Rawls's fifth primary good concerns the social bases of self-respect, that is, "those aspects of basic institutions normally essential if citizens are to have a lively sense of their worth as persons and to be able to advance their ends with self-confidence."[19] This is a striking requirement (particularly the reference to self-confidence) because it seems unlikely that seventy-five years ago agents in an original position would designate this as a primary good. That Rawls does so now is to his credit, but he is able to do so only given relatively recent advances in social theory and moral psychology that insist on the importance of intersubjective recognition for psychosocial development.

In the preceding paragraphs, I have suggested, through an argument with Rawls, that efforts to construct a reasonable and well-ordered polity need the resources provided by an empirically funded social theory and moral psychology. In particular, a strong feel for the full range of forces that shape human social relations, including psychological forces, is invaluable. Cosmopolitanism cannot simply propose "political" as opposed to "metaphysical" schemes, therefore. A coherent object of theoretical and practical concern (something to know and something to work on), must incorporate, and continually, the ongoing empirical findings of social theory and moral psychology and thus concern itself with totality in some rich and meaningful manner.

To think of the role of character in cosmopolitanism, return to Terrence and the notion that cosmopolitans are not indifferent to the welfare of their fellow citizens, presuming all cosmopolitans will affirm some version of this commitment. More specifically, let us specify a range of activities that cosmopolitan concern requires, and in a reciprocal manner; that is, each cosmopolitan must be able to receive what she or he also gives, namely: (a) sufficient interest in another's welfare to meaningfully attend to it; (b) the hermeneutic ability to track another's well-being; (c) the hermeneutic ability to understand how another accounts for his or her own well-being; (d) the ability to provide an account of the other's well-being; (e) the ability to work through those points where the accounts in (c) and (d) conflict; and (f) the ability to learn from and act on the results of (e).[20]

I do not suppose that the preceding list will surprise anyone. I elaborate it because it suggests that cosmopolitanism requires a certain set of capacities and thus a certain kind of character. Thus, while Benhabib is right to claim in *Another Cosmopolitanism* that the demos is not an ethnos, in a certain regard the demos needs to be present as an ethos in a majority of its constituencies.[21] Benhabib may concur, and I obviously think she must, but like many, she tends to talk about social wholes and actors without articulating the intricacies of the kinds of actions cosmopolitanism demands. For example, while she asserts that only "polities with strong democracies are capable of . . . [a] universalist rearticulation through which they refashion the meaning of their own peoplehood," she has less to say about the demands this places on personhood, although, to be fair, she does insist that many of the principal players in France's L'Affaire du Foulard proved unable to undergo the kind of "learning processes" required for there to be a genuine dialogue about all the meanings in play when students wear head scarves in French schools.[22]

In a way, everyone acknowledges the centrality of character in political life, albeit not always directly. Rawls, for example, asserts in *Justice as Fairness*: "If citizens of a well-ordered society are to recognize one another as free and equal, basic institutions must educate them to this conception of themselves."[23] Fair enough, but "conception" is not really on point, and the term betrays a weak moral psychology. What is required is not only a certain self-concept; the full-blooded capacities to reach mutual recognition are required. In Judith Butler's language from *Precarious Life*, what is required is a kind of "recognition that does not substitute the recognizer for the recognized."[24] Agreed, but also, the chief variables in this crucial difference are largely bound to character, to ethos, to a range of habits, capacities, and phronetic actions that effect a kind of self-transcending form of sociality.[25] Moreover, the issue cannot rest with the attainment of certain hermeneutic and reasoning capacities. One must also, as Benhabib's language of "learning processes" indicates, be capable of meaningfully changing one's behavior as a result of the enactment of cosmopolitan concern.

I have been trying to articulate part of what is involved in proposing cosmopolitan citizenship as a coherent object of theoretical and practical concern (though we could also speak of praxical concern). In closing, let me identify two implications of setting character at the heart of cosmopolitan concern, and in a manner that recalls some of what classical cosmopolitanism teaches. First, appreciating the kind of character that cosmopolitanism requires makes evident that being a "citizen of the cosmos" (or "the world") is a task, not just a given or earned standing in an ethical and/or political community. Moreover, if one embraces "citizen of the world" as a kind of legal standing, one is also embracing, at least at the level of rationality, the tasks that that identification entails, several of which I have enumerated. This is to say that while citizenship brings rights and liberties, it also brings responsibilities, some of which we, at least for the time being, will not know how to fulfill, and often because our grasp of global political phenomena is poor. A good deal of social-theoretical work (or eco-social-theoretical work given the ecological situatedness of social orders), thus awaits whoever wishes to instantiate and enter a cosmopolitan political order.

Second, because cosmopolitanism names a task with irreducible personal dimensions, whoever wishes to *not* be indifferent to their fellow citizens needs to be able to "speak their language" in the full, metaphorical reach of that phrase. To this end, I find the search for "common universal principles that encompass all human activities," which Garrett Wallace Brown and David Held associate with "cultural cosmopolitanism," to be limiting at best.[26] On the presumption that even global persons need to meet by way of logos, and a living one at that, global literacy is more to the point. And since nothing stands still for very long, the education in mutual respect that Rawls envisions, at least in a culturally cosmopolitan setting, must prove to be lifelong (though we might also speak of mutual response-ability, as many Levinas-inspired theorists do, e.g., Kelly Oliver). Not that one has to travel far to feel the need for a kind of literacy that many of us woefully lack, myself included. Atlanta, Georgia, or the greater Atlanta area is home to almost six million people, many of whom were not born in the United States or speaking English. They came to Atlanta from China, Mexico, Ghana, El Salvador, Viet Nam, Liberia, India, Pakistan, Argentina, and that is to name only the most conspicuous populations. But if the global is also local, the local is also global, as any credible social theory can prove. UPS, Coca-Cola, AT&T, The Home Depot—these Atlanta corporations extend the agency of their employees and customers well beyond the greater metro area. As I noted, political disorientation is rampant. But this is just to close by suggesting, again, that cosmopolitanism must concretely attend to the social forces enveloping our political present, as well as to the kind of character that could prove equal to the shifting occasions that such a world presents.

JOHN LYSAKER is Professor of Philosophy and Chair of the Department of Philosophy at Emory University. His principal philosophical interests include philosophical psychology, aesthetics, social and political philosophy, and nineteenth- and twentieth-century continental and American philosophy. His most recent book is *After Emerson* (Indiana University Press, 2017).

Notes

1. Habermas presents this claim in "Interpreting the Fall of a Monument," collected in: Jürgen Habermas, *The Divided West* (Cambridge: Polity, 2008), 28–29.

2. The research cited was conducted by economists Thomas Piketty and Emmanuel Saez. See Avi Feller and Chad Stone, "Top 1 Percent of Americans Reaped Two-Thirds of Income Gains in Last Economic Expansion," *Center on Budget and Policy Priorities*, September 9, 2009, www.cbpp.org/cms/index.cfm?fa=view&id=2908.

3. This is not to say that global warming only flows from global capital. Even very local capital, and at the level of individual consumption, is party to this phenomenon.

4. Matthew J. Slaughter, writing for the United States Council for International Business (USCIB), uses "10% direct ownership" to define multinationals. See "How US Multinational Companies Strengthen the US Economy." The paper is available courtesy of the USCIB website, www.uscib.org/docs/foundation_multinationals_update.pdf.

5. Three articles in particular helped us clarify the summary that follows. A. A. Long, "The Concept of the Cosmopolitan in Greek & Roman Thought," *Daedalus* 137, no. 3 (Summer 2008): 50–58; John Moles, "Cynic Cosmopolitanism," in *The Cynics: The Cynic Movement in Antiquity and Its Legacy*, ed. R. B. Branham and M-O. Goulet-Cazé, 105–20 (Berkeley: University of California Press, 1996); Martha Nussbaum, "Toward a Globally Sensitive Patriotism," *Daedalus* 137, no. 3 (Summer 2008): 78–93.

6. The play is available at www.gutenberg.org/files/22188/22188-h/files/terence3_4.html.

7. Chremes position would thus support Jeremy Waldron's claim that proponents of what he and others term identity politics are wrong to defend "presenting oneself and one's cultural preferences *non-negotiably* to others in the present circumstances of the world"; see Jeremy Waldron, "What Is Cosmopolitanism?," in *The Cosmopolitan Reader*, ed. Garrett Wallace Brown and David Held (Cambridge: Polity, 2010), 165. While I share the sentiment, I doubt *preference* is the right moral psychological term in this context, if only because it detaches a preferring ego from all of its cultural commitments, whereas it is likely that certain cultural commitments are constitutive of whatever ego identity one has. In other words, Waldron underplays the ways in which his cosmopolitanism requires a kind of identity or, as I would have it, character.

8. In Chapter 4 of this volume, Jacquelyn Ann K. Kegley follows and builds on such an interpretation as a means of reconciling the concept of "world-citizen" with more place-bound attachments.

9. Kwame Anthony Appiah, *Cosmopolitanism: Ethics in a World of Strangers* (New York: W. W. Norton, 2006).

10. Ibid., 113.

11. One could argue, of course, that respect for actual human beings lies precisely in such dialogues, particularly since the capacity for the logos is what actually makes us "human beings," according to classical cosmopolitanism. Appiah does not make this point; however, it is not inconsistent with what he does propose.

12. Friedrich Nietzsche, *The Gay Science*, trans. Walter Kaufmann (New York: Random House, 1974), 167.

13. As an example of a contemporary affirmation of logos (as the universality of rational speech), see Chapter 3 by Juan Carlos Pereda Failache in this volume. Pereda locates this universality in the practice of giving reasons, which may avoid grounding rationality in a metaphysical principle or divine order.

14. I have also articulated some general views on normativity and its relation to logos in the recent article, John Lysaker, "Praxis as Form: Thirty Notes for an Ethics of the Future," *Journal of Speculative Philosophy* 25, no. 2 (2011): 213–38.

15. John Rawls, *Justice as Fairness: A Restatement* (Cambridge, MA: Harvard University Press, 2001), 5. While Rawls is not a contemporary cosmopolitan, his work does fund various contemporary versions, for example, Charles Beitz's, and his distinction between metaphysical and political approaches to political theory remains widely influential. I thus think it important to address his concerns when insisting on the centrality of any concepts in political philosophy.

16. Ibid., 81.

17. Ibid., 41.

18. Ibid., 136. Rawls also states: "A political conception of justice must take into account the requirements of social organization and economic efficiency" (ibid., 123).

19. Ibid., 56, 59.

20. It is worth stressing the sociality of these unapologetically logocentric labors. As David Held notes, albeit in a manner more bloodless than we would prefer, the "pursuit of impartial reasoning is a social activity"; see David Held, "Principles of Cosmopolitan Order," in *The Cosmopolitan Reader*, ed. Garrett Wallace Brown and David Held (Cambridge: Polity, 2010). 239.

21. Seyla Benhabib, *Another Cosmopolitanism* (New York: Oxford University Press, 2008). I will leave open the question of whether this need for a certain kind of character requires cosmopolitans to affirm something like a conception of the good life, thus abandoning another core Rawlsian commitment, namely, the eschewal of comprehensive doctrines.

22. Ibid., 66, 69, and 56–57.

23. Rawls, *Justice as Fairness*, 56.

24. Judith Butler, *Precarious Life: The Powers of Mourning and Violence* (London: Verso, 2006), 48.

25. For examples in this volume of arguments that describe cosmopolitan character in this strong sense of habits and practices, see Chapter 2 by Noëlle McAfee (cosmopolitan imaginary), Chapter 12 by Jessica Wahman (cosmopolitan-as-guest), and Chapter 13 by Jennifer Hansen (cosmopolitan hope).

26. See their introduction to *Cosmopolitan Reader*, 10.

2 Home, Hospitality, and the Cosmopolitan Address

Noëlle McAfee

MARSHALL MCLUHAN BEGAN his curious little book of 1967, *The Medium Is the Massage*, with an epigraph by Alfred North Whitehead: "The major advances in civilization are processes that all but wreck the societies in which they occur."[1] For McLuhan's purposes, the meaning is clear. The old world became undone by the literacy that the printing press created. Literate readers of the Bible no longer needed to defer to priests for the word of God, which led to the Protestant Reformation and shortly thereafter to new ideas about government legitimacy, heralding the English, American, and French revolutions. Invented during the Holy Roman Empire, the printing press put an end to that empire and made the Renaissance and then liberal democracy possible.

The new communicative technology of McLuhan's day was the television, which turned the world, he said, into a global village. All those other people I could previously ignore? Now I turn on the television, and they are in my living room. "Our new environment compels commitment and participation," McLuhan writes. "We have become irrevocably involved with, and responsible for, each other."[2] It is tempting to become a determinist about technology, to think that new material conditions will necessarily give rise to new behaviors. But this equation leaves out a vital factor, human imagination, not just the ability to represent in one's mind what one has seen elsewhere but the ability to imagine something radically new, something entirely different from what already exists, like the end of racism or democracy throughout the Middle East. To become open to undetermined change requires what Cornelius Castoriadis called a radical imaginary, which can open up the possibility of radically new realities, such as marriage equality for all.

In this chapter I explore this radical imaginary and show how it is working at this point in time as the world is transitioning from a nation-state mentality to a more global one. I show that it is our human situatedness plus our ability to address others across borders that help create a new cosmopolitan political imaginary. So I proceed as follows: After laying out my starting premises, I explain what I mean by *cosmopolitanism* and the idea of a cosmopolitan political or social imaginary. Then I develop the concept of a cosmopolitan address, which I then use to rethink the idea of hospitality. I close with some implications that this view has for how to respond and think about fragile movements from authoritarian to democratic life.

Starting Points

To begin, here are my three starting points: First, most of my work, this piece included, rests on an empirical claim—that most people want to have a hand in shaping the social and political world they share with others. This sort of claim has shown up throughout the history of philosophy, as early as Aristotle's claim that we are political animals, that because we have the gift of speech we can and do make claims about justice. In modern moral philosophy, empirical claims are often embedded in moral psychology. Even in Kant's metaphysics of morals, there is an unstated claim that people want, that is, desire, to be treated as ends, never merely as means. In other words, Kant must have been observing empirically, not just rationally, that people want to be able to shape their world. So, too, in Marx's observations on alienation, the flip side of which is engagement, a live connected relationship with one's fellows, work, products, and all humanity, not just in any way but in a way that signals that one is a being who can and should be able to chart one's own direction. We postmetaphysical philosophers might look askance at all this talk of "authorship," like a philosophy of the subject, but even without any metaphysical baggage we can observe empirically that a good life is one that is made by oneself with one's fellows, not by others. This is a deep-seated political germ, as Castoriadis might put it, that can take many forms.

Second, one can observe a continuum that can be traversed in many directions between the psyche, the social, and political. With Michel Foucault I agree that we are subjected to and shaped by social forces; but I also think (with Jeffrey Goldfarb, who also follows Hannah Arendt on this) that power runs the other way, too, that our radical imagination allows us to make and remake our world. Still there is no guarantee that we will be free to imagine new things for, as Sigmund Freud's work shows, failures to sublimate well, instances of traumas unworked through, develop pathologies that show up in the public sphere. As I see it, the public sphere is a shared circulation of the signs of our attempts at being fully human in the Aristotelian and Arendtian sense of flourishing through political deliberation and participation with others.

Third, I think that things like rights, dignity, subjectivity, the public sphere, and the cosmos are made, not found. They are meaningful fictions: *fictions* because they don't have any independent ontological status; *meaningful* because through their performance we make some sense of and give meaning to our lives. At every step, when I say "the whole world" I am knowingly speaking a fiction.

There never is a whole world watching, and the concept itself of a unitary whole world is as much a fiction as the concept of a person with infinite dignity. In none of this am I making any transcendental claims to truth about the world or human nature. I am describing the ways we make up our freedom, create it, sometimes out of nothing but hope. It is an act of hospitality, making at home those of us who at the moment have none.

Political Imaginaries

Even with these three starting points, which I think are shared widely across cultures, there is a vast array of differences in political cultures. By "political culture" I mean the expectations that prevail in any given community about who has political efficacy and how things get done, for example, the more democratic a political culture is, the more people presume that agency and power are cultivated and shared horizontally. But throughout much of the twentieth century, political power was theorized largely as a matter of vertical power, whether that of the state over the people or the possibility of the people overthrowing the state. Political power came to be seen as something that ran up and down a political society, not laterally throughout civil society. Power was about control. Gone was any understanding that had been cultivated by the civic republican tradition of power as an energy or ability to make something *new* happen. Political power was simply the ability to control or divvy up an existing bundle of goods and distribute scarce resources. Legitimacy, then, was a matter of justifying state power.

A key aspect of any given political culture is the expectations it sets up about how problems should be addressed and who has the authority to address them. These sets of expectations comprise the "political imaginary" of a polity. Nancy Fraser understands this as the "taken-for-granted assumptions," mind-sets, attitudes, catchphrases, and images about how politics works. These assumptions inform the ways in which social problems are named and debated, and, as Fraser puts it, they "delimit the range of solutions that are thinkable." "They are often distilled in catch phrases and stereotypical images, which dominate public discourse. Taken together, such catch phrases, images, and assumptions constitute the political imaginary."[3] If politics describes the task of deciding and acting in the midst of uncertainty or disagreement on matters of pressing and widespread concern, political imaginaries delineate who the key actors and deliberators are, the norms according to which agents interact, and the kinds of power they employ. A political imaginary will rarely be recognized as such. Rather, it will be taken as "just the way things are," "the ways politics work," and "how things get done." Political imaginaries constitute our place in a political world, simultaneously constituting our own political subjectivity, our political relationships to others, and our political culture.

If this is so, if the prevailing imaginary guides people's expectations and actions, how does significant change happen? This is the question that Castoriadis took up for much of his life. Along with others, he used the term *imaginary* to describe this mental model of how things are, but he also used it, with the adjective *radical*, to describe how people are able to imaginatively construct something new. Our radical imagination is our capacity to question our current laws of existence, institutions, and representations of the world, and create new ones.[4] In this sense it calls into question current institutions and practices and helps create new ones. In other words, the radical imagination is an *instituting* imagination. A familiar word for this radical imagination is *autonomy*, which Castoriadis borrows from Kant but uses in a new way; for Castoriadis autonomy can put everything in question, and there is no universally "right" answer to what should be. The radical imagination of one era may create the instituted status quo that a radical imagination of another era may overthrow. Nothing is sacred. Moreover, Castoriadis focuses on the collective capacity to create a new world, much as Arendt did, that is squarely focused on the political. But like Kant's idea of autonomy, it is undetermined, that is, it is not a causal effect of material or other circumstances. In fact, the very meaning of it is that it is a capacity to imagine things being radically otherwise than they are now.

Along such lines, the feminist philosopher Lorraine Code uses the phrase *social imaginary* to describe "a transformative, interrogating, and renewing *imaginary*—a loosely integrated system of images, metaphors, tacit assumptions, ways of thinking—a guiding metaphorics that departs radically from the imaginary through and within which epistemologies of mastery are derived and enacted."[5] Where Code uses this language to describe an alternative way of knowing, I use it here to describe another way of relating to others in the world, that is, as an opening into new ethical engagements.

Following Fraser, Code, and Castoriadis, I believe we can employ the concept of an imaginary to think about the ways that peoples of the world are appealing and responding to one another—as citizens not just of a country but of the world—able as well as obligated to call and respond to others globally. This would be an imaginary that is cosmopolitan in Appiah's sense of the world as a potentially moral community, however imperfect. A *cosmopolitan* social and political radical imaginary foregrounds transactions and relationships among citizens of the world even as they hang on to their thick local attachments.

Cosmopolitanism is not so much a fact or an achievement as it is a way of thinking about our relationships to others in the world. It is not a fixed state or quality but something we performatively create in response to the call of others—in response to being arrested or seized by the plight of others and their claim to have the right to be accorded dignity and respect. Cosmopolitanism is an interrelational effect of our responses to others. A cosmopolitan social imaginary is not a new thing, but the shape it takes now is new. In ancient times it took the form of identification with human beings as such; in early Christianity *cosmopolitanism* meant an understanding of all people being God's creatures; and in modernity it was a matter of all having the same kind of rational nature. These were various views of how, despite ethnic and national differences, no matter how foreign someone else seemed, there was something saliently *alike* about us all.

More recently cosmopolitanism has grown out of a political imaginary of a global world. In the past one hundred years, new forms of communication have, to borrow Marshall McLuhan's phrase, turned the world into a global village. Whether or not this is completely true, the concept of a global village has a powerful hold on us, just as the photo of the earth taken from space in 1968 and published on the cover of the *Whole Earth Catalogue* profoundly shaped popular consciousness, literally showing the world without borders.[6] Today's cosmopolitan social imaginary, I venture, is mediated through new technologies that create powerful communities of action, such as the global mobilization to help deal with the Indian Ocean tsunami in 2004, and tools for community organizing, including movements opposing authoritarian regimes forming nearly overnight. But even without calamities and popular uprisings, the internet, or more specifically Web 2.0, has changed our relations with people around the globe. Our professional networks are increasingly international. Our philanthropy and political activism largely ignore borders. We can spend our free time playing games with anyone awake at the same time anywhere in the world. Without the state as intermediary, we are creating wider and denser horizontal networks with other human beings all over the world.

The Cosmopolitan Address

Cosmopolitan appeals do not issue from everywhere but from somewhere. A cosmopolitan appeal always has an address, a place from which it is issued, as well as an address to which is it being sent. To explain, let me recount what is now a familiar story.

On December 17, 2010, at 10:30 in the morning, a municipal inspector for the Tunisian town of Sidi Bouzid, along with her assistants, arrived at the cart of Mohamed Bouazizi, a fruit vendor. The inspector and her colleagues started harassing the vendor for not having a permit—even though reportedly no one ever knew whether a permit was really required—and confiscated his fruit, which he had just bought on credit the night before for the equivalent of $200.[7] Bouazizi had been working odd jobs since he was ten years old, and he had dropped out of school so he could support his mother, uncle, and five siblings. Now at twenty-six he was just scraping along well enough to support his family and set aside some money to eventually buy a truck. Where other vendors would often pay off the inspectors and police with a bribe or a bag of fruit, Bouazizi stood his ground and refused to pay. This time, when the inspector started taking his apples, he tried to take them back. Reportedly, the inspector slapped him, her aides beat him, and then the inspector and aides left with his fruit and his electronic scale. Humiliated and angry, Bouazizi went to the municipal building and demanded his property, to no avail.[8] Then he went to the governor's office to complain, but he was refused an audience. At around noon, standing outside the governor's office, he drenched himself in paint thinner and set himself on fire.

That afternoon, after he'd been taken to the hospital with burns over 90 percent of his body, his relatives and friends gathered outside the governor's office and began throwing coins at the gate, yelling, "Here is your bribe." Others joined them; the protests grew, and the police started beating the demonstrators and firing tear gas. The protests spread across the country, demanding the end of the regime that had led to widespread corruption, high unemployment, inflation, and scant political liberty. After Bouazizi died in the hospital on January 4, the protests against the twenty-three-year dictatorship of President Zine el-Abidine Ben Ali intensified. On January 14, unable to counter the huge surge of popular sovereignty opposed to his regime, the president fled the country. Shortly after protests began in Tunisia, Algerians began protesting the nineteen-year-old state of emergency in their country, which they succeeded in ending. These were followed by protests (in roughly chronological order) in Jordan, Lebanon, Mauritania, Sudan, Oman, Saudi Arabia, Egypt, Yemen, Iraq, Bahrain, Libya, Kuwait, Morocco, and Syria. During subsequent months, these led to the overthrow of the government in four countries (Tunisia, Egypt, Libya, and Yemen) and significant governmental changes in five others (Jordan, Oman, Bahrain, Kuwait, and Morocco).[9] Some revolts turned out well, as in Tunisia, which as of June 2015 was still a secular democracy. At the other extreme, there is the civil war raging in Syria and the rise of the Islamic extremist insurgency known as ISIS. As the Arab Network for the Study of Democracy reports, since the end of 2010, the Arab world "has been living amongst a wave of uprisings aimed at toppling authoritarianism and transitioning toward democratic regimes, an ongoing movement that has, thus far, achieved only partial success."[10] While partial, this new wave of democratization is ongoing.

Up until Bouazizi set himself on fire and set off the Arab Spring, the idea that the citizens of the Arab world might rise up and call for the end of authoritarian regimes was, to put it mildly, barely thinkable, or at least exceedingly utopian. The political imaginary of the Arab world accommodated a narrow range of possibilities: authoritarian rule in bed with the West, corrupt and dictatorial secular rule at war with the West, or fundamentalist religious rule at war with modernity. There was no space in this imaginary for citizen action to oust authoritarian power. Bouazizi's match somehow sparked a radically new imaginary in which people began to think and act on how things *ought* to be rather than suffer through how they were.

How did this happen? What was it about Bouazizi's match that set off the change? As I see it, Bouazizi's act enacted the contradiction he was living. Situated outside the gate of the governor's office, barred from power, bereft, ignored, and humiliated, Bouazizi addressed the governor in the most extreme manner imaginable. His self-immolation was a paradoxical claim of being human and deserving of respect. It was a very particular, situated appeal to universality. The Tunisian fruit vendor who set himself on fire enacted an extreme announcement borne of daily humiliations. The only way he saw to announce that he should be treated as a human being, as somebody with dignity and rights, was to annihilate himself.

The story of what is now called the "Jasmine Revolution" captures the doublesidedness of what I call the cosmopolitan address, both the address from which one speaks and the act of addressing the world. This is the paradoxical performance of citizenship that is being reenacted nearly every day now as people take to the streets to claim their dignity in situations where they have none. Because they want dignity and freedom, they are acting like free, dignified people. They are addressing their dictators, or the police, but also one another and the world. The cosmopolitan address is the demand to be seen as somebody in situations where one is not. This is what resonates in the more recent #BlackLivesMatter movement, announcing one's dignity in a world that denies it.

What has been happening in the Middle East echoes what happened in Eastern Europe in 1989 and in the preceding decades, as recounted by sociologist Jeffrey Goldfarb. Drawing on Erving Goffman and Hannah Arendt, Goldfarb describes "the interactive constitution of public life and its culture,"[11] the ways in which people, during the height of their unfreedom, comported themselves and interacted in small but important ways that performatively created their freedom. Goldfarb points to the guiding imperative of the Polish Solidarity movement, as articulated by Adam Michnik, "to act as if one lived in a free society."[12] Many would buy illegal books from booksellers as if it were a legal transaction; they would attend salons to discuss cultural matters as if such activity were allowed. As far back as the 1970s in Poland, democratic opposition participants "published their names and address in their illegal publications."[13] Through such actions, "acting as if they lived in a free society, they were creating a regularized pattern of social interaction, an institution in fact, which was a component part of a free civil society."[14] Acting as if they were free, Goldfarb observes, they became so.

I would say that such performances of freedom are cosmopolitan addresses. Issuing from situations of unfreedom, they make a claim to freedom. A cosmopolitan address is threefold, with no clear temporal structure except that one phase turns to the next and so on. First, it is the address from which one speaks. In a repressive society, this is a situation of unfreedom, of being denied recognition of one's full humanity, which I take to be the ability to have a hand and a voice in shaping one's world with others. In such situations one is really not at home; one is kind of an exile in place, alienated, there but not there, *unheimlich*. Second, it is the speech itself, whether in words or deeds, the claim itself that one is a human being, or that one is free, or that the king can and should be toppled—all in spite of, in fact *to spite* the situation. In this second aspect, the cosmopolitan address is the announcement of the situation that *ought to be* other than the one that is. Rather than announce a fact it announces an aspiration and opens up the possibility that this aspiration might come to be. In this sense the announcement is always ethical rather than constative. Here we can draw on Christine Korsgaard's reading of Kant, or Levinas's claim in *Otherwise Than Being* that ethics is the call to make things otherwise than they are. Third, the cosmopolitan address is the phenomenon of addressing and being addressed. Thanks to the cosmopolitan social imaginary, we can imaginatively send an address to all humanity, however fictively. In this third aspect, a cosmopolitan address is addressed to all; anyone might find oneself addressed. This can happen turning the page of a newspaper to find an image that breaks one's heart. In this moment one is arrested, seized; one finds oneself addressed, commanded to do something. When we find ourselves seized by an address and we set about responding, we are choosing to both instantiate the dignity of the other being and enact our own humanity. This is what we mean by *humane*, to act like a human being in the face of some kind of devastation.

The Tunisian fruit vendor's addressee was only partially or at least indirectly the governor. It was to the world that might in turn *judge* the governor as being inhumane. The Polish Solidarity movement, too, was addressing the world, knowing that the party leaders would find that the whole world would be watching if it were to try to take down the labor movement. The #BlackLivesMatter movement following the police killing of the young black man Michael Brown is largely an appeal to the world for racial justice. As an appeal to others around the world, a cosmopolitan address calls on others to respond, which in a sense is the very meaning of *cosmopolitanism*. As John Lysaker notes in Chapter 1 of this volume, even in the natural law tradition a cosmopolitan imaginary locates all people as sharing equally in the category "citizen": "all persons share this location, and thus humans share a certain nature or 'humanity.'"[15] To be human, of course, has two sides: living up to the ideal for oneself and coming to the aid of others so that they may do the same. If we neglect the latter, we can never attain the former. Hence, a key part of cosmopolitanism is hospitality, to which I turn next.

Hospitality

Now I propose that we rethink the idea of hospitality in light of a cosmopolitan social imaginary and address. What duties does it introduce? How does it unsettle or dispossess us when we are being addressed? Hospitality in the cosmopolitan social imaginary is a call to the following:

- Host refugees and stateless ones, to provide sanctuary (along the lines that Derrida suggests in his essay on cosmopolitanism).
- Aid those in other states who need help (which in international law is formulated as the Responsibility to Protect, or RtoP, a principle articulated after the genocide in Rwanda).

Hospitality has ancient roots, featuring prominently in Homer's Odyssey. This cardinal virtue of the ancients was foremost designed to appease the gods. In the modern era of nation-states, it is been an extension of rights to those who are not member of a community. Its most famous formulation is the one that Immanuel Kant gave in his essay *Perpetual Peace*:

> Hospitality means the right of a stranger not to be treated as an enemy when he arrives in the land of another. One may refuse to receive him when this can be done without causing his destruction; but, so long as he peacefully occupies his place, one may not treat him with hostility. It is not the right to be a permanent visitor that one may demand. A special beneficent agreement would be needed in order to give an outsider a right to become a fellow inhabitant for a certain length of time. It is only a right of temporary sojourn, a right to associate, which all men have. They have it by virtue of their common possession of the surface of the earth, where, as a globe, they cannot infinitely disperse and hence must finally tolerate the presence of each other.[16]

Note the conditions that restrict hospitality: (a) the stranger cannot lay claim to residence in a foreign land unless there had been some kind of treaties between states ensuring such a right, but (b) one may refuse to receive the stranger only when this will not cause him destruction.

Kant's claim is that we need not harbor such foreigners indefinitely (i.e., by granting them resident status), but we must protect them from destruction. This entails the duty to provide sanctuary for those who come upon our shores, that is, when they are in our national territory. But what comes of this duty when the stranger is still in her homeland but we find ourselves seized by her address? When we find ourselves, thanks to a global social imaginary and new media, witnessing her possible destruction? What if the foreigners are not visitors, but members of other polities who for some reason are in imminent danger? Even something as minimal as Kantian cosmopolitanism, it seems, entails that we go out of our way to protect these other beings from mortal harm.

I would like to affirm this, even if it means doing a little violence to Kant's intent. Given the contemporary global, cosmopolitan, social imaginary, we are in relation with others, and hence we will, in fact, find ourselves feeling obligated to tend to them. The images of the tsunami, Katrina, the London Underground bombing, Tahrir Square, all these images and faces literally arrest us. Had the international community not responded with an outpouring of aid or solidarity, or whatever is called for, it would have been found guilty of neglect. (And this is precisely the position the international community is in at this point, as I write, in its response, or lack of response, to the Syrian crisis.)

The kind of cosmopolitanism I am describing surmounts one of the difficulties that has beset cosmopolitan theory: whether it prioritizes global citizenship over local affiliations, thin commitments "to all" over thick commitments to kith and kin. The view I am describing allows for us to be citizens of a certain place as well as citizens of the world. Cosmopolitanism need not be an alternative to community or the nation-state; it can be a supplement, one that grows more robust over time. My primary identity/ethnos may be as an American, but I can still find myself obligated—as an American or Greek or whatever my identification—to care for others. Hospitality is an ethics that emerges from being at home and from having one's own culture. As Derrida puts it: "'To cultivate an ethic of hospitality'—is such an expression not tautologous? . . . Hospitality is culture itself and not simply one ethic amongst others. Insofar as it has to do with the *ethos*, that is, the residence, one's home, the familiar place of dwelling, inasmuch as it is a manner of being there, the manner in which we relate to ourselves and to others, to others as our own or as foreigners, *ethics is hospitality*."[17] We are in a position to offer hospitality only when we are at home with ourselves, Derrida continues, that is, "*l'être-soi chez soi—l'ipseite même*—[at home with] the other within oneself."[18] Or, put another way, *if* we are at home in/with our own culture, we will open our doors and offer aid to others.

While holding too close to home, to "one's own," seems to sunder any cosmopolitan ties, relinquishing home—or being banished from it—leaves one bereft of the possibility of addressing the world. A cosmopolitan address has to issue from some particular place even as it calls for the world to live up to something better than what is the case, something that we might recognize with our moral imagination, in our aspirations or ways of thinking through how things *ought to be*. The cosmopolitan address is at the same time particular and universal.

But there is a danger here. To the extent that we moderns are all bereft of the place and rootedness of premodernity, to the extent that we are thrown into a bureaucratized world shorn of place and ties, we are all refugees announcing to others that we would like to belong, not to everywhere, which is the flip side of nowhere, but to somewhere. The danger of this rootless position is that it is tempting to cling to particularity, to stop addressing the world and address instead only those we imagine to be our own. Without a cosmopolitan appeal, the call for home becomes close-minded and even hateful.

While the balance is hard to find, by having some particular place I call home I can exercise an ethics of hospitality. But even a nomad can be hospitable, provided he or she extends graciousness and solicitude to those he or she encounters.

Implications

As soon as I saw what was happening in Tunisia and the way this movement was beginning to ripple across the Middle East, I flashed back to 1989. At that time, pockets of nascent civil society movements in Poland, Czechoslovakia, East Germany, and all the other eastern bloc Soviet satellite countries stood up to their governments and denounced them as illegitimate. They said out loud what had long been thought: that the so-called people's governments of these countries were not in fact authorized by the people. Recall that it was commonplace for communist parties to call themselves the people's party, never mind that Marx would have rolled over in his grave. What became of communism under Lenin, then Stalin and Mao, bore little resemblance to a government that really stood for the working class or was prepared to "wither away" anytime soon. Rather than develop conditions for true equality and freedom, they took their cue from despots and tyrants. The first thing such rulers do is close down free space. Dictators intuitively seem to know what the philosopher Hannah Arendt noted: that power springs up among people when they speak and act in the company of others. This was the power that King George feared when he instituted the "Black Acts," which made illegal the town meetings in colonial America. When these people get together, George must have realized, they create a kind of power that could threaten his rule, his power being the threat of force, theirs being a civic or public power.

Before and since, dictators of most any political persuasion have done the same thing. They prevent public association and gatherings where alternative power might form, hence the crisis in Tiananmen Square in China in 1989 or the importance of Tahrir Square during Egypt's uprising. The Syrian government understands this all too well. Citizens under siege are in mortal danger in the basements of their own homes. Unable to venture out, they haven't been able to create the public square or public imagery or "space of appearance" for politics. The best they can do, at this point, is ferry to safety those international journalists brave enough to enter the country in hopes that their story will be told internationally, while the Free Syrian Army engages in the other form of power, the power of force.

A major part of public power is the power of the people together to deliberate and judge, to decide whether laws and governments are legitimate. This is the meaning of popular sovereignty as opposed to the sovereignty of a king. In a system that even pretends to be democratic, its claim is that the public has authorized the political system. Without public authorization, the system cannot claim to be legitimate unless it can simply silence any public opinion. But once the silence is broken, once thousands of people flood the streets in opposition, the lie is revealed for what it is. This is what brought down the regimes of Eastern Europe, what was so frightening for the authorities then and now in China, what caused Tunisia's and then Egypt's presidents to step down. Their presidencies were shams, and the laws that kept them in power were corrupt. Public power created in the streets and public squares called the lie. Oddly, the same phenomenon was *not* at work in Libya, and I think that this is because Qaddafi never pretended to be democratically supported. There was no sham to unveil. His rule did not rest on any claim of popular sovereignty. But the uprising in Libya made manifestly clear that his government was illegitimate. The people who were taking to the streets at their own peril were making a cosmopolitan address almost as extreme as the Tunisian fruit vendor's. They were saying, in effect, that while the tyrant might destroy them, they were free. From their vulnerable and partial situation, they were making a call to all who would listen that they had the dignity and right to rule themselves, that they were citizens, not subjects, people, not things. This cosmopolitan address is a claim of popular sovereignty that trumps any dictator's claim to nation-state territorial sovereignty.

This cosmopolitan address calls for humanitarian intervention, perhaps even justifies the use of force, such as the institution of the no-fly zone in Libya. Since the genocide in Rwanda, the international community is beginning to recognize its RtoP citizens of regimes that are not protecting them. But well before things ever get so dire, wherever there is a cosmopolitan appeal, those addressed have a responsibility to protect. The international community did so in Libya. Now the question is whether it will do so in Syria. In any case, the radically cosmopolitan imaginary supports such intervention.

But this is not carte blanche for the international community to engage in regime change. Some conditions should be honored. First, there needs to be a genuine appeal from the people living in these regimes. Second, nonviolent means should be employed early and vigorously before force is considered. Third, transnational nongovernmental organizations should take a lead role, especially by trying to strengthen the country's civil sector so that it has the capacity to rebuild itself in a more democratic fashion. As an activist from the campaign to end Pinochet's dictatorship in Chile said, the aim should not be just to overthrow a dictator but to create a country that will not tolerate one.

In a world constituted by a cosmopolitan social imaginary, ethics is a call to all others, however fictively constructed, to make things otherwise than they are. Those situated as powerless can performatively announce and help create their own humanity. And those addressed have a duty to respond, no matter where nations draw their borders. Unlike the days when hospitality was only extended when a stranger came ashore, now hospitality calls for making the other at home wherever he or she might be.

NOËLLE MCAFEE is Professor of Philosophy at Emory University. She is author of many publications focused on social and political philosophy, feminist theory, psychoanalytic theory, and contemporary European and American philosophy, and her most recent book is *Democracy and the Political Unconscious*.

Notes

1. Marshall McLuhan and Quentin Fiore, *The Medium Is the Massage: An Inventory of Effects* (New York: Bantam Books, 1967).
2. Ibid., 24.
3. Nancy Fraser, "Clintonism, Welfare, and the Antisocial Wage: The Emergence of a Neoliberal Political Imaginary," in *Marxism in the Postmodern Age: Confronting the New World Order*, ed. Antonio Callari, Stephen Cullenberg, and Carole Biewener (New York: Guilford Press, 1994), 493.
4. See Cornelius Castoriadis, *World in Fragments: Writings on Politics, Society, Psychoanalysis, and the Imagination* (Stanford, CA: Stanford University Press, 1997), 17.
5. Lorraine Code, *Ecological Thinking: The Politics of Epistemic Location* (Oxford: Oxford University Press, 2006), 29.
6. See Stewart Brand's account and a photo of the cover at http://click.si.edu/Story.aspx?story=31.
7. This account is based on Kareem Fahim, "Slap to a Man's Pride Set Off Tumult in Tunisia," *New York Times*, January 21, 2011, http://nyti.ms/1BGHvV7; see also and the Wikipedia entry for Mohamed Bouazizi, https://en.wikipedia.org/wiki/Mohamed_Bouazizi.
8. That he was humiliated by a woman is especially important in this story—particularly in that he seemed to equate what this woman did to him with what the state had done to him—humiliated him, emasculated him. There is a very interesting inquiry to be made about how the Middle East revolutions were fueled by emasculation, but I cannot do that here.
9. See the timeline in the Wikipedia entry on the Arab Spring at http://en.wikipedia.org/wiki/Arab_Spring.
10. Hassan Krayem, "The Arab Spring and the Process of Democratic Transition," in *The Arab Spring: Revolutions for Deliverance from Authoritarianism: Case Studies*, ed. Hassan Krayem, trans. Jeffrey D. Reger (Beirut: Al Sharq, 2014), 13.
11. Jeffrey Goldfarb, *The Politics of Small Things: The Power of the Powerless in Dark Times* (Chicago: University of Chicago Press, 2006), 27.
12. Ibid., 44.

13. Ibid., 33.
14. Ibid., 16–17.
15. See Chapter 1, page 14 of this volume.
16. Immanuel Kant, *Perpetual Peace*, trans. Lewis White Beck (New York: Library of Liberal Arts, 1957), x.
17. Jacques Derrida, *Cosmopolitanism and Forgiveness* (London: Routledge, 2002), 16–17.
18. Ibid., 17.

3 Cultural Heritages and Universal Principles

Juan Carlos Pereda Failache

SOCIALIZATION PROCESSES normally imply that we stimulate and praise—or discourage and scorn—some of our desires. And something comparable happens to our beliefs, emotions, interests, and, of course, to our actions. A tradition or cultural heritage is not just something out there; it entails a complex, and usually implicit, social normativity. However, communities also make explicit, in a fragmentary way, that normativity by means of codes, regulations, exhortations, suggestions, prohibitions, historical narratives, monuments, songs—all in a more or less vague and inconsistent manner. Is this how a public normativity becomes rooted in every person's life?

What Matters and What Doesn't

More often than not, we trust the way our cultural heritage approves or disapproves of many things. Such confidence takes the task of assessing what matters and what does not, and so human animals get their bearings from a young age—and sometimes through most of their lives—by sticking to the normativity that stems from the cultural heritage to which they belong. This is why from the point of view of the first person people don't perceive the specific quality of many of those deeply entrenched desires, beliefs, and emotions—not to mention other possible options to them.

So it comes as no surprise that from the point of view of the third person all those apparently disparate ways of valuing and living by codes and norms from different cultural heritages constitute a ubiquitous normative pluralism. But surely such pluralism is not just external. It doesn't come across only to those who contrast different cultural heritages from the point of view of the third person, as historians or anthropologists do when they compare societies from different ages or places in the world. On the contrary, in almost every modern society that pluralism has also become something internal. It is a part of the problems that people frequently must face in everyday life when they adopt the point of view of the first person. (And perhaps a qualification is in order here, for it seems likely that more or less conflicting evaluations have been the case since the dawn of human interrelations.)

We must be careful to notice that, among many other obstacles, the term *normative pluralism* makes reference to a changeable phenomenon, ranging from cultural discrepancies that apparently should not cause any trouble (as in the case of food and clothing variations) to harsh conflicts about values and norms that groups of people from different cultural backgrounds consider irreconcilable. However, in spite of these disagreements, a spontaneous, general, and passive confidence in the normative guidelines of one's society becomes, again and again, an inevitable starting point. From where else could we start?

But even that general confidence in some normative principles teeters from time to time. Disagreements and conflicts about different ways of trusting in what personally and socially matters and in what doesn't matter, or doesn't matter much, have produced practical troubles, serious conflicts, and even puzzlement. Among many other things, one can recall here the prudential, political, or moral conflicts that frequently have a large effect on the lives of individuals and social groups. As a result, people switch their trust to other guidelines, and sometimes even the whole field of values and norms suffers a major transformation. So, if we start classifying—rather coarsely—the ways we trust, we must take notice first of an attitude of trying to cling to tacit agreements according to a general credulity principle.

Acting consistently in accord with such a principle seems to mean at first sight rejecting any experience that does not coincide with the social normativity in which we have grown up. Some people even make it a matter of principle to maintain for their whole lives the very same views they learned as children at home. But even the sensible traditionalist cannot escape from unconventional options and dilemmas, for cultural heritages, as well as the social normativity they imply, are not closed systems. That is why even the most consistent traditionalist will have to sometimes face difficult choices between one and another value, or between norms for action. And if she is not willing to resort to violence or arbitrariness, she will have to justify her choices: she will have to give, and give to herself, reasons and arguments. But this means the end of blind loyalties. From that moment on, the traditionalist has adopted up to a point the principle of trust as presumption.

Adopting this principle implies that one is disposed to considering reasons against and for the received and trustworthy presumptions—hence the term "presumption." And any serious consideration of reasons against held beliefs will put us in a position of having to answer to those reasons using more or less complicated arguments. According to this second attitude, every time that a problem or disagreement arises with the general confidence in the guidelines offered by any cultural heritage, instead of appealing to violence or arbitrariness the members of that cultural heritage will have to drop the fragment of contested normativity and adopt a fragment of reflective normativity.

Should we add, then, to what matters at a personal or social level the practice of giving reasons and arguments, at least as norms that unavoidably must also matter? But the word *add* is confusing here because it is difficult to imagine a language, and therefore a cultural heritage, deprived of questions like "Why?"—and thus deprived of the practice of giving reasons and arguments. However, we might assign to that practice different application areas and different appraisals. Let's suppose now we attribute to that practice a more or less decisive importance. How do we justify choosing this over other ways of dealing with conflicts?

The Importance of Giving Reasons and Arguments

Many times we are likely to ask questions such as "Why do you say that?"; "How do you know that?"; and "What are your reasons for saying that?" Those questions are usually answered with sentences whose contents are provided by a perception, a memory, or some kind of testimony. But why and how can these different sources support a knowledge claim? To become reasons, those sentences often operate as true propositions that keep some kind of epistemic connection—induction, deduction, abduction, probability, and the like—with other held propositions. This is why a reason might be construed as an enthymematic proposition, or as pointing to an enthymeme. Thus, an argument is a set of claims provided by several reasons that work together to form the premises that somehow support a conclusion.

However, let's suppose someone has gathered the premises "All men are mortal" and "Socrates is mortal," and then announces: "According to my collection of premises, I reach the conclusion 'Socrates is mortal,' though I understand that you might use my collection in some other way." How come this sounds weird to us? Or suppose someone claims to have reasons to believe that Acapulco is a beach on the Pacific Ocean because that's what she learned in school, a reliable friend told her so, she checked out the fact in a prestigious encyclopedia, or she sailed all along the Pacific Coast and disembarked in Acapulco. And now she says something like, "I have gathered many reasons to believe that Acapulco is a beach on the Pacific Ocean, but those reasons are only valid for myself and no one else."

In both cases we might answer to these "private reasons collectors" as follows: "I don't know what you are talking about. If you do have reasons, you should be able to explain them to me, and even if they were extremely difficult, I could come to understand and share them with you if we apply ourselves properly to the task. If what you have are really reasons, then they are not your reasons, as the stamps in your stamp collection are your stamps. They are simply reasons." This reply entails that having any remarks (empirical proofs, testimonies, an expert report, and so on) put forward as reasons or as arguments must take us to presume that anybody able to understand the language in which those reasons are being stated will reach a conclusion in the same way that we do.[1] Let us enunciate now the following condition for using reasons and arguments:

(1) If X is a reason or an argument to believe A, for any person P X must be a reason or an argument to believe A.

As we can see, the universality presumption is part of the concepts of reason and argument. But then this also holds for our reasons and arguments for acting. Therefore,

(2) If X is a reason or an argument to do A, for any person P X must be a reason or an argument to do A.

So suppose someone has a good reason for not going to that great party in order to keep a promise to visit an ill—and disagreeable—aunt. Isn't this person acting on considerations that, if questioned, would also be considered as applicable for any other individual in similar circumstances? But again, why are reasons and arguments valid at all? These concerns are better approached through other related worries. If a belief is called into question under ordinary circumstances, why should the most adequate answer be to give reasons to defend or to replace that belief? Furthermore, why is solving conflicts by using reasons or arguments so appreciated? Notice that underlying these concerns one can find the following question: "Why do we have to support the beliefs and actions we need for solving our problems and conflicts with reasons and arguments valid for anyone under similar circumstances?" But again questions like this seem odd, for if they carry the intention of undermining the practice of giving reasons and arguments—and so their answers are supposed to convince us about something—then we should try to dissolve them: we should try to show that they entail some kind of contradiction. Obviously these questions take for granted precisely what they seek to challenge, namely, the value of reasons and arguments. But if we thought that reasons and arguments had no value, why should we care for asking people for reasons and arguments? And if we thought that they are worthy, why then should we ask for their value?

Agreeing to all this seems to recommend that the practice of giving reasons and arguments be part of what unavoidably must also matter for any cultural heritage. Let us see how this can be done.

A First Universal Principle Candidate?

Here is a possible description of a candidate for a first universal principle:

> Whenever you face problems that cast doubts on your confidence in the norms and values accepted by your cultural heritage, whether because you have found those norms and values problematic or because they seem to clash with the norms and values of other cultures, try to stand back from yourself and give yourself reasons and arguments just as if you were any other person. However, don't stop listening to what other people have to say, and, if necessary, engage with them in argumentative practices.

This principle does not apply only to isolated cases. It rather implies a complex perspective by which we address other people's desires, beliefs, and actions, as well as the institutions and regulations of their society. Let us call this "the perspective of reasons or arguments." What does this view entail?

As suggested before, once we assume this perspective we give up violence and arbitrariness as instruments for dealing with conflicts. So, instead of beating people to keep them silent or trying to subjugate a society by war, we must face our problems by means of reasons and arguments. But there is also a positive aspect to this perspective. To explain it, let me return to my former examples. The reasons that support (1) and (2) lead us to the suggestion that there can be a convergence among personal proofs, testimonies, and the expert's knowledge: Generally speaking, we assume that an agreement is possible among the most diverse reasons and arguments. For instance, we take for granted that anybody who studies Mexico's geography and then checks out the data by herself will confirm that Acapulco is a Pacific Ocean beach. And the same seems to go for the many reasons and arguments that we use to support an action—like keeping a promise. The negative and positive aspects of this perspective are like both sides of the same coin: we turn our backs on violence and arbitrariness and commit ourselves to a perspective in which anyone can participate. Nevertheless, doesn't this path lead us to the inclusion in this perspective of a self-correction principle of reasons and arguments?

By following this principle, if those participating in the practice of giving reasons and arguments consent to the internal dynamics of such practice—that is, if they are willing to respond to reasons and arguments with other reasons and arguments—sooner or later the normative discrepancies and errors will be identified and corrected. The participants in this activity will correct themselves. But is there such an "internal dynamics," or is it a "necessary" feature at all?

Of course, it might be objected that any close look at the practice of giving reasons and arguments in everyday life, and in political and religious disputes—as well as in scientific debates—casts doubts on the alleged connection between the practice of giving reasons and arguments and the configuration of a perspective in which any individual eschews violence, cooperates with others, and corrects herself, all at the same time. Perhaps the connection seems plausible only when we bear in mind the very abstract models based on that practice—as in the reasoning schemes included in logic textbooks. But if we look at the past, or at our present-day argumentative practices, we may be tempted to deny any contribution made by them to the creation of a perspective in which we can all agree, work together, and correct ourselves. And maybe we even feel we should disregard the positive aspect of the universality principle for reasons and arguments as just one more groundless utopia—a simple delusion. Moreover, if the reasons of any individual depend on the rest of her psychological states, then surely those reasons and arguments will tend to confirm those very states. Or at least they won't exceed the limits—however vague—set by the individual's other psychological states. Therefore, how can anybody self-correct herself in a radical way?

To respond to these concerns, it is important to take account of the importance of the point of view of a second person—the points of view of other persons—in the first universal principle candidate (as formulated above). The last part of that principle directs us to continue listening to what other people have to say—particularly persons who hold views other than ours own—and, if necessary, to engage with them in reason-giving and argumentative practices. With this importance of the points of view of others firmly in mind, let me now try to defend this principle—and therefore the perspective of reason giving and practices of arguments. Now, to defend the principle of the importance of giving reasons and making arguments informed by the perspectives of others is not to defend the view that giving reasons and making arguments are self-correcting. Indeed, it would be delusional to think that merely articulating reasons and offering arguments to others are ways all by themselves to resolve social differences and problems. They are not. It would also be counter-productive to hold this view, because it deadens our sensitivities to the reasons and arguments offered by others. Once arguments are set in motion—the practice of making arguments as distinct from the results of this practice considered in abstract isolation from the practice itself—obviously they do not operate as a perpetuum mobile that needs no external source of energy to keep going on. On the contrary, argumentative practices depend at every moment on the energy—and on the good and bad contributions—of the people participating in them. Hence the obligation of each participant to listen to the others, even sometimes against their strongest desires—the obligation of the point of view of the first person to open up to the point of the second person in order to qualify, correct, or even replace desires, beliefs, and emotions.

All these things—listening even against our strongest desires, qualifying or even replacing beliefs and emotions—assume that both the others and myself are not passive animals, but agents. Furthermore, as agents we are as sensitive to perceptions, desires, beliefs, and emotions as to reasons and arguments. Suppose we do have such sensitivity. What consequences can be drawn from an agency with such faculties? Here's a possible answer, a second universal principle candidate:

> Whenever you face problems that cast doubts on your confidence in the norms and values accepted by your cultural heritage, whether because you have found those norms and values problematic or because they seem to clash with the norms and values of other cultures, remember that you're an agent.

These two prospective universal principles—or mediator principles between conflicts and problems—have many points in common, or at least a number of connections between them. For instance, see the following section.

On the Art of Knowing When to Restrain Oneself

Let's bring to mind the circumstances in which we appeal to this form of art. Sometimes we are in a situation where we need to lower the voices that make up the point of view of the first person and prevent us from hearing what the point of view of a second person is really trying to communicate. It is often as if we had in our heads a bunch of very noisy radio sets from which we can hear all kinds of voices and conversations. And some other times it's like all we can hear is one single radio repeating the same piece of information over and over again. The art of knowing when to restrain oneself is the art of silencing those inner voices so we can listen to the voices coming from the outside: the voices coming from the point of view of the second person that sometimes surround and even confront our deafened and self-absorbed first-person point of view.

Following the first and second principle demands that the point of view of the first person put aside its idiosyncratic beliefs, desires, emotions, and expectations in order to be able to listen both to the reasons and arguments it can discover by itself when acting just like any person and to the reasons and arguments provided by the others.

Clearly, this art of restraining oneself is not an easy task to perform. More often than not, the point of view of the first person avoids any kind of questioning. And it is not only difficult to detach oneself from one's desires and beliefs to identify the errors they might contain; it is also very hard to think dispassionately about matters related to what we consider as characteristic to us—as our own culture or our own country. (This is why emphasizing the other's faults serves the purpose of hiding our own imperfections. Hence the consoling effects in our community provided by the media frenzy every time horrible things happen in the surrounding world.)

Besides, no one can ignore that the will is a fragile and erratic faculty (constituted perhaps by second-level reflections on one's own desires?). If the point of view of the first person does not put into practice on a regular basis the art of knowing when to restrain oneself—making little efforts to argue against itself—it will easily fall prey to self-deceptions, to colorful rationalizations intended to protect it from real or imagined evils. Sadly, we are often more prone to rationalizations than to reasons.

Fortunately, whether we admit it or not, the others are there as agents, just as the first and second purported universal principles indicate. And they usually stay there, even against my best efforts to ignore them, and they remind me that I am also an agent, that I can change, a little or a lot. Sometimes even a distracted look from the second person can discern a solution to the first person's problems, a solution that the first person cannot notice from his or her comfortable, self-satisfied position—the inner radios are on full volume. This is the reason why sometimes only the irruption from the outside by the other, in conflicts and cooperative tasks, can prevent the first person's reasons from becoming mere rationalizations. But how can this ability to restrain ourselves become more stable? How can we preserve and even broaden the holes in the walls we build around ourselves?

The Institutionalization of the Art of Restraining Oneself, and a Third Universal Principle Candidate

The second person, the other, the others, are the equals the first person, and that's why the first person can assume as one's own many of the other's presumptions. But they are also different people, sometimes so different that the first person is amazed by the other's seemingly peculiar desires, beliefs, and emotions. And on occasions one finds it hard even to make sense of a desire or a belief of a second person. But there's more to this. The assumptions of many of the others are, predictably enough, each different, given the diverse natural and cultural backgrounds from which they come. More often than not, a first person has to face an irreducible, and at times diffuse, multitude of "yous" that she cannot control, and that irritates, amazes, comforts, and accompanies her, and that sometimes represents a real challenge to her. The first person learns from this that not only is she vulnerable to the acknowledgment or lack of acknowledgment from the others; she is affected by their ignorance, rejections, and threats. She might also find out—in a borderline case—that she is exposed to those actions that seek to destroy her. So what can we do if we cannot help being part of a group of people like this?

A recurrent practice to help restrict the tragic character of some of these circumstances is the institutionalization of the art of restraining ourselves with the intention of reconstructing social normativity and our trust presumptions; that is, trying to modify the limits between what unavoidably matters and what doesn't matter. For example, by the institutionalization of restraining ourselves we might not only learn—in our work, our neighborhood, or at the club—to restrain our displeasure or even our disgust at the sight of, for instance, certain sexual preferences; we might even be required to do so by the law of our society. Nor is it the case that we only learn to appease our spontaneous desires to reduce to silence those religious opinions we do not share and consider silly and barbaric; by certain political processes we even honor the existence of freedom of speech and freedom of worship.

There are many other examples of these social attempts at instituting the restriction of even our most intense desires, deep-rooted beliefs, and vigorous emotions. But is there a common principle shared by these and other similar ways of trying to restrain the dynamics of many cultural heritages? Here's a third universal principle candidate to arbitrate disputes between individuals, groups, and their institutions:

> Whenever you face problems that cast doubts on your confidence in the norms and values accepted by your cultural heritage, whether because you have found those norms and values problematic or because they seem to clash with the norms and values of other cultures, treat those problems with the arguments and other tools that anyone living in a democracy would justify and promote.

JUAN CARLOS PEREDA FAILACHE is Professor of Philosophy at Universidad Nacional Autonoma de Mexico Instituto de Investigaciones Filosoficas. His publications concern issues of rationality and models of reason, ethical theory, political theory, and intercultural challenges and opportunities. His many books include *Los aprendizajes del exilio* and *Sobre la confianza* (Siglo XXI, 2008).

Note

1. This point is explored in related but different contexts in several other chapters in this volume. See, for example, Cynthia Gayman's discussion of varieties of pluralism (Chapter 14) and Erin Tarver's account of multiple publics (Chapter 15).

4 Not Black or White but Chocolate Brown

Reframing Issues

Jacquelyn Ann K. Kegley

> Life is neither black nor white, but chocolate brown.
> —Hegel

IN CONCERT WITH the classic American philosophical tradition, I argue that philosophical inquiry is best advanced when one avoids black-white thinking and the trap of false alternatives. Much of the contemporary, as well as historical, discussion of cosmopolitanism has framed the debate in terms of a dichotomy between cosmopolitanism and nationalism. But both concepts are complex and thus clarity is demanded in delineating what notions are being opposed as opposites or in dichotomy. Further, both concepts are often oversimplified. Thus, cosmopolitanism is generally seen as promoting moral obligations to all human beings as contrasted to obligations to one's groups or significant circle of others and favoring some suprastate political arrangement while excluding considerations of loyalties to a nation-state.[1] Few, if any, advocates of cosmopolitanism would promote such a view. Likewise, nationalism has taken on many forms in recent political thought, but within the variety is an underlying dichotomy between "nation," conceived as an ethno-cultural entity, and a more civic version focused on "nation" as grounded in self-determination and based on civic duties and protections. Again, clarity of concept is needed to further intelligent debate.

The debate between cosmopolitanism and nationalism can, in some manner, be viewed as the old individual versus the community debate. This perspective also is oversimplified and poses false alternatives. In my view the cosmopolitan debate today needs to be reframed in terms of a balancing of cosmopolitan, universal, and expansive views of moral and political obligations and loyalties with equal regard for particular, individual, regional, and national loyalties. In concert with communitarian views, one can agree that individuals are socially grounded to the core, that we become persons because of the social settings and contexts in which we mature. Yet there is human creativity and choice in developing a life plan, and identity and a healthy individualism requires transcendence both of self and community and/or social group interests. Though it is true that language and ethnicity provide rich resources for the crafting of self-identity, it is also true that individuals can and do forge individualistic as well as communal-based identities different from and even in opposition to their ethno-cultural setting. An enlightening example of this is religious loyalties that often transcend geographical, national, or cultural grounding, for example, Christianity and Buddhism, or even Islam and Judaism.

Further, with the American philosopher Josiah Royce and others, one can argue for a view of human nature as capable of developing wider loyalties, moving from one's immediate group, family, or clan to broader communities and finally to a universal community. Such a broader loyalty does not destroy one's more limited loyalties but rather enriches them. Further, this kind of transcending of an inner circle of obligations can and should involve the fostering and valuing of diversity of many kinds: peoples, lifestyles, religions, and political and social arrangements. Thus, in concert with Anthony Appiah, I argue for a "rooted cosmopolitanism" that highlights our obligations to others beyond our immediate circle while also taking seriously the significance of individual human lives and values and the importance of group identities and commitments.[2] However, with Royce, and perhaps unlike Appiah, I hold that such "rooted cosmopolitanism" is a difficult task and requires strong effort and constant vigilance and dialogue with others. It is my judgment that such a view, though demanding, is eminently worthwhile and much needed in today's world.

In what follows, I first briefly describe various notions of a strong version of nationalism. The first view sees nation in terms of an ethno-cultural state. There are also forms of nationalism rooted in concerns for social justice, namely, defending minority rights or seeking redress for past injustice. There is also the argument that nationalism has been successful in the past in promoting equality and democracy, and some even argue that nationalism has played a key role in the success of capitalism and the promotion of economic growth.

Second, I discuss the notion of self-creation and identity formation, focusing on social and communal roots, especially on the notion of "place" as providing an answer to two central questions: "Where am I?" and "Who am I?" In this discussion, it is argued that although "place" locates one and provides a sense of identity, it is a "human creation," a location suffused with the human. A "place" is fashioned and refashioned by the individuals occupying that location and thus it is not correct to see "place" as owned or created only by the original occupiers or as resisting creative change and advance.[3] As Jose Medina notes (Chapter 7), paraphrasing Megan Craig (Chapter 9), "We belong to places, but they don't belong to us, no matter how intimately 'ours' they may feel."[4] My analysis draws on recent sociological research on "the South" as a place and a piece on "The World Trade Center Wall," by Bruce Janz.[5] The latter piece allows us to discuss the idea that there can be a passing in and out of being a place. In Appiah's words, "cultures" can travel.[6] In arguing for transforming and transporting of "place," we will not ignore that dislocation and marginalization can occur with loss of "place."[7] "Place" is an important concept for human beings, and this importance needs to be honored in arguing for any form of cosmopolitanism. Also, there must be room in our "rooted cosmopolitanism" for claims of social justice about displaced minorities and indigenous groups.[8]

Third, I discuss the notion of wider loyalties, of building a "moral cosmopolitanism" from the ground up, beginning with a strong sense of loyalty and love for one's immediate community, region, or land, and expanding loyalty outward to encompass broader loyalties and commitments. I draw on the work of Royce, on community and loyalty as well as more recent arguments such as those of Hilary Putnam and Richard Rorty.[9] Sissela Bok speaks of transcending through "concentric circles."[10] In this context, I argue for a "rooted cosmopolitanism" and a notion of a "cosmopolitan place" and worldview.

The Arguments for Nationalism: Community, Nation, and Self-Identity

A central argument against cosmopolitanism and for nationalism, particularly in its strongest form, centers on the intrinsic value of community, viewing it as a strongly knit moral community sharing the same language, customs, traditions, and values. A prominent obligation of each member of such a community is, in fact, to cherish, preserve, reinforce, and protect the essential elements of their community. Community is valued for three interconnected reasons. First, it is seen as essential to the development of self-identity because, as communitarians argue, we become the kind of persons we are because of our social settings and contexts. Second, and closely connected, is the notion that communities with rich, shared traditions, customs, and language provide one with a "thick" strong sense of morality, in contrast to a thinner set of universal values such as "freedom" and "equality." Thus, as Charles Taylor puts it, "The language we have come to accept articulates the issues of the good for us."[11] And, finally, because the community provides an identity that includes a set of values, it also gives the conditions for the flourishing of members of the community.

A crucial next step in this argument is to promote a nationalist format for preserving and encouraging such identity, namely, it is asserted that communal life should be organized around particular national cultures. The assumption is that the ethno-cultural nation is necessary for adequate individual and communal life. This idea is best expressed by A. Margalit, in his essay "The Moral Psychology of Nationalism," when he writes: "The idea is that people make use of different styles to express their humanity. The styles are generally determined by the communities to which they belong. There are people who express themselves 'Frenchly,' while others have forms of life that are expressed 'Koreanly,' or . . . 'Icelandicly.'"[12] A final step in this argument for an ethno-cultural nationalism is to argue that the ethno-cultural community has the right to have an ethno-national state, and the citizens of the state have the right and obligation to favor their own ethnic culture in relation to any other.

Political theorists not relying on a communitarian basis but who believe nationalism is viable often argue from a stance of seeking political justice. One group sees the demand for a nation as prior to the choices of particular individuals, for example, in the context of a social contract, and others argue for the notion of a right to collective self-determination.[13] Social justice, in the eyes of some, also demands some kind of redress for past injustices, and thus, for example, if a minority group is oppressed by the majority in a manner that almost every minority member is worse off than most majority ones, simply in virtue of belonging to the minority, then it is argued that nationalist minority claims are morally plausible and maybe even morally compelling. Freedom to conduct one's daily life is a goal, and equality, some argue, demands that steps be taken to protect the right of a minority group to its own institutional structure. This, in turn, recommends that nation-states turn themselves into more moderate multicultural ones.[14] Finally, there are arguments for nationalism based on the idea of success. Craig Calhoun argues that the nation-state has been successful in the past in promoting equality and democracy and that it seems essential today to safeguard the moral life of communities and to protect communities from the threats of globalization and assimilation.[15] Liah Greenfield, though critical of nationalism, has connected the success of capitalism and the growth of the economy with nationalism, using the United States as a paradigm case. She writes, "The unprecedented position of the economic sphere in the modern consciousness is a product of the dynamics of American society, in turn shaped by the singular characteristics of American nationalism."[16]

These are all strong arguments for some form of "nationalism," and yet the banner of nationalism in current history has led to devastating consequences, including horrific examples of ethnic cleansing. In light of this, some political philosophers have argued for some mixture of liberalism-cosmopolitanism or patriotism-nationalism. B. Barry, for example, lauds "a remarkable mixture of cosmopolitanism and parochialism" and believes this characterizes America's national identity.[17] Charles Taylor claims, "We have no choice but to be cosmopolitan and patriots."[18] Finally, Hilary Putnam proposes a loyalty to what is best in the multiple traditions that each of us participates in, a middle way, he sees, between narrow-minded patriotism and a too abstract cosmopolitanism.[19] Here again, however, the framing is in terms of a dichotomy between nationalism and cosmopolitanism. Might not a different framing be possible?

Individual Identity, Place, and Rooted Cosmopolitanism

The notion that human identity is tied to place has a long history. Thus, for Aristotle, "where something is" constitutes a basic metaphysical category (*Categories* 2a1, 5a9–14). For many indigenous groups, such as the aboriginal Australians, all life is inextricably bound up with the land.[20] In these cultures, the child's core identity is determined by his or her place of derivation. "Life is annexation of place."[21] In contemporary times this connection of human identity with place is exemplified in preoccupation with genealogy and tracing family, as well as in the sense of loss or dislocation often noted as a feature of contemporary life.[22] *Remembrance of Things Past* by Proust is essentially an invocation and exploration of places, and through these places, the persons who appear with them. Proust's novel is an embodiment of the ideas of Gaston Bachelard, who, in *The Poetics of Space*, posits the idea that the self is discovered through an investigation of the places it inhabits. It is in this work that we find two new phrases, *topophilia* (love of place) and *topoanalysis* (the investigation of places).[23] For Proust and other authors such as Toni Morrison, William Faulkner, and Salman Rushdie, human life is essentially a life of location, of self-identity found in place and of places somehow suffused with the human.[24]

Place, indeed, plays a crucial role in human experience. It seems vital to human identity and yet it can also engender a strong sense of ownership and an exaggerated contrast between locals and outsiders. It also leads to notions of sovereignty and control of all that might be essential to the place such as culture, language, tradition, money, movement in and out of place, and people allowed to belong, or even to visit. To highlight aspects of place and identity, I turn to some recent studies of "the South," a distinct region of the United States. Such a move seems justified by the conclusion of one study entitled "The Cardinal Test of a Southerner: Not Race but Geography."[25] John Shelton Reed writes:

> The sociological apparatus built around the notion of "ethnic group" can be applied profitably to the study of white Southerners. The group, we have seen, is characterized by a surprisingly high level of identification by its members, cross-cutting (as an ethnic group identification should) class, sex, and age lines. Although this identification undoubtedly responds to the currents of American sectionalism, it is not dependent on one's holding a "correct" ideological position. Its roots must be sought elsewhere. The ethnic analogy suggests that one turn to the group's history or the socialization processes that lead both Southerners and non-Southerners to think of Southerners as different.[26]

And, as the title suggests, it is not a matter of race but geography. Thus research has shown that large number of African Americans have either returned to the South or chosen to migrate there, and they are as likely as whites to claim the South as home.[27] Whatever one's race, class, sex, the sense of place seems to be central to each southerner's biography; a "southern sense of place" is feeling that your identity is grounded in the region. A southern sense of place is not only southerners' commitment to their homes and lives but also, in a much larger sense, to the region of which they are a part. "A place is not a place until people have been born into it, grown up in it, lived in it, and died in it—have both experienced and shaped it as individuals, families, neighborhoods, and communities over more than one generation."[28]

Further, there is in the South a distinct question of us versus them, of "been heres" versus "come heres," "newcomers" versus "old-timers." Native southerners claim ownership of the region, resist efforts to change it, and certainly assert the right to determine how it should be changed, if at all. A good example of the resistance and resentment toward "outsiders" is seen in the bumper sticker message: "We don't care how you did it up north." Yet there is a great deal of migration into the region as well as remigration back home, as indicated by the return of many African Americans. Key questions include the following: Can one ever claim to be southern if they were not born in the South and did not spend much of their life in the region? Can one claim a new place? Does one become one with the place or do they expect the place to become one with them? The answer is, of course, that places become humanized. Human beings change their places. In the article "Southerners All," it is claimed that "southern identity is the collective accomplishment of all in the region . . . no single group owns it . . . it belongs to all because the region itself is fashioned and continually refashioned by all."[29]

Places as tokens of identity change all the time. This is exemplified in a recent discussion of the wall of the World Trade Center by Bruce Janz, who claims that the wall was a physical site of a place but now has become a place. He calls it the "Classic American Story of triumph over insurmountable odds—the Wailing Wall, the Alamo, *Independence Day*—it is the localization and focal point of shared meaning, a place that makes identity available to be shared."[30] In this connection, he says, the thing of interest is the passing in and out of being a place. He writes: "Places are in flux, sliding in and out of existence."[31] He reminds us of Locke's view of place, which was a relational one: it is a matter of interaction; humans change the meaning of place all the time. He writes: "The World Trade Center wall is a good example of the interaction between geography and discourse. It emerges as a place not because it did not exist before, or because it was hidden from view, but because a particular mode of reflection brought it into being."[32] Janz reminds us that place can play many roles. One of these roles, in his view, is to oppose the anomic effects of globalization: "In an increasingly homogenized world, place celebrates difference. And place resists the central assumption of globalization that we are transcending place and particularity altogether. Knowledge and human experience is still rooted, and the simultaneously comforting and disorienting fact that one can eat the same McDonald's hamburger in any one of a hundred countries does not diminish this."[33] Place is an undeniably important element in any discussion of nationalism or cosmopolitanism. Place, argues Janz, exists at the edge of particularity and universality and it resists reductionism. Further, it changes with humans and with changes in their meaning and it can give a voice to a host of identities. "As that wall [at the World Trade Center] has become a place, it has become a focal point for human anguish and heroism. . . . It has given a voice to a host of identities (New York, American, victim, hero, marginalized, etc.)."[34] Place gives identity but it also transcends identities. We must not allow nationalism to circumscribe place and believe that it does not allow for a cosmopolitan approach, or even a cosmopolitan place.

Thus, we can join with Appiah in forging a notion of a cosmopolitan patriot, namely, by "entertaining the possibility of a world in which everyone is a rooted cosmopolitan, attached to home of his own or her own peculiarities, but taking pleasure from the presence of other different places, that are home to others."[35] Appiah's father noted wisely that "there was no point in roots if you can't take them with you."[36] Thus, Gertrude Stein is reported to have remarked, "America is my country and Paris is my hometown."[37] Roots and cultural practices do travel, and cultural hybridization occurs. One need only to reflect on the richness of culture in the United States, one developed and refined by numerous immigrants who brought their cultures and roots with them. Appiah speculates, correctly, I believe, that behind many objections to cosmopolitanism is the anxiety about the disappearance of cultures. As places change, so do cultures; some may disappear or become enveloped in a rich mosaic of another form of culture. Appiah writes: "The disappearance of cultural forms is consistent with a rich variety of forms of human life, because new cultural forms that differ from each other are being created all the time as well."[38] Further, as a cosmopolitan patriot moves from place to place he would accept a citizen's responsibility to nurture the culture and politics of his new home. Thus, cosmopolitanism is consistent with many different local ways of being. Further, Appiah would argue that the notion of a homogeneous "common culture" is a fantasy that does not fit reality; no nation today truly fits this idea. Thus, a cosmopolitan patriot can celebrate the varieties of human life while being rooted in one local society or a few and committed to carrying out civic, social, and moral responsibilities to that society.

A Moral Cosmopolitanism

In addition to grounding in "rootedness," a viable form of cosmopolitan, in my view, is also a moral cosmopolitanism, committed to the central values of human dignity and autonomy and human choices about ways of life. Rooted cosmopolitanism can and should support a variety of human forms of life, and the state should carve out the space within which we explore the possibility of freedom.[39] What is needed is not citizens centered on a common culture or shared core values, but citizens committed to common institutions and to conditions necessary for a common life. These conditions are "shared democratic habits." Among these habits is a requirement that we engage respectfully with our fellow citizens who disagree with us.[40] The notion of a nationalism based on a common culture promotes a notion of a society in which every political dispute can be resolved because everyone has been constrained to accept a common sense of the meaning of life. This is contradictory to both healthy nationalism and cosmopolitanism.

In my view, another aspect of a "moral cosmopolitanism" would be to respect and advocate for basic human rights. Here one would side with Martha Nussbaum in arguing for cosmopolitanism that asks persons to respond to the human, above and beyond the claims of nation, religion, and even family. The central idea is equality, namely, counting people as equals in the moral sense so that nationality, ethnicity, religion, class, race, and gender are "morally irrelevant."[41] She writes: "A crucial question for a world citizen is how to promote diversity without hierarchy . . . The challenge of world citizenship is to work toward a state of things in which all of the difference will be nonhierarchically understood."[42] It is to respond to the human, regardless of its variety of embodiment.

Among those who oppose cosmopolitanism are the strong communitarians who argue that such universal human response is not a viable notion because our obligations to compatriots and more local people crowd out any obligations to benefit human beings as such. Further, they hold that there can be no obligations except where there are close, communal relationships. Elaine Scarry has argued for the narrowness of human imagination by noting that both philosophical and literary descriptions of such imagining show the "difficulty of picturing other persons in their full weight and solidarity. This is true even when the person is a friend or acquaintance; the problem is further magnified when the person is a stranger or foreigner."[43] Scarry also argues that one can be in the presence of another person who is in pain and not know it. Further, the ease of remaining ignorant of another person's pain even permits one to inflict it.

One would not deny Scarry's claims, but yet one would also argue that persons can stretch their imagination and empathetic feelings. Richard Rorty, for example, argues for literature as a vehicle of stretching the human imagination, particularly with regard to pain and suffering. Both Rorty and Scarry cite *Uncle Tom's Cabin* as a literary work that broadened people's views of the suffering and pain of others and, in fact, incited constitutional and legal changes that eliminated the inherently aversive structural positions of "foreignness."[44] And in this volume, Noëlle McAfee conceives of a cosmopolitan imaginary that allows for us to be citizens of a certain place as well as citizens of the world.

Nussbaum responds to Scarry's concern about limited imagination by suggesting that large-scale and compelling art is generally concerned with the recognition of the common in the strange and the strange in the common. She argues that Dante, for example, was a poet of his time but not only. She writes: "We never meet a bare abstract human being."[45] She argues that human infants have universal needs for food, comfort, lights, and so on. They immediately respond to a human face. Further, she notes that children's stories do not bind the mind to the local. "Good family tales are rarely about Cambridge, Massachusetts."[46] Nussbaum refers to the human concentric circles of relationships as always developing simultaneously and in a complex and interlacing movement. One learns a language before a national song, and all know hunger and loneliness. She reminds us of the "goyim," those persons who risked death to save Jews. She writes, "These people [the goyim] were able to function as world citizens because they had not permitted the original awareness of common need and vulnerabilities to become encrusted over by demands of local ideology. They were able to respond to human face and form."[47] Human beings are capable of moving through concentric circles, of expanding loyalties. Royce developed the idea of building community through "loyalty," but a loyalty that also demanded one to expand that loyalty to other communities and other individuals. Royce's moral principle, "loyalty to loyalty," is a demand that one honor and seek to understand the loyalties of others, although also condemning destructive loyalties. Above all, loyalty to loyalty demands a concentrated effort to expand community through mediation and interpretation, expanding the circle of concern and commitment.

In concert with the notion of a rooted cosmopolitanism, Royce argues that one must begin with the individual in her immediate social context—family, neighborhood, village, and province. The forming of "creative individuals" and the skills for creative action necessarily starts with the family, the school, sports, or other kinds of club, for these are the formative crucibles for coming to self-consciousness. Family, however defined, is the original community, and it should provide the conditions that initiate the development of genuine unique selves, allowing its members to engage in processes that are a subtle blend of imitation and creativity, contrast and defiance. Further, a family, like any "genuine community," should operate by the principle of loyalty to loyalty, which asks each member to expand one's circle of concern and commitment, while also maintaining commitment to the original community.

Further, a genuine community, whether local or cosmopolitan, should be characterized, says Royce, by an emphasis on the contrasts between various individuals. A genuine creative individual, in Royce's view, is one who is able to generate a multiplicity of viable potential strategies for serving a cause or a project or solving a problem, thus enhancing her opportunity for effective action. This is also true for community—the "effectiveness of human action at the level of community will be enhanced by a pluralism of ideas and strategies which can be realized only through the cultivation of individual differences."[48]

Royce, in my view, was an advocate for rooted cosmopolitanism. He argued for building wholesome communities at the beginning level—family and province. He wrote extensively on the notion of "wholesome provincialism." Stuart Gerry Brown has argued that the values represented in Royce's wholesome provincialism are individual freedom and democracy. He writes:

> The dearest social values are the liberty and dignity of the individual man and the democratic method of arriving at social decisions. In order to preserve and enhance these values, we must re-emphasize, re-dignify, and re-vitalize the smaller units of society which are known as provinces, for within the provincial life individual variety will most surely flourish. A democratic nation requires variety of province just as a democratic province requires a variety of individuals; a world order which is at once free and democratic will require variety of nations.[49]

A final level of creative community building for Royce was to create a world community. This action was described in several of his works, but most especially in his 1916 *The Hope of the Great Community*. Royce warns against any notion of cosmopolitanism that would urge people to eschew their national identities and consider themselves only as "citizens of the world."[50] He views such a notion of global community as too abstract, too utopian and as an understanding of relationships that is too thin. Rather, Royce views global community as emerging by "uniting the already existing communities of mankind into higher communities."[51] The unity envisioned by Royce is an aesthetic unity, a unity that encompasses variety and rich diversity. This unity would respect the internal motives for loyalty and modes of expression of the loyalty exhibited in each community; it would be a plurality of morally autonomous communities. A truly international community as envisioned by Royce would find a way to respect the liberty of individual nations. Royce writes:

> Therefore, while the great community of the future will unquestionably be international by virtue of the ties which will bind its various nationalities together, it will find no place for that sort of internationalism which despises the individual variety of nations, and which tries to substitute for the services of those who at present seek merely to conquer mankind, the equally

worthless desire of those who hope to see us in future as "men without a country" . . . There can be no true international life unless the nations remain to possess it.[52]

Of course, to achieve such a unity with plurality will involve much creative interpretation and dialogue.

Finally, Royce, through his extensive work on "interpretation" and "mediation," provides a solid basis for creating community out of conflict and thus for working to build a global community. Such a global community would not develop out of political institutions, but rather will be the result of deliberative dialogues among autonomous international agents acting together in communities of interpretation. In addition to creative community building, Royce's views are clearly relevant to the need today to address the various tragic conflicts so besetting our world. Thus, in a very fine essay on power and compassion, Shibley Telhami, author of *The Stakes: America and the Middle East*, argues for the need to build bridges of mutual understanding by establishing dialogue with various stakeholders.[53] Royce's ideas on dialogue and interpretation are also reflected in the work of Reverend Alec Reid, a Catholic priest who played a crucial role in bringing peace to the Irish situation and is now working on the Basque controversies with Spain.

With Royce, I believe a "rooted cosmopolitanism" is possible and needed today. It will take much work on the part of many, but creative thought and action are what philosophy should be about. It is my hope that many will seek to take on the task.

JACQUELYN ANN K. KEGLEY is Professor in the Department of Philosophy and Religious Studies at California State University, Bakersfield. Her philosophical areas of specialization include American philosophy (and particularly the thought of Josiah Royce), philosophy of race, bioethics and philosophy of medicine, and technology and philosophy of science. Her most recent book is *Josiah Royce: In Focus* (Indiana University Press, 2008).

Notes

1. In her discussion of climate change, Nancy Tuana similarly addresses the problem of a simple dichotomy between national and global allegiances. She refers to a cosmopolitanism that simply opposes itself to nationalism as "too thin" (see Chapter 11, page 184 of this volume) in its failure to address multiple levels of interdependence. I similarly argue in what follows that a meaningful cosmopolitanism must be rooted in a variety of connections and loyalties.

2. Kwame Anthony Appiah, *Cosmopolitanism: Ethics in a World of Strangers* (New York: W. W. Norton, 2006).

3. In Chapter 6 (85), Vincent Colapietro argues that "place" should not be thought of as a location at all but as a set of "processes and practices." While, for reasons that will become evident, I find the concept of location useful to an understanding of place, Colapietro's attention to process can help to account for the possibility of creative change and undermine notions of ownership.

4. See Chapter 7, page 107 of this volume.

5. Larry J. Griffin, Renae J. Evenson, and Ashley B. Thompson, "Southerners All," *Southern Cultures* 16, no. 1 (Spring 2012): 6–25; Bruce Janz, "Walls and Border: The Range of Place," *City and Community* 4, no. 1 (March 2005): 87–94.

6. Appiah, *Cosmopolitanism*.

7. Tony Swain, *A Place of Strangers* (Cambridge: Cambridge University Press, 1986).

8. See W. Kymlicka, ed., *The Rights of Minority Cultures* (Oxford: Oxford University Press, 1995); M. Moore, ed., *National Self-Determination and Succession* (Oxford: Oxford University Press, 1998).

9. See Hilary Putnam, "Must We Choose between Patriotism and Universal Reason?," in *Cosmopolitics: Thinking and Feeling beyond the Nation*, ed. Pheng Cheah and Bruce Robbins, 91–97 (Minneapolis: University of Minnesota Press, 1998); Richard Rorty, "Justice as a Larger Loyalty," in *For Love of Country*, ed. Joshua Cohen, 45–58 (New York: Beacon, 2002).

10. Sissela Bok, "From Part to Whole," in *Cosmopolitics: Thinking and Feeling beyond the Nation*, ed. Pheng Cheah and Bruce Robbins, 38–44 (Minneapolis: University of Minnesota Press, 1998).

11. Charles Taylor, *Sources of the Self* (Cambridge: Cambridge University Press, 1989), 35.

12. Avishai Margalit, "The Moral Psychology of Nationalism," in *The Morality of Nationalism*, ed. R. McKim and J. McMahan, 74–87 (Oxford: Oxford University Press, 1997).

13. See especially A. Buchanan, *Justice, Legitimacy, and Self-Determination* (Oxford: Oxford University Press, 2004); C. Gans, *The Limits of Nationalism* (Cambridge: Cambridge University Press, 2003). For a work on the right to succession, see A. Pakovi and P. Radan, eds., *Creating New States: Theory and Practice of Succession* (London: Ashgate, 2007).

14. W. Kymlicka, ed., *The Rights of Minority Cultures* (Oxford: Oxford University Press, 1995); W. Kymlicka, *Multicultural Citizenship* (Oxford: Oxford University Press, 1995); and W. Kymlicka, *Politics in the Vernacular* (Oxford: Oxford University Press, 2001).

15. See C. Calhoun, *Nations Matter: Culture, History, and the Cosmopolitan Dream* (London: Routledge, 2007); A. Mason, "Political Community, Liberal-Nationalism and the Ethics of Assimilation," *Ethics* 109:261–86.

16. L. Greenfield, *The Spirit of Capitalism: Nationalism and Economic Growth* (Cambridge, MA: Harvard University Press, 2001); L. Greenfield, *Nationalism and the Mind* (Oxford: Oneworld, 2006).

17. B. Barry, *Culture and Equality* (Cambridge: Polity, 2001).

18. Charles Taylor, *Reconciling the Solitudes* (Montreal: McGill University Press, 1993), 121.

19. Putnam, "Must We Choose," 114.

20 See Fred R. Myers, *Pinpui Country, Pinpui Self* (Canberra: Australian Institute of Aboriginal Studies, 1986).

21. Swain, *Place of Strangers*, 3.

22. See Peter Read, *Returning to Nothing: The Meaning of Lost Place* (Cambridge: Cambridge University Press, 1996).

23. Gaston Bachelard, *The Poetics of Space*, trans. Maria Jolas (Boston: Beacon, 1994).

24. For an extensive discussion of Place, see J. E. Malpas, *Place and Experience* (Cambridge: Cambridge University Press, 1999).

25. John Shelton Reed, "The Cardinal Test of a Southerner: Not Race but Geography," *Public Opinion Quarterly* 57, no. 2 (1973): 232–40.

26. Ibid.

27. See William W. Falk, Larry L. Hunt, and Matthew O. Hunt, "Return Migrations of African-Americans to the South: Reclaiming a Land or Promise, Going Home, or Both? *Rural Sociology* 69 (2004): 490–509; William W. Falk, Larry L. Hunt, and Matthew O. Hunt, "Who Is Headed South? Return Migration in Black and White," *Social Forces* 85 (2008): 95–119.

28. Wallace Stegner, *Where the Bluebird Sings in the Lemonade Springs* (New York: Random House, 1992), 165.

29. Larry J. Griffin, Ranae J. Evenson, and Ashley Thompson, "Southerners All," *Southern Cultures* 11, no. 1 (Spring 2005): 6–15, 23.

30. Bruce Janz, "Walls and Borders: The Range of Place," *City and Community* 4, no. 1 (March 2005): 87.

31. Ibid.

32. Ibid., 88.

33. Ibid., 92.

34. Ibid., 93.

35. Kwame Anthony Appiah, "Cosmopolitan Patriots," in *Cosmopolitics: Thinking and Feeling beyond the Nation*, ed. Pheng Cheah and Bruce Robbins (Minneapolis: University of Minnesota Press, 1998), 91.

36. Ibid.

37. In the 2006 motion picture *The Devil Wears Prada*, the character Christian Thompson, played by Simon Baker, attributes to Gertrude Stein the statement "America is my country, but Paris is my hometown." See also Appiah, "Cosmopolitan Patriots," 91.

38. Appiah, "Cosmopolitan Patriots," 92.

39. Ibid., 102.

40. Ibid., 103.

41. Martha Nussbaum, "Reply," in *For the Love of Country*, ed. Martha Nussbaum and Joshua Cohen (Boston: Beacon, 1997), 133.

42. Ibid., 138.

43. Elaine Scarry, "The Difficulty of Imagining Other People," in *The Handbook for Interethnic Coexistence*, ed. Edward Weiner (New York: Continuum, 1998), 40.

44. Ibid., 99–100.

45. Nussbaum, "Reply," 141.

46. Ibid., 142.

47. Ibid., 144.

48. Griffin Trotter, "Royce, Community, and Ethnicity," *Transactions of the Charles S. Pierce Society* 30, no. 3 (1994): 254.

49. Stuart Gerry Brown, "From Provincialism to the Great Community: The Social Philosophy of Josiah Royce," *Ethics* 59, no. 1 (October 1948): 14–34.

50. Antonio-Jose Orosco, "Cosmopolitan Loyalty and the Great Global Community: Royce's Globalization," *Journal of Speculative Philosophy* 19, no. 3 (2003): 205. Orosco discusses the cosmopolitan ideas of Martha Nussbaum in this context. Additionally, this concern with such an untethered cosmopolitanism may be akin to John Stuhr's criticism (though he comes to a different conclusion than I do here) that those who assume themselves to be at home anywhere would fail to "know their place" (see Chapter 17, page 284 of this volume).

51. Josiah Royce, *The Hope of the Great Community* (New York: Macmillan, 1916), 49.
52. Ibid., 50–51.
53. Shibley Telhami. *The Stakes: American and the Middle East* (Boulder, CO: Westview, 2002); Shibley Telhami, "Of Power and Compassion," in *The Philosophical Challenge of September 11*, ed. Tom Rockmore, Joseph Margolis, and Armen Marsobian, 70–80 (London: Blackwell, 2004).

5 Pragmatism and the Challenge of a Cosmopolitan Aesthetics

Framing the Issues

Robert E. Innis

The Problem: Scharfstein's Challenge

In his *Art Without Borders: A Philosophical Exploration of Art and Humanity*, Ben-Ami Scharfstein, writing against the background of his deeply pragmatic *The Dilemma of Context*, contends, "Art is not a single problem, nor does it have a single solution, rational or mystical."[1] Art's multiple contexts, and types of contexts, are, he argues, the sources of this radical plurality, which characterizes thought itself. In this, art mirrors life itself. Nevertheless, in spite of the admitted plurality, he issues a call for an "open aesthetics" and an "aesthetic pluralism" and asks, "Is there really an aesthetics that cuts across all human cultures?"[2] It may be that there is, but it is not immediately clear how "openness" and "pluralism" can be accommodated to the putative demand of cosmopolitanism to be "universal" and not "provincial."

This, as I see it, is the core issue of the project of developing a "cosmopolitan aesthetics," an aesthetics that is not limited to, or based on, any one "place," either *temperamental, geographical, conceptual,* or *political*. These types of places are deeply intertwined, as the contributions to this volume show, and each marks a space of difference with potentially, but not necessarily, deleterious consequences.[3] We can find such places other than our own, whatever they may be, "strange" and often treat them and those who inhabit them as dangerous or threatening to our entrenched forms of self-understanding, which get valorized in forms of power and dominance embodied in state institutions to control the other. A cosmopolitan aesthetics would recognize in a spirit of affirmation the validity or value of temperamental differences, accept the rootedness of aesthetic values in different ecological or geographical frames, acknowledge that the conceptual tools used in aesthetic theories have links to other conceptual commitments, especially metaphysical world visions, and need not have the same weight or focus in every tradition and their paradigmatic art forms, and be wary of political enforcement of "official art."

Scharfstein points out the ineluctable and irreducible "difference between generalizations and their examples,"[4] a difference known to everyone who has read a book on aesthetic theory or reflected on their own aesthetic experience. Theories need exemplifications, to be sure, but aesthetic theories are notoriously connected with the tastes and preferences of the theorist, a point foregrounded in Hume's classic essay on the standard of taste. But exemplifications likewise need theories, in some sense of that term, in order to be placed in an intelligible context and validated. A cursory look at John Dewey's examples, including the original illustrations in *Art as Experience*, or in Santayana's own "cosmopolitan" *The Sense of Beauty*, bears out this reciprocity between theory and exemplification, but one could choose practically any book at random, from any tradition from Aristotle to the present day, to illustrate the point. It is to Scharfstein's great merit—and a challenge to us—that he tries to avoid both the perils of an ungrounded or unreflecting provincialism and an aesthetic version of the Hegelian complaint about Schelling's Absolute, that it was "the night in which all the cows are black."

Still, the nonflattening universal implications of a cosmopolitan aesthetics is gestured toward in Scharfstein's not unambiguous remark that "it is its universalization that distinguishes aesthetic from ordinary experience."[5] Here the reference point of universalization is not *art* in an essentialist sense, but a principled contrast drawn between dimensions, phases, or types of exemplified experiences (of certain types of objects or situations, whether art in any predefined sense or not). Aesthetic experience, as well as its objects, has to have more than a merely local or idiosyncratic appeal if the notion of some kind of universality or intelligibility is to have any validity at all. Art and aesthetic experiences, while necessarily embedded in, as well as creating, particular contexts, must in some sense be able to transcend these contexts and their boundaries, or at least in principle not be limited to them. They must be in some way open to everyone, but not necessarily on their own terms. And there has to be a context, or at least an interpretive process, that contextualizes these contexts, perhaps a kind of meta-context that allows mutual and nonreductive engagement. But, I propose, this meta-context does not have to be universal theory but a set of hermeneutical practices that Gadamer characterized as the "fusion of horizons."[6] Such practices will accept the permanent tension between "cosmopolitan," "open," and "universal." "Cosmopolitan" foregrounds the self-conscious or self-reflective nonprovinciality of an aesthetic theory or aesthetic practice; "open" foregrounds the consequent unbounded willingness to accept new instances of aesthetic values; and "universal" foregrounds the aspect of general import of aesthetic products or their demand on us for recognition.

While clearly not identical, these labels have substantial overlap and relations of mutual implication.

Scharfstein's challenge is clear. A cosmopolitan aesthetics must find a way of surmounting multiple boundaries: (a) between historical artistic traditions, with radically different forms of art and their cultural, including philosophical, matrices; (b) between forms and genera of art and their rankings; (c) between the experience of art and other forms of (aesthetic and nonaesthetic) experience; (d) between art and non-art. Obviously it is not possible to deal with all these issues in the course of a single chapter. Nor could Scharfstein in the course of five hundred dense and nuanced pages. It is primarily, though not exclusively, the first type of boundary I am concerned with, although each boundary type bears on the problem at hand. It is a commonplace in the history of art, and of the forms of experiencing associated with it, that different cultures have deep preferences as to paradigmatic art forms as well as different levels and standards of excellence and achievement. Whether music, literature, painting, sculpture, architecture, or whatever is the highest form of art and the source of the greatest pleasure and insight is not central to the specific theme at hand. But, once again, such rankings, or temptations to such rankings, illustrate the substantive problems facing the intertwined themes of a cosmopolitan, open, and universal aesthetics. Moreover, the concept of aesthetic *experience* does not initially have to be connected to art at all, but, as Dewey clearly showed in *Art as Experience*, is more general than art. As to drawing a line between art and non-art, unless one has an antecedently accepted universal concept of art as such, which one does not have to have, the task would seem not just impossible but unnecessary.

Some Analytical Complexities

It is clear (and Scharfstein's book confronts this boundary problem unflinchingly) that there are many artistic traditions and many different institutionalized and entrenched "habits of attending" in and to the world. These traditions make up a kind of aesthetic "pluralistic universe," a vast stream of eddies and currents of products and contexts that intersect, fuse, repel, and challenge one another. There are many different aesthetically relevant conceptions of art and the aesthetic, with multiple focal points that compete and strive to subordinate or reduce the others to themselves. For example, the classical Western aesthetic tradition's focus on "beauty" is entangled with other putatively general analytical and critical categories such as "form," "meaning," "expression," and so forth, which struggle for conceptual primacy and strive to put beauty in its place, and perhaps even "dis-place" it.[7] But such categories have more than merely local validity and appeal, and they challenge us to "dis-locate" ourselves from our self-evident, individually and socially egocentric, premises.

Stendhal in his work *Love* famously wrote, in the existential, not the analytical mode, that "Beauty is only the promise of happiness." But he also qualified this assertion: "There are as many styles of beauty as there are visions of happiness."[8] But I think that focusing on beauty as essentially or necessarily connected with happiness restricts the content of a promised, or hoped for, cosmopolitan aesthetics. While beauty and happiness, on the one hand, are clearly not merely local categories, nor, on the other hand, do they have, if we follow Stendhal, a univocal meaning. It could be objected that Stendhal is trying to explicate the already contentious, obscure, and problematic by recourse to the even more contentious, obscure, and problematic, that is, the putatively objective and normative—*beauty*, by something subjective and variable—*happiness*?

Stendhal, a cosmopolite himself, is, however, clearly onto something by trying to hold on to both poles. One might think it self-evident that one would never pursue beauty if doing so did not offer some intrinsic, internal, noninstrumental reward, such as "happiness." But beauty is also clearly not a mere tool for obtaining something else external to it. Still, as the sinologist François Jullien has convincingly argued in his *Vital Nourishment: Departing from Happiness*,[9] there is a way of thinking of the "vital nourishment" we get from art and the aesthetic as precisely involving *departing* from happiness rather than seeking it. Perhaps, following Jullien, one is seeking—or even not seeking—something else entirely, for example, "ontological attunement" or a way of manifesting and participating in the invisible "originative matrix" of the visible, as in the Taoist tradition and, to a certain extent, in the Confucian tradition's concern with being in balance with "the way of Heaven." And while there is a radical theological divide between Plotinus's framing of art and beauty (and its Christianizing continuation in Augustine and the high Scholastic tradition) in terms of eternal forms and our participation in them and the Taoist framing of parallel issues in terms of processivity, there are nevertheless remarkable intersections in terms of contemplating the cosmos as a play of forms emerging from and manifesting a primal unity, as John Scotus Eriugena proposed in *De Divisione Naturae*.

Crispin Sartwell has shown, in *Six Names of Beauty*,[10] how different cultural matrices, with their different terminological accents and focal points, can supply other, albeit not completely foreign and novel, conceptual tools that foreground or place other aspects of our encounters with beauty, or at least one of its placeholders, and in this way effectively explodes a unitary meaning to such a term. Sartwell "rotates" the notion of beauty through six frames and matrices that locate various experiential occasions and their objects and place them in the spectrum of our lives, both individual and social. Beauty is explored: (a) as satisfaction of an existential lack, hence the link between happiness and beauty (Plato's *Symposium* and Stendhal's this-worldly quest); (b) as openness to sensory glowing and blooming, to forms of appearing as appearing;[11] (c) as the experienced decentering, transcending, even loss, of the self toward "the holy"; (d) as participation in ideality and rational order; (e) as engagement in forms of modest, even "poor," everydayness; and (f) as pursuit of wholeness, health, and environmental harmony.

Just as in the Islamic tradition Allah has many names, not even the sum of which can encompass his unlimited reality, so even the most cursory look at the history of aesthetic reflection reveals an open spiral of corresponding partial mappings of "beauty" or its correlates or substitutes. The aesthetic dimension spreads itself over the whole field of experience and the multiple contexts in which it occurs.

Engaging Boundaries and Affinities: An Exemplification

A truly cosmopolitan aesthetics, or any aesthetics claiming some sort of universal relevance, then, would acknowledge and accept differences but learn not to pass beyond or over them but to pass *between* them or even over *to* them, as Sartwell did in his "album of instances."[12] To that effect I would like to show, in a test case, how by relying on some critical elements primarily from John Dewey's pragmatist and experiential approach to the aesthetic we can establish deep and hidden affinities of general import and mutual confirmation between Dewey's analytical scheme as found principally in *Art as Experience* and the philosophical approach embodied in one major strand of Chinese art and aesthetics as propounded by François Jullien in *The Great Image Has No Form or On the Non-object through Painting*. Such a comparison and contrast throws strong light on how a Deweyan pragmatist aesthetics can supply essential analytical tools for a cosmopolitan aesthetics. It can further an understanding of an aesthetic tradition and metaphysical vision that emerged in radically different circumstances from the pragmatist philosophical tradition. But nevertheless, especially in their philosophical naturalist forms, they ultimately have much in common and, in terms of comparative philosophy, are mutually enriching.

To turn, then, immediately to the first point of contrast and contact, Dewey speaks, in *Art as Experience*, of "the penetrating quality that runs through all the parts of a work of art and binds them in an individualized whole.... The different elements and specific qualities of a work of art blend and fuse in a way which physical things cannot emulate. This fusion is the felt presence of the same qualitative unity in all them."[13] Dewey's phenomenological point is quite general, not restricted to the aesthetic dimension and indeed can be applied to our perception of physical things and problematic situations of all sorts.[14] For Dewey, the center of any occasion of experience is an "intuited enveloping quality," which runs through all its differentiations. "The resulting sense of totality is commemorative, expectant, insinuating, premonitory." But, as Dewey says, "there is no name to be given it."[15] It is what it is, with its own "idiom" that stamps it with individuality.

This sense of totality, Dewey writes, is the "background" that "enters into and qualifies everything in its focus, everything distinguished as a part and member."[16] Dewey puts at the heart of his aesthetic project, appropriating and extending James's rich phenomenological descriptions, the essential openness of experience as a process that "grows by its edges" with an aura or margin of felt tendencies and transitive relations. The following text helps us see a first fertile point of intersection, or overlap, between Dewey's valorizing approach to aesthetics from the experiential side and Jullien's presentation of Chinese literati painting from the metaphysical side. The problem of a cosmopolitan aesthetics will be seen, even starting "low" on the experiential level, to bear on the problem of a metaphysical or cosmic vision embodied in and informing aesthetic and artistic contexts. Dewey writes in two long passages that frame a large part of the following discussion:

> We are accustomed to think of physical objects as having bounded edges; things like rocks, chairs, books, houses, trade, and science, with its efforts at precise measurement, have confirmed the belief. Then we unconsciously carry over this belief in the bounded character of all *objects* of experience (a belief founded ultimately in the practical exigencies of our dealings with things) into our conception of experience itself. We suppose the experience has the same definite limits as the things with which it is concerned. But any experience the most ordinary, has an indefinite total setting. Things, objects, are only focal points of a here and now in a whole that stretches out indefinitely. This is the qualitative "background" which is defined and made definitely conscious in particular objects and specified properties and qualities.
>
> For although there is a bounding horizon, it moves as we move. We are never wholly free from the sense of something that lies beyond. Within the limited world directly seen, there is a tree with a rock at its foot; we fasten our sight upon the rock, and then upon the moss on the rock, and perhaps then take a microscope to view some tiny lichen. But whether the scope of vision be vast or minute, we experience it as a part of larger whole and inclusive whole, a part that now focuses our experience. We might expand the field from the narrower to the wider. But however broad the field, it is still felt as not the whole; the margins shade into that indefinite expanse beyond which imagination calls the universe. This sense of the including whole implicit in ordinary experiences is rendered intense within the frame of a painting or poem.[17]

Dewey's phenomenology is concerned, from the experiential side, with the feeling of "the unlimited envelope" that becomes, or is made, intense in our experience of an object of art but is also present in other occasions of experience, especially of landscapes, the paradigm Chinese art form. Jullien argues that Chinese landscape painting will try to paint—*as a nonobject*—this unlimited envelope, such that it makes manifest that, to repeat Dewey's words in the preceding texts, "we are never wholly free from the sense of something that lies beyond." Everything experienced as a focal object, Dewey writes, is "part of a large whole and inclusive whole." Dewey then avails himself of the fundamental Jamesian triad of theme-field-margin. The focal object is a Jamesian theme, the part of the stream of consciousness that "focuses our experience." The theme is located within a "field," which may be narrower or wider. But, Dewey writes, "however broad the field, it is still felt as not the whole; the margins shade into that indefinite expanse beyond which imagination calls the universe."[18] Hence, still speaking from the experiential perspective, Dewey remarks, "About every explicit and focal object there is a recession into the implicit which is not intellectually grasped. . . . The sense of extensive and underlying whole is the context of every experience and it is the essence of sanity."[19] The "sanity" referred to here is a feature of experience, but, if we can trust Jullien, it has ontological and existential relevance, without being reduced to the realm of "subjectivity."

Chinese literati painting, according to Jullien, "unfocuses" our experience from "the object" and the semiotically charged task of "representation," one of the great themes of Western art and its philosophical companion and tutor. In *The Great Image Has No Form*, Jullien characterizes classic literati painting as an attempt to silence and soften "representation's power to figure"—that is, to present objects—and to bring us, paradoxically, by means of an image of the "great image" that has no form to the "brink of the undifferentiated."[20] This is the Chinese equivalent of Peircean firstness as metaphysical category. To be sure, according to Jullien, while "the concrete is refined but not left behind . . . once we get to China . . . we leave behind the autonomous consistency of forms, and the status of the perceived object dissolves," although in light of the development of abstract painting such a dissolution of the object is not unique to Chinese painting.[21] In Jullien's conception, Chinese painting has as its goal to make manifest "breath-resonance/energy-consonance," and this is "ineffable" and "nonsubstantial" in the strong sense. It is, as the *Tao de Ching* says, beyond names and, as Jullien contends, beyond images, too. What is made manifest in the painting is, according to Jullien, the "undifferentiating-harmonizing fount" that is no 'objective that' able to be pointed to.[22] "If there is a 'that' which Chinese painting paints, it is truly the primordial 'that' of breath-energy, from which the world endlessly comes forth and which animates the world."[23]

This is another way, in my opinion, of speaking in a different rhetorical (creative metaphorical) register about *natura naturans* or *nature naturing* that is the core concept or principle of philosophical naturalism. It likewise takes, in the Chinese context, a nontheistic form. Breath-energy is not a substance, not a thing, not a cosmic person, not the "the wholeness of the divine All" of the Stoics, Jullien remarks. It escapes, maybe even sidesteps, the grip of onto-theology altogether. It is beyond being and nonbeing. While Dewey clearly admits the deep affinity between the "mystical" sense of participation in an encompassing whole and the deep structures of aesthetic perception, he is also close to the Chinese position as laid out by Jullien: "China is not haunted by that hidden God" of traditional philosophy. "It has no interest in deciphering the Promise nor has it been anxious about Lack."[24] That is, it is not "symbolic" or "compensatory" or waiting for a "revelation" from or of another world. And neither is a Deweyan or Dewey-inspired naturalist aesthetics or metaphysics.[25] Jullien argues that for Chinese painting the painted world—the world itself—is the "phenomenal site of a transformation" and its "object—or rather its nonobject—is what he calls "the fount of invisibility."[26] But that fount, following Jullien, in spite of being manifested, does not enter into the realm of form, even if it is impossible for us to leave this realm. "That is the realism inherent in painting,"[27] even if form itself is not the "non-objective-object," which appears *in* and *through* it, but not *as* it.

Still, I think that there is a deep, even if seemingly paradoxical, affinity between Dewey's experiential approach and the Taoist "recession" from experience, an affinity that reveals something fundamental about the project of a cosmopolitan, open, and non-content-determined universal aesthetics. Dewey, for example, remarks in *Art as Experience* that "emphasis on spaciousness is a characteristic of Chinese paintings," that "move outwards" and, for example, in the case of panoramic scroll paintings "present a world in which ordinary boundaries are transformed into invitations to proceed."[28] Participation in an unfolding process has a remarkable similarity to Dewey's profound and pivotal notion of "organization of energies" that marks both the artwork and the participant observer who is turned into a live creature by the work.

Clearly, however, Dewey's aesthetics, extending James's crucial insights into the dynamic structures of experiencing, is on one level oriented toward perceptual completion or at least completion in perception—or, paradoxically, an experience of "incompletion." It sees art's fundamental role as capturing objects in their intensity and in their surrounding fields in terms of their "shades of expression," that is, their forms of appearing. But it, no more than the literati paintings that Jullien brings forth for discussion in their philosophical import, is not essentialist and does not intend to find fixed objects or fixed meanings. In fact, Dewey thought it was precisely art's role to disabuse of the notion that objects had permanent, fixed properties. Indeed, Peircean semiotics proposes that the complex semiotic structure of art works induces an unending play of interpretants, or proper significate effects.[29] The following passage from Jullien about China is, in many, though not in all, ways, deeply compatible with the essential thrust of a pragmatist aesthetics: "China never conceived of the contemplation of images as an operation of recognition or as the pleasure of recognition. The aim of figuration is not to fix essences but to record the play of energies in continuous interaction, whose coherence figuration unveils and indicates how to use."[30] The Western tradition, with its organizing principle of representation, certainly has implemented a metaphysical project clearly different from the Chinese, until it ran its course and, with the rise of abstraction, found its pleasure not in the contemplation of objects but in the energies of objects and in the principles by which objects obtain their energies and their nonobjective reverberations. While representation certainly is a legitimate goal of painting as an art (and of other art forms of course), it does not entail production of an exact copy. It is a re-presentation, not a duplication. The relation of representation to figuration, to be sure, is defined by their relative placement within different conceptual systems and, as we will see, different material practices. But acceptance of the aesthetic validity of one does not contravene acceptance of the other.

An historically sensitive and pragmatist cosmopolitan aesthetics would not try to fix essences in an ontologically constituted and critically oriented meta-context or meta-frame, a project that Jullien ascribes essentially to the West in general and to Greece in particular.[31] Such an ascription is clearly true to one of the central features of the classical strand in Western aesthetic theory, the normative status of which was gradually weakened by artistic practices, in multiple genera, within that tradition itself, as has been charted by art historians in great detail. While Aristotelian *mimesis* and the Chinese project of *figuration*, Jullien rightly argues, have important and quite different conceptual contexts and ontological points of origin, still the differences are not absolute if we attend to the processual side of Aristotle's own dynamic vision of nature and his criticism of any aesthetic norms beyond nature itself. And we have to accept Jullien's claim that he is not proposing any intrinsic superiority of one over the other.[32] It is true that the Chinese tradition, as characterized by Jullien, places the origin of painting in the "great Process of the world, which exceeds human beings to the point of being 'unfathomable' and encompasses all human activity,"[33] but this is not a position foreign to, for example, major strands in the Romantic tradition of nature painting or to such theorists-artists as Goethe. Again, Jullien claims that China "conceived and justified the power of images in a completely different way" from the Greeks, for in their case "lying at the heart of the image is not some capacity both representative and cognitive but rather an efficacy."[34] But, one could ask, is not this clearly and emphatically nonmagical efficacy the phenomenon of the "organization of energies," the play of felt "tendencies," that lies that at the core of Dewey's James-based aesthetics? Is not the artwork, and the participants, both creative and receptive, the "locus" of this "play"?[35]

Jullien speaks of the Chinese image phenomenon "as an energetic condensation and as a convocation of powers" that early on "took its distance from the requirement for resemblance, or at least from resemblance of form," without, however, repudiating them altogether. The philosophical premise of this distance taking is that the painted image bears on the "Great Emptiness" that is the "nonobject par excellence," a focal point of the Taoist philosophical position.[36] The consequence for the philosophical aesthetics immanent in and governing the pictorial traditions Jullien is proposing in contrast to the dominant Western tradition is that "rather than the imitation of an external object set up as a model and considered only from a perceptual point of view, what is at issue is the power of figuration that anticipates the entreaty emanating from beings and things and joins with them in the internal aspiration that makes them exist, leading them to deploy."[37] This entreaty is a spiritual resonance that strives to achieve a kind of closure but not completeness, a closure that is always finite and transitory. Such a resonance gives the processive figuration—*not the figure*—a live presence, which also, Jullien argues elsewhere, accounts for the absence of the nude in Chinese painting.[38] "If spiritual resonance does not emanate from all sides, you will deploy the resemblance of form to no avail."[39]

Spiritual resonance is a phenomenologically apt notion, a kind of Chinese analogue to Dewey's point about the felt difference between living and dead *forms* of appearing. Forms do appear, to be sure, but the *form* of appearing can lack energy or power to quicken us by being too easy or slack, with no auratic margins of implications such as James describes in the famous chapter of *Principles of Psychology*. In such cases, there is nothing in the "presentation," nor the representation, that elicits from us a response that leads us on and *into* a field of felt implications.[40] The contrast Jullien makes between resonance and resemblance is a fruitful one, but the relation between them, as Jullien shows in spite of himself, is not absolute. Jullien writes that resonance is the "prolonged reverberation of an internal timbre, while resemblance is the specific reproduction of external traits. Resonance opens onto infinite vibration, while reproduction dries up on the surface."[41] Paradoxically, infinite vibration and resonance belong first and foremost to the object and only as a consequence to the perceiver. The object appearing is a dynamic, even at times evanescent, locus or congelation of activity and power, which emerges from and makes appear its ground, which, on the Chinese view, is *no-thing-at-all*, the cosmic marginal field.

As to the second pole of the resonance-resemblance contrast, Jullien writes of a "resemblance that does not resemble," that is not compelled by (formal) resemblance but "deploys indefinitely *through* form."[42] Indeed, in the case of painting, true resemblance, according to Jullien, "lies in that allusivity to the invisible dimension that permeates the concrete particularity of all the strokes."[43] This "concrete particularity" is, looked at from the point of view of pragmatist semiotics, the signifying power resident in the "material quality" of the image-sign, what Meyer Schapiro ascribed to the two principal nonrepresentational components in an image-sign, namely, the "vehicle" that makes forms appear and the "field" in which they appear that becomes progressively more and more "framed." The persistent emphasis of the Chinese literati paintings that Jullien has taken as his theme is paradoxically to paint within, or construct, a frame that makes appear on the margins another frame that can never be encompassed. It is out of this frame that an infinite vibration emerges and is embodied in concrete, though transient, forms. So paradoxically, resemblance, as correspondence to its object, can be seen to be at work even when there is no object at all, and in this way it is precisely in the materially visible's allusive power that it is able to make manifest the invisible.

Readers of the two chapters in *Art as Experience* on the common and varied substance of the arts will recall that Dewey makes much of the fact that "every product of art is matter and matter only," and that "sensitivity to a medium as a medium is the very heart of all artistic creation and esthetic perception."[44] Indeed, as Dewey writes, "media and esthetic effect are completely fused."[45] This is precisely the point Jullien is making. Dewey saw Peirce's great contribution to an experiential philosophy to lie in his theory of quality, including the material quality of any sign-configuration: that everything, every situation, every object, every moment of consciousness, every life, has its own distinctive *quale*, and a fortiori so does every work of art.[46] The concrete particularity of the stroke in Chinese painting is based on the embodied, that is, indexically configured, semiotics of the wrist and the utilization of the method of 'one stroke' by which a medium becomes the locus of an appearing of something, but not some thing, that cannot itself appear but is still made manifest. This profound notion of the stroke has been explored in the rich text of Shih Ta'o on the philosophy of painting.[47] Such a notion reminds one familiar with Peirce's idea of firstness as a plenum of possibility of his striking image of the "mark" on the cosmic slate board that introduces "difference" in the plenum, setting possibility "into play," that is, into actuality. Whether the mark comes from an original "sporting" without agency or from an immanent agency at work in the world is, of course, not unambiguously settled by Peirce. According to the Western tradition, the agent is the artist; however, the artist may be inspired by an outside power (the Muses or divine inspiration) or dependent on the available material means of introducing differences on the marked surface, whatever it should be, and thus creating a material field of appearances, as Schapiro has shown.

In connection with the foregoing idea of the mark or the stroke, when Jullien offers up the contentious, yet defensible, assertion that the essence of Chinese painting is *de*-picting, that is, *un*-picturing, he argues that it rests on an (achieved) effortless fusion of wrist, brush, and ink, culminating in, or exemplified in, the ink wash, which has its own "qualitative feel" or "distinctive quality," which every material configuration has. Jullien writes with respect to the aesthetic revolution of the Tang dynasty in the eighth and ninth centuries:

> It was exclusively to the ink wash that the Chinese literati assigned the play of variation between pale and dark, wet and dry, "between there is-there is not," to render the evanescent character of things in the process or emergence or resorption. These things, born of the gradual saturation of the silk or paper by the ink, deploy in a haze, and this halo keeps them evasive.... Depending on the state of dilution of the ink, these gradations foster the continuous transition of beings and things from physical concretion to spirit dimension.[48]

Of course, looked at semiotically, this is the *indexical* dimension that supports, in its qualitative materiality, the *iconic symbolization* of the nonobject. Jullien remarks, however, that it is the brush, not the form, that is paired with ink, with the implication that the Western approach pairs color with the form, the brush being a mere instrument. This is an enlightening difference and clue to how to read the produced image, but its import is as much hermeneutical as it is metaphysical, both dimensions, as Jullien shows, being intertwined in the respective ultimate premise systems of the various aesthetic traditions of practice and concomitant theory. The fusion of the metaphysical and the aesthetic in the joining of brush and ink in Chinese painting in the following passage has distinctively Peircean overtones. "Chinese painting was being conceived ever more consciously, not as a practice of representation that transfers given forms from the model to the support, but as an operation of actualization and engenderment in which what takes precedence is its character as a differentiating process from an undifferentiated foundation-fount, in this case silk or paper."[49] Such a materially embodied semiotic-constructive process is, Jullien asserts, isomorphic with the Chinese conception of world process or cosmic processivity. Production and process run together.

According to Jullien, "every engenderment of the line in the art of painting and writing stems in the first place from the integration of a vital rhythm and not from a capacity to represent."[50] Writing in *Art as Experience* that rhythm is "ordered variation of energy" Dewey goes on to further say that "variation is not only as important as order, but it is an indispensable coefficient of esthetic order."[51] Variation in the material foundation-fount engenders Jullien's integration of a vital rhythm which Dewey also characterizes as "rationality among qualities,"[52] *not* the representation or construction of an ideal preexisting order of objects and forms. The integration Jullien refers to involves, or stems from, "the figuration of a continuous transformation of forms in accordance with the rhythm animating them and not from the reproduction of forms to be contemplated, whether ideal or perceived, given or invented (but always definitive, perfect). In short, they confirm that in China, painting stems more from a kinetic-energetic apprehension than from an aesthetic perception."[53] Such a notion of kinetic-energetic apprehension is in full accord with Dewey's reflections on resistances, tendencies, intensities, and the essential materiality of the art product, which, to be sure, becomes the artwork in being experienced and "worked out" in the hermeneutical process of interpretation communities whose worldviews are embodied in these works. This aesthetic effect has metaphysical implications for Dewey just as much as it does for the Chinese traditions presented by Jullien. This effect, as Dewey characterizes it, "is due to art's unique transcript of the energy of the things of the world." It is not a transcript of things alone, or even primarily, but of their energies, and it "operates by selecting those potencies in things by which an experience—any experience—has significance and value."[54] It is to these potencies that we are to respond with "commensurate perception" and to which we are to surrender ourselves "in devotion."[55]

On Blandness and the Circle of the Perceived

Jullien wrote a provocative book on "blandness" as a central category of Chinese aesthetics. It seems both to refute the notion of a "distinctive quality" as marking any work of art and any experiential occasion and to exemplify it at the same time. Blandness as an aesthetic category in Chinese thought, Jullien remarks in a striking metaphor, strives toward the limpidity of water and utter transparency, where everything is in balance and nothing stands forth. It is, however, for most aesthetic theories, including the pragmatist aesthetics developed by Dewey, precisely the standing forth that gives each work of art its unique "affective tone" and "idiom." But are we really faced with a contradiction or irreducible contrast here? The paradox of blandness is that it is both noticed and not noticed at the same time. Blandness is the "quality" of being "just right," but one cannot put it into words. As Jullien puts it, blandness's "sole characterization is to elude characterization."[56] This is, as I see it, actually a positive, not a negative, quality.[57] Jullien writes, in a passage that captures the upshot of the types of intersections adduced in the preceding pages, that "the motif of the bland distances us from theory but does not, at the other end, commit us to mysticism." The bland, however, does not eschew discourse or render experience vacuous. "With the bland, we remain in the realm of perceived experience, even if it situates us at the very limit of perception, where it becomes most tenuous."[58] The circle of the perceived is our experiential home and the locus of the aesthetic, but *its* circle is the ever-receding horizon or margin, where tenuousness opens onto plenitude, a phenomenon that galvanized Emerson.

A cosmopolitan aesthetics must be prepared to accept and attend to occasions of experiencing in all their manifold forms of appearing. Such an "open aesthetics," in Scharfstein's sense, is not a theory composed of universal concepts that apply in all contexts. Rather, it is a practice of self-reflective engagement that prepares us for an inexhaustible set of encounters with, and production of, forms that carry and express what James called the infinite "iridescences of consciousness." It is marked by a radical perspectival and experiential pluralism.

Cosmopolitan aesthetics is not itself an aesthetic theory. Scharfstein is right, and the conflicts of aesthetic theory bear witness, that there is no one-size-fits-all framework that can unify aesthetic and artistic traditions. Each aesthetic tradition has its matrix of premises and ways of working that make these premises appear. The conceptual, as opposed to the aesthetic and hermeneutical, task of a cosmopolitan aesthetics is to engage these premises and to make them explicit, something that I have tried to illustrate in this chapter. While the primary hermeneutical task is to engage the art works themselves in their own terms, the job of philosophy is to reflect on the premises embodied in the works themselves. But, as Jullien puts it, in the Chinese mode, "tasting substitutes for knowing; it is the only true aspiration."[59] Philosophy, in the pragmatistic mode, encompasses both tasting and knowing and does not set them in opposition. A truly cosmopolitan aesthetics in the pragmatist mode is a variegated set of hermeneutical exercises in learning to attend to the world and to attend to our modes of attending, including becoming aware of their limits, their heuristic powers, their material supports, and their affinities. A pragmatist aesthetics, in both its receptive and constructive phases, would focus specifically on the heightening of these iridescences and thus lead to transformations in our consciousnesses from the "local" to the "nonlocal." It would also, and most importantly, allow us to accept irreducible differences as enriching rather than as leading to existential and interpretive frustration or to psychic or sociocultural violence. But it would not lead to a slack relativism nor an easy irenic reconciliation of truly opposing metaphysical visions. The real oppositions have to be properly identified and submitted to critical examination.

In light of competing metaphysical lattices or frames, each with its own distinctive heuristic powers, the very idea of a cosmopolitan aesthetics is an injunction to engage in hermeneutical and existential self-reflective *practices*. There is no privileged *conceptual* "place" for a cosmopolitan aesthetics. A cosmopolitan aesthetics is in principle at home nowhere and everywhere, even where it does not feel at home. Cosmopolitan aesthetics in the pragmatist mode is the aesthetics of the rooted wanderer who has given up seeking, but without despair, anxiety, or frustration, to find a permanent place to lay his head. The flux of experience and the emergence of novel forms with their distinctive qualities pulls us on. As Jullien says, "When, rather than favoring one flavor over another, we remain equally open to all of them, we evolve freely through the different flavors and so do away with their incompatibility."[60]

Putting such an injunction into practice is the essence of a cosmopolitan aesthetics.

ROBERT E. INNIS is Professor Emeritus of Philosophy at the University of Massachusetts, Lowell and Obel Foundation Visiting Professor at Aalborg University.

His work focuses on semiotics, philosophy of language, art, and politics, and his many books and articles include *Pragmatism and the Forms of Sense: Language, Perception, Technics* (Pennsylvania State University Press, 2002) and *Susanne Langer in Focus: The Symbolic Mind* (Indiana University Press, 2009).

Notes

1. Ben-Ami Scharfstein, *Art Without Borders: A Philosophical Exploration of Art and Humanity* (Chicago: University of Chicago Press, 2009), 179.
2. Ibid., 404.
3. Readers of this chapter will easily see how the theme of an aesthetic cosmopolitanism most explicitly bears on and is supplemented by the focal points of other contributions. But special links are John Lysaker's notion of cosmopolitanism as a kind of philosophical praxis and not just a theory (Chapter 1); Megan Craig's analysis of loss of a place, which expands on the metaphor of place in my own analysis (Chapter 9); Jessica Wahman's connection of cosmopolitanism with homelessness, a category adduced at the end of this chapter in the sense of aesthetic homelessness (Chapter 12); Vincent Colapietro's sense of indwelling and moving across different grounds with their sedimented histories (Chapter 6); and John Stuhr's rejection of a theoretical solution "from above" and "across the board" to the issue of the conflicts between particular contexts (Chapter 17). Clearly, my argument does not bear in any substantial way on the connections between aesthetics and the social or political dimensions of life, although I have discussed these connections at some length elsewhere, especially in Part II of Robert E. Innis, *Pragmatism and the Forms of Sense: Language, Perception, Technics* (University Park: Penn State University Press, 2002).
4. Scharfstein, *Art Without Borders*, 434.
5. Ibid., 420.
6. Hans-Georg Gadamer, *Truth and Method* (New York: Seabury, 1975).
7. Clearly, some approaches and categories are richer than others. "Form," "meaning," and "expression" are semiotic in essence, but they also have to have experiential cash value. I have explored many aspects of these terms in my *Consciousness and the Play of Signs* (Bloomington: Indiana University Press, 1994); see also my *Pragmatism and the Forms of Sense, Susanne Langer in Focus: The Symbolic Mind* (Bloomington: Indiana University Press, 2009). I developed a multilayered conceptual scheme in my "Dimensions of an Aesthetic Encounter: Perception, Interpretation, and the Signs of Art," in *Semiotic Rotations: Modes of Meaning in Cultural Worlds*, ed. Jaan Valsiner, Sun-Hee Geertz, and Jean-Paul Breaux, 113–34 (Charlotte: Information Age, 2007); and in my "The 'Quality of Philosophy': On the Aesthetic Matrix of Dewey's Pragmatism," in *The Continuing Relevance of John Dewey: Reflections on Aesthetics, Morality, Science, and Society*, ed. Larry Hickman, Matthew Caleb Flamm, Krzysztof Piotr Skowroński, and Jennifer A. Rea, 43–60 (Amsterdam: Rodopi, 2011).
8. Stendhal (Henry Beyle), *On Love*, translated from the French with an introduction and notes by Philip Sidney Woolf and Cecil N. Sidney Woolf (Plymouth: Mayflower, 1915); originally published as *De l'Amour* in 1822 (chap. XVII).
9. François Jullien, *Vital Nourishment: Departing from Happiness*, trans. Arthur Goldhammer (New York: Zone Books, 2007).
10. Crispin Sartwell, *Six Names of Beauty* (New York: Routledge, 2006).
11. See Martin Seel, *Aesthetics of Appearing* (Stanford, CA: Stanford University Press, 2005).

12. There is operative here a kind of hermeneutical principle of charity, which is meant to root out all temptations to theoretical self-assertion, without falling into an easy relativism and avoiding the hard work of an honest engagement with "the other." Indeed, it only when we have passed over to another frame that we recognize the outlines and limits, and powers, of our own.

13. John Dewey, *Art as Experience* (New York: Perigee, 2005), 200.

14. See my *Consciousness and the Play of Signs*, 44–68.

15. Dewey, *Art as Experience*, 200.

16. Ibid.

17. Ibid., 200–201.

18. Ibid., 201.

19. Ibid., 202.

20. François Jullien, *The Great Image Has No Form or On the Nonobject through Painting*, trans. Jane Marie Todd (Chicago: University of Chicago Press, 2009), 33.

21. Ibid., 95, 98.

22. Ibid., 98.

23. Ibid., 99.

24. Ibid., 102.

25. See not only Dewey's *A Common Faith*, 2nd ed., introduction by Thomas M. Alexander (New Haven, CT: Yale University Press, 2013); but also the deeply moving paragraphs at the end of his *Human Nature and Conduct*, with an introduction by Murray G. Murphey (Carbondale: Southern Illinois University Press, 1983), where he indicates the task of salvaging the great ciphers of transcendence in a naturalistic mode.

26. Jullien, *Great Image*, 104.

27. Ibid.

28. Dewey, *Art as Experience*, 217.

29. I am referring here to the iconic, indexical, and symbolic dimensions of the artwork and the corresponding affective, energetic, and logical interpretants. See my "Dimensions" and "Quality of Philosophy" for a more detailed discussion.

30. Jullien, *Great Image*, 108.

31. See François Jullien, *Detour and Access: Strategies of Meaning in China and Greece*, trans. Sophie Hawkes (New York: Zone Books, 2000).

32. Jullien emphasizes, perhaps not completely convincingly, that what he is drawing is a principled contrast without implying a judgment of superiority of the Chinese tradition to the Western, Greece-derived tradition. The further question, however, which we are pursuing, is whether the contrasts, while being principled, are as absolute as Jullien claims. The Western tradition, as interpreted by Jullien's clearly Heidegger-inspired reading of it, may have resources that allow us to mediate the contrasts without radical reduction or deletion. This is the great task of a comparative philosophy in general. David Hall, Roger Ames, and Robert Neville stand as pioneers in this respect. See also Robert Neville, *Boston Confucianism: Portable Tradition in the Late-Modern World* (Albany: SUNY Press, 2000).

33. Jullien, *Great Image*, 108.

34. Ibid., 109.

35. The category of "play," of course, has been developed and applied fruitfully to the aesthetic dimension by the Kantian tradition and then transformed, once again, by penetrating essays by Hans-Georg Gadamer. See especially the essays in his *The Relevance of the Beautiful*, trans. Nicholas Walker, ed. Robert Bernasconi (Cambridge: Cambridge University Press, 1986); and Hans-Georg Gadamer, *Truth and Method*, 2nd rev. ed. (New York: Continuum, 2004).

36. Jullien, *Great Image*, 110.
37. Ibid., 111.
38. François Jullien, *The Impossible Nude*, trans. Maev de la Guardia (Chicago: University of Chicago Press, 2007). This book continues to rotate, in a lower register, the themes of *Great Image*.
39. Jullien, *Great Image*, 112.
40. Once again, the principal theme of Seel's *Aesthetics of Appearing*.
41. Jullien, *Great Image*, 114.
42. Ibid., 117.
43. Ibid., 113.
44. Dewey, *Art as Experience*, 197, 207.
45. Ibid., 207.
46. For a detailed exploration of Dewey's valorization of Peirce, see my '"Quality of Philosophy."
47. See Earle L. Coleman, *Philosophy of Painting by Shih Ta'o* (The Hague: Mouton, 1978).
48. Jullien, *Great Image*, 194.
49. Ibid.
50. Ibid., 203.
51. Dewey, *Art as Experience*, 170.
52. Ibid., 175.
53. Jullien, *Great Image*, 203.
54. Dewey, *Art as Experience*, 192.
55. Ibid., 193.
56. François Jullien, *In Praise of Blandness: Proceeding from Chinese Thought and Aesthetics*, trans. Paula M. Varsano (New York: Zone Books, 2004), 23.
57. Ibid., 27.
58. Ibid., 33.
59. Ibid., 123.
60. Ibid., 121.

PART II

TAKING PLACE SERIOUSLY

Introduction

José Medina

THE CHAPTERS in this part of the book cover various themes concerning making and unmaking places, being placed and displaced, orienting and disorienting yourself and/or others, remembering and forgetting places, connecting and disconnecting places, finding a home and being homeless, and so on. In different ways, all the chapters on place in this part of the book stage an original and provocative philosophical dialogue on the notion of place between classic American philosophers such as Emerson, Peirce, James, Addams, and Dewey, and a wide range of contemporary theorists: cultural critics and phenomenologists (Colapietro and Craig), global ethicists and critical theorists (Tuana and Corbí), and race theorists (Edmonds and Medina). In these suggested critical dialogues, the insights of classic and contemporary American philosophers are expanded, enriched, supplemented, interrogated, and challenged; they are put to the test by addressing the real-life problems and experiences of placement and displacement of particular groups of people: being displaced as a result of the destruction of one's land (Craig and Tuana), concrete experiences of trauma such as that of Jean Améry in a Nazi concentration camp (Corbí), the education of migrant communities in the Americas (Edmonds), and racial ignorance among different ethnic groups in southern Spain and the United States (Medina).

I want to call attention to three overlapping and converging themes that connect the chapters in this part of the book. A first salient theme is the *performativity* of place, that is, how places are constituted and reconstituted by activities. This theme is present—at least implicitly—in all the chapters, for all of them rely on practice-based accounts of place developed within the pragmatist tradition. These chapters put the emphasis on situated activities of place-*making*, on interactive ways of creating and re-creating, of opening and occluding, shared spaces. The most explicitly and fully developed account of place in terms of activities is provided in Chapter 6 by Colapietro's interactionist and dynamic view of place as "a verb," as constituted by ways of doing and dwelling. Colapietro's chapter is itself a journey, performing the *wayfaring* that is argued to be place-constituting. This view is often echoed in all the other chapters of this part of the book.

A second recurrent theme is the *heterogeneity* and *multiplicity* of place. The authors underscore that places have multiple histories and trajectories, that they are the sites of dramas and struggles in which different ways of dwelling converge and sometimes clash. The pluralistic views presented and defended here emphasize that a place is always multiple and heterogeneous because it can be differently inhabited by heterogeneous beings and their multiple ways of dwelling. This is the basis for the ethics and politics of coinhabitation that Colapietro proposes and that other authors also address in their discussions of specific challenges of coinhabitation that arise in relation to itinerant communities, racially stigmatized groups, traumatically harmed subjects, and economically and ecologically displaced populations.

A third recurrent theme in this part of the book is the *elusiveness* of place: places cannot be owned or monopolized; we belong to places, but they don't belong to us. Ways of orienting yourself or finding your bearings within a place always go hand in hand with ways of becoming disoriented and losing your bearings. The authors explore ways in which people feel oriented and disoriented within a place, often simultaneously; they also interrogate the power struggles that make up a place and how the comfortable inhabitation of some comes at the cost of the discomfort—and in some cases even the displacement—of others. Although there are robust discussions of finding your place and feeling at home in the chapters that follow, they also focus on a range of phenomena concerning displacement, feeling disoriented and out of place. Some of these chapters (6, 7, and 8) focus on being disoriented and out of place (whether at home or away from home), exploring the cognitive and affective dynamics underlying the interrelated ways in which we orient and disorient ourselves and others as we make and unmake places. Others (Chapters 9, 10, and 11) focus on radical forms of being displaced or losing one's place in the world, and even losing the world as such, whether as a result of human atrocities (such as torture or war), or as a result of ecological phenomena (such as climate change) in which human practices, institutions and policies are also implicated. But besides these thematic threads, there are many connections and ways of orienting oneself in and across these chapters.

I hope the reader can find her or his way and a home within these chapters, but I also want to emphasize that, as many of their authors argue (and Colapietro's Chapter 6 performatively demonstrates), the most unexpected cognitive and ethical achievements can come from getting lost, feeling disoriented, and striving toward new forms of orientation that reconfigure who one is and one's place in the world. I hope the reader has the courage to get lost in these chapters and to venture into new and unexpected connections that she can bring to these chapters and the chapters to her. As one possible synoptic view that may have some value for navigating the labyrinth of interconnected reflections offered here, let me call attention to some key themes, challenges, and provocations that can be found. In relation to these themes, challenges, and provocations, the chapters encourage readers to find their own ways of entering and inhabiting the questions they raise and the paths for philosophical reflection on place that they offer.

This part of the book opens with the practice-based account of place provided by Vincent Colapietro's "ambulatory" approach in "Toward a Politics of Cohabitation: 'Dwelling' in the Manner of Wayfarers." Colapietro offers an account of place "as a verb"—that is, as constituted by practices, ways of doing, or "ambulatory processes." On the basis of this pragmatic account of place, Colapietro argues for a shift from a politics of occupation to a politics of coinhabitation. In his critical elucidation of our practices of making and unmaking places, Colapietro pays special attention to the experiential and affective ties we develop toward the places we inhabit and share with others. Sentience, organic development, and animality figure prominently in Colapietro's understanding of "place" and in the ethics and politics of coinhabitation he proposes. With his proposal, Colapietro calls for solidarity in sharing "places" as sites of multiple forms of activities or "dramas"; and he tightly connects this global form of solidarity to environmental and ecological concerns about earth as a "global home," arguing for a shift from cosmo-politanism to "geo-politanism": "Being citizens of the cosmos is one thing, being coinhabitants of the earth quite another" (Chapter 6, page 98).

The epistemic side of the ethics and politics of coinhabitation is explored in José Medina's "Cosmopolitan Ignorance and 'Not Knowing Your Place.'" Medina contends that coming to terms with our own ignorance about place and taking steps to repair it are crucial ingredients of our local and global responsibilities toward multiple communities. He urges us to become critically reflective of our ignorance about seemingly familiar and seemingly unfamiliar places that unites us with and separates us from particular groups of people. Medina argues that getting to know a homely place is both a cognitive and an affective achievement, and that it always remains partial, precarious, and unfinished. Medina emphasizes that the ignorance/knowledge of one's place is crucially mediated by the imagination, and he tries to show how different racial imaginations coinhabit a place as their home while constituting it quite differently. To develop a critical and responsible relationship with a homely place, Medina argues, it is important to develop the ability to imagine it from different perspectives and to have diversified emotional (*dis*-identificatory) relations with it, instead of having rigid emotional attachments that go along with a homogeneous imagination and with monolithic relations of identification or counteridentification with that place. "Taking critical distance from our feelings of belonging and not-belonging, from our relations of identification and counter-identification with places, involves a difficult process of *self-estrangement* [that] is crucial for developing a responsible epistemic relation with a place" (Chapter 7, page 114). Following Jane Addams, Medina argues for a duty of self-estrangement that demands that we reimagine places and make them appear as newly strange to us so that we can then refamiliarize ourselves with them in more critical and responsible ways. He develops this argument by examining how racial exclusions become inscribed in the imaginative relations that people can have with a so-called *white city*, uncovering the bodies of ignorance that go into the making of such racialized construction of a place and raising challenges for the kinds of collective imagination and collective action needed to resist it and overcome it. He argues that our ignorance about the places we call "home" is intertwined with our ignorance about the places we see as foreign and alien to us. According to Medina's argument, getting to know one's place is an endless task, which we must assume as an ongoing responsibility to one's place(s) and its(their) multiple constituencies.

Converging with the upshot of Medina's discussion, Jeff Edmond's "America and Cosmopolitan Responsibility: Some Thoughts on an Itinerant Duty" also calls attention to the endless nature of our responsibility to coinhabit places responsibly, and underscores the critical force contained in the *unfinished* nature of a place and in experiences of disorientation and of not feeling quite at home. Edmond's analysis and argumentation bring these issues to the very idea of *America*. Elucidating how our agency in our everyday activities today operate simultaneously locally and globally in "the food we eat, the clothes we wear, the news we hear, the music we listen to," and so on, Edmonds argues that the tension between the local and the global is "a problem that structures the very idea of America from the outset [as] a continent of both indigenous peoples and immigrants" (Chapter 8, page 124). Claiming that the distinctive challenge of American philosophers is "to provide some help in understanding how to live through this tension," Edmonds develops a critical discussion of the notions of place and community offered by different American philosophers, from Emerson and Dewey to Anzaldúa and Mignolo, urging us to rethink the relationship between American provincialism and cosmopolitanism. Edmonds develops his critical insights through a provocative discussion of the challenges faced by migrant populations in the Americas, focusing in particular on the education of migrant workers and the possibilities for the formation of itinerant American identities and communities through new educational practices that can offer multiple ways of developing a sense of belonging. Edmonds sees the convergence of American provincialism and cosmopolitanism in the dynamic relation between the settled and the unsettled: in the critical reconstruction of old habits, we are forced to adjust habitual forms of life to changing conditions and we are led to take responsibilities that go beyond our (settled) selves and our (settled) communities and cultures. Following Emerson, Edmonds argues that, paradoxical as it may seem, the cosmopolitan insights of American philosophy have to be grounded in its provincialism. He contends that, as Emerson suggested, the American problem is "one of constantly misunderstanding one's own home and one's own self because of the influence of old habits." And, he argues, if American philosophy is provincial, it is "also cosmopolitan precisely because it [feels] unsettled in this new place, even as it [considers] it to be a home."

The constitutive tension between the settled and the unsettled in our relationship to places is also the focus of Megan Craig's "Loss of Place." Combining insights from James and Levinas, Craig argues for "the inevitability of losing one's place and the ethical imperative to acknowledge the precariousness and potential injustice of every claim to a place" (Chapter 9, page 139). Craig develops a psycho-phenomenological analysis of three distinctive places and the experiences of loss associated with them: the stairwell of an urban skyscraper, a farm, and a village in northern Alaska. Craig's analysis underscores the constitutive fluidity of places and the human contours of this fluidity. Combining insights from Emerson, Bachelard, and Deleuze and Guattari, Craig examines "the entanglement and precarious balance of places and lives" under extreme conditions of loss and displacement. She elucidates how places alter instantaneously and dramatically as a result of natural disasters (tsunamis, earthquakes, tornadoes, or hurricanes) or unnatural disasters (Waldo's death or the collapse of the World Trade Center). She argues that most experiences of loss and disaster entail a combination of the unnatural and the natural, and that they force us to interrogate the meanings of the words *natural/unnatural, human/inhuman*. Craig's argument about the inevitability of losing our places underscores the fragility of the interdependence between human lives and ecosystems, and calls for creative ways of reimagining places and of orienting and disorienting ourselves in them: "in a world bound together by ecosystems whose slightest variations provoke trembling everywhere, one needs a certain aptitude for revision and revolution, something learned in part by reading, traveling, and other means of decentering oneself" (Chapter 9, page 156).

Chapters 10 and 11 use concrete experiences of "losing the world" and being displaced to criticize and correct principle-based cosmopolitan approaches: Josep Corbí focuses on experiences of torture in his critique of Kantian cosmopolitanism, while Nancy Tuana examines experiences of being displaced as a result of climate change in her critique of principle-based cosmopolitan approaches. In "The Loss of Confidence in the World," Corbí explores the normative presuppositions and implications of experiencing a traumatic experience in which the possibility of a *human* world seems to disappear. Analyzing Jean Améry's reflections on his own experiences of torture, Corbí argues that the concepts of maintaining "a human world" and having "confidence in the world" involve normative expectations concerning being protected from harm and protecting others. These expectations, he argues, are traumatically broken in experiences of harm (such as torture) not only by those directly involved in the production of the harm in question but also by all those others who (knowingly or unknowingly) do nothing to stop it. Thus, Corbí's analysis raises critical questions about *complicity* that need to be addressed in order to fully understand experiences of harm and the shared responsibilities concerning the restoration of confidence in the world. As he puts it, the normative expectations that are constitutive of an experience of harm reveal a cosmopolitan aspiration insofar as they constitutively involve an appeal to others ("third agents" who are neither victims nor producers of harm) to work toward the creation (or the restoration) of a human world. In Corbí's view, this cosmopolitan aspiration originates in and remains grounded in the normative expectations experienced by particular subjects, but it goes beyond the particular person who holds those expectations and concerns everyone. Corbí's experiental cosmopolitanism stands in sharp contrast with Kantian views that demand impartiality and do not make room for normative expectations of protection anchored in situated identities.

This part of the volume closes with another set of challenges, criticisms, and correctives of cosmopolitan views issued in the light of a different kind of traumatic experience of "losing the world": the displacement of vulnerable populations as a result of climate change. In "Climate Change and Place: Delimiting Cosmopolitanism" Tuana discusses the conceptual and normative challenges that arise around the phenomenon of climate change for cosmopolitan perspectives. She argues that taking *place* seriously calls for a more robust conception of interdependence than the one traditionally offered by cosmopolitanism: "By attending to the ways we are in place and recognizing the deep interdependence of humans and environments, we come to appreciate the importance of an enriched conception of inter-relationality that goes beyond the human interdependencies that are the focus of cosmopolitanism" (Chapter 11, page 182). Tuana argues that only a thick account of interdependency that pays attention to human-environment interactions (and not just to human interdependencies) can properly accommodate the embodied and affective components of the impacts of climate change. Focusing on the rich interconnections between people and places, Tuana criticizes a wide range of principle-based cosmopolitan responses to climate change (such as those of Pogge, Held, and Caney), from human rights to justice-based to consequentialist approaches. Through a discussion of the experiences and vulnerabilities of those who have been displaced, Tuana's chapter teaches us how we can better understand "how places matter as well as our deep interconnectivity with the world that we are in and of," giving us hope for "sustainable modes of being in place" (Chapter 11, page 192).

6 Toward a Politics of Cohabitation
"Dwelling" in the Manner of Wayfarers[1]

Vincent Colapietro

This chapter is first and foremost a reflection on place, precisely as a verb—that is, not as an antecedently fixed container or enclosure, but as a historically evolved and evolving set of processes and practices. While unavoidably abstract in some respects, it is pointedly political and, to a less extent, polemical. For I am taking this occasion to urge a shift from a politics of occupation (including dwelling) to one of cohabitation, based on a reconstructed self-understanding of ourselves as *wayfarers* in a sense to be defined later. I am also urging a shift in focus from the cosmos to the Earth and thus, by implication, from abstract invocations of the cosmopolitan ideal to concrete preoccupation with the actual planet on which life in its staggering proliferation and innumerable forms, as we know it, has evolved. Given this reorientation in our reflections about what is most mundane, intimate, and fateful, place does more than afford sites in which we dwell; it does more than facilitate processes of dwelling, moving, and in particular wayfaring. It is unidentifiable and unintelligible apart from those processes and practices in which animals make their way in and through the world.

Consider a particular example of a privileged class of human beings. Travel is often an integral part of the life of most professionals, including professors in the humanities. We frequently travel long distances to attend conferences or simply present papers. After we arrive, part of the time we sit more or less comfortably, but for us even sitting so is not an instance of being motionless. We shift our positions, turn our heads, perhaps even nod off, only to be startled by some inner impulse or outer sound to bolt upright. The objects of our visual attention attain whatever stability and clarity they possess by virtue of the unperceived movements of our somatic selves, not least of all the continual, subtle adjustments of our eyes to a world in the making.[2] Every mode of perception occurs as a result of our *immersion* in the medium of perception,[3] hence as a consequence of our evolved skills to move more or less fluently through diverse media. In the first instance, perception is itself not a mode of cognition, but a manner of acting (not so much a response to stimuli as an integral part of an ongoing stream of human conduct).[4]

Our modes of perceiving, acting, dwelling, and moving about have in recent decades become especially intense sites of critical interrogation. Such interrogation encompasses reflecting on the possibility of attenuating the tyrannical claim of any particular here, so that *elsewhere* might become a more effective presence in our entangled lives. The very ideal of the cosmos being transformed into a polis—or simply our capacity to conceive the cosmos[5]—depends on at least news traveling to us from afar, reaching us from remote places, and (in doing so) making us aware of the expansive context in which any specific locale must be set in order for us to have some determinate sense of our actual place. As important as space and place in their imaginary and virtual registers are, the actuality of *this* place merits attention. For instance, recalling that this is the bar where historically significant riots erupted in response to harassment by the police, or this is the auditorium in which a revolutionary figure was assassinated helps us know where we are, hence enables us to situate ourselves more thoughtfully than would be possible apart from such recollection. The paradox here is that the actual and the imaginary are woven together: to know where we actually are we must imagine this place as the scene of those riots or of that murder or of some other critical events and eventualities. Our sense of actuality does not preclude imagination; rather it utterly depends on our capacity to make the absent present, there there-and-then integral to the significance of the here and now, the lives of far distant strangers constitutive of the actual places we inhabit and traverse. In other words, a thick sense of actuality requires a mobile exercise of imagination.

The solid does not necessarily melt into the ethereal, though this is indeed a possibility. But solidity is severed from stasis. Terra firma itself must be translated into dynamic terms. Our image of the Earth as a sphere hurling in space also depends as much on our movements as the Earth's own. No less than *place*, *polis* is not a noun but a verb. It names a set of processes and practices. Anything to which we can point as integral to (say) a place or a polis is a distinct phase in an ongoing history. The purpose of my chapter is not to prove this claim, only to render this suggestion plausible.

To know a place is to be able to get around there. But, in this instance, getting around is not going in circles, however much the image of an expanding or contracting spiral might trace the trajectories of our travel. We are able to get around anywhere by virtue of having gone along the routes afforded by the contours of a locale.[6] Going along and getting along are perhaps more intimately connected than we realize. While we tend to use the expression "getting along" primarily (if not solely) in reference to how people are faring in their relationships to one another, there is no insurmountable obstacle to extending it to the relationship between people and places. Some days New York and I did not get along at all: we had a rather bitter lover's quarrel. On one such occasion, it all began by being stood up by a subway train. On countless other occasions, we got along quite well. Of course, *getting along* with a place cries out for clarification. I might—indeed, I cannot help but—bring to any place a set of expectations and desires that to some extent put me at odds with the opportunities and affordances of a locale. In the best of cases, an intimate, transformative process unfolds, one in which my affective and practical ties to a place are deepened and expanded (this often involves the alteration of my expectations, desires, and demands); in the worst of cases, a place affords me so little of what I desire or demand that I sever my ties with that place.

As noted at the outset of this chapter, *place* here signifies a verb. In my judgment, at least, this invites, perhaps even demands, a shift from a politics of occupation or dwelling to a politics of cohabitation. In turn, this drives toward a reconstruction of our self-understanding, in particular, a vision of ourselves as wayfarers. Such a reconstruction is achieved by taking not only life but also animality with the utmost seriousness. The way in which an organism is in an environment is dramatically different from the way coins are in a pocket or pencils in a container. In the life of animals, place as a verb is, without exaggeration, *dramatically* manifest: movement is almost unavoidably dramatic. An example from one of Dewey's late manuscripts makes this point in an especially memorable way. After recalling an account of experience in which experienced is reduced to a small number of discrete properties ("What I actually experience [when I look at a chair] is only a very few of the elements that go to make up a chair, namely, that color . . . that shape, etc."), Dewey insists:

> I would rather take the behavior of the dog of Odysseus upon his master's return as an example of the sort of thing experience is [or should be] for the philosopher than trust to such statements. A physiologist may for his special purpose reduce Othello's perception of a handkerchief to simple elements of color under certain conditions of light and shapes seen under angular conditions of vision. But the actual experience was charged with history and prophecy; full of love, jealousy, and villainy, fulfilling past human relationships and moving fatally [or fatefully] to tragic destiny.[7]

As George Santayana notes, the transition from vegetative to animal life "literally turns everything upside down." How is this so? "The upper branches, bending over and touching the ground, become fingers and toes; the roots are pulled up and gathered into a snout, with its tongue and nostrils protruding outward in search of food; so that besides the up-and-down and inwards-and-outwards known to the plant, the animal now establishes a forward-and-back—*a distinction possible only for travelers.*"[8] Such an organism "is now in perpetual motion, following his nose, which is itself guided and allured by all sorts of scents and premonitions coming from a distance" (ibid.). The capacity to respond to what is distant and, in the case of some animals, to what is absent itself goes a great distance toward generating a distinctive form of animal life.[9] But our energetic responses and pursuits, flights and attacks, even to what is far away are precisely what traditionally gets overlooked. For the dominant metaphor for our deepest attachment to specific locales (that of being rooted in a place) is one in which just this most salient feature of human life is in effect erased. It is to this metaphor that I now turn, but only as a way of moving toward movement itself.

Buried Alive?

In 1901, after being away from home for nearly two years, William James wrote: "I long to steep myself in America again and let the broken rootlets make new adhesions to their native soil. A man coquetting with too many countries is as bad as a bigamist, and loses his soul altogether."[10] Whether or not we ought to transform ourselves into rooted or (for that matter) rootless cosmopolitans,[11] the fact is that many people feel themselves to be rooted to particular locales (no matter how expansive or inclusive their sympathies and identifications). So, too, many others feel the need to uproot themselves, to wander far from the places of their origin and, then again, far from wherever they begin to feel too comfortable. This is true even if the metaphor of rootedness, though not easily eradicated, is not altogether apt.

As is so often the case, the metaphors in which we are most at home are not necessarily the ones in which our own experience of (say) their attachment to a place is best articulated.[12] Hence, we need to be especially attentive to the ways in which our metaphors and, more generally, our concepts depict as static what is inherently and irrepressibly dynamic or even truly alive;[13] also alert to the ways our metaphors in effect depict as antecedently fixed what is historically emergent,[14] as objects sharply demarcated from one another what are processes so inextricably entangled as to constitute a meshwork.[15] "Philosophy should seek," as James insists, "this kind of living understanding of the movement of reality, not follow science in vainly patching together fragments of its dead results."[16] But a living understanding is necessarily a participatory achievement, attained only by immersing ourselves in the ongoing flux of some actual history.[17] It is also unquestionably a mobile affair: not only are things in the making but our invincibly finite, partial, and perspectival understanding of them is itself in the making.[18]

Whatever else places are, they are sites of activity, loci for dramas, above all, those improvised scenes in which the unintended consequences of our most careful deliberations quickly acquire (no matter how slow our acknowledgment) their fateful significance.[19] Places are not carpentered and furnished stages, but media *in* and *through* which whatever possesses a recognizable identity (no matter how brief or even contested) not only move but (by virtue of their movements in and through these media) have their being. Hence, places in the sense intended here are always in some manner and measure inseparable from these activities. This is true even though (say) our ability to read in our study at home *or* at work, in a library *or* café, engenders the illusion that these activities have little or nothing to do with the sites in which they are taken up and carried on.[20] The scenes of *our* strivings and exertions, *our* achievements and failures, *our* fulfillments and frustrations, exhilarations and devastations are not external to these very processes. The scenes are themselves a meshwork of processes facilitating, thwarting, sustaining, and in countless other ways contributing to what we do, undergo, and indeed are. They are far less the planks of a stage on which we enact the improvised dramas of our everyday lives,[21] far more often characters (often quite significant ones) in these very dramas. They are forces with which we contend and cope, but also often ones by which we are supported and sustained. If the Earth is our habitat (as it assuredly is), then our lives are better understood as instances of inhabitation than dwelling. Just as a house may not be a home, a home need not be a house or anything constructed primarily by humans. The Earth *is* in some sense our home or habitat. Regardless of the extent to which the dominant scenes of our everyday lives are the protected enclosures of a built environment, human life is always to some extent lived "in the open."[22] To suppose we live primarily within the confines of humanly constructed enclosures (even when we do actually live the bulk of our lives indoors) fails to give both the natural materials out of which these human dwellings are made *and* the natural processes by which these human artifacts are supported their due (it fails to give these materials and processes their due).[23] Our primordial capacity to live in the illiminable open of the natural world completely colors even our most evolved forms of dwelling in the protective enclosures of our built environment.[24] Our historical failure to appreciate the radical implications of our actual locus in the terrestrial world has resulted in grossly distorted images of consciousness, mind, agency, subjectivity, and much else (arguably, all else). We are manifestly inhabitants of the Earth and, as such, ineluctably live in the open. Even so, our traditional categories in effect allow us only to portray ourselves as *exhabitants*, to depict the immediate foreground of our most spontaneous entanglements as an alien sphere in which mindful agents such as human beings appear to themselves,[25] by virtue of consciousness and mind, to be cosmological anomalies.[26]

While there is much to learn from Heidegger on this score, the Heideggerian question of *dwelling* must nonetheless be transformed into the pragmatist question of *inhabiting*,[27] and, in turn, this pragmatist question must be heard above all as one preoccupied with *co*inhabiting. Our main focus ought to be not on the places in which we dwell, but the entangled paths being forged and retraced by our irrepressible movement through terrestrial media, our dwellings being themselves principally occasions for the confluence of forces and, within this confluence, for the distinctive exertions of the human animal.

It is thus to movement, activity, and process—hence to entanglement, involvement, and participation, also incorporation, alteration, and simply relationality—that we must attend. But, of course, these are precisely the aspects of our world on which the pragmatists insisted.

In general, metaphors allow us to obtain a critical distance from some of our most intimate activities (not least of all thinking itself), thereby providing us with much needed perspective. In the history of pragmatism, they have been nothing less than pivotal. In "How to Make Our Ideas Clear," one of the central metaphors for thinking is drawn from music,[28] whereas the inaugural and indeed orienting one in "Philosophical Conceptions and Practical Results" is trailblazing.[29] "Philosophers are," James asserts in this text, "after all like poets. They are path-finders." The words of both fulfill "the same function. They are ... so many spots, or blazes—blazes made by the axe of the human intellect on the trees of an otherwise trackless forest of human experience." As such, their words "give you a direction and a place to reach."[30] In this as in so many other respects, the congregation of latter-day pragmatists has followed James rather than Peirce: the metaphor of finding our way has tended to be more dominant than that of music. But, with respect to both, temporality is central; not only temporality, but also an array of processes, above all, transition, transposition, transformation, and transfiguration, as well as reconstruction, recovery, renewal, and recognition (note the prefixes—*trans*- and *re*-). Our general reliance on metaphors is, hence, noteworthy, but the particular metaphors deployed by the pragmatists are, for our purpose, far more so.

This is especially true of the Jamesian metaphor of thought as ambulatory. But even here Peirce appears, once again, to have already been where James eventually arrived. In any event, he quite early described his thought as "pedestrian,"[31] while James later characterized his account of knowing as "ambulatory." Moreover, Peirce took his distinctive version of the pragmatic approach to philosophical questions and arguably also his categoreal scheme to be first and foremost examples of a *lanterna pedibus* (specifically, a lantern for the feet of inquirers).[32] Using a related (if only distantly related) figure of speech, Dewey identified the function of his metaphysics as providing "a *ground-map* for the province of criticism, establishing base lines to be employed in more intricate triangulations."[33] That is, the function of Deweyan metaphysics is not to provide a single blueprint for a multistory edifice, resting on an absolutely secure foundation; rather it is to offer us a plethora of maps and, beyond this, a pluralistic understanding of our cartographic endeavors themselves.[34] The architectural metaphor so dominant in so much traditional philosophy is thereby displaced by the ambulatory one so congenial to American thinkers, whose actual lives were illustrative of long voyages, extended sojourns, and other forms of coming and going.

Peircean pragmatism at least is, by unembarrassed avowal, a *pedestrian* affair. He stressed that "the *history* of words, not their *etymology* . . . [is] the key to their meanings."[35] But he also appreciated that the roots of words are part of their history and, in addition, often used words for the purpose of evoking the earliest stages of their unfolding histories. Such is manifestly the case in his use of "pedestrian" to describe his philosophy. His critique of Cartesianism is in effect an attempt to overturn the doctrine of intuitionism and, thereby, to uproot the metaphor of seeing. Our minds are discursive, not intuitive: we deceive ourselves if we take the instantaneous, effortless sighting of an object in optimal conditions as our model. To attain anything, our minds are forced to run about and, in the process, not infrequently the fate of getting lost befalls us. Logic, the principal passion of Peirce's intellectual life, is only possible because symbols allow us to identify the steps by which we attempt to reach a conclusion—and to retrace those steps countless times. Learning where a path leads is, at bottom, the primordial experience of learning the highest ideal of a philosophical life—having the courage to follow the evidence wherever it leads. In any event, reasoning in Peirce's sense means going step-by-step, with the initial ones always being inescapably tentative (for the first step in human reasoning can never be anything but a conjecture or hypothesis). Logic is an attempt to map those steps in such a manner as to reveal any possible missteps. The overarching goal of Peircean logic is not to provide a calculus facilitating ease and speed of inference, but rather to equip us with an *analytic* tool enabling us to break down an inferential sequence into its most critical steps, for the sake of discerning wherein we might have gone astray. The point of his system of Existential Graphs and other experiments in logical symbolization is to break down complex instances of argumentation into a sequence of elementary steps in order to ascertain whether a mistake or misstep has occurred.

Thus, it is that I want in this chapter (in its entirety, no more than selected pages from a log of my recent meanderings) to call your attention to not simply movement but those forms of movement characteristic of our and other species. Our talking and (inextricably connected to this) our very form of rationality might have far more to do with walking than we appreciate. Indeed, our form of rationality might be of a piece with our motility (Santayana, Woodbridge, Merleau-Ponty). So, on this occasion, I invite you to meander a while longer with me along pathways with which you are familiar, all too familiar, so that the shock of perception requires the deliberate cultivation of that all too rare capacity—the ability to see what stares us in the face.

The philosophical wayfarer in effect offers more or less detailed sketches of the conceptual terrain over which she or he has traveled. But even in making this suggestion I am once again guided by Peirce and, for that matter, also by Wittgenstein. In a series of drafts for a work entitled "Reason's Rules," he elaborates a metaphor especially worthy of our attention on this occasion. MS 598, to focus on one of the drafts in this sequence (MSS 596–600), is a remarkable manuscript for various reasons, not least of all that Peirce explicitly grants his reader the *first word*.[36] "'The author,' the reader will properly remark, 'professes to have something to say. Before I listen to him, I want to know, in a general way, what it is he has to tell me.'"[37] Peirce's reply to his imaginary reader might be considered an echo of a famous passage from Wittgenstein's later writings,[38] were it not written first.

> The author replies: Of course, I have something to say to you, but I have nothing to tell you. I invite you to journey with me over a land of thought which is *already more or less known to you* [emphasis added]. It is a land where I have sojourned long, and I wish to point out objects for you yourself to see, some of which, I am pretty sure, have hitherto escaped your attention. I promise you they shall be interesting in themselves, and also that they shall be such as shall concern the interests in which you are already engaged to know better than you do. *It will be important that you keep an itinerary as we go along* [emphasis added], and be aware of just where we find each object that concerns us. Otherwise we should bring back from our journey nothing but vague and confused ideas. We must keep something of a log-book of all the courses and distances of our travels ... [and] we want, in the first[,] to settle just where our starting-point is.[39]

We must keep a log not simply to record what we have observed, but also as an instrument of observation. Writing is itself an instrument of attention,[40] not simply the means by which we record observations allegedly made with eyes unaided by pen, pencil, or keyboard. The self-imposed task of describing in painstaking detail what we encounter in our wanderings is, on this account at least, an indispensable aid to discerning observation. Careful expression requires of us careful observation.

Any useful log is likely to include, in some form, at least rudimentary maps. In general, maps are in (or, better, *from* or *by*) the hands of pragmatists not so much summations of where we have been as indications of where we have yet to go. They are far less records of past travels than directives for future ventures. To be sure, detailed diagrams of past wayfarings are indispensable tools for our future ventures; but they are just that—tools. Self-warranting cognitions are replaced by self-corrective processes and, among all the mundane examples of such processes, none is more down to earth or significant in its implications than those of getting lost, discovering this, and then altering our course to insure the likelihood of arriving at our destination. But the very notion of travel has to be reenvisioned as an open-ended process not suffered as an onerous exertion for the sake of an external terminus: "If it is better to travel than arrive, it is because traveling is a constant arriving, while arrival that precludes further travel is most easily attained by going to sleep or dying."[41] Arrival in the pragmatist sense is thus not a cessation of movement, but an alteration of the scene and (almost certainly) an alteration also of the very form of motion. Ours is not only a world of things in the making but also one of organisms on the move, to no slight extent, agents on the make. The immobile state of any living animal is always temporary and indeed comparative: vitality precludes any more enduring or complete form of immobility. What is true of the human animal is, *mutatis mutandis*, also true of countless other species of animals. A far wider, deeper, more detailed, and more differentiated account of animal life is called for than I am equipped to provide. While my primary focus here is on the human, this should not be taken to be an exclusive preoccupation. The live of any human animal is inextricably bound up with those of other animals and indeed plants, as well as inanimate beings.

For an animal to be rooted in the earth entails it being buried alive, at least partially. In making this point, I am not trying to be a crude literalist. My own meaning is mainly metaphorical—life in general and human life in its most salient features get buried by an uncritical reliance on the all too commonplace metaphor of human rootedness. We need to recover our land legs and the restless feet so crucial for our characteristically ambulatory existence. The Cartesian *cogito* so proudly triumphant over the most extreme skepticism is a thoroughly diminished being, a truly punctual self (to use Charles Taylor's arresting expression), lacking hands and feet, arms and legs, head and genitalia. In contrast, human beings as conceived by the American pragmatists are more or less fully equipped organisms making their way *through* the world (i.e., getting along on the earth). Experience is, as the word *Erlebnis* suggests, what we have lived *through* and, in turn, what we have lived through is largely a function of what we have gone through, almost always in the literal sense of this expression (hence, the sense straightforwardly related to *going*). Indeed, our life is an endless series of comings and goings.

Land Legs and Restless Feet

In all too many of our theories, then, we have in effect buried ourselves alive and, even worse, made of life (above all, animal life in all its fleeting mobility) something less than life. To have acquired sea legs is to have regained the ability to walk steadily, albeit on the deck of a ship. But, given the incredible neglect of traditional philosophy, we need to recover something even more basic—what might be called land legs. Yet what needs to be recovered is not the ability to walk on land, rather simply the realization of just how integral this capacity is to our inhabitation of the Earth.[42] We have glanced at the extent to which this ability served the pragmatists as a metaphor. The literal sense of this human capacity however demands painstaking attention.

It should come as no surprise to anyone acquainted with American thought that so robust a naturalist as Santayana gave just such attention to this matter. Though brief, he penned a brilliant essay entitled "The Philosophy of Travel," asking at the outset, "Has anyone ever considered the philosophy of travel?" (Philosophers attain their status in no small measure by the memorable way in which they pose seemingly simple yet largely, if not entirely, overlooked questions. Regarding travel, Santayana clearly exemplifies this.) For vast stretches of Western thought, at any rate, the music of the celestial spheres received far more attention than the movement of terrestrial animals. But given its importance in our lives, travel, ranging from the most rudimentary forms of locomotion to the most dramatic instances of migration, calls for reflection. Or, as Santayana wryly puts it, the philosophy of travel "might be worth while. What [indeed] is life but a form of motion and a journey through a foreign world?" Santayana goes so far as to suggest, "locomotion—the privilege of animals—is perhaps the key to intelligence."

"In animals," Santayana stresses, "the power of locomotion changes all this pale experience into a life of passion; and it is on passion, although we anæmic philosophers are apt to forget it, that intelligence is grafted." So, he goes on to suggest, "instead of saying that the possession of hands has given man his superiority, it would go much deeper to say that man, and all other animals, *owe their intelligence to their feet.* No wonder, then, that a peripatetic philosopher should be the best."

The person who travels somewhere *in order to travel* in a manner uniquely afforded by that locale—for example, to travel to a particular mountain for the purpose of climbing it, to a particular city for the aim of being aimless and meandering there, to make a pilgrimage—is identified by Santayana as "a genuine traveler" (for this individual travels "for travel's sake"). We are driven to such travel "because the world is too much with us, and we are too much with ourselves. We need sometimes to escape into open solitudes, into aimlessness, into the moral holiday of running some pure hazard, in order to sharpen the edge of life, to taste hardship."[43] While Emerson was disposed to condemn travel as a "fool's paradise,"[44] Santayana appears to be disposed to characterize it as a sage's retreat.

The philosophy of travel, then, helps us to obtain a perspective on our mode of habitation, which is always a matter of cohabitation. When dwelling is conceived in reference to rootedness, human and indeed most other forms of animal life are reduced to that of vegetation, whereas when dwelling itself is envisioned as an activity, moreover, one enabling a vast array of other intertwined practices, the lives of animals are seen for what they are—dramas of movement, entanglement, extrication, and transposition. The Earth's own movements provide a matrix and arena for all Earthlings, most manifestly, for those whose very being is bound up with making their way through the intermediate zone of the "weather-world" (Ingold, Colapietro). That is, for those whose status is that of wayfaring.

At least part of the meaning of a traveler in this sense overlaps with what Ingold designates as a wayfarer. Wayfaring is never a mere means to an external destination. It is rather the consummatory experience in which each distinct phase of a wayfaring venture is itself "a constant arrival." It is possible even in the apparent enclosures of built environments, for these often familiar sites reveal as much as any other human habitation that places primarily afford paths along which we can move in habitual but also novel ways. Human habitation is a restless affair (some of us are even restless sleepers, when we manage to succumb to the relief of slumber); moreover, it is truly a process in which the participants constitute by the interwoven lines of their ongoing activities the very sites of their enmeshed coming-to-be. What is manifestly true of the air and the earth in conspiring to refashion each other, is equally true of us in relation to earth, air, and hence weather. Our breathing in effect testifies to nothing less than this, our moods arguably to much more. We unquestionably are in our most sublime pursuits no less than our most mundane routines Earthlings. This is of course not an exceptional status. Countless other beings are Earthlings and a deliberately cultivated sense of this fact might contribute an effective sense of our solidarity with these beings.

We and innumerable other beings are, to repeat, inhabitants of the Earth, and this means that we do not so much live on the surface of this planet but in and through terrestrial processes of incomprehensible complexity. There is an inhabitable zone between the Earth's crust and the higher reaches of its atmosphere where we tend to reside. It is more medium than stage—that through which we ceaselessly move rather than that on which we stand still. We are bound to the Earth in such a manner that our distinctive form of terrestrial habitation provides boundless possibilities for human movement. For this and countless other reasons, then, rather than urging a cosmo-politan ideal, I want to endorse a geo-politan one in which a geocentric consciousness operates as a healthy provincialism (Royce).[45] But our province turns out to be nothing less than the Earth in its entirety, rather than something as limited as a specific region or something as limitless as the universe itself. The world or cosmos might be in our imaginations, "in the angle at which it touches our own manner of being."[46] But the Earth is in its actuality just this—and far, far more (not least of all an endangered wilderness). Humans are unquestionably mortals, but of equal certainty we are Earthlings. Our modes of inhabitation and habituation are one with our ambulatory ventures and wanderings, trailblazing and wayfaring (James, Ingold). A geo-politan ideal is consequently the one most suitable for ambulatory agents who have all too frequently deluded themselves into seeing themselves as celestial creatures unconfined by the omnipresent constraints of earthly existence. In addition, this ideal conscientiously preserves possibilities for wayfaring (in contradistinction from transport), bears witness to being astonished, not merely surprised,[47] and undertakes ever anew the work of acknowledging more fully the practical implications of the most salient features of our terrestrial life—not least of all, natality, embodiment, habituation, motility, food, sexuality, and mortality.[48]

In recent years, however, philosophers have joined anthropologists, geographers, and others in stressing the importance of place. But the work of philosophers might greatly benefit from a wider consultation with other theorists, just as these theorists have in many instances learned much from philosophers. The anthropologist Tim Ingold in particular is not only a philosophically literate anthropologist but also an astutely critical philosopher. This is nowhere more apparent than in his response to Edward Casey's claims regarding place. "Time and again, philosophers have assured us that, as earthbound creatures, we," Ingold observes, "can only live, and know *in* places. Thus, according to Edward Casey, place is 'at once the limit and the condition of all that exists. . . . To be is to be in place.'"[49] This is alleged to follow from one of the (if not *the*) most salient features of human existence: "We are in place, the argument goes, because we exist as *embodied* beings." But the distinctive form of human embodiment is that of a mobile and specifically ambulatory actor.[50] "Now embodied we may be, but that body . . . is not," Ingold insists, "confined or bounded but rather extends as it grows along the multiple paths of its entanglement in the textured world."[51] This makes all the difference in the world—more precisely, all the difference for how we conceive our being in the world—and, of utmost significance, for how we imaginatively yet actually *inhabit* the Earth. "Thus [for us] to be . . . is not to be *in* place but to be *along* paths. The path, not the place, is the primary condition of being, or rather of becoming."[52] One of the most famous metaphors used to describe pragmatism itself, crafted by Papini and adopted by James—the image of a corridor in a hotel opening onto various chambers[53]—identifies a passageway, a hall affording access to a variety of rooms. It is not itself a chamber or room but a means of access to where we might come to reside for a while. The hallway is a pathway, the rooms off the hallway separate from one another yet connected by it. More generally, places themselves come into being as a result of movement. Of course, the Earth is not devoid of enclosures hollowed out or otherwise constructed. But these have to be accessible to their inhabitants and, ideally, inaccessible or, at least, difficult to reach by the predators of their inhabitants. The hallway in a hotel is hence just a more developed form of pathway. That it not infrequently is part of what feels like a labyrinth is noteworthy, but there is no space here to probe this. The places in which organisms dwell are, first and foremost, sites of activities (even in they are primarily domiciles, sleep being a crucial activity for countless organisms). However readily and fully the ambience of an organism affords[54] opportunities for that actor's movements to encircle themselves[55] and thereby institute sites of inhabitation, these sites are not antecedently there but historically emergent.[56] They are established and maintained by an ongoing series of intermeshing processes in which human organisms are far from the sole architects.

Conclusion

Is it truly necessary to go over the same ground, generation after generation, to return to the same topoi and strive to think anew what even the most penetrating and insightful of human minds have failed to discern in its full sweep and most salient details?[57] One might as well ask whether inhalation or exhalation is yet again required, since it has been reenacted countless times before (Emerson, Dewey). For the geo-politan the most pressing issue is that of cohabitation.[58] The most exhilarating experience is however the unconstrained movement of the human psyche, in the various media in which this restless being undertakes its diverse ventures. The universe may be so much cosmic weather (in Chauncey Wright's telling expression), but the immediate site of human habitation is the highly variable zone where atmospheric processes are enmeshed with geological ones to generate among other large-scale processes,[59] none more significant than *terrestrial* weather. Nature as the source of metaphors displays an extraordinary fecundity.[60] It does so however because of its Protean guises,[61] because of its apparently inexhaustible fecundity. It is an arresting scene of myriad processes of re- and trans*figuration*.[62] While *nature* might be a name for excess,[63] it definitely is one for metamorphosis. As the origin of the word attests, it signifies what comes and what ceases to be and, by implication, what ceaselessly changes all the while it endures in a more or less recognizable manner. Things in the making are things becoming otherwise than they have been.

    Many philosophers have imagined we have the capacity to assume the role of a spectator, surveying a scene from which we have extricated ourselves or, in any event, can extract ourselves. *Spirit* is Santayana's name for this stance or capacity. There is nothing unduly misleading about this as long as we realize that even the role of the spectator is, at bottom, a mode of participation.[64] In any event, spirit in Santayana's sense provides its consolation and enthrallments, its ravishing vistas and incomparable essences, but psyche is the only habitat for any spirit or consciousness available to us. And *psyche* is only the name for a living being and, in our case, an ingenious one (Vico), endowed with irrepressible impulses to make of the sites of our habitation improvised scenes of an unfolding drama, in which entrances and exits are but the more obvious instances of human motility. But, alas, it is time for me (at least momentarily) to exit this discourse, thereby allowing space for others. But, first, a brief summation of my main points might prove useful.

The cosmopolitan ideal tends toward abstractness, thus thinness, while the geo-politan orientation drives toward concreteness, hence thickness—a point that resonates deeply with analyses by José Medina (Chapter 7), Megan Craig (Chapter 9), Nancy Tuana (Chapter 11), and John Stuhr (Chapter 17) in this volume. The cosmos names an antecedently established order inherent in the totality of things to which we are destined to conform or destroy ourselves, while the Earth is the proper name of a historically evolved and evolving planet, itself the matrix and ambivalence for innumerable forms of life. Life is one with movement of some sort. In the case of animals, it is (following Aristotle and Santayana) a self-propulsion in and through a world of hazard, opportunity, and indifference. The task of thinking, pressed on us by the exigencies of living, is far less that of learning to dwell here and now in accord with the dictates of the cosmos as it is to coexist here and there, now and then, with innumerable beings whose lives are bound up with our own. Our ambulatory processes and other modes of wayfaring exhibit place to be not an enclosure but a partner in a dance, one without which our own exertions would be utterly vain. As Dewey notes: "Breathing is an affair of the air as truly as of the lungs; digesting an affair of food as truly as the tissue of the stomach. Seeing involves light just as certainly as it does the eye and optic nerve. Walking implicates the ground as well as the legs; and speech demands physical air and human companionship and audience as well as vocal organs."[65] In walking, the ground, the "surface" of the Earth, is a dynamic partner in what must be seen as a cooperative activity. The ambulatory process of thought and, in turn, the critical topoi of discourse disclose just how much thinking is a movement akin to walking, on the one hand, and how walking itself can be nothing less than a process of thinking. Our intellects are, as Thoreau suggests, as much snouts and forepaws as anything else. That is, they are organs enabling us to burrow more deeply into the Earth. The transcendence of the particularities, contingencies, and transience of this place, especially in the name of such an abstract ideal as the cosmos, must give way to modes of "dwelling" that show themselves to be, at every turns, forms of wayfaring. Being citizens of the cosmos is one thing, being coinhabitants of the Earth quite another. Hence, one of the first yet critical steps toward a politics of cohabitation, toward geo-politanism, is realizing the practical difference between being attuned to the harmony inherent in the totality of things and becoming ever more responsive, critical, and differential in our evolved and evolving relationships to our coinhabitants. That, at least, is the perspective advocated in this chapter.

VINCENT COLAPIETRO is Liberal Arts Professor of Philosophy and African American Studies at Penn State University. Focusing on pragmatism, semiotics, and philosophy and psychoanalysis, his many books and articles include *Fateful Shapes of Human Freedom: John William Miller & the Crises of Modernity* (Vanderbilt University Press, 2003).

Notes

1. The figure of the wayfarer signals my debt to the anthropologist Tim Ingold, while reference to ambulation signals my debt to the pragmatist William James; see especially his *Pragmatism & the Meaning of Truth* (Cambridge, MA: Harvard University Press, 1975). "Cognition, whenever we take it concretely, means," James notes, "determinate 'ambulation,' through intermediaries. . . . As the intermediaries are other than the termini [*a quo* and *ad quem*], and connected with them by the usual associative bonds . . . there would appear to be nothing especially unique about the processes of knowing. They fall wholly within experience; and we need use, in describing them, no other categories than those which we employ in describing other natural processes" (247). The figure of the wayfarer is one of a living being who moves *along* paths and *through* the world in such a way that the life of being is one with its movements and engagements. For such beings, the environment is not their surroundings but "a zone of entanglements"; see Tim Ingold, "Bindings against Boundaries: Entanglements of Life in an Open World," *Environment and Planning A* 40 (2008): 1796; cf. Jo Ann Boydston, ed., *Dewey Experience and Nature, the Later Works* (Carbondale: Southern Illinois University Press, 1988), 1:387. They live (at least, in part) out in the open and "in the open world there are no insides and outsides, only comings and goings"; see Tim Ingold, "Earth, Sky, Wind, and Weather," *Journal of the Royal Anthropological Institute* (2007): S31. Wayfarers moreover are capable of being astonished, not merely surprised; see Tim Ingold, "Rethinking the Animate, Re-Animating Thought," *Ethnos* 7, no. 1 (March 2006): 18–19. My two debts however come together in Ingold's own bold claim: "Walking along . . . is not the behavioural output of a mind encased within a pedestrian body. It is rather, in itself, a way of thinking and knowing—'an activity [as J. Rendell notes in *Art and Architecture: A Place Between*] that takes place through the heart and mind as much as through the feet'"; see Tim Ingold, "Footprints through the Weather-World: Walking, Breathing, Knowing," *Journal of the Royal Anthropological Institute* (2010): S135. "For the wayfarer, movement," Ingold emphasizes, "is not ancillary to knowing—not merely a means of getting from point to point in order to collect new data of sensation for subsequent modeling in the mind. Rather, moving *is* knowing. *The wayfarer knows as he goes along.* Proceeding on his way, his life unfolds. . . . Thus the growth of his knowledge is equivalent to the maturation of his own person" (S134).

2. See Tim Ingold, "Epilogue: Towards a Politics of Dwelling," *Conservation and Society* 3, no. 2 (2005): 501–8.

3. See Tim Ingold, "The Eye of the Storm: Visual Perception and the Weather," *Visual Studies* 20, no. 2 (2005): 102.

4. See John Dewey, *The Earl Work*, ed. Jo Ann Boydston (Carbondale: Southern Illinois University Press, 1972), 5:96–102; John Dewey, *The Middle Works*, ed. Jo Ann Boydston (Carbondale: Southern Illinois University Press, 1988), 12:128–32; Alva Noë, *Action in Perception* (Cambridge, MA: MIT Press, 2004), chap. 1.

5. This term is problematic insofar as it implies an overarching order or harmony of the totality. If the universe is, as William James insisted, a *multiverse*, then can it be a cosmos? Is not chaos a better name for this multiverse? Chaos can generate order, but in time it undoes what it generates.

6. One of the main emphases of this chapter is that, in the first instance, routes result from movement. Of course, boulevards, streets, and other routes have been established by the innumerable movements of pedestrians and vehicles. But this only means that historically instituted routes have acquired a sanctioned status (consider here laws prohibiting jaywalking). A wayfarer nonetheless can venture around even in a city whose streets are laid out in a grid.

7. John Dewey, *Experience and Nature, the Later Works*, ed. Jo Ann Boydston (Carbondale: Southern Illinois University Press, 1988), 1:367–68.

8. George Santayana, *The Birth of Reason & Other Essays*, ed. Daniel Corey (New York: Columbia University Press, 1968), 7, emphasis added.

9. Dewey, *Experience and Nature*, chap 5.

10. Quoted in Ralph Barton Perry, *The Thought and Character of William James* (Boston: Little, Brown, 1935), 316. This entire letter can be found in William James, *The Letters of William James*, ed. Henry James (Boston: Atlantic Monthly, 1920), 2:150–52.

11. See Kwame Anthony Appiah, *Cosmopolitanism: Ethics in a World of Strangers* (New York: W. W. Norton, 2006).

12. "All 'homes' are," James insists, "in finite experience; finite experience as such is homeless. Nothing outside of the flux secures the issue of it" (*Pragmatism*, 125).

13. It is, however, instructive to recall that "people do not always agree about what is alive and what is not, and . . . even when they do agree it might be for entirely different reasons" (Ingold, "Rethinking the Animate," 10).

14. See Dewey, *Experience and Nature*, 34, 389.

15. Wherever there is life, "there is a trail of movement or growth. Every such trail traces a relation. But the relation is not *between* one thing and another—between the organism 'here' and the environment 'there.' It is rather a trail *along* which life is lived: one strand in a tissue of trails that together make up the texture of the lifeworld. That texture is what I mean when I speak of organisms being constituted within a relational field. It is a field not of interconnected points but of interwoven lines, not a network but a *meshwork*" (Ingold, "Rethinking the Animate," 13). Elsewhere he notes, "The network metaphor entails that the elements connected (whether people or objects) are distinguished from the lines of their connection. . . . To the extent that actor-network theorists [such as Bruno Latour in "On Recalling ANT"] have repudiated this distinction, they are—by their own admission . . . no longer dealing with networks at all. Latterly, Latour [in such works as *Reassembling the Social*] . . . has suggested that actors are knotted from the constituent lines of their relations . . . and are thus networks or part-networks in themselves. . . . This position would come close to mine were it not for the persistent confusion of knots with nodes, and hence of the meshwork with the network" ("Bindings Against Boundaries," 1805n7). See also Tim Ingold, *Lines: A Brief History* (London: Routledge, 2007), 98–100.

16. William James, *A Pluralistic Universe* (New York: Longmans, Green, 1977), 188. In *Pragmatism*, James speaks of "living reason" (138). This is also an expression used by Peirce; see, for example, Charles Sanders Peirce, *The Essential Peirce*, ed. Nathan Houser and Christian Kloesel (Bloomington: Indiana University Press, 1992), 1:59. Roughly equivalent ones can be found in the writings of Josiah Royce, George Santayana, and G. H. Mead, as well as in those of Henri Bergson, Giovanni Papini, and José Ortega y Gasset. John E. Smith develops the pragmatist notion of living reason. He insists on the need to distinguish between "first, formal reason . . . and, second, living reason or reason as the quest on the part of the concrete self for intelligibility"; see John E. Smith, *Experience and God* (New York: Fordham University Press, 1995), 111. The latter is "a living movement of thought related individual to a thinking self; it starts from certain direct experiences and moves toward the discovery of rational pattern and meaning within these experiences" (ibid.).

17. "The man thinks he can know," Emerson observed in his journal, "this or that, by words & writing. It can only be known or done organically. He must plunge into the universe, & *live in its forms*—sink to rise. None any work can frame unless himself become the same"; see Joel Porte, ed., *Emerson in His Journals* (Cambridge MA: Harvard University Press, 1982), 452; emphasis added. It is primarily for this reason that in "The American Scholar" he asserts: "I do not see how any man can afford, for the sake of his nerves and his nap, to spare any action in which he can partake. It is pearls and rubies to his discourse. Drudgery, calamity, exasperation, want, are instructors in eloquence and wisdom. The true scholar grudges every opportunity of action past by, as a loss of power"; see Larzer Ziff, ed., *Ralph Waldo Emerson: Selected Essays* (New York: Penguin, 1982), 92.

18. "What really *exists*," James rightly stresses in *A Pluralistic Universe*, "is not things but things in the making" (117). Although the language is different, the point Ingold presses is substantively the same as the one James asserts: "And as the environment unfolds, so the materials of which it is composed do not *exist* . . . but *occur*. Thus, the properties of materials, regarded as constituents of the environment, cannot be defined as fixed, essential attributes of things, but are rather processual and relational. They are neither objectively determined nor subjectively imagined but practically experienced. In that sense, every property is a condensed story. To describe the properties of materials is to tell the story of what happens to them as they flow, mix, and mutate" ("Earth, Sky, Wind, and Weather," S14).

19. See Dewey, *Experience and Nature*, 368; John W. Miller, "Afterword," in *History as System and Other Essays Toward a Philosophy of History*, ed. Jose Ortega y Gasset, trans. Helene Weyl (New York: W. W. Norton, 1961), 259; John W. Miller, *The Philosophy of History* (New York: W. W. Norton, 1981), 81, 94; and Vincent Colapietro, *Fateful Shapes of Human Freedom: John William Miller and the Crises of Modernity* (Nashville, TN: Vanderbilt University Press, 2003), 124, 181, 205.

20. We fall prey to an analogous illusion regarding the innumerable associations in and through which human identity is constituted. Because an individual can be dissociated from this, that, and the other grouping," as Dewey observes in *The Public and Its Problems*, "there grows up in the mind an image of a residual individual who is not a member of any association at all. From this premise, and from this alone, there develops the unreal question of how individuals come to be united in societies and groups" (*The Later Works*, 2:355). Such considerations force us to recognize that "an individual, whatever else it is or is not, is not just the spatially isolated [or isolatable] thing our imagination inclines us to take it to be" (ibid., 352). Indeed, any spatially isolatable being is, at bottom, a functionally enmeshed process weaving itself and being woven into the densely textured world of ongoing, constitutive processes.

21. "How to spend a day nobly, is," Emerson insists, "the problem to be solved, beside which all the great reforms which are preached seem to me trivial. If any day has not the privilege of a great action, then at least raise it by a wise passion. If thou canst not do [that], at least abstain. Now the memory of the few past idle days so works in me that I hardly dare front a new day when I leave my bed. When shall I come to an end of these shameful days, & organize honour in every day?" (*Emerson in His Journals*, 222).

22. See Ingold, "Earth, Sky, Wind, and Weather," for example, though he develops this theme in a number of other essays.

23. As recent natural disasters so dramatically disclose, the inescapable fact is that the built environment is itself *in the open*. And, as Dewey notes, "through science we have secured a degree of power of prediction and of control; through tools, machinery and an accompanying technique we have made the world more conformable to our needs, a more secure abode. We have heaped up riches and means of comfort between ourselves and the risks of the world. We

have professionalized amusement as an agency of escape and forgetfulness. But, *when all is said and done, the fundamentally hazardous character of the world is not seriously modified, much less eliminated*" (*Experience and Nature*, 45, emphasis added).

24. "In "Bindings Against Boundaries," Ingold asks: "Do we follow Heidegger in treating the open as an enclosed space cleared from within, or Kant (and, following his lead, mainstream science) in placing the open all around on the outside?" (1796). But, rather than following the lead of either, he takes up suggestions made by J. J. Gibson in his ecological approach to human perception; then, by way of his critique of Gibson's own position, Ingold progresses "beyond the idea that life is played out upon the surface of a furnished world." Put positively, he arrives at realization "we need to attend to those fluxes of the medium we call weather." "To inhabit the open is," he insists, "to be immersed in those fluxes. Life is lived in a zone in which earthly substances and aerial media are brought together in the constitution of beings which, in their activity, participate in weaving the texture of the land" (ibid.). Cf. Charles Scott, *The Lives of Things* (Bloomington: Indiana University Press, 2002).

25. Breathing is an example of such an entanglement, walking another. "Breathing," as Dewey so acutely observes in *Human Nature and Conduct*, "is an affair of the air as truly as of the lungs; digesting an affair of food as truly as of tissues of the stomach. Seeing involves light just as certainly as it does the eye and optic nerve. Walking implicates the ground as well as the legs; speech demands physical air and human companionship and audience as well as vocal cords" (*The Middle Works*, 14:15; cf. *Experience and Nature*, 21). In general, then, "functions and habits are ways of using and incorporating the environment in which the latter has its say as sure as the former" (ibid.). Cf. Ingold, "Footprints."

26. See Dewey, *The Middle Works*, 10:3–48. Dewey points out that "the description of experience [which we have inherited as much from the empiricists as from any other school of philosophers] was arrived at by forcing actual empirical facts into conformity with dialectic developments from a concept of a knower outside of the real world of nature" (*The Later Works*, 10:18). This knower is, without exaggeration, an extra-terrestrial or (to use Ingold's term) *exhabitant*. But "if biological development [or Darwinian evolution, at least in its broad outlines] be accepted. The subject of experience is at least an animal, continuous with other organic forms in a process of more complete organization. An animal in turn is at least continuous with chemico-physical processes which, in living things, are so organized as really to constitute the activities of life with all their defining traits" (ibid., 26). Even after the intellectual domination of religious traditions in which terrestrial life was denigrated was significantly weakened, the received view of the human knower was still shaped by the conception of the self as "a stranger and pilgrim in this world" (25).

27. Ingold, "Bindings Against Boundaries," 1808n11. Cf. S. Hinchliffe, "'Inhabiting': Landscapes and Natures," in *Handbook of Cultural Geography*, ed. K. Anderson et al., 207–25 (London: Sage, 2003).

28. Peirce, *The Essential Peirce*, 1:129. Of course, music in a way involves movement. It is the temporal art par excellence and its power is linked to its ability to convey a sense of transitions of the most subtle and complex as well as jarring and emphatic manner.

29. See Max Fisch, *Peirce, Semeiotic, and Pragmatism* (Bloomington: Indiana University Press, 1986), chap. 15.

30. William James, "Philosophical Conceptions and Practical Results," *University Chronicle* 1, no. 4 (September 1898): 257, 258, and 288. The map is not the terrain, the blazes on the trees but pointers, not the forest in its fullness: the words of the poets and philosophers "do not give you the integral forest with all its sunlit glories and its moonlit witcheries and wonders. Ferny dells, and mossy waterfalls, and secret magic nooks escape you, owned only by the

wild things to whom the region is a home. Happy they without the need of blazes! But to us the blazes give a sort of ownership. We can now use the forest, wend across it with companions, and enjoy its quality. It is no longer a place merely to get lost in and never return" (ibid., 288–89).

31. Joseph Brent, *Charles Sanders Peirce: A Life* (Bloomington: Indiana University Press, 1998), 13, 16. "Genius is," Peirce alleges, "above reasoning" (quoted in ibid., 340). That is, it does not amble toward, but flies to its conclusion. As used by Peirce, *reason* traces its roots to the medieval distinction between *ratio* rather than *intellectus* (the former being essentially discursive, whereas the latter is intuitive). This can be the source for confusion, since the Kantian distinction between *Vernunft* and *Verstand*, especially as received by American thinkers through S. T. Coleridge's creative appropriation of it, reverses to some extent the significance of *ratio* in its scholastic sense. That is, *Vernunft* (or Reason) in Coleridge and Emerson's sense is closer to the medieval meaning of *intellectus*, than *ratio*. *Discursus* is a process of running about, hence one requiring time and effort.

32. Peirce, *The Essential Peirce*, 2:399. See also my essay, "A Lantern for the Feet of Inquirers," *Semiotica* 136, nos. 1–4 (2001): 201–16.

33. Dewey, *Experience and Nature*, 309, emphasis added.

34. This form of cartography is connected to what Dewey identifies as the denotative method. The denotative or "empirical method points out when and where and how things of a designated description have been arrived at. It places before others a map of the road that has been travelled; they may accordingly . . . . Re-travel the road to inspect the landscape for themselves. Thus the findings of one may be rectified and extended by the findings of others" (*Experience and Nature*, 389).

35. Charles Peirce, *Selected Writings*, ed. Philip P. Wiener (New York: Dover, 1958), 403; see also Charles Peirce, *Semiotic & Significs: The Correspondence Between Charles S. Peirce & Victoria Lady Welby*, ed. Charles S. Hardwick and James Cook (Bloomington: Indiana University Press, 1977), 79.

36. Authors inescapably are forced to grant their readers the *last* word and any number of words between their opening sentence and concluding one. But to acknowledge explicitly from the outset the voice of the reader is far from commonplace. Peirce even gives a formal title to his imagined reader—Reader *Loquitur* (MS 596; cf. MS 682 [Houghton Library, Harvard University])—thereby also explicitly acknowledging than the function of the reader is not only to listen but also to talk back.

37. Charles S. Peirce, MS 598, "Reason's Rule" (Houghton Library, Harvard University), 1.

38. In the preface to his *Philosophical Investigations*, Wittgenstein confessed: The "very nature of the investigations . . . compels us to travel over a wide field of thought criss-cross in every direction—The philosophical remarks in this book are, as it were, a number of sketches of landscapes which were made in the course of these long and involved journeying"; Ludwig Wittgenstein, Philosophical Investigations, trans. G. E. M. Anscombe (New York: Macmillan, 1958), ix.

39. Peirce, "Reason's Rule," 1–2. For comparison, see also Dewey, *Experience and Nature*, 389.

40. In her 1988 Tanner Lecture ("Unspeakable Things Unspoken"), Toni Morrison asserts: "Writing is, *after* all, an act of language. But *first* of all it is an effort of the will to discover" (146). Upon the death of John Updike, Garrison Keillor stresses: "Writing is an act of paying attention"; see "Appreciation for a Great Appreciator," *A Prairie Home Companion*, February 3, 2009, www.publicradio.org/columns/prairiehome/the_old_scout/archives/2009/02/03/appreciation_for_a_great_appreciator.shtml.

41. Dewey, *Human Nature and Conduct*, 195.

42. There is an ableist bias in this claim. Not all human beings are ambulatory agents; some are not able to comport themselves in this manner, but their compensatory modes of inhabiting the world are worthy of being recognized and not merely seen as deficiencies.

43. George Santayana, *The Birth of Reason & Other Essays*, ed. Daniel Corey (New York: Columbia University Press, 1968), 10–11, 5, 8, 9, emphasis added, 13–14.

44. Ziff, *Ralph Waldo Emerson*, 198.

45. While finding myself driven to the "desperate expedient" of coining a new word (as Kant identified neologisms), I quickly discovered that this term had been not only invented by someone else but also was already trademarked! It is used for a company devoted to providing "Satellites; satellite communication apparatus and instruments, namely, transmitters, transceivers, antennae, signaling devices, analogue and digital display units, computer terminals and keyboards; satellite communication terminals; communications apparatus and instruments, namely, transmitters, transceivers, antennae, signaling devices, terminals, analogue and digital display units, computer terminals and keyboards; telephones; telex machines and facsimile machines, etc." (https://trademarks.justia.com/761/86/geopolitan-76186292.html).

46. Dewey, *The Later Works*, 5:123.

47. Painters "aim to recover, behind the mundane ordinariness of the ability to see things, the sheer astonishment of that experience, namely of being able to see. This is what Merleau-Ponty . . . calls [in "Eye and Mind"] the magic or delirium of vision. Astonishment . . . is the other side of the coin to the very openness to the world. It is the sense of wonder that comes from riding the crest of the world's continued birth" (Ingold, "Rethinking the Animate," 18). Students of pragmatism will be reminded of James's own use of this metaphor: "We live, as it were, upon the front-edge of an advancing wave-crest, and our sense of a determinate direction in falling forward is all we cover of the future of our path" (*Pragmatism*, 234). In his hands no less than in Ingold's, this points to the world itself coming into being, moreover, our presence at, and contribution to, this "continued birth": "Somewhere being must immediately breast nonentity. Why may not the advancing front of experience [the front edge of this wave-crest] carrying its immanent satisfactions and dissatisfactions, cut against the black inane as the luminous orb of the moon cuts the cærulean abyss? Why should anywhere the world be fixed and finished? And if reality genuinely grows, why may it not grow in these very determinations which *here* and *now* are made?" (ibid., 222, emphasis added).

48. In human beings, "the organs of fertility, which were the flowers, sunning themselves wide open and lolling in delicious innocence, are now," Santayana wryly observes, "tucked away obscurely in the hindquarters, to be seen and thought of as little as possible." He immediately adds: "This disgrace lies heavy upon them, prompting them to sullen discontent and insidious plots and terrible rebellions. Yet their unrest is a new incentive to travel, perhaps the most powerful and persistent of all: it lends a great beauty to strangers" (*Birth of Reason*, 7).

49. Quoted in Ingold, "Bindings Against Boundaries," 1808. The text cited by Ingold is Casey's *Getting Back into Place* (2009), 15–16.

50. Of course not all human beings are ambulatory agents, but the exceptions prove the rule.

51. In *Essays in Radical Empiricism*, James suggests: "Philosophy has always turned on grammatical particles. With, near, next, like, from, toward, against, because, for, through, my—these words designate types of conjunctive relation arranged in a roughly ascending order of intimacy and inclusiveness"; see William James, *Essays in Radical Empiricism* (New York: Dutton, 1971), 26. This chapter, in large measure inspired by Ingold's work, is an attempt to show how philosophy at this juncture might turn on the word *along* and words related to movement and direction.

52. Ingold, "Bindings Against Boundaries," 1808. "Where there's a road there has been," John William Miller contends, "going. The wilderness is then less bewildering. Where there is a way, a procedure, a control, there has been a traveler. No way, no road, has manifestation as absolute prospect. The road is the course taken to have arrived. Without direction, there is no going, neither departure nor arrival. A road is retrospective. It is the *continuance* of a doing.... Any path, any way or road entails not only the verb, but also the past tense of the verb" ("Afterword," 102, emphasis added; cf. my *Fateful Shapes*).

53. See James, *Pragmatism*, 32.

54. As much as obstacles and impediments, environments offer (to use J. J. Gibson's apt term) *affordances*. Before any traveler or wayfarer forges a path, there is not a path but a series of affordances inviting and facilitating living organisms in their terrestrial meanderings.

55. "Places are," Ingold suggests, "formed through movement, when a movement *along* turns into a movement *around*, precisely as happened in our initial experiment of drawing a circle. Such a movement around is place-binding, but it is not place bound [hence the title of the article in which these claims are being made—"bindings against boundaries"]. There can be no places were it not for the comings and goings of human beings and other organisms to and from them, from and to places elsewhere" ("Bindings Against Boundaries," 1808). The "experiment" to which Ingold alludes in this passage needs to be recalled here. At the outset of the article, he asks his reader to draw a circle and then poses the question, "How should we interpret this line?" His answer helps us not only see the circle as the trace of a gesture but also see our own distinctive emphasis as akin to a dominant note in American pragmatism. Strictly speaking, the circle "is the trace left by the gesture of your hand.... However, viewing the line as a totality, ready drawn on the surface, we might be inclined to reinterpret it quite differently—as a trajectory of movement but as a static perimeter.... With this figure we seem to have set up a division between what is on the 'inside' and what is on the 'outside'" (ibid., 1796). Upon this reinterpretation, however, we have turned "the pathways along which life is lived into boundaries within which life is contained. Life, according to this logic, is reduced to an internal property of things that *occupy* the world but do not properly *inhabit* it. A world that is occupied ... is furnished with already-existing things. But one that is inhabited is woven from the strands of their continual coming-into-being" (1796–97). The circle is first and foremost the trace of a gesture, that is, of a movement. The fixed form is derivative, the more or less fluid act primary. But this view is akin to that of the pragmatists. Already in *The Principles of Psychology*, James suggested: "Life is one long struggle between conclusions based on abstract ways of conceiving cases [or affairs], and opposite conclusions prompted by our instinctive perception of them as individual facts"; see William James, *The Principles of Psychology* (Cambridge, MA: Harvard University Press, 1981), 1266. The abstract view is abstract by virtue of ignoring the processes and relationships in which some object emerge and endure, for however long they do.

56. Dewey, *Experience and Nature*, 34.

57. In *What Is Philosophy?*, Ortega stresses: "in philosophy a straight line is usually not the shortest road. The great philosophic problems yield to conquest only when they are treated as the Hebrews treated Jericho—by approaching them in concentric circles which become ever tighter and more suggestive"; see José y Gasset Ortega, *What Is Philosophy?*, trans. Mildred Adams (New York: W. W. Norton, 1960), 30.

58. Of humanism, James asserts: "Ethically the pluralistic form of it takes for me a stronger hold on reality than any other philosophy I know of—it being essentially a *social* philosophy, a philosophy of '*co*,' in which conjunctions do the work" (*Pragmatism*, 238).

59. It is, Ingold contends, "by walking along from place to place, and not by building up from local particulars, that we come to know what we do. Yet as we walk, we do not so much

traverse the exterior surface of the world [or Earth] as negotiate through a zone of admixture and interchange, between the more or less solid substances of the earth and the volatile medium of air" ("Footprints," S121–S122). This makes of walking a process of *wayfaring*, rather than one of *transport*.

60. In addition to characterizing nature in terms of commodity, beauty, and discipline, Emerson portrays nature as language (*Selected Essays*, 48–55). Nature is, in other words, a source of symbols. More precisely, it is both inherently expressive and an indispensable resource for human articulation. But, from Emerson's perspective, the function of symbols is itself linked to the dominant emphases of this chapter. This is nowhere more evident than in his insistence in "The Poet" that "all symbols are fluxional; all language is vehicular and transitive, and is good, as ferries and horses are, for conveyance, not as farms and houses are, for homestead" (ibid., 279). It is however no less so than in his claim: "The use of symbols has a certain power of emancipation and exhilaration for all me. We seem [in this use] to be touched by a wand which makes us dance and run about happily, like children. We are like persons who come out of a cave or cellar into the open air" (276). The themes of movement and living out in the open are obviously sounded in such passages.

61. What is true of nature, is at least equally true of experience and thus our experience of nature (moreover, human experience as itself a natural process). As Dewey notes, "Coarse and vital experience is Protean; a thing of moods and tenses" (*Experience and Nature*, 367).

62. There are not too more distinctively pragmatic prefixes than *re-* and *trans-*.

63. William James, *A Pluralistic Universe* (New York: Longmans, Green, 1977), 129. "Every smallest state of consciousness, concretely taken, overflows," James insists, "its own definition. Only concepts are self-identical; only 'reason' deals with closed equations; *nature is but a name for excess*; every point in her opens out and runs into the more; and the only question, with reference to any point we may be considered, is how far into the rest of nature we may have to go in order to get entirely beyond is flow" (ibid., emphasis added).

64. Once again, it is instructive to recall the words of Ingold: "all science depends on observation, and all observation depends on participation—that is, a close coupling, in perception and action, between the observer and those aspects of the world that are the focus of attention. If science is to be a coherent knowledge practice, it must be rebuilt on the foundation of openness rather than closure, engagement rather than detachment. . . . Knowledge must be reconnected with being . . . thought with life" ("Rethinking the Animate," 19). It however may be that observation is itself a mode of participation, not simply a process depending on other ones (such as action) identified as instances of participation. Of course, Santayana in defending the place of Spirit is not concerned with scientific observation, but rather a contemplative stance.

65. Dewey, *Human Nature and Conduct*, 15.

7 Cosmopolitan Ignorance and "Not Knowing Your Place"

José Medina

> In supposing themselves at home everywhere, would-be cosmopolitans fail to know their place.
> —John J. Stuhr, "Somewhere, Dreaming of Cosmopolitanism"
>
> No less than *place*, *polis* is not a noun but a verb. It names a set of processes and practices. Anything to which we can point as integral to a place or a polis is a distinct phase in an ongoing history.
> —Vincent Colapietro, "Toward a Politics of Cohabitation: 'Dwelling' in the Manner of Wayfarers"
>
> If place is as fluid as experience, then there is literally no place like home, no *place* like the home we remember and dream.
> Every place has multiple histories, stories of attachment and ownership, of usurpation and surrender. We belong to places, but the places themselves, even the ones we think of as most intimately "ours" don't belong to anyone.
> —Megan Craig, "Loss of Place"

As Vincent Colapietro urges us to do, *place* should be thought of a verb, as referring to activities, and more specifically shared activities or social practices. As Colapietro puts it: "Whatever else places are, they are sites of activity, loci for dramas, above all, those improvised scenes in which the unintended consequences of our most careful deliberations quickly acquire (no matter how slow our acknowledgement) their fateful significance" (Chapter 6, pages 88–89). Whereas in traditional views *place* was conceived as "a fixed container or enclosure," Colapietro proposes a pragmatic reconceptualization of *place* as "a historically evolved and evolving set of processes and practices."[1] Colapietro's dynamic and interactionist perspective urges us to shift the focus of our reflections on place from occupation to coinhabitation. This chapter aims to be a contribution to the kind of pragmatist politics of coinhabitation that Colapietro proposes. The pragmatist approach I use also endorses the thoroughgoing pluralism that

Megan Craig alludes to when she remarks that "every place has multiple histories."[2] The multiplicity and fluidity of places make them forever elusive: we belong to places, but they don't belong to us, no matter how intimately "ours" they may feel; we may call them "ours," but this does not designate a proprietary relation.

Places are elusive for all of us, but not to the same degree or in the same sense. Although we are all placed and displaced in various ways, some people are radically displaced; radical dislocation can be disabling and damaging. There are many forms that the phenomenon of displacement can take. In her phenomenological account Craig focuses on displacement as the *loss* of place, that is, cases in which people are displaced because their place has "disappeared, eroded, or ceased to be," or because they have been forced to leave it behind. But one can also be *displaced within a place*, that is, without abandoning the place one inhabits but being prevented from making that place one's own, being trapped in a context where one has no opportunity to find or make a home. This is the phenomenon of displacement I want to focus on as an ethical and political problem. And I want to emphasize from the start that this is not a problem only for those displaced or marginalized within a place but also for those who coinhabit that place and remain complicit with—or oblivious to—the exclusion or marginalization. It is a problem that ultimately concerns people in other places, as well, given the relational nature of place—and therefore of processes of placement and displacement—as I argue in the following. The kind of exclusion or marginalization involved in being displaced within a place is a key problem for a pragmatist politics of coinhabitation, and a problem with wide ramifications that is both local and global.

By focusing on how places are constituted by different forms of exclusion and marginalization I want to call attention to the intimate connection between processes of being placed and processes of being displaced. Placing and displacing peoples and their ways of life go together. Any community—no matter how open and inclusive—will allow some ways of inhabiting places by some people and not some other ways by some others. Every form of inclusion is at the same time a form of exclusion, and, therefore, processes of placing and displacing are unavoidably interrelated. This is the first thing we must recognize in order to inhabit places responsibly and to be attentive to the different forms of exclusion and marginalization that have become inscribed in those places. As John J. Stuhr puts it in Chapter 17 of this volume: "The alternative we face to some form of inclusion/exclusion is some other form of inclusion/exclusion. There is no live, nonabstract politics that does not involve practices of exclusion. To realize this is to take a step toward knowing—and changing—one's place."[3] What traditional cosmopolitan views forget or don't know is precisely this deep connection between being placed and being displaced. This is a key component of what I call *cosmopolitan ignorance*.[4] This ignorance involves a failure in our ethical and political responsibility of knowing and being sensitive to multiple and interrelated histories of placement and displacement. The contribution I want to make to a pragmatist politics of coinhabitation concerns the danger of inhabiting the world comfortably without any regard for the impact of our inhabitation on others, that is, the danger of making a place our home without taking into account whether or not others with whom we share spaces feel at home in them. This is a disregard for interdependence that results in irresponsible inhabitation. And of course the ethical and political problem becomes more acute when we arrange our practices and our cognitive and affective ties so that we feel at home not just in particular places, but in *the whole world*, while there are others who do not feel at home anywhere. This is what Stuhr denounces about the cosmopolitan aspiration of being at home everywhere. He replaces this aspiration with the following key "challenge facing pluralistic democracies today": "What social practices would lead the included to feel—and I want to stress affect rather than cognition—the importance of the concerns and lives of the excluded?" (Chapter 17, page 291 of this volume). I fully agree with Stuhr that this is the challenge of responsible coinhabitation. And, as Stuhr emphasizes, meeting this challenge successfully should be understood in the following way: "To succeed is not to find one's self at home everywhere in the world; it is to feel one's self *not quite fully or ever at home* any place in the world."[5] It is the kind of epistemic and affective discomfort involved in not feeling "quite fully or ever at home" that can enable us to inhabit places more responsibly that I will discuss below under the rubric of "perplexity."

In this chapter I want to link the *cosmopolitan ignorance* that (mis)leads agents to inhabit the world irresponsibly (that is, without due sensitivity to multiple others) to the *local ignorance* of one's own place that leads to irresponsible coinhabitation at the local level. Ignorance is both local and global, indeed truly cosmopolitan (perhaps even more so than knowledge). We may think it is easy to ignore what happens far away but not what happens under our very noses, and yet our ignorance of our own world, of our most familiar places, is often truly remarkable; moreover, this local ignorance is often related to our more global ignorance of other less familiar places and global contexts, or so I argue.

There are many ways in which we can talk about "knowing (or not knowing) your place": knowing your way about, knowing your placement within a social hierarchy, knowing your standing within a group (e.g., your family or a group of friends), and so on. I focus on a specific sense of knowing your place in the world that is both local and global simultaneously, and it brings out the interrelations between the local and the global level. This is what I call knowing a place in the world that you can call your own, that is, knowing your home within the world. It is in this sense that we can be said to know (or not know) our neighborhood, our city, our state or country, or our region of the world, as places that we can call our own, as our homes. Knowing your place in the world, in this sense, can be understood only relationally, for knowing a place that you can call your own in its particularity involves knowing it in relation to other locations, as being similar, different, and variously related to other places. These interrelations among places within which our own place needs to be located are both *synchronic and diachronic*. Synchronically, knowing the place you call home means knowing how it is currently related to many other places and how it is constituted by those relations: relations of geopolitical proximity/distance, of cultural proximity/distance, of economic interaction, and so on—in short, relations of dependence and independence of various sorts. The challenging task of getting to know your place, or deepening the knowledge of your place, is the task of learning to navigate the complex network of heterogeneous relations within which that place emerges and is sustained. On the other hand, diachronically, knowing your place over time involves knowing how to trace its historical trajectories, how to appreciate its continuities and discontinuities, so that we are able to project this place into the past and into the future and to relate its present shape and configuration to other possible ones.

So conceived, getting to know your place in the world is indeed an *endless task*. Although this kind of knowledge will never be completed, we can always keep perfecting it. Our knowledge of our homes in the world always have different degrees of depth, ranging from the most superficial and one-dimensional to the most critically digested and multifaceted. But no matter how knowledgeable we become and how successfully we may have fought against misconceptions, illusions, and insensitivities at home, some opaque corners and blind-spots always remain in our homely gaze. However we relate to our homes in the world, we always live in them with some degree of blindness. The best we can hope for is a mixture of lucidity and blindness that does no harm (or as little as possible) to ourselves and to others. Our places in the world have different degrees of transparency and opaqueness to us. But we have to take responsibility for what is transparent and what is opaque to us. Our gaze is unavoidably selective, illuminating for us certain things while obscuring others; we have to take responsibility for how it is selectively pointed in certain directions and not others, for how certain aspects and relations of what we call our place acquire visibility (even hypervisibility), while others are rendered invisible. This chapter tries to contribute to this kind of critical interrogation of what we know and don't know about our places in the world, aiming at providing some critical tools for developing responsible epistemic relations. How does one take responsibility for what one knows and does not know about their place in the world? In the first section, I draw on some insights from recent epistemologies of ignorance in order to start answering this question. Then in the second section, I sketch a normative and relational account of ignorance/knowledge of one's place that tries to address normative questions and provide a robust notion of epistemic responsibility. Finally, in the last section, I offer a brief illustration and derive from my analysis some conclusions for a pragmatist politics of coinhabitation.

Ignorance/Knowledge, Epistemic (Dis)Comfort, and Responsibility with Respect to One's Place

As I have argued elsewhere, following Wittgenstein and Foucault,[6] *spaces of knowability and unknowability* are produced simultaneously, and the epistemic agency that subjects have within a discursive practice is such that their knowledge and ignorance are co-constituted: their epistemic lucidity and their epistemic blindness go hand in hand, mutually supporting each other. As another epistemologist of ignorance, Shannon Sullivan, puts it, "Rather than oppose knowledge, ignorance often is formed by it, and vice versa."[7] For this reason, in "White Ignorance and Colonial Oppression" Sullivan suggests that we talk about "ignorance/knowledge," instead of talking about ignorance and knowledge separately, so that we undo certain epistemic illusions: in particular, "the purported self-mastery and self-transparency of knowledge, as if nothing properly escaped its grasp."[8] The dangerous epistemic illusion of self-mastery and self-transparency often appears when one feels comfortable about what one knows and does not know about their homely places. This kind of *epistemic comfort* typically signals that one has failed to interrogate one's ignorance/knowledge and to take responsibility for it. What is needed in order to disrupt this problematic comfort and to start taking responsibility is a process of self-estrangement, which can be prompted by experiences of *perplexity*. This is well illustrated by Sullivan's candid account of her ignorance/knowledge of the United States and its colonial past and present. "Why I Know So Little About Puerto Rico" (which is the subtitle of Sullivan's essay) describes the perplexity that she felt when she watched the Puerto Rico basketball team defeat the United States in the 2004 Summer Olympics. Sullivan was perplexed because she could not understand how Puerto Rico could have "its own team, separate from the US" and how a country could "be beaten by itself in the Olympics."[9] Sullivan was troubled by her "vague knowledge that Puerto Rico is somehow part of the US." She soon found out that Puerto Rico had in fact been granted a limited form of self-government since 1948. But the general questions that Sullivan raises are: How can a well-educated person in the United States live so comfortably and for so long with a notable ignorance about Puerto Rico and its relation to the United States? How can one manage to keep this ignorance hidden or invisible so that it does not make one feel uncomfortable about the contours of one's ignorance/knowledge of one's country? Is one responsible for this kind of ignorance? And how can one be led to rethink one's positionality in the world?

As recent epistemologies of ignorance have taught us, a crucial corollary of bringing together ignorance and knowledge is that there is no such thing as epistemic innocence, for we always operate from a space of knowability and unknowability simultaneously. And this problematizes the notion of *culpable ignorance*. On the one hand, as Lorraine Code has observed, there is no such thing as "an innocent position from which 'we' could level charges of culpability."[10] Therefore, as Code insists, in dealing with the epistemic aspects of particular forms of oppression, we should be very careful not to indulge in the naive charge of epistemic culpability "they should have known better"; for very often subjects *could* not have known otherwise (at least not by themselves and without altering the bodies of knowledge and ignorance they have inherited), and, therefore, the charge of culpability becomes vacuous. On the other hand, however, interstices within discursive practices as well as alternative practices are often available; they present opportunities for *epistemic resistance*, for challenging ignorance/knowledge structures, and genealogical investigations can be used to point out how these subjugated knowledges could have been used, how people could have known otherwise by drawing on them. Foucaultian genealogical investigations try to mobilize the power of resistance that subjugated knowledges have.[11] As Sullivan puts it, echoing Foucault: "The creation of ignorance/knowledge through relations of force often is unbalanced and unequal, as is the case in colonized lands. But as a dynamic, relational process, it involves the active participation of all 'sides' and includes the possibility of resistance to and transformation of the forms of ignorance/knowledge produced."[12] Counterpublics and countermemories enable us to see how different possibilities of resistance appear for differently constituted and situated subjects as they develop different forms of agency with respect to power/knowledge, or rather, power/ignorance- knowledge.

In his now classic *The Racial Contract*,[13] Charles Mills put white ignorance in the agenda of critical race theory. Following a long tradition in African American philosophy, Mills argued there that privileged white subjects have become unable to understand the world that they themselves have created. He called attention to the cognitive dysfunctions and pathologies inscribed in the white world, not merely as side effects but as constitutive features of the white epistemic economy, which revolves around epistemic exclusions and a carefully cultivated racial blindness. As Mills suggests, American white ignorance is a form of self-ignorance that includes as a crucial component the ignorance of the nonwhite aspects of the United States and its history. In "White Ignorance" Mills emphasizes the role that official histories and hegemonic forms of collective memory play in sustaining white ignorance, and also the crucial role that countermemory needs to play to resist and subvert the epistemic oppression that condemns the lives of marginalized people to silence or oblivion. As Mills puts it, we have "both official and counter-memory, with conflicting judgments about what is important in the past and what is unimportant, what happened and does matter, what happened and does not matter, and what did not happen at all."[14] Mills argues that the postbellum national white reconciliation was made possible and was subsequently maintained thanks to "the repudiation of an alternative black memory."[15] There have been all kinds of mechanisms in white epistemic practices that have contributed to maintain this repudiation in place: blocking black subjectivities from giving testimony, keeping black testimony—when given—out of circulation,[16] exercising an epistemic assumption against its credibility, and so on. In multiple venues of epistemic interaction in the white world, from the streets of white suburbs to the lecture halls of the academy, black voices have been traditionally minimized and heavily constrained in their ability to speak about their own experiences,[17] when they have been allowed to speak at all.

As recent epistemologies of ignorance have clamored, we have to take *responsibility* for what we know and for what we do not know; this applies also to our knowledge and ignorance about the places that we call "home." But this complex responsibility is not properly understood if it is conceived in purely cognitive terms, as Mill's "cognitive therapy" might suggest.[18] I emphasize two crucial features of our epistemic relations to the places we manage to inhabit as our home, showing how these features expand our epistemic responsibilities beyond a narrow cognitive repertoire such as our repertoire of beliefs. In the first place, the ignorance/knowledge of one's place is crucially *mediated by the imagination.* As Moira Gatens, for one, has put it, the imagination enables one "to exist in a particular way in relation to one's context."[19] And as we saw earlier, the relational nature of our epistemic attitudes toward our place in the world requires that we envision the network of relations in which our place is inscribed, and that we project that place and its relations into the past and into the future. All this requires the imagination, and it is for this reason that our epistemic relation with a place is always an *imaginary* relation.

In the second place, being able to recognize a place as your home—for example, your hometown, your home country—is both a *cognitive and an affective achievement.* On the one hand, knowing a homely place requires cognitive attitudes and habits that enable you to recognize a particular place as your own. Perceptual habits, memory, our ability to decipher signs, and so on, are among the crucial cognitive skills that we need to recognize our places in the world. But, on the other hand, recognizing a homely place is also an affective achievement and it requires affective attitudes that enables us to position ourselves emotionally in relation to that place. We always have emotional investments in our homely places in the world. This does not mean that we must have positive affective attachments to these places. Sometimes we love our homes, and sometimes we don't. But our homely places in the world are never neutral to us; they can evoke affective reactions of various sorts, but not indifference.[20] It is, in fact, important to develop the ability to have diversified emotional responses to our homely places, to be able to feel a wide range of emotions about them, instead of having rigid emotional attachments that go along with homogeneous and monolithic relations of identification and counter-identification with one's place. As I have argued elsewhere, rigid relations of identification and counteridentification are problematic and constrain our cognitive-affective relations and our agency.[21] *Disidentification* is a mechanism that enables us to introduce fluidity and flexibility in our relations of identification and counter-identification with places in the world: by disidentifying with our countries, cities, neighborhoods, and so on, we acknowledge our emotional investments in them, without thereby being blind to the different ways in which we may want to distance ourselves from a particular configuration of that place. We identify but with a difference; we acknowledge our relation of identification with that place while critically distancing ourselves from some of its aspects or relations. And a similar kind of fluidity and heterogeneity can be introduced in relations of counter-identification with places we regard as foreign: we can regard a place as foreign while at the same time developing an intimate familiarity with it, noticing that we do not belong there but being able to envision what it can mean to inhabit it, and thus taking critical distance from our imagined distance or unfamiliarity with that place.

Taking critical distance from our feelings of belonging and not-belonging, from our relations of identification and counter-identification with places, involves a difficult process of self-estrangement. This process of self-estrangement is crucial for developing a responsible epistemic relation with a place: we need to learn to distance ourselves from the relations of identification and counteridentification that we forge with places in the world, so that these places can appear as newly strange to us and we can then refamiliarize ourselves with them. This is the *duty of self-estrangement* that I want to present as a key aspect in acquiring responsibility for our epistemic relations with places in the world.

The Duty of Self-Estrangement, or How to Start Developing Responsible Relational Attitudes Toward Homely (and Unhomely) Places

Given the imaginary and hybrid (i.e., cognitive-affective) character of our epistemic relation to homely (and unhomely) places, taking responsibility for that relation must involve at least two things. In the first place, we have to take responsibility for our actual imaginative relation with such places *and* for not having other kinds of imaginative relations that we *could* have; that is, we have to take responsibility for what we imagine and for what we fail to imagine. And, in the second place, since our epistemic relation to a homely place in the world involves a hybrid set of attitudes that are both cognitive and affective, we also have to take responsibility for having the particular cognitive and affective attitudes that we do have *and* for not having other possible ones that we *could* have. So, when we say that we have to take responsibility for our knowledge (as well as for our ignorance) of our places in the world, this means at least the following things: first, that we have to take responsibility for the kind of geopolitical imagination we have developed and for its limitations; second, that we have to take responsibility for our cognitive and affective achievements and failures in our relations to the places we become attached to.

Note the crucial *counterfactual* dimension of this responsibility as I have formulated it. A crucial part of acquiring responsibility for our epistemic relation to a place is the obligation to consider alternative ways of relating to that place and inhabiting it, as many alternatives as possible. But of course our imagination is always limited, and so are our cognitive and affective capacities. So how can we carry out this counterfactual responsibility? How do we determine which possible imaginary relations and cognitive-affective attitudes to consider and be open to? This is contextually determined by the experiential possibilities that appear in our individual and collective horizons and can enrich our individual and collective lives. But the contextual interaction and mutual interrogation of diverse ways of inhabiting a place can only happen if subjects make themselves vulnerable and lose their epistemic comfort, that is, if they are willing to expose themselves to other experiential perspectives and other imaginary ways of relating to a place. To inhabit places responsibly, we have to seek opportunities to become *perplexed* about our ignorance/knowledge of such places; we have to learn to work with those experiences of perplexity—instead of blocking them, hiding them, or escaping from them—so that those experiences can become the starting points of constructive processes of self-estrangement in which we can learn about the presuppositions and implications of our cognitive, affective, and imaginary relations to places.

In *Democracy and Social Ethics*, Jane Addams described experiences of perplexity as the kind of existential discomfort that constitutes the initial stage of ethical inquiry.[22] Perplexity and self-estrangement are of the utmost importance for cognitive, affective, ethical, and political learning. The experiential disruptions that arise in interaction with significantly different others are precious opportunities for developing an awareness of our interdependence and a critical consciousness of the limitations of our perspective vis-à-vis that of others. By seeking these experiences of perplexity and disruption and using them as a mechanism of learning, we can cultivate a social sensibility that opens our eyes, ears, and hearts to other ways of thinking, feeling, and living. This is absolutely crucial for developing responsible relational attitudes towards places, that is, attitudes that are responsive to the experiences and concerns of others who inhabit them. An important failure of responsibility takes place when we become insensitive to ways of relating to a place that are at odds with ours, when we no longer cultivate an openness to being challenged and affected by alternative experiential perspectives, when we lose the capacity to become perplexed and to do anything constructive with that perplexity.

Arrogantly assuming that we know a place without contrasting and interrogating such alleged knowledge (and its companion forms of ignorance) involves cognitive and affective deficits as well as a deficit in the imagination. Such excessive epistemic comfort leads people to become cognitively and affectively numbed; it also leads to the occlusion of relational possibilities that the imagination can offer for cohabitating within a place. The unquestioned epistemic comfort that a subject can take in her knowledge of a place involves a lack of concern for the limitations, presuppositions, and lacunae or blind spots of that knowledge. It also involves an important shortsightedness about the cognitive-affective relations on which it rests and the kind of imagination (or imaginary inhabitation) it involves. We need to cultivate epistemic discomfort through processes of self-estrangement so as to produce the kind of critical awareness and sensitivity that can lead to being responsive to other possible ways of inhabiting places, to other experiential perspectives that can be part of those places or be affected by them. In linking our ability to experience self-estrangement in our epistemic relation to a place with our ability to make such places hospitable for multiple forms of sociability and inhabitation, my argument gives support to two of the key political duties that J. Tully has argued for in his account of "critical freedom": first, the duty to cultivate "the ability to see one's own ways as strange and unfamiliar, to stray from and take up a critical attitude towards them and so open cultures to question, reinterpretation, negotiation, transformation and non-identity," and, second, the responsibility to acknowledge that everyone is entitled to "the aspiration to belong to a culture and a place, and so to be at home in the world."[23]

Not knowing your place, experiencing epistemic discomfort about your location, even being disoriented, can be a good thing. But too much of it is also a problem. Let's not forget that feeling comfortable in the world is a luxury that many subjects do not have. And those who feel displaced or out of place should not be asked to confront the duty of self-estrangement in the same way. How can we demand more self-estrangement from those who have been alienated in and from their places? Let's not romanticize the wonders of discomfort, for, as those who have felt nothing but discomfort well know, far from being renewing and habilitating, discomfort can be deeply oppressive and paralyzing. We need to strike a balance between comfort and discomfort, so that we become capable of losing epistemic comfort without thereby losing our bearings and feeling completely out of place. Indeed, the duty of self-estrangement should be properly qualified and often relaxed when it is *contextualized*. It matters deeply whether we start from a place of comfort or a place of discomfort. Whether and how an agent enters the duty of self-estrangement depends crucially on her trajectory. But only in extreme cases in which the subject has been unable to identify with *any* place and to develop a functional imaginative relation to a place and healthy cognitive and affective ties to it, only in that case, would I say that the duty of self-estrangement should be completely suspended. In other cases, the key is to understand the duty of self-estrangement as demanding that we make our familiar attitudes unfamiliar, whether these attitudes are positive and comfortable or negative and uncomfortable. Taking distance from one's discomfort is indeed a different and more problematic thing than that of taking distance from one's comfort. But finding ways of interrogating one's discomfort is important so that one can recognize the specific cognitive and affective deficits and the specific failures of the imagination that have led to it and support it. When subjects are not in a position to take critical distance from their epistemic discomfort, this should become a collective responsibility, so that they can receive the proper social support and we can collectively learn about the presuppositions and implications of their inability to recognize a place as their own.

One may think that in cases where the subject has been, not just displaced (having a home, but not being able to occupy it), but always out of place, eternally homeless, without the possibility of identifying with any place at all, there is no task to undertake either individually or collectively because there is nothing to develop a responsible epistemic relationship with, nothing to know. But this is false. There is here an even more pressing task to undertake, even though it is a task that the out-of-place subject cannot assume the burden of all by herself. It is a counterfactual task that calls for collective responsibility, collective imagination, and collective action. The task is to figure out what would count as a place in the world that this subject can properly relate to, a place she can inhabit comfortably and call her own, even if it is a place that has never existed and needs to be created.

I now turn to the challenges that arise for reimagining a place in a way that can effectively resist exclusions. I focus on racialized ways of imagining places that exclude or marginalize oppressed groups, paying special attention to imaginative strategies—such as the imaginative conceptualization of a city as a "white" city—that racially homogenizes a place and arranges an oppressive racial geography.

Perplexity and "White" Cities

We need to work with our perplexities; they provide the starting points and the raw materials of the ethical and political tasks with which we are confronted. But we are often numbed to feel perplexity, to even register that something does not fit and runs contrary to well-entrenched expectations. And when we do notice and feel perplexed, we often do not know what to do with that perplexity and fail to question the assumptions of our perspective. Take, for example, the racialization of a place, which can be so insidious that it remains mostly hidden, invisible, and unnoticed by those who dwell in that place even though it is everywhere (or *precisely because* it is everywhere) in their daily lives. There may be all kinds of things that run contrary to the bodies of ignorance produced by the racialization of a place, but people may not notice them, or may notice them without feeling much perplexity at all, or may feel perplexed and do nothing about it. Think, for example, of the "whitening" of a city and how difficult it can be for the city dwellers to interrogate such dominant racialization of their familiar spaces even if they run into opportunities for such interrogation. Let me use as an illustration my hometown, Seville, in southern Spain, which has been the home of many ethnic groups and cultures throughout the centuries. Surprisingly (or perhaps not so much), Seville has been persistently imagined by mainstream Spanish culture as a white city (as most Spanish cities have). The traces of nonwhite peoples and cultures are regarded as anomalies of one sort or another. Even the abundant Arab elements in southern Spanish culture—in its architecture, its cuisine, its music, and so on—are not taken to define its cities, but are rather regarded as picturesque gifts left by a foreign culture that overstayed its visit, gifts that now beautify cities like Seville, Cordoba, or Granada.

Perhaps the most radical erasure of all from the collective memory of Seville is that of its black inhabitants. Despite the fact that there are at least some prominent black icons in the city that should remind people of its black past. For example, in my childhood neighborhood, Triana, we have a black cultural icon, el Negro de Triana, who was buried in 1503 with high honors in the neighborhood's main church (Santa Ana). His name is Iñigo Lopes, and people talk about him as if he were the only person of color who was brought to Seville during the colonization of the Americas, while in fact during that period there were entire neighborhoods of people of color in Seville, Triana being only one of them.[24] Sevilleans rarely know this today, but when they find out, their perplexity does not seem to lead to a deep redescription of their town and its history. Even the very few journalists and historians who have been writing on this recently do not seem to take it as an opportunity to question the myth of Seville as a white city.[25] Even more perplexing is for people to find out that Seville's black neighborhoods were not simply a product of Spain's colonial activities in the Americas, for their existence predates 1492.

It is actually surprising that few Sevilleans today know about this since it is well known that one of the oldest religious associations in the city is called the Brotherhood of the Black Peoples of Seville (Hermandad de los Negros de Sevilla, which today is colloquially referred to as Los Negritos). This association was founded in the last decade of the fourteenth century (the exact year being unknown) by the black peoples of the city who lived *extramuros*—outside the walls of the city—which is the only place they could live unless they were part of the domestic service of a house within the walls. The local historian Isidoro Moreno has shown how the foundation of this religious association transformed the lives of black Sevilleans and also the city as a space of multiracial coinhabitation.[26] As a group, the members of this association could enter the walls of the city for something other than work and they could participate in processional activities at the cathedral. Thanks to this association, black Sevilleans could acquire collective property and have collective rights. As individuals, they could not buy property or initiate lawsuits; however, collectively, as a religious organization with legal standing, they could do so. In this way black Sevilleans were able to dwell regularly and even own spaces *intramuros*—within the walls of the city—and to make different parts of the city (and not only the black neighborhoods) their own homely place.

Unfortunately, this long battle that black Sevilleans initiated in the fourteenth century to make the city their own and to gain agency within it is still unfinished. And their struggles have been, for the most part, forgotten. It would be productive to reflect on the spatial symmetry between the black neighborhoods of Seville in the fourteenth century and the black and brown neighborhoods of Seville today. In both cases there are numerous populations of nonwhite Sevilleans living in the outskirts of the city, although the outskirts of today are quite a few kilometers away from the historic walls of the city. It is said daily (in the local newspapers, in the local radio and TV channels, on the streets) that this is a *new* phenomenon, that Seville did not use to have nonwhite neighborhoods or spaces with a considerable concentration of black and brown Sevilleans. Sevilleans from all races, classes, and walks of life can become perplexed when confronted with the black past of the city. Not only middle-class white Sevilleans who have been acculturated into a sense of belonging but even those who have been marginalized within the city seem to assume that Seville has been, for the most part, a white city and are perplexed when they find out otherwise.[27] It is not easy to reverse the long history of dominant identifications that have reclaimed the city for some groups and not for others. The dominant mentality that started to be impressed on Sevilleans since 1492 after the expulsion of the Jews and the Arabs also whitened the city and invited imaginary relations between the city and other places that remain largely uninterrogated today. Sevilleans have been trained to look north for identifications and south for counteridentifications. Through the centuries, waves of white immigration from the north have been seen as the rightful occupants of the city, whereas waves of nonwhite immigration from the south (especially from North Africa, but also from sub-Saharan Africa) have been seen as perpetual foreigners.[28]

As the whitening of Seville illustrates, the racialization of a city is likely to be supported by uninterrogated imaginary relations among places and populations and, therefore, by both local and cosmopolitan ignorance. In the neocolonial times of today, it is pressing to initiate processes of self-estrangement that can help us interrogate our imaginary and cognitive-affective attachments to places, so that we can—individually and collectively—start developing epistemically responsible attitudes toward those places that some can call "home" and others cannot.

A coeditor of this volume, **JOSÉ MEDINA** is Professor of Philosophy at Northwestern University. Drawing on American and European critical theorists, he has published primarily in social and political philosophy (including social epistemology), speech act theory, feminist theory, queer theory, and critical philosophy of race. His articles in these areas have appeared in journals such as *Critical Philosophy of Race, Inquiry, Metaphilosophy, Philosophical Studies, Philosophy and Social Criticism*, and *Social Epistemology*. His books include *Speaking from Elsewhere* (SUNY Press, 2006), and *The Epistemology of Resistance* (Oxford University Press, 2012), which received the 2012 North-American Society for Social Philosophy Book Award. He is currently working on issues concerning epistemic injustice and "epistemic activism" in relation to race, gender, and sexuality. His current projects in critical race theory, decolonial theory, and gender and queer theory focus on how social perception and the social imagination contribute to the formation of vulnerabilities to different kinds of violence and oppression. These projects also explore the social movements and kinds of activism (including *epistemic* activism) that can be mobilized to resist racial and sexual violence and oppression in local and global contexts.

Notes

1. Chapter 6, (85).
2. Chapter 9, (150).
3. Chapter 17, (291).
4. What I am calling *cosmopolitan ignorance* is well explained by the distortions and misunderstandings that Stuhr finds in traditional cosmopolitanism. As he puts it in Chapter 17 of this volume, the "cosmopolitan notion that one is, or may be, at home everywhere rests on a misunderstanding of home in the sense in which homes are places.... Places are ways of living, ways of being, worlds of experience, worlds of relations.... Some (but not all) of these places are homes for some folks sometimes, but the would-be cosmopolitan who would be always at home everywhere and every place is an impossibility. To be at home some place (or places, including hypermobility and virtual communities) is to be not at home in—and through—other places" (283). Cosmopolitans forget their own placement, the proper contextualization of their aspiration: "The dream of being a citizen of the world, someone at home in every place, is always dreamed somewhere. It is always a dream of some citizens and some places" (284).

5. Chapter 17, page 292 (my italics).
6. See my *Speaking from Elsewhere: A New Contextualist Perspective on Meaning, Identity, and Discursive Agency* (Albany: SUNY Press, 2006); and my *The Epistemology of Resistance: Gender and Racial Oppression, Epistemic Injustice, and the Social Imagination* (New York: Oxford University Press, 2012).
7. Shannon Sullivan, "White Ignorance and Colonial Oppression: Or, Why I Know So Little about Puerto Rico," in *Race and Epistemologies of Ignorance*, ed. Shannon Sullivan and Nancy Tuana (Albany: SUNY Press, 2007), 154.
8. Ibid.
9. Ibid., 153.
10. Lorraine Code, "The Power of Ignorance," in *Race and Epistemologies of Ignorance*, ed. Shannon Sullivan and Nancy Tuana (Albany: SUNY Press, 2007), 226.
11. A good illustration here is Ladelle McWhorter's *Racism and Sexual Oppression in Anglo-America: A Genealogy* (Bloomington: Indiana University Press, 2009). In this book the author tries to uncover the forgotten and marginalized memories of racial and sexual minorities, reopening spaces of resistance against racism, heterosexism, and their interrelations.
12. Sullivan, "White Ignorance and Colonial Oppression," 155.
13. Charles Mills, *The Racial Contract* (Ithaca, NY: Cornell University Press, 1997).
14. Mills, "White Ignorance," 29.
15. Ibid., 30.
16. As Mills puts it, "the 'testimony' of the black perspective and its distinctive conceptual and theoretical insights will tend to be whited out. Whites will cite other whites in a closed circuit of epistemic authority that reproduces white delusions" (ibid., 34)
17. As Mills points out, "slave narratives often had to have white authenticators, for example, white abolitionists" (ibid., 32).
18. The underlying cognitivism of Mill's epistemology of ignorance has been criticized by some of the contributors to Sullivan and Tuana's 2007 *Race and Epistemologies of Ignorance*. See esp. chapter 3, by Harvey Cormier. What I offer here can be taken as a critique of this cognitivist bias, but also as an extension of Mills's proposals.
19. Moira Gatens, *Imaginary Bodies: Ethics, Power and Corporeality* (New York: Routledge, 1995), 127.
20. As Gatens has argued, following Spinoza, embodied ignorance/knowledge has a strong affective dimension. Our "embodiment" involves an intimate connection with one's context, for one's embodiment is not simply one's individual body, but it also includes "the *total* affective context of that body" (ibid., 131). This has also been emphasized by transactional views of embodied identities such as Sullivan's "White Ignorance and Colonial Oppression."
21. See my article, "Identity Trouble: Disidentification and the *Problem* of Difference," *Philosophy and Social Criticism* 29 (2004): 655–80.
22. Jane Addams, *Democracy and Social Ethics* (Urbana: University of Illinois Press, 2002).
23. J. Tully, *Strange Multiplicity: Constitutionalism in an Age of Diversity* (Cambridge: Cambridge University Press, 1995), 206, 202.
24. To be accurate, at the time—in fact, until the twentieth century—Triana was considered an adjacent village separated from Seville by the river, and not one of its neighborhoods.
25. See, for example, the article on the Negro of Triana published in the cultural pages of the national newspaper *EL PAIS* on August 12, 2000.
26. See Isidoro Moreno, *La Antigua Hermandad de los Negros de Sevilla. Etnicidad, Poder y Sociedad en 600 Años de Historia* (Seville: Universidad de Sevilla Press, 1997).
27. I am thinking, in particular, of the Gypsy populations of Triana and other neighborhoods, who have been exploited to give color and cultural depth to Seville, but who have been

relegated to marginal spaces within the city, reaffirming the idea that the city—especially the core of the city, downtown Seville—does not belong to them, but to the white middle and upper classes.

28. For a lucid discussion of the stigma of being a perpetual foreigner, see Edwina Barvosa, *Wealth of Selves: Multiple Identities, Mestiza Consciousness, and the Subject of Politics* (College Station: Texas A&M University Press, 2008); David Kim and Ronald Sundstrom, "Xenophobia and Racism," *Critical Philosophy of Race* 2, no. 1 (2014): 20–45.

8 America and Cosmopolitan Responsibility
Some Thoughts on an Itinerant Duty

Jeff Edmonds

> Caminante, no hay camino,
> Se hace camino al andar.
> —Antonio Machado

> Hope's just a word
> that maybe you said
> or maybe you heard
> on some windy corner
> 'round a wide-angled curve.
> —Bob Dylan

THE QUESTION of the nature of cosmopolitanism and its relationship to place is not just a question of how these logical categories might be properly determined and defined. While it would be perhaps convenient for philosophers to share a definition of cosmopolitanism and come to agreement on its limits and possibilities, philosophical convenience or agreement is hardly the reason the question of cosmopolitanism is worth talking about.

The conversations on cosmopolitanism rise out of the practical problems of a world that is increasingly mobile, changing, and intimate. Cosmopolitanism is a lived condition—the name of a problem that perhaps cannot be intellectually defined, but which is lived constantly. The food we eat, the clothes we wear, the news we hear, the music we listen to remind us constantly of the fact that our lives overflow the boundaries of locality and that we are therefore confronted with cosmopolitan questions as a matter of the ethics of daily life. To be a moral agent today is to make decisions that have effects that operate at the level of locality and echo far beyond locality. To take up the question of cosmopolitanism is to make this latent fact of twenty-first-century life into a subject of reflection in order that we might more clearly understand and respond to the ever-pressing moral duties that the task of living better together imposes.

While the ethics of cosmopolitanism are a problem for us today, the question of the duties and responsibilities of cosmopolitanism is hardly new. The cosmopolitan tension between the longing for locality and the moments of experience that threaten or unsettle a sense of locality is a problem that structures the very idea of America from the outset. America is a continent of both indigenous peoples and immigrants. It is both deeply settled and deeply unsettled. America is a concept that still today denotes both the static and hegemonic notion of empire and the dynamic and democratic notion of possibility. To be an American philosopher and to take up the question of cosmopolitanism is to attempt to provide some help in understanding how to live through this tension—at least through some of its American manifestations—and how to turn its energy toward good ends.

An example that demonstrates both the difficulties and possibilities of cosmopolitanism is the ongoing difficulties around migrant populations in the Americas in general and in the United States specifically. A *New York Times* article by Patricia Lee Brown raised the problem of the education of the children of itinerant families.[1] The article described a system of educational practices that was out of sync with almost every aspect of the way of life of migratory farmworkers. Although there is a $394 million migrant education program administered by the federal government, the institutions put into place through that money are unable to take into account the way of life of the migrant community that it serves. While family units are mobile, schools are stationary and place based. Though the children of farmworkers are bilingual, teachers are monolingual. Money goes to provide a system of schooling that does not meet the population's needs, and meanwhile 97 percent of migrant families live at or below the poverty line.

The disjunction between the needs of the community and the form of schooling causes several problems. These schools struggle with students who enter school in the middle of the semester, leaving and transferring to a different school a few months later. Those who choose to remain in one place to take advantage of the stability of the school must live with distant relatives and friends as their mothers and fathers leave to follow the movement of the harvest. The program tries to make up for the lack of stability of the community through ideas like tutoring and summer school. These attempts aim to make the transitions between schools easier for the students, but of course these programs are merely stopgap measures. They are not programs designed for a fundamentally itinerant life; they were invented to help students who pass through temporary mobility make a transition to a new and stable place.

Just as traditional institutions of school are unable to meet their educational responsibilities, traditional institutions of law are unable to guarantee the rights of citizenship. Despite the fact that the children of immigrants are technically legal U.S. citizens, parents choose not to take advantage of these rights for fear that by entering the names of their children into the bureaucratic rolls, their status as illegal migrants will be discovered and they would face the consequences. Families who have migrated across borders end up with a variety of citizenship statuses, including no national citizenship at all.

When Steve King, Republican representative from Iowa and vice chairman of the House immigration subcommittee, introduced a bill that would repeal "birthright citizenship," arguing that "lawbreakers shouldn't be rewarded," he showed little concern for education within these communities and offered no alternative way of considering the proper basis of citizenship.[2] However, there is one moment of his thought that is correct: in an increasingly mobile world, linking political civil rights and responsibilities to a territorial place or birthright seems increasingly arbitrary and unresponsive to the actual conditions of contemporary life.

I begin by outlining this scenario because I believe it is representative of the general problem that cosmopolitanism attempts to address. The problem, in its most general form, is the adjustment of habitual forms of life to changing conditions. Though cosmopolitanism has been defined in many ways in these chapters, Cynthia Gayman's (Chapter 14) phrasing of cosmopolitanism as a moral demand conveys most directly the urgency of the problem that cosmopolitanism presents. Cosmopolitanism simply means that "we have obligations to others beyond the boundaries of our local communities, cultures, and nations."[3] This moral claim is a result of coming to terms with the "necessity of life" that Dewey describes so eloquently as the general form of education.[4] The fact of life as growth naturally demands that we take on the responsibility of moving beyond ourselves. Cosmopolitanism, as Gayman reminds us, is the general attitude of taking conscious and reflective responsibility for this natural demand of life—that it critically reconstruct its habits.

American philosophies have been uniquely attuned to this natural demand. When they have taken up issues of ethics, politics, metaphysics, and epistemology, they have done so with an eye toward how old habits of thinking about these themes might be reconstructed in light of the new conditions found in the Americas. American philosophers in the nineteenth and twentieth centuries were particularly critical of a philosophical tradition that would speak from nowhere and to and for everyone, preferring instead to begin with the image of the organism in an environment as the starting point of philosophy.[5] The American project favored instead the critical examination of the methods, ideas, and effects of philosophy in light of the problems and challenges posed by the challenges of migrating to a new place.

In this sense, the great strength of American philosophy was its provincialism, and it somewhat paradoxically gained its critical teeth and philosophical imagination—the responses to the cosmopolitan demand of going beyond one's place—through this provinciality. Here is Emerson, urging us to stop traveling so much and to create a way of thinking more in tune with our own place: "if the American artist will study with hope and love the precise thing to be done by him, considering the climate, the soil, the length of the day, the wants of the people, the habit and form of the government, he will create a house in which all these will find themselves fitted, and taste and sentiment will be satisfied also."[6]

As José Medina reminds us in Chapter 7, this task of getting to know one's place is endlessly vexed, involving both synchronic and diachronic relations that can never be fully known or mastered and thus demand a sort of ongoing responsibility to one's place.[7] Medina is right to point out that just because we have arrived to or live in a certain place—even call it home—we are not necessarily any less ignorant about it. Indeed, this is precisely the point that Emerson urged on us in his own writing, that the American problem was one of constantly misunderstanding one's own home and one's own self because of the influence of old habits. If American philosophy was provincial, it was also cosmopolitan precisely because it felt unsettled in this new place, even as it considered it to be a home. Perhaps it is precisely this sense of "not knowing one's place" that led to the preoccupation with environing conditions that is a hallmark of American thought.

These more general philosophical points are highlighted and deepened by our contemporary situation. The variety of new modes of technology, new business relations, new forms of government, new ecological relations, the migration of peoples, and shifting modes of war and imperialism have muddied the borders of America such that it is no longer clear that the concept of "America" refers to anything resembling a territory or place. America seems less and less to be *located*, more and more to be a wandering concept: a place without a home.

If these facts are true, then American philosophies can no longer rely on a notion of a radically different place as a tool for philosophical reconstruction. Instead, to maintain their critical vision, American philosophies have to liberate themselves from a narrow conception of the place of America through self-criticism. We must be attuned to the way in which habits of language continue to link America with the geographic borders of the United States. But beyond that, we have to be aware of how our very own notions of place, associated concepts like "local," "global," or "cosmopolitan," and political institutions and laws that are built and administered through these concepts are funded by experiences of particular places and territories. As Megan Craig reminds us in Chapter 8 of this volume, "We are destined to lose our places, even as we are condemned to stake them. Place cedes to place, at a pace one can never predict or imagine."⁸ Yet, despite all the difficulties and responsibilities and impossibilities that place poses to us, as itinerant thinkers living within a fractured place, we must predict, imagine, and judge. Even if it is our destiny to lose it, we have to construct and reconstruct a home for our thought.

In what follows, I want to look at two thinkers—Walter Mignolo and Gloria Anzaldúa—who undertake this work of reconstructing America. Both of these thinkers ground their thought in the Americas, and each might also be placed as philosophers in the sense that they each take up a project of criticism. Neither, however, would be wholly at home with the labels "American" or "philosopher," as their projects are uniquely attuned to the deeply problematic aspects of American life and indeed of philosophy itself. In this way, Mignolo and Anzaldúa seem representative of the sort of cosmopolitanism that I have been articulating. Theirs are attempts to find new metaphors for understanding what it means to philosophize from a locality and to fund the understanding of America from a different site of experience.⁹ Mignolo wants to look at the place of America from the standpoint of the intersection of the modern dream of European salvation with the colonial project of imperialism. His America is not the neatly composed set of nation states. It operates at the borders of those territories, at the sites where the very designation of a place as American is contested. Anzaldúa's work from the US-Mexico border also attempts to begin an analysis of American life from the people who live within contested cultural spaces. Her mestiza consciousness denotes a place of fundamental ambiguity, a home that is simultaneously a frontier, a battle, and a site of ongoing transformation. Each of these places departs from a geopolitical mapping of empty space that underlies the dominant conception of America and provides new possibilities for reconstructing the American project of a critical provincialism in light of the ongoing moral challenge of cosmopolitanism.

Mignolo: Place as Dialectic of Justice

The key distinction in Mignolo's *The Idea of Latin America* is the difference between invention and discovery. The book methodically and comprehensively reconstructs the concept of America away from the idea of a static place that had been discovered and toward the notion of America as an invented concept. If we are understanding cosmopolitanism as the moral responsibility to travel beyond location and to critically rupture and renew spaces, then Mignolo's work is squarely cosmopolitan.

Mignolo shows us how the notion of America as a discovered country posits it as a primal space of total renewal; it idealizes it from the point of view of European settlers and from the standpoint of modernity. This standpoint tends to take what Mignolo calls "egology" and "theology" as the starting points for analysis, and it paints the world—and particularly America—as a blank slate for the renewal of the self, on the one hand, and a new religion, on the other. Mignolo sees the concept of America as "a key turning point in world history," marking the beginning of modernity as the project of European salvation.[10] From the standpoint of imperial Europe, the "discovery" of America as a place promised a new world in which the modern project of the renewal of the self and the renewal of religion could be practiced.[11] At the heart of his critique of the idea of discovery is the insight that there is no such thing as a pure and untrammeled place that might be discovered. Instead, we are always moving—meandering, to use Colapietro's word—from place to place.[12]

Mignolo prefers to see America as invented rather than discovered. This way of attending to America allows him to interrogate the idea of America from the perspective of the needs, desires, and stakes involved in its invention. He is able to unlink the idea of America from an imagined empty New World, a promised land for social renewal, and look at it as an invented idea that underwrites certain practices. Within the modern logic of salvation and not necessarily opposed to it, Mignolo finds a colonial logic. He traces a two-sided concept. On the one hand, the invention of the concept of America historically worked to spur European culture to and through a modern cosmopolitan project of renewal and self-overcoming through the movement to a new place. But on the other hand, sometimes through the very same processes, the concept of America worked according to what Mignolo calls "an embedded logic that enforces control, domination, and exploitation disguised in the language of salvation, progress, modernization, and being good for everyone."[13] Exactly how the concept of America works—the truth-effects of this invented idea of America in a pragmatic sense—depends in large part on the situation in which it is deployed, the historical line that is invoked when it is deployed, and the audience toward whom the term is directed.

Mignolo uncovers the pragmatic logic of coloniality through what he calls "a shift in the geography of reason."[14] The fundamental thesis of Mignolo's analysis is that to unlock the colonial picture of America, it is essential to shift analysis from a fascination with the self and with theology, both of which disguise their geopolitical underpinnings to what he calls a "de-centered" analysis that is "geopolitically rooted in the histories of the borders, and not in territorial histories created by European and US expansionism."[15] To expose the antidemocratic effects of America, in other words, Mignolo argues that it is essential to look at the way in which America denotes not only a place or a region of the world but an activity that works at borders. So long as the postmodern project of pluralism is thought as something that happens *within* a contained space, "as a diversity of representations within a Euro-centric frame of reference," analysis only works to repeat the idea of a discovered America.[16] In his attention to marginalized communities of resistance to American progress and colonialism, the shift in the geography of reason, Mignolo encourages us to move away from the idea of America as a territory or region and toward the idea of America as a sort of working edge. Mignolo teaches us to see America not as a preexisting place or locality, but as a historical and effective concept that, as Foucault described, "is not made for understanding; it is made for cutting."[17] Pluralism, from the perspective of coloniality, does not unfold within a space or a place, but at the edges of a territory as it is being established.

It is important to note that for Mignolo the colonial narrative of America is written both "with and against" the narrative of modernity. Although at certain moments in his text, he seems to indicate that the narrative of European salvation through the colonization of America was a mere disguise for acts of violence and oppression, Mignolo does not advocate abandonment of the dream of modernity. Indeed, he wants to point out the way in which modernity disguises its brutality under the idea of America and simultaneously uses actual American experiences to critically renew the possibility of pluralism, democracy, and freedom. Mignolo's criticism of representations of America is intended to deepen Enlightenment commitments to justice, and at one point he even quotes Kant's "What Is Enlightenment," using it as a critical tool.[18] He is unbending on one point, however. For Mignolo the experience of the colonial wound—not the transcendental ideal of enlightenment—is the founding moment of a political analysis that advocates for the critical decolonization of the Americas and a truly pluralistic democracy. Mignolo puts this critical starting point in no uncertain terms:

> *Decolonization of knowledge and of being* (and more generally, of politics and the economy) cannot be thought out and implemented other than from the perspective of the *damnés* (and not from those of the World Bank or from an updated Marxism or a refreshed Christianity); that is, from the perspective, provided by years of modern/colonial injustices, inequalities, exploitation, humiliation, and the pains of the colonial wound, of an-other world where creative care for human beings and the celebration of life will take precedence over individual success and meritocracy, and the accumulation of money and of meaning (e.g., personal CVs, the personal satisfaction of celebrity, and all other ways in which alienation is being reproduced and encouraged).[19]

Mignolo's challenge to American philosophy, then, is straightforward. It is a question of how to think of its ongoing reconstruction in a way that doesn't alienate itself from the conditions of its reconstruction. If we take the cosmopolitan demand seriously, we have to be attentive to the ways in which American thinkers like Emerson, James, and Dewey localize American philosophy within a settled place. Their work needs to be supplemented by the work of other Americans like Anzaldúa, Mignolo, Enrique Dussel, and Eduardo Galeano. Of course, this is not simply an issue of an intellectual canon, nor is it a call to abandon the idea of American philosophy. Cosmopolitanism does not ask us to leave behind the idea of place; it demands that we keep moving from place to place, constructing a living and ambulatory understanding in response to living change. By returning to the classical American pragmatists through the work of other American philosophers and the problems they encounter, these texts take on new resonances, meanings, and possibilities.

It is, however, precisely at this highest moment of critique of the notion of American philosophy that a pragmatist American philosopher ought to pause and consider whether Mignolo's criticism remains pragmatic. Why, exactly, should we be committed to a nonalienated project of American reconstruction? Even if it were possible to take up the concept of America absolutely critically with respect to its colonial consequences, in full awareness of the violence, oppression, and injustices that this concept has produced, should we accept this as the critical ideal? It seems to me that attending to the very experiences of the *damnés* would call on us to pragmatically temper our critical goals. What we see when we go to experience is: What? That experience is simply a mess and that intellectual clarity of the sort that Mignolo idealizes is hard to find.

When we consider the complexity of the environing conditions of colonialism—that is, when we actually go to the real place of colonialism, an uncomfortable question emerges. Is the purity of Mignolo's critical ideal simply the repetition of the project of Enlightenment modernity instead of its actual reconstruction? At the level of ordinary experience, it is almost impossible to distinguish the experience of the colonial wound from the American promise of salvation. Indeed, it is when the two are fundamentally opposed that they lose their political efficacy—the wound gets amplified into something like a trauma that cannot be healed, and the promise of salvation becomes hollow and otherworldly. When Mignolo's critical ideal of colonial justice comes up against the messy tangle of actual life, our pragmatic commitments demand that we cleave close to life, choosing to butcher the ideal and remain clear eyed about the fact that history cannot be so cleanly separated into oppressors and oppressed, colonizers and colonized.

So, while Mignolo does see modernity and coloniality as two sides of the same coin, I am afraid that this coin is problematic on both sides. When Mignolo goes to the site of colonial experience, he finds, always, dominating effects of modernity. And when Mignolo criticizes the way in which modernity hides its colonial projects, modernity is always treated as a mask that hides the true reality of oppression. When Mignolo tells the history of the development of Latin America, it is the dialectical relation that tends to dominate, relentlessly seeking oppositions and drawing conclusions such as this: "Today the 'Americas' are divided. One is the temple of neo-liberalism while the other provides the land, natural resources, and cheap labor, as well as emerging, contesting states and myriads of social movements."[20] While the coloniality-modernity dialectic is powerful and jarring, what makes it jarring is its ideological character. It jars us because of the way in which it sums up a vast plurality of experiences, many of which are ambiguous in nature, in terms of a simple opposition between oppression and salvation. Mignolo takes us to the experience of the oppressed, but the upshot of that experience is always to confirm a clear dichotomy between the oppressors and the oppressed: Is this a place at all?

Anzaldúa: Place as Ambiguous Path

Mignolo's critique, like those of his European predecessors, Kant, Marx, and Hegel, leads with the nonplaces of logic and modernity in order to critically reconstruct American narratives of colonialism. For all its insights into the Latin American experience, Mignolo's thought is also firmly and deeply rooted in a critical tradition that came out of European experiences. For this very reason, Mignolo's thought works well to turn traditional critical theory toward Latin American issues, but its Germanic logic also ensures that it operates according to laws and limits that find little connection with life in Latin America. Mignolo's dialectic moves as predictably as Kant's clock in Königsberg, but its dualistic rhythms and strict conceptual categories are perhaps less useful for analysis of the polychronic, multinational, mestiza, colonial, indigenous paths of Latin American experience.

Mignolo's approach is, in short, limited and determined by its locality. If we are following Gayman in articulating cosmopolitanism as the moral duty to critically rupture locality and place by traveling to new places, then we ought to look to how the European materialist dialectical logic might be ruptured or challenged by an analysis that follows a more Latino/a logic. Anzaldúa's analysis of the political scene at the US-Mexico border refuses a dialectical treatment. She advocates what she terms the *"El camino de la mestiza*/the Mestiza Way," choosing to articulate her political methodology in terms of a path to be traveled, rather than in terms of an ideology to be exposed, overcome, or relieved from alienation.[21] In fact, Anzaldúa's conception of mestiza consciousness works outside or beyond the concept of alienation by attempting to reconfigure oppressive circumstances as possibilities. In her polymorphous logic, which follows a polymorphous experience, oppression does not necessarily invoke salvation or alienation. It is, instead, a way of life among other ways—a way that makes its way by burrowing down into the interstices of place, rather than seeking to rise out or rewrite experience through the logical clash of categories.

In articulating the Mestiza Way, she writes: "Her first step is to take inventory. . . . Just what did she inherit from her ancestors? This weight on her back—which is the baggage from the Indian mother, the Spanish father, which the baggage from the Anglo?"[22] Anzaldúa depicts the critical problem of dealing with historical inheritance as one of sorting through the contents of the baggage we carry with us, discriminating the useful from that which simply weighs us down—looking for what will work to allow us to keep moving, keep living.

Thus, the mestiza consciousness is both outraged by oppression and accepting of its circumstances. It stoically affirms its place on the border while simultaneously communicating its outrage with the violations that border perpetrates. Anzaldúa continues, "*Pero es difícil* differentiating between *lo heredado, lo adquirido, lo impuesto*. She puts history through a sieve, winnows out the lies, looks at the forces that we as a race, as women, have been a part of."[23] Unlike Mignolo, who draws clear lines, Anzaldúa's critical mestiza consciousness has trouble differentiating between what's been inherited, acquired, or imposed. This is part of the work of consciousness, but this work is not cashed out always in terms of a fight for justice (though it is sometimes, particularly in its indictment of white racism.) Her path of analysis is not one of seeing the truth of the situation, unmasking the oppressive America beneath the lies of the American dream. It is, instead, figured through the metaphor of the sieve: the nuggets worth keeping may have been acquired in each of the three ways, through choice, through inheritance, or through imposition—the difficulty is in taking something forward. Hers is not a project of truth, but a project of walking a *camino*, finding a way.

Indeed, we see Anzaldúa in good pragmatic fashion accepting *both* the European project of modernity *and* the *nahual* process of transformation. Anzaldúa continues: "She becomes a *nahual*, able to transform herself into a tree, a coyote, another person. She learns to transform the small 'I' into the total Self. *Se hace moldeadora de su alma. Según la concepción que tiene de sí mismo, así será.*"[24] The project of America is building a relationship with a particular place and the beings that populate it. It is the *nahual* path of transforming one's self. But it is also the Emersonian/Cartesian project of egology and theology, of finding the universal through the self. Anzaldúa embraces the ambiguity of her cultural inheritance in the last lines that she writes. I translate them here: "One becomes a crafter of one's own soul. One becomes what one has conceived one's self to be." In the recognition that ethics is a task of creation, not just critique, one finds the signal of a mature politics grounded in lived realities. She is attuned to the ambiguity of her inheritance, but committed to the articulation of a singular voice.

In Anzaldúa's writing we see a different sort of cosmopolitanism. She breaks open the notion of America from within, rupturing and rebuilding locality from a place. It is in this sense that her writing is cosmopolitan—not in the Kantian sense of rising out of a place toward a universal, but in using the very notion of place to uproot settled conceptions of place. The logic of her critique is not dialectical, but confrontational. She speaks as a contextualized subject out of and through an experience. This is very different from the way in which philosophy tends to cosmopolitanize from without. Her criticism from the borderlands does not find it lacking with respect to a universal conception of justice. On the contrary, she asserts through the fullness and vibrancy of her place-based subjectivity the very hollowness of cosmopolitanism as universalism. Like Whitman a century earlier, she sounds a barbaric yawp that rattles the old customs through affirmation of the particularity of the self. This is a fundamentally American move, and Anzaldúa's poetic genius might be termed Emersonian: "So when the soul of the poet has come to ripeness of thought, she detaches and sends away from it its poems or songs,—a fearless, sleepless, deathless progeny, which is not exposed to the accidents of the weary kingdom of time; a fearless vivacious offspring, clad with wings (such as the virtue of the soul out of which they came), which carry them fast and far and infix them irrecoverably into the hearts of men."[25] Whatever universality Anzaldúa's cosmopolitanism attains, it does so through the Emersonian "ripeness" of its subjectivity; its fullness of poetic voice is the mark of its universality. If her discourse ruptures locality, it is only by bringing the fullness and ripeness of that locality forward in a way that "infixes" that locality as a place in the hearts of men.

Anzaldúa's critical strategy, then, is not suspicious. She does not look to uncover a violent America hidden beneath a progressive America. Her strategy is to affirm the fractured reality in which she lives, affirm a pluralistic self that is informed by multiple cultures and that cannot be fully reconciled. Anzaldúa's approach to cosmopolitanism is therefore more poetic than dialectical, more affirmative than critical; Borderlands/*La Frontera* is a text about learning to live within a fractured cultural environment without coming to hate one's self. The book does not end in a call to justice or an end to domination, but in an image of *renacimiento*, rebirth, an agricultural image that embraces her locality and celebrates the place where she lives. The critical work of the book is in expanding an erased space—the two-dimensional national border between the United States and Mexico—and showing this borderlands to be an actual place, one worth living in and celebrating, for all of its flaws. The *renacimiento*, the hopefulness that she offers, is not one of unalienated life free from oppressive circumstances and conflict, but the smaller project of affirming as valuable the specific conflicts that Chicanos face, seeing their struggle as valuable in its own right.

In Anzaldúa's depiction of the borderlands, we find a different way of responding to the cosmopolitan demand. It is akin to Jennifer Hansen's articulation of cosmopolitan hope: "redrawing the boundaries of the familiar in order to see what is better."[26] Anzaldúa writes from a threatened locality, not in terms of a project of expansion but from the standpoint of a form of life worth preserving and undertaking. She responds to the obligation of cosmopolitanism by *offering* those of us who live outside of that space a justification for it. She reaches across the borders of her locality with a gift, inviting us into the shape of the soul that occupies it. Anzaldúa, like Mignolo, privileges the border space as a site of cultural renewal, but different from Mignolo, she takes up the responsibility of cosmopolitanism affirmatively, writing from within that space and to articulate the precise values of that space, affirming its particular struggles and laying out a provisional path forward.[27]

Toward a Nomadic Conception of America

I opened this chapter with a particular problem, the problem of educating an itinerant community. I suggested that this problem was not just a matter of allocating resources but could be traced to a habit of thinking about education and law as operating within a particular sort of space. Both the school and legal institutions imagine a sort of preestablished space within which they do their work. Migrant communities threaten the integrity of that space and indeed of law itself, which is why they earn the label of "alien." Their act indeed breaks the law in the sense that it exposes the sense in which law is not universal but depends on a geopolitical space for its application. So, the migrant is treated not as a citizen but is literally alienated. Hers is another world entirely, a nonplace in which the bureaucratic functions of government get no traction.

The school, too, imagines a community in which it works. Around the school we imagine family structures with some degree of stability. The school depends on a home that has a place for the homework it assigns. Further, the school assumes a type of regularity of life: the idea of a curriculum that a student could follow, year after year, accumulating knowledge from the bottom up, so to speak, imagines a stable student that would attend more or less the same type of school for a long period of time. The contemporary school functions only in certain environments, and the idea of an itinerant population does not fit the institution that has been built.

Our ideas of law and of education—ideas fundamental to democracy—are funded by our own experiences of place, and the extent to which we can imagine new institutions depends on the possibility of seeing places in different ways. When Dewey took up the question of the relationship between school and society, he was deeply attuned to the fact that the effectiveness of a school relies on the social environment in which it sits. A school, as an institution, must respond to a place. The problem of educating itinerant communities is a subspecies of a more general problem. Dewey puts it like this: "A society is a number of people held together because they are working along common lines, in a common spirit, and in reference to common aims. The common needs and aims demand a growing interchange of thought and a growing unity of sympathy. The radical reason that the present school cannot organize itself as a natural social unit is just because this element of common and productive activity is absent."[28] A social place is a set of working problems and goals. It denotes movements within experience that are active and organizing, and the organization of any educational institution rises naturally out of the social needs of that community. The problem of educating itinerant workers cannot be fully addressed by a federal migrant education program—at least insofar as that education program conceives itself as concerned with curricula, teachers, and schooling institutions that are already in existence. The problem is a matter of American cultural habits and whether they are still open to the sort of cosmopolitan reconstruction toward which Emerson and Dewey pointed more than a century ago and toward which Mignolo and Anzaldúa point in more recent contexts. The larger problem is how to invite these people, these migrant farmers, into the projects and possibilities of society—and how to reimagine our own social goals, projects, and possibilities in ways that allow for their critical contribution. In other words, the problem of schooling is only reflective of a much larger socio/educational problem, the problem of a place that is hostile to their life, and it will not be addressed until that larger problem is addressed.

I have tried to show that one obstacle to addressing this larger problem is a problematic conception of the place of America, which shuts down cosmopolitan responsibility. Here is where the philosophical conversation on cosmopolitanism determines its effectiveness. Can philosophy in general or American pragmatism specifically continue to crack open conceptions of America that foreclose cosmopolitan responsibility? In order to do so, it is likely that American pragmatism or American philosophy as such has much to learn from its Latin American critics.

The question of place, of constructing a critical provincial voice, does not lie primarily in opposing the local to the global. A place is not a static spot on a map, but a territory of becoming. What makes a place distinctive are the problems, struggles, and transformations of the people who live in that place. The critical struggle of determining the problems and struggles that define the place of America has both a negative and positive side. From the negative side, Mignolo teaches us to track the ways in which we assume that other social forms identify with our projects. America is a place for European social renewal, but it is also a place where people have struggled against that dream for the preservation of their own ways of life. By disarticulating the concept of America from the "discovery" of the whole of the Western Hemisphere and looking at it as an invented concept, Mignolo teaches us how to track the differentiated effects of that invention and uncover the ways in which America has masked a colonial history. The value of the idea of America in the halls of Washington looks very different from the value of the idea from the perspective of the soy farmers in Paraguay. The work of American philosophy demands bringing those differences to light as part of the ongoing reconstruction of America as a society yet to be formed.

From the positive side, Anzaldúa teaches a sort of solastalgic phenomenology of the lost Americas.[29] If one problem of the idea of America is that it is too commonly thought in terms of a US project of European renewal, we need philosophers who are able to describe different projects for America and articulate both their debt to and departure from the organizing myths of American life. Anzaldúa takes a place that is commonly depicted as oppressed, chaotic, dangerous, and wild, and she delicately and defiantly paints a portrait of a society with its own *camino*, one opposed in some ways to a European or white racist project, but one that does not take its moment of departure from that opposition. It instead affirms its own life. Through her phenomenology of Chicano/a life, Anzaldúa shows its value and invites us to consider how our projects might not just save the folks in the borderlands but learn from them.

In "Neither Here nor There: Mexican Immigrant Workers and the Search for Home," the ethnologist Steve Striffler writes:

> Instead of assuming a strong coherence between a particular place and a particular set of shared values, the notion of "community" that develops [in itinerant communities] is grounded in a common experience of displacement and fractured reality. Put another way, what ultimately ties these immigrant workers together may not be that they are from Santo Domingo in the physical sense of having been born there; rather, what ties them together are common experiences and understandings that do not allow immigrants to be either here or there; that deny them the possibility of being there, of remaining in their Mexican pueblos, while at the same time making it very difficult to be here, to work, go to school, to belong in any meaningful sense of the word in US communities where they are marginalized by ethnicity, nationality, and language.[30]

The life of itinerant peoples in the Americas is not bound together by physical space, but by common experiences. In this case, the experience is one of a fractured reality, the lack of a social home. This is the experience that characterizes the place of itinerant population in America. In order to share the common and productive activity that Dewey notes as a precondition of education, the centers of America might also embrace the fractures that have always been at the basis of the American experiment. We find them in classical American philosophy from the outset, just as the same fractures populate ordinary life across race and class in America. Cosmopolitanism is a problem for all of us—the challenge is whether it rises to the level of a moral problem, which is to say a problem that forces difficult encounters, intelligent readjustment of practice, brave and patient consideration, democratic deliberation—the noble things that America has sometimes been able to achieve.

Cosmopolitanism and the itinerant life is not a narrow experience; in a world of rapid change, war, economic instability, hyperbolic media, and wide-ranging social interaction, we are all, to some degree, itinerants. The idea of America wanders on. This cosmopolitan nomadism is not new, but it must be renewed in the light of new conditions and the decay of old conditions. Our project as American philosophers is to try to trace its path and, if not direct it, travel alongside and offer some help, some consolation, some goodwill, and indeed reminders of the moral duties that cosmopolitanism imposes. Perhaps if we take this nomadic, fractured, and displaced experience as the fundamental ground of twenty-first-century space, we might stumble across a notion of place that would begin to allow us to more ethically and intelligently treat the path of America, both centrally and at its margins.[31]

JEFF EDMONDS is Academic Dean and Dean of the Freshman and Senior Classes at the University School of Nashville, where his teaching includes both philosophy and physics. In addition to philosophical work in philosophy of education, ethics, and political philosophy, Edmonds is the author of *The Logic of Long Distance: Connecting Running and Philosophy* (www.logicoflongdistance.com).

Notes

1. Patricia Leigh Brown, "Itinerant Life Weighs on Farmworkers' Children," *New York Times*, March 12, 2011, www.nytimes.com/2011/03/13/us/13salinas.html.
2. Ibid.
3. Chapter 14, 242.
4. John Dewey, *Democracy and Education* (New York: Free Press, 1916), 1.
5. See, as one of innumerable examples, John Dewey's criticism of old modes of philosophizing and description of experience in "The Need for a Recovery of Philosophy." "Any account of experience must now fit into the consideration that experiencing means living, and that living goes on because of an environing medium, not in a vacuum"; in *The Middle Works of John Dewey (1916–1917): Journal Articles, Essays, and Miscellany Published in the 1916–1917 Period*, ed. Jo Ann Boydston (Carbondale: Southern Illinois University Press), 10:7.
6. Ralph Waldo Emerson, *Self-Reliance and Other Essays* (New York: Dover, 1993), 35.
7. See Chapter 7 of this volume.
8. Chapter 9, 153.
9. Here, Vincent Colapietro's description of "living understanding" as a "mobile affair" seems particularly apt. See Chapter 6 of this volume.
10. W. Mignolo, *The Idea of Latin America* (London: Blackwell, 2005), 8–9, 65.
11. American philosophers from Emerson to Dewey have operated according to this mythology. One need only draw a path from Emerson's "Self-Reliance" to Dewey's *A Common Faith* in order to see the way in which American philosophies have taken up the modern project of egology and theology under the conditions of this new place.
12. See Chapter 6 of this volume.
13. Mignolo, *Idea of Latin America*, 6.

14. Ibid.
15. Ibid., 8–9.
16. Ibid.
17. Michel Foucault, "Nietzsche, Genealogy, History," in *The Foucault Reader*, ed. Paul Rabinow (New York: Pantheon, 1984), 88.
18. Ibid., 55–56.
19. Ibid., 156
20. Ibid., 50.
21. Gloria Anzaldúa, *Borderlands/La Frontera*, 2nd ed. (San Francisco: Aunt Lute Press, 1999), 104.
22. Ibid.
23. Ibid.
24. Ibid.
25. Ralph Waldo Emerson, "The Poet," in *Selected Writings of Ralph Waldo Emerson*, ed. William Gilman (New York: Penguin 1965), 333–34.
26. See Chapter 13, page 222 of this volume.
27. In this sense, Anzaldúa's work resonates quite profoundly with the work that Nancy Tuana has done on climate change and place. See particularly Tuana's analysis of solastalgia in Chapter 11 of this volume.
28. John Dewey, *The School and Society*, in *The Middle Works of John Dewey (1899–1901): Journal Articles, Books Reviews, and Miscellany Published in the 1899–1901 Period, and the School and Society, and the Educational Situation*, ed. Jo Ann Boydston (Carbondale: Southern Illinois University Press, 1976), 10.
29. See Chapter 11 of this volume.
30. Steve Striffler, "Neither Here nor There: Mexican Immigrant Workers and the Search for Home," *American Ethnologist* 34, no. 4 (2008): 685.
31. Gilles Deleuze's "Treatise on Nomadology—the War Machine," from *A Thousand Plateaus: Capitalism and Schizophrenia* (Minneapolis: University of Minnesota, 1987), offers some promise for further conception articulation of this sort of "nomadology" and its promise for a different conception of politics.

9 Loss of Place

Megan Craig

Each of us has a place we presently occupy, a place from whence we came, and an ambiguous place toward which we are heading. Even if the present place is makeshift or temporary, if one is a refugee or homeless, being in the world entails occupying, however minimally, some shred of ground. Heidegger underscored this fact of existence by the term *Dasein*: "being-there." One is always emplaced one way or another in the wider world. Levinas responded to Heidegger by noting that wherever one finds oneself, the "there" of "being-there" entails the usurpation of someone else's place.[1] Quoting Pascal at the beginning of *Otherwise Than Being or Beyond Essence*, Levinas wrote, "That is my place in the sun. That is how the usurpation of the whole world began."[2] There is no clearing for Being in Levinas's work. Instead, there is only the contested and crowded space of human beings encountering each other and competing claims to entitlement. This chapter follows in the spirit of Levinas's thought insofar as it focuses on the inevitability of losing one's place and the ethical imperative to acknowledge the precariousness and potential injustice of every claim to a place. Many endangered places on earth urgently require stewardship and protection. But the challenges posed by a shrinking and warming planet also call for practice in the arts of ceding one's place, losing, getting lost, and letting go.

I will not say more about Levinas here. Instead, I venture a psycho-phenomenology revolving around three distinctive places: the stairwell of an urban skyscraper, a farm, and a village in northern Alaska. I have chosen these places because of their differences but also because, individually and collectively, they demonstrate something about the essential fluidity of place. In *The Principles of Psychology*, William James coined the phrase "stream of thought" to describe the moving, eventful experience of thinking and the interpenetrating nature of ideas.[3] Places are similarly fringed and interconnected. This makes the containment or ownership of any place problematic, if not impossible. The wall is never high or wide enough. The fence needs perpetual mending. Places expand and contract in cycles of transmutation, shifting beneath one's feet. The geological/physical fact of the moving quality of place (its elemental and material volatility, its susceptibility to erosion) stands in tension with an impulse of sedentary creatures, who long to put down roots, settle, and stake out their own ground. In general, such creatures (human beings foremost among them) are far more adept at moving in than at moving out or moving on.

In a late essay entitled "On a Certain Blindness in Human Beings," James wonders whether a person can cultivate an ability to unsettle herself and to see beyond the centrality of her own place or the borders of her own life. One of the ways he thinks vision is expanded is by traveling, which upends habitual practices of attention. Reading is another form of travel, and for that reason, I have included descriptions of actual places in this text to help facilitate the sense of being transported elsewhere (out of the text, out of philosophy). The chapter proceeds in three sections framed by cinematic snapshots. The first deals with the entanglement and precarious balance of places and lives brought into focus under extreme conditions of loss or displacement with help from Emerson's essay "Experience." The second looks at Bachelard's analyses of the place called "home" in light of the emotional attachments and psycho-physical implications of one's earliest shelters. The final section turns to Deleuze and Guattari's *A Thousand Plateaus* to consider the fluidity of place from a global perspective informed by the threats of climate change and the accelerating melting of vast parts of the earth. In the snapshots between these sections, I explore variable experiences of loss relative to particular places (urban, rural, remote) and their distinctive speeds of dissolution (fast, slow, glacial).

Staircases: Places Between

I have lost my place, or in other words, I have lost my way. Losing one's place is sometimes tied to an experience of the ruin, disappearance, or dissolution of a physical structure or a geographic location. Places are lost to nature: to fire, wind, and sea (as, for example, the disappearance of the fishing town of Kesennuma and a significant portion of the coast of northern Japan in March 2011). Other places vanish under the pressures of human hands: mountains blasted apart for mining, fields and waterways deserted to chemical runoff, cities invaded, sacked, leveled, and burned. In other instances, places undergo less dramatic changes that render them slowly, subtly erased.[4] Even in cases where one can point to the ground or map the coordinates of where a place once was, every loss of place entails something more than the loss of a particular building or swath of land. Recovery is never as simple as rebuilding or returning, since everything, including the one who would attempt to return, has irrevocably changed.[5]

One can experience a loss of place without having lost anything that could be named or located. It is, therefore, impossible to discern whether losing one's place is tied more firmly to the loss of a particular geographical spot or to a general loss of orientation that is more pervasive and less physically precise. Place, as

Vincent Colapietro insists, is "a verb—that is, not as an antecedently fixed container or enclosure, but as a historically evolved and evolving set of processes and practices."[6] Because places are malleable and fluid, they are activated in multiple ways, and losing one's place, similarly, takes myriad forms. Perhaps this is why any overarching theory of either place or loss will feel woefully ungrounded and ill equipped to deal with the intricate physical-psychological texture and ambiguous thresholds of each place, each loss. Perhaps an account of the loss of place should take the form of what Wittgenstein called "an album"—snapshots of places that once were, or postcards written from places that are no longer.

Three of the great literary/philosophical images of being lost entail (explicitly or implicitly) a sense of vertigo. The first image comes in the opening lines of Dante's *Inferno*: "Midway in the journey of our life I came to myself within a dark wood, for the straight way was lost. Ah, how hard it is to tell the nature of that wood, savage, dense, and harsh—the very thought of it renews my fear!"[7] Dante describes a wavering road, an impenetrable wood, and the terror of finding himself abandoned to grope in the dark. The second image comes at the start of Descartes's second *Meditation*, when, increasingly overwhelmed by doubt, he writes: "It feels as if I have fallen unexpectedly into a deep whirlpool which tumbles around me so that I can neither stand on the bottom nor swim up to the top."[8] Unable to find solid ground, Descartes articulates the classic symptom of vertigo: a pervasive dizziness that renders the whole world liquid and insubstantial. The third image of being lost comes from Emerson's 1884 essay "Experience," which opens with the deceptively simple question, "Where do we find ourselves?," followed by the tentative answer: "In a series of which we do not know the extremes, and believe there is none. We wake and find ourselves on a stair; there are stairs below us, which we seem to have ascended; there are stairs above us, many a one, which go upward and out of sight."[9] As with Dante, Emerson recounts an inability to see where things are leading or to recount how he arrived at the present moment. The road is neither straight nor flat. He has lost his way, and being lost coincides with a deprivation of sight, memory, and language (stuttering, stammering, he can neither climb nor speak). Like Descartes, Emerson cannot articulate the "extremes" of the situation. He is unable to discern a top or a bottom that might provide orienting points of landing or destination. In his opening question, Emerson also voices the paradox of "finding oneself" lost. That is, being lost, or losing one's place, is simultaneously the occasion of a certain discovery.

Dante finds himself in a dark wood, Descartes finds himself submerged in a whirlpool, and Emerson finds himself in midair. Transported out of their element, they are forced to move in ways that are awkward and unfamiliar (groping, drowning, hovering). But they are not without *any* place; in fact, their experiences of lostness take shape in distinctive, evocative places (forest, water, air).

These are uncanny places that resist demarcation or dwelling.[10] The experience of lostness is therefore not without place, just as the dissolution of one place does not leave a nowhere.[11] Place cedes to place. Lostness is itself a placement in an unknown or unfamiliar place, a *replacement* that reconfigures one's sense of order and identity.

The reconfiguring is acute in Emerson's example, which (of the three I have cited here) is perhaps the most disorienting and extreme description of being lost. This is so, in part, because Emerson's displacement is precipitated by the death of his child (something we learn a few pages into his essay). Places are tied to the intersections of lives that render them habitable. The loss of a place indicates a rupture of personal identity and coincides with a loss of connection with other lives (a dispersion or disbanding of life). For this reason, Emerson's essay and his image of a staircase provide clues to the complex intertwining of places and the lives they shelter.

Emerson finds himself suspended on an ephemeral stair, as if paralyzed on a rung of Martin Puryear's 1996 sculpture, *Ladder for Booker T. Washington*. Puryear's ladder, installed in the cavernous second-floor atrium of the Museum of Modern Art for his 2008 retrospective, is composed of undulating pieces of ash and maple. Suspended from the ceiling several feet off the ground, the ladder stretches three stories high, suggesting a seemingly infinite climb. The first rung hangs just out of reach, curtailing any possibility of ascension and underscoring both the comedy and pathos of an insurmountable ladder to nowhere. Subsequent rungs narrow in a wobbly arabesque of pale, twisting wood that could never support the weight of even the frailest human body. The whole apparatus exudes a ghostly, antigravitational quality. Like Emerson's stair, it hovers ethereally in midair, connecting nothing, and devoid of a substructure that might render it functional.

The figure of a stair, whether a ladder or a staircase, is itself terribly complicated. In *The Poetics of Space*, Gaston Bachelard associates staircases with "primal images," arguing that "a few steps have engraved in our memories a slight difference of level that existed in our childhood home."[12] Early experiences of verticality and depth lodge themselves in memories of particular steps (the haunting stairs leading up to the attic or down to the basement), and these experiences are coincident with the development of an increasingly complex, rugged emotional landscape, one characterized by peaks and valleys, highs and lows. Steps and stairs relate to the earliest experiences of verticality and the effort of climbing (or the trauma of falling). One of the forty-seven dreams of his own that Freud analyzes in *The Interpretation of Dreams* entails finding himself stalled on a staircase he had been bounding up, suddenly unable to move. One might also recall the staircase Socrates attributes to the prophetic stranger, Diotima, as she describes the ascent from beautiful bodies to beautiful ideas—an ascent that culminates in a "sea of beauties." The stair arrives at a sea—as if the steps that seemed to be rising were in fact descending all along.

Stairs are a means of changing levels, moving up or down. They accentuate the incremental effort of mobility, marking each step with a vertical rise. When a baby learns to crawl or toddle, stairs present innumerable difficulties. Similarly, in old age, stairs are avoided or replaced with lifts and ramps. Those with heavy baggage, baby carriages, in wheelchairs, on crutches, or with other issues of mobility must find novel ways of ascending and descending stairs, often enlisting the help of others. A stairway, intended as a utilitarian place of passage for those with specific physical capabilities, signals an ambiguous place, a place between places, on the way up or down. To hesitate on a stair, therefore, is to stall in a more profound (and precarious) way than any indecision that takes place on level ground. A place composed solely of stairs would be a place where nothing ever settles. Emerson's stairway, suspended in midair, stands open to the elements, like a fire escape unhinged from its building.

In choosing a stair as the opening image of "Experience," Emerson gives us a figure for the continuous but often rough and traumatic nature of experience. The things we think should link together, one after another in a smooth sequence, fail to cohere, so that life lacks the closure of the circles so prevalent across Emerson's writings. Returning to a longer excerpt from the beginning of Emerson's essay, one can sense his longing for firm footing, and his simultaneous resignation to the inescapable transience of all things:

> Where do we find ourselves? In a series of which we do not know the extremes, and believe that it has none. We wake and find ourselves on a stair; there are stairs below us, which we seem to have ascended; there are stairs above us, many a one, which go upward and out of sight. But the Genius which according to the old beliefs stands at the door by which we enter, and gives us the lethe to drink, that we may tell no tales, mixed the cup too strongly, and we cannot shake off the lethargy now at noonday. Sleep lingers all our lifetime about our eyes, as night hovers all day in the bough of the fir-tree. All things swim and glitter. Our life is not so much threatened as our perception. Ghost-like we glide through nature, and should not know our place again.[13]

Like a tightrope walker suddenly fixated on the tension of the rope, Emerson is roused by the sensation of standing on a ledge. Unable to discern how he got there, he recalls "the old beliefs" about the soul's initial journey into the world. Socrates relates one such story, "the myth of Er," at the close of *Republic*. He describes Er returning from the dead as a messenger from the gods, sent to relate the stories of the souls' rewards and punishments in the afterlife. After the souls have picked a pattern for their new life, they are made to cross a vast desert ("through terrible stifling heat") and finally led to the banks of the river Lethe. As the parched souls drink from the river, they forget everything that has happened to them. The more they drink, the less they remember of their past lives and passages through the afterlife (condemning them to repeat the same mistakes over and over). Every soul has lived more lives than it can recall, and its fate is tied to experiences it can neither recount nor imagine. Emerson envisions himself as one of those souls who drank most deeply from the river, so deeply that nothing in life seems solid or certain: "all things swim and glitter."

The image of the stair illustrates the precarious balance of a soul that has lost its sense of orientation and terra firma, as if a chasm has erupted to reveal the fluid core of the earth. The soul deprived of memory is without any sure footing and denied the possibility of "know[ing] [its] place again." In old age or through some malady or accident, one can lose the links of memory, which serve as crucial steps between experiences. Even without any acute memory loss, memories fade over time and become harder to retrieve. Without the footholds provided by memory, the soul lives untethered and displaced. Memory becomes constitutive of every sense of place, as though place only takes shape relative to previous places, in a web that extends infinitely. Memory safeguards places we no longer physically occupy as sites of possible return. In Emerson's case, everything has become shadowy, like the heavy boughs of the fir tree. His next step only leads up or down if he can remember whether his previous step was above or below.

What occasions such an experience of the dimming of the world and the feeling of waking on a stair? Emerson opens his essay with the image of suspension in the midst of climbing or descending that becomes a figure for life lived in the wake of a particular experience, namely, the loss of his son, Waldo. A few pages into the essay Emerson explains:

> The only thing grief has taught me is to know how shallow it is.... In the death of my son, now more than two years ago, I seem to have lost a beautiful estate,—no more. I cannot get it nearer to me ... something which I fancied was a part of me, which could not be torn away without tearing me nor enlarged without enriching me, falls off from me and leaves no scar. It was caducous. I grieve that grief can teach me nothing, nor carry me one step into real nature.[14]

His prose jars in its dispassionate remove from the depths of mourning, his too-neat equation of his son with "a beautiful estate—no more," and his curt assessment of grief's futility; its inability to provide any "step" forward or back. Two years after the death of his son, grief did nothing to restore Waldo, nor did it reignite the brilliance of the world diminished in the wake of his death. Emerson offers a deft diagnosis of loss in four scant lines. In grief, one finds oneself stalled and cut off from the forward momentum of life. (One day the sun shines and you realize, as if an epiphany, it's May already and you haven't changed your shirt for days or stepped outside in weeks.) Emerson emerges from his own grief like someone sobering up in the harsh light of day, unable to fathom how he arrived here. Like Whitman, he stands "baffled, balk'd, bent to the very earth / Opress'd with myself that I have dared to open my mouth / Aware now that amid all that blab whose echoes recoil upon me I have not once had the least idea of who or what I am."[15]

Waldo constituted a sense of place, Emerson's "beautiful estate." This could be read as the superficial equation of his son with his property, but "estate" derives from the Latin *status* and *stare*, to stand. An estate is not just any place, but a place in and through which one finds the confidence to stand up, and the loss of which leaves one crushed and bereft of home. In another image, he describes his child as a piece of himself, flesh of his flesh, a limb, or more literally a bough (as if Emerson is the shadowy fir tree invoked in the opening lines). And yet severing the limb was not lethal; the tree, even the one that has been radically pruned, incorporates the gash leaving "no scar." Two years on, the loss of his son has proved no more substantial or lasting than any other experience, no more *real*. Stung by the meaninglessness of loss, he laments that the loss of his child failed to become a point of contact with something real or to provide a lasting sense of something *really having happened*. The experience that should have altered everything, the death that should have meant the end of life, ends everything in some sense, and yet nothing ends. The stairs continue to descend to deeper depths and higher heights, and as he writes in "Circles," "We do not guess to-day the mood, the pleasure, the power of to-morrow."[16]

Emerson extracts a positive lesson from loss's inability to be definitive or final, namely: loss is subject to the same laws of nature that dictate life's ever-forward momentum, its great logic of "eternal equilibrium."[17] Life itself fails to stall or settle into any definitive, permanent shape or resting place—and this is the source of both despair and hope. It is a source of despair because one wants everything to stop and register the profundity of each loss. But it is a source of hope because no loss, however devastating or disorienting, is allowed the power to dictate the shape of all life. Emerson chooses to emphasize the hope to be found in nature's forward march and life's fluid indeterminacy. His is not a starry-eyed optimism, but a hard-won belief in the efficacy of the surplus and plurality of experiences. Near the close of "Experience," he replaces the figure of the stair with an image of finding himself at sea, declaring: "Suffice it for the joy of the universe that we have not arrived at a wall, but at interminable oceans." The gloom of the essay's opening lines turns into an increasingly exhilarated embrace of life's unexpected turns, its sheer enormity, culminating in Emerson's final cry, "Never mind the ridicule, never mind the defeat; up again, old heart!"—a call to move despite setback or collapse, to hoist anchor and set sail.[18]

The best one can do in the face of life's relentlessness is to be, as much as possible, poised for the next transition, ready to take another step into the unknown. Experience as Emerson conceives it opens ambivalently and often chaotically onto more experience—no experience is the last or the final one. His description of experience should help us appreciate that one's place, though singularly meaningful, is never a bare or discrete locale. Stairs must be linked in a series to form a staircase—one stair on its own is no longer a step. Emerson helps us appreciate that experience links forward and back to "an interminable ocean" of other experiences. The same could be said of memories, which can flood the psyche in a rush of images (one taste of a madeleine dipped in tea for the whole of childhood), or of places, which join together in a patchwork of arenas and interlocking public and private spheres. Places, like experiences itself, are entangled with multiple places, so that any shift or loss of place reverberates in unpredictable ways. Every place entails a set of connections and relationships that include, perhaps above all, relationships with other people and other forms of life. This is why the loss of place and the feeling of vertigo are so intimately tied to the loss of a person—explicitly so for Emerson (and each of the images of being lost from Descartes and Dante entail being left seemingly alone). A place devoid of its inhabitants loses its living clamor, like an abandoned house. Place is about the lives lived together in the environments that sustain, nurture, and ground them. There is no place entirely unpopulated or empty. Place is inhabited and habitable. Places are textures woven by interpenetrating lives—and perhaps this is why the places in which Emerson, Descartes, and Dante find themselves lost (the stair, the sea, the forest) are mythical figures of place that seem infinite or unbounded—places that seem (though they are not) abstract and remote.

First Snapshot: World Trade Center. Disaster.

Stairs are places in between. They are like the "conjunctive relations" James describes as "places of flight:" transitory and innately resistant to being occupied or immobilized by thought.[19] While the stairs in a home or apartment building have an intimate connection with daily trips up and down, most stairwells in modern office buildings go largely unused; they are a means of emergency exit. I am thinking now of the stairs in the north tower of the World Trade Center, massive columns of stairs into the sky.[20] I remember stories about someone running those stairs in preparation for the annual race up the Empire State Building: stairs as StairMaster. Others probably smoked in the stairwells, made private calls, had illicit rendezvous, went to cry. At least one person smuggled things up and down the stairs: Phillipe Petit took the freight elevator to the top for his tightrope walk between the towers in 1974, but he stashed his cables and supplies in the stairs. Upon his arrest, he was handcuffed by the police and brusquely pushed down the stairs, an experience he drolly recalled as the most dangerous part of his routine. But in principle, no one took the stairs. Even the elevators were divided into groups: one for the lower floors and another high-speed device to carry you above the seventieth floor, as if even machines had to split the labor of such an epic climb. And yet, for almost an hour on the morning of September 11, it was a building reduced to its stairs, to its places between, its lines of flight. Below the ninety-first floor, everyone took the stairs that descended all the way down and into the subway, only to proliferate in a maze of tunnels and rise again out of the ground.

To think about places is to remember specific places, and those that no longer exist are etched in memories of particular days: the weight of a door and the key in its lock, the terrible August heat in the plaza, the lemon glare on the East River, storms when the tower was socked in, faces in the elevators, the creaks of the building swaying in the wind. One afternoon the windows streamed with rain, and combined with the structure's soft moans (steel, concrete, glass straining to hold together against the forces of gravity) the building seemed alive, pitiable, sweet. It was brute, dumb matter. But also an access to a perspective, a place in the sky, a semiterrestrial, semicelestial intersection, angel and beast.

And then it vanished. Not all at once, and not instantaneously (even though now, years on, it seems like the blink of an eye). In a slow-motion peeling apart from the top, the column rained down in streams of rubble and cascading billows of grit and smoke. People fleeing were encrusted midstep. Where did the buildings go? Was there still a place in the sky, reserved there like a seat in a theater? Or perhaps a vacuum of air, like a breath inhaled and never released. And could one go back—by plane or helicopter, by hot air balloon, on the wing of some mythical bird? Sometime later I remember seeing a photograph of the north tower seemingly rising out of a sea of gold. It was Agnes Denes's work: *Wheatfield—A Confrontation, Battery Park Landfill, Downtown Manhattan, 2 Acres of Wheat Planted and Harvested, Summer 1982*. Denes, a pioneering environmental and conceptual artist, planted two acres of wheat on an abandoned landfill in Battery Park, adjacent to the World Trade Center towers (which were erected in 1974). The plot yielded one thousand pounds of wheat, which Dene harvested and then exhibited and replanted around the world to raise awareness of hunger and land use. Images of her work from above show a surreal swathe of gold dipping into the Hudson River and hugging the urban cityscape. Some ground-level images depict Denes riding a red tractor in the middle of the field. I could imagine the land being tilled, the seeds scattered, the feathered tips inching their way up, enveloping the city in their hazy glow. The opposite of a disaster: the tilling, planting, growth and harvest would have taken time; it would have been slow.

The same place can be landfill, a wheat field, apartments, a mall, a festival, a catastrophe, a morgue, a cemetery, a hole, a museum. The land was something else before; the land is something else now. A place passes into another place, cedes its place, is replaced. When this is sudden, when it is a disaster, then it's hard to recall what the place was like before. Memory and place fall and rise together. Is any disaster natural? Was the place ever there at all? And where exactly: What inch of sky? Holding the key to a door that no longer exists, I am retracing the steps down the hall, etching them in memory. But memory itself is not a stable place (is it a place at all?), and the places we lose suddenly become sites of eruptive imagery, psychic sinkholes that require repeated excavation, as if the buildings must be rebuilt and dismantled piece by piece in the work of imagination and dreams.[21] Every place is the grave of multiple places, a memorial—if we only knew the names to inscribe, the stones to lay.

"There's No Place Like Home."

If places are as fluid as experience, if they are "sites of activity, loci for dramas," as Vincent Colapietro observes (see Chapter 6, page 88 of this volume), then there is literally no place like home, no place like the home we remember and dream. Is home any sturdier a place than a stair? Emerson provides an opportunity to think about places between and the ties between loss, memory, and place. If stairs are paradigmatically inhospitable, a home is paradigmatically a resting place. It is where one returns or retires at the end of the day, a place with special gravity.

Bachelard begins *The Poetics of Space* with descriptions of houses and ends in the corners, recalling the dust in the cracks in the floorboards. Although the title of his text employs the term "space" (*L'Espace*), Bachelard writes about *places*, in particular, the places that give rise to the most intense memories and that inhabit one's dreams. As Bachelard describes it, the childhood home is the first place, and it informs every experience of place. Put otherwise, one's sense of place is first located and generated in relation to specific sensory-motor experiences and particular architectural/natural structures (smells, colors, sounds—the feel of a creaking stair, a canopy of trees, the sheltering nooks under tables and chairs, the smell of raisins in the cupboard). Bachelard describes the way that the first home molds the body and the psyche to its contours, as if we are made in the image of our first shelters. He invokes Victor Hugo's descriptions of Quasimodo's relationship to Notre Dame: "It is useless," Hugo writes, "to warn the reader not to take literally the figures of speech that I am obliged to use here to express the strange, symmetrical, immediate, almost cosubstantial flexibility of a man and an edifice."[22] The body bends into the space it is given, like a child curling into the corner of her bed.[23]

Following Bachelard, we could imagine a palatial body, a hut body, a cave body, a duplex body. Whatever the particular dimensions or characteristics of one's first home, this place looms larger in memory and in imagination that any other place, and it determines more about one's own shape (of body, of soul). It occupies a wider expanse of the unconscious and thereby requires more intense or extensive "topoanalysis," the procedure Bachelard describes as "the systematic psychological study of the sites of our intimate lives."[24] Such "sites" are places in the strongest sense of the word: singular, lived, and irreplaceable. Returning to the images of one's first home (however fleeting, marginal, or impermanent that home may have been), is a means of examining one's attachments, fears, dreams, and aptitude for intimacy. As Bachelard notes, the places one lived as a child seem immense: the vast rooms, the stairs that rise forever. This may be why returning to the actual, geographical, sites of one's childhood can be so disorienting, as everything appears miniaturized and ill suited to the large-scale dimensions of one's dominant memories. But Bachelard reminds us that the smallest places (drawers, nests, shells) are often the most evocative, the most psychologically vast, and "home" might be lived in the "intimate immensity" of any corner of the world.[25]

Any sense of place, then, is tied to a foundational or primal sense of home, and home itself is tied to the earliest memories of intimacy and protection. Every experience of displacement registers, at some level, as a loss of home—a loss that often occasions a wider and more generous sense of the world and its inhabitants.[26] We build our capacities for exposure on a foundation of loving enclosure. It is not hard to imagine that a child who is denied intimacy and protection lives without sheltering memories and becomes subject to a pervasive sense of displacement, a radical, if not literal, homelessness. Or perhaps she retreats into the corners of her mind, fabricating in daydreams places she can inhabit, building interior rooms, becoming an architect of invisible cities.

Bachelard's analysis of intimate places focuses on the mere and the small. It is not a description of the places where lives intersect, but a focus on the withdrawal of the soul into its own safe enclosures, like the retreat of a mollusk into its shell. His work does not help us to think about intensely populated places (cities, subways, public schools for example) and their unique demands. But he does help us think about the ways places are lived and vividly internalized by children and the impact of such places on the rest of life. Bachelard also reminds us that a sense of home is not reducible to any specific architectural structure or any geographic location on a map. As in Emerson's case, one's "estate" might be located in another person. One's home might be nothing more than a voice or a face, the smell of the sea, a shade of orange that colored the walls of one's first room.

Second Snapshot: The Farm. Disappearance.

Sometimes places erode over long periods of time so drawn out and incremental that one cannot say when a place stopped being one place and become another.[27] Things accumulated, borders blurred, chaos (a new order) encroached. I am thinking of a farm, a swath of land rolling across multiple slopes where dairy cows, tractors, hens, pumpkins, beans, all took their turns. Nothing happened. Seasons came and went, the creeks froze and thawed, the sap ran in the spring and the beavers dammed their way into new, wet labyrinths each year. Perhaps that was how it started, with the beavers. The pond was low one year, and the next year it was a swamp. By the third year, the swamp was studded with saplings. No one wanted to mow the outer field, and so it welcomed the impenetrable thicket of brambles in at the edge . . . an inch or a foot or a meter lost to the woods here and there. There was no epic battle to recount, no date of surrender, no singular event. The apple trees caught something and lost their will to fruit. The driveway needed plowing, but instead they shoveled a narrow path to the door and the truck stayed in the field, reclaimed under a blanket of snow.

When the time came to divide the land, there seemed to be less of it than anyone remembered. Couldn't it be surveyed again, measured and studded with neon flags to signal where one property begins and another ends (but to whom? the deer, the mouse, the brush, the rain)? And whose was it to will or to give away?

Things happened so slowly that they didn't happen at all. They unfurled, they seeped. Histories went untold, buried, forgotten. Once it was a place where the Mohawk tribe ("Keepers of the Eastern Door") hunted and lit their ceremonial fires. Later the cows thought it was theirs, their hooves digging into the wet earth as they wandered off to give birth in the lowest parts of the field. Later still it seemed to belong to the hands that worked it, dug, turned and planted it. The seeds put down roots and thought the place was theirs. The house and the barn weathered and grew into the landscape until they seemed like ancient ruins from a lost time, temples from another world.

Every creature has a claim; every season has its sleepers and its wakers. One by one they stake their ground, taking their place in the sun. Every place has multiple histories, stories of attachment and ownership, of usurpation and surrender. We belong to places, but the places themselves, even the ones we think of as most intimately "ours," don't belong to anyone. Perhaps this realization takes a long time. The chronology of loss can be sudden or slow, but the realization of a place having disappeared or slipped through one's hands is always dramatic in the end. This is not unlike the death of someone preceded by a long sickness, a slow demise. In some sense there is plenty of time to prepare, and one knows the end before it arrives. Nonetheless death is always surprising and sudden. In the case of the land that changes hands—morphing incrementally from the wild to the field, from the field to the farm, from the farm to a subdivision . . . and beyond—one cannot say exactly when the change happened. What was the last tie to the place, the one that couldn't be cut without losing the place altogether?

City and Sea

Places are fluid. They move and shift, just as bodies change and grow, erode and decay. The houses Bachelard envisions in memories and daydreams acquire an unnatural ideality, a sheen and permanence only possible in the safe and abstract confines of the mind. (As Proust wrote, "the true paradises are the paradises that have been lost."[28]) Yet memories (even the strongest ones) fade, and the world is composed of places that are in the process of becoming ruins or the sites of yet other places.

In *A Thousand Plateaus*, Deleuze and Guattari set out to examine forces of organization and disorganization as they manifest themselves in bodies broadly construed (bodies of water, political bodies, human bodies, animal bodies, artistic bodies of work, etc.). They describe the rhythms of accumulation (or building) and ruination (or erosion) as forces of "territorialization" and "deterritorialization," respectively. In their introduction they write: "It is not a question of this or that place on earth, or of a given moment in history, still less of a category of thought. It is a question of a model that is perpetually in construction or collapsing, and of a process that is perpetually prolonging itself, breaking off and starting up again."[29] A larger part of the project of *A Thousand Plateaus* entails conceiving bodies as forces rather than *things* and describing the interpenetrating rhythms and intensities traversing all matter (rendering even the most seemingly inert matter poised for movement). If places are not "this or that place on earth," that is because the earth itself has no bedrock, no solid ground. Although, like Bachelard, Deleuze and Guattari employ the word *space* more often than *place*, their account helps to underscore the fluidity and essential impermanence of every place, while radicalizing Bachelard's intuition (via Victor Hugo) that places and bodies are "consubstantial."

A "territory" is a particular kind of place, one that has been bounded and claimed by distinctive forms of life engaged in idiosyncratic practices. Deleuze and Guattari's favorite examples come from territorial animals (such as the Stagemaker bird, or coral fish). In each case, the animal develops ways of making a physical trait explicit and expressive, as the color of the coral fish becomes a sign of its belonging to a particular part of the reef. Deleuze and Guattari define "territorialization" as "an act of rhythm that has become expressive."[30] The animal stakes a place as soon as it finds a means of exhibiting ownership, using its body to mark, or "sign" its land. Such demarcation of particular territories entails a simultaneous change in the animal and change in a place, an intertwining of organism and environment. Echoing Bachelard's descriptions of the body's intimate relationship with its first house, and emphasizing the degree to which animal and environment are co-creative, Deleuze and Guattari explain: "Climate, wind, season, hour are not of another nature than the things, animals, or people that populate them, follow them, sleep and awaken within them. The becoming-evening, becoming-night of an animal.... Five o'clock is this animal! This animal is this place!"[31]

Territories develop where creatures practice and privilege modes of ownership, but even as the most fiercely territorial animals mark their land, the land itself shifts beneath them. It is as if the "signatures" (the "territorializing marks"[32]) that Deleuze and Guattari describe as essential to every animal's territory are being inscribed in water or sand (and this may account for the nearly desperate, repetitive behavior of territorial animals). This is also why Deleuze and Guattari end up describing almost every place in terms of water, ice, or desert (inadvertently or not). The marks of ownership are constantly being effaced, and therefore must be endlessly redrawn. In 1981 Deleuze devoted a small book to the work of the painter Francis Bacon, for whom deserts inform the barren, color-field landscapes for his contorted figures, as jets of water stream from and through bodies in effacing rivers of gooey paint.

The description of the coincident forces of territorialization and deterritorialization becomes more explicit in a chapter devoted to what Deleuze and Guattari term "the smooth and the striated." In their fourteenth Plateau, "1440: The Smooth and the Striated," they devote a section to what they call "the maritime model" to examine the differences between the sea and the city (the fluid and the solid respectively, which turn out to be radically implicated in one another and nearly indistinguishable by the end of their analysis—a strange hybrid—Atlantis). In order to set up an instructive (though false) opposition, they define the ocean as "the smooth space par excellence," and the city as "the striated space par excellence."[33] The ocean resists articulation, decomposition, and ownership. Even at the edges of the sea, the tide lines change, so that property rights only extend to the trace of the last wave. Put otherwise, the ocean for Deleuze and Guattari represents an extreme case of deterritorialization—an antiterritory or a place that resists placement, resisting possession (and the true nomad is the one who is always, even on dry land, at sea). By contrast, the city is defined by a grid, an organization that extends horizontally and vertically as place is carved into more and more discrete units, each unit made articulate with a number, a tenant, a landlord. Every inch of the city is "signed." Deleuze and Guattari recount an imaginary history of the "citification" of land, which begins with the first bare furrow in the earth (the first mark on the ground) and becomes the deeply ploughed lines of a farm—the hallmarks of the first settlements.

As they begin to undermine their own dualistic opposition between city and sea, Deleuze and Guattari describe the ways that cities themselves contain areas analogous to the smooth space of the ocean—chaotic zones of disorganization, "an explosive misery secreted by the city."[34] Whether in the form of shifting shantytowns of the homeless or razed lots and abandoned buildings where birds and plants, rats, and other forms of life establish an urban "wild."[35] Likewise, they describe the probing of the ocean with more advanced forms of sonar, the waters themselves bending around the forms of increasingly powerful nautical machines. Their point is that radical organization tends to engender its own forms of disorganization, eroding from within, while the smoothest parts of the sea lay themselves open for (and even invite) striation.

Still, it is not hard to discern the prioritization of the smooth over the striated in *A Thousand Plateaus*, despite Deleuze and Guattari's insistence that both are necessary (inevitable) and cannot be definitely differentiated from one another. They insist that "smooth spaces are not in themselves liberatory," but they consistently stress the value of "deterritorialization" as a means of resistance to the forces of oppressive inertia.[36] (Such an emphasis strangely recalls Emerson's claim that "People wish to be settled; only as far as they are unsettled is there any hope for them."[37]) Cities are sites of radical organization, and Deleuze and Guattari prefer the risks and adventures of more chaotic, unpredictable forms of non-dwelling—the relationship the nomad has to the steppe and the desert, to places that inherently resist demarcation. It is for this reason that they advocate "nomadology"—a project of unsettling oneself and finding novel ways of reinstating or releasing a disequilibrium that becomes productive of new "lines of flight."

The sea resists striation, even as it is probed with navigational devices, allocated and plumbed, drilled, polluted. And yet there are no places (not even the deepest places in the sea) that are entirely smooth. Deleuze and Guattari show the chaotic and fluid aspects of places and the inevitability of the gridding and girding of space—the building and dwelling that tame and transfigure the wild and render space into habitable place. No place is stable or for all time. We are destined to lose our places, even as we are condemned to stake them out. Place cedes to place, at a pace that one can never predict or even imagine.

Snapshot 3: Shishmaref. Dissolution.

The city is a place where things happen fast; buildings go up and down in a matter of weeks. Time unfurls more slowly on the farm, a place that lives according to the pace of the seasons, speeding up in the spring and the fall, slowing down in the heady summer heat and the deep winter's cold. Loss of urban places and loss of rural places have their own distinctive chronologies, their own mechanisms of attachment and habitation; and once lost, they require their own works of mourning. In northern Alaska, time spreads out and moves so slowly, glacially, that it exceeds any human frame. One needs other means of measurement, other mechanisms of observation, to say what is happening, or when, or where.[38] Some places are connected to a time immemorial, a prehistoric time, and becoming sensitized to their changes will require a more radical, expansive memory and imagination. On the ice, change seems so slow it can't be called disaster or disappearance. It is melting, giving way . . . dissolving. But not over the course of days or years. The icy village of Shishmaref, perched on an island in the middle of the

Seward Peninsula, once lived at earth-speed, closer to the speed of boulders and mountains. Hence its aura of permanence, its ancient rituals and rites. It seemed immune to the forces of erosion, exempt from the cycles of discovery and loss at work on every place. If loss occurs at a pace slower than can be measured by a single human life (taking longer than eighty years or so), then it becomes very difficult to discern or appreciate as happening at all.

But the changes that were happening so slowly are speeding up, and the places that once seemed permanent are dissolving more and more quickly. Elizabeth Kolbert, who devotes a chapter of her book *Fieldnotes from a Catastrophe* to Shishmaref, explains it this way: "The oceans are becoming not just warmer, but more acidic; the difference between daytime and nighttime temperatures is diminishing; animals are shifting their ranges poleward; and plants are blooming days, and in some cases weeks, earlier than they used to . . . while in many parts of the globe [these changes] are still subtle enough to be overlooked, in others they can no longer be ignored. As it happens, the most dramatic changes are occurring in those places . . . where the fewest people tend to live."[39] Kolbert tells us that 591 people lived in Shishmaref, all of them forced to relocate to the mainland in the summer of 2002 following a fall dominated by relentless storms and twelve-foot waves.[40]

Places that seem inhospitable are easier to ignore or abandon: tundras, deserts, blighted cities, contaminated land. These are forgotten places of the world. They lack the familiar structures that provide a sense of scale and orientation—instead there are huts, tents.[41] Without robust signs of settlement, these kinds of places linger at the outer margins of perception, treated as zones of passage and denied the privileges of any definite place, except by those who live there, who know they inhabit sacred ground. They are the most abstract or distant places, the ones that few of us have been. Kolbert goes on to describe the melting of permafrost in northern Alaska, a dissolution of the frozen core of the land that dates back to beginning of the last glacial cycle. If the permafrost thaws, Kolbert notes, it will be doing so "for the first time in more than a hundred and twenty thousand years."[42]

Shishmaref was living at the edge of the very last of those years, and soon the island was submerged by the surrounding sea. Its ice was less reliably frozen year by year (and the inhabitants invented new names for the ice, as if naming it better might keep it in place), until, piece by piece, the island washed away. What didn't happen for hundreds of thousands of years happened quickly in the end, too quickly to reverse or to forestall. Time sped up, accelerated by human hands. Perhaps it is the nature of every loss that the demarcation between presence and absence, between here and there, is painfully stark and decisive once it happens. Still, it is hard to say when the loss began or when it will end.

Places dissolving are hard to discern, but like every other place, they are interconnected. The loss of Shishmaref is something more than the loss of a place where 591 people made their lives hunting and fishing, living from the land. A place is always local and inextricably bound to the lives intersecting within a given location, but it is also bound to neighboring places—a patchwork of places fringed on all sides, with no hard lines of demarcation, not even when they are physically walled off from one another (as at the southern borders of the United States or Israeli settlements). Places are all, to some degree, wet, and capable of seeping into one another, blurring their own lines. No place changes, therefore, without changing surrounding places. And when a place dissolves, the loss reverberates in unforeseeable ways. In the case of Shishmaref, the repercussions are dramatic, global. The ice that melts over the course of thousands of years raises the level of the seas, which wash ashore with greater frequency and intensity, eradicating whole swaths of coast, altering the earth's rate of revolution, changing the length of days, shifting the plates of the globe and transfiguring the very ground of every place. Perhaps every place is part stair, part home, part sea—a collection of moving forces we try, sometimes desperately, to hold together.

I never knew this place. I can't imagine it. And yet I can almost picture the melting drawn out over thousands of years, like a Japanese scroll painting being unfurled for such a long time that one can no longer remember the intricate mountain and the lone figure with a cane winding his way upward at the beginning. Over time, the scroll unrolled more and more quickly, until it was frantically spilling onto the floor. The last scene was the only one etched in memory, and it appeared too wet to decipher—a blur of inky waves.

Postscript

In examining a staircase, a farm, and Shishmaref, I have tried to show the differential speeds of places and the varying psychic works of responding to unique kinds of loss. Sometimes places alter instantaneously and dramatically, as in the case of Waldo's death and the collapse of the World Trade Center. These seem like unnatural disasters insofar as they challenge or reverse the expected course of things. They intervene suddenly and inexplicably in the midst of life, forever altering one's sense of continuity. Natural disasters—tsunamis, earthquakes, tornadoes, hurricanes, and other storms caused by extreme weather or other atmospheric or geographic changes—are no less difficult to endure or to process. Yet they lack the sting of feeling that one could have intervened or done something differently to alter the course of things. They transpire according to what Werner Herzog called "the overwhelming indifference of nature."[43] I am not, however, suggesting that loss fits neatly into two distinct categories. Most experiences of loss and disaster entail a combination of the unnatural and the natural, or the natural ceding to the unnatural as it did in the wake of Hurricane Katrina: one storm displacing people only to leave them further exposed to negligence and neglect. Most disasters force a questioning of the meaning of the very words *natural, unnatural, human, inhuman*—and a host of other terms that may have once seemed secure.

In a digital age characterized by dizzying speed and a collapsing sense of distance, the earth has flattened, and places have become both more and less important than ever before. They are more important because they testify to the irreplaceability of material, physical ground, in contrast to the infinite interchangeability of virtual places. They are less important because one can be anywhere with the click of a button, allowing a person to occupy one place on earth while roaming across the globe. One could argue about the degree to which surfing the web is real travel, but the fact remains that the internet has facilitated a unique cosmopolitanism that has far-reaching (both positive and negative) implications for the sense of home, belonging, responsibility, and place. Disasters are broadcast in real time, linking people in a global network of impact. Places that once seemed remote become accessible. Experiences of loss that would previously have been locally confined and inflected transfigure in their conveyance across media across the world.

It may be uniquely difficult to find one's place in the modern world, when the very concept of *a place* feels outdated. Yet places continue to recede and to change, at rates that are faster than anything human beings have experienced in their relatively short history on the planet. Such acceleration remains difficult, if not impossible, to appreciate, since it relates to the Earth: the place we all call home, the most concrete yet abstract place of all. No place is secure or final. The various authors I've followed here help us face the inevitability of losing our places, even as they stress or even celebrate the positive dimensions of displacement—its ethical and creative force. There are less hopeful things to say about loss and place, especially for the vast numbers of animals and human beings who have been and are in the midst of being violently forced from their places. Disasters never reconcile neatly into lessons learned, except for those who never lived them in the first place. But in a world bound together by ecosystems whose slightest variations provoke trembling everywhere, one needs a certain aptitude for revision and revolution, something learned in part by reading, traveling, and other means of decentering oneself. Perhaps one also needs real life experiences on the ground as a means of honing local knowledge and being present to changes that transpire incrementally, below the radar of any new media, beyond the broadband of every network. It is hard to accept that no place, not even the one I love the most fiercely, belongs to me. But it is as futile and tragic to grip a place as it is another living creature. The relevant question, then, is not whether to let places go (as if one had a choice in the matter), but how and when to do it in such a way that they, and you, can live by changing.[44]

MEGAN CRAIG is a painter and Associate Professor of Philosophy and Director of the Master's Program in philosophy and art at Stony Brook University. The author of *Levinas and James: Toward a Pragmatic Phenomenology* (Indiana University Press, 2010), her philosophical writings focus on aesthetics, sensibility, memory, ethics, French phenomenology, and American philosophy.

Notes

1. There are several precedents for Levinas's thinking about crowded spaces and the priority of the other, but perhaps none is as influential as Bergson's descriptions of pure duration and his refutation of empty space as abstract and merely conceptual. In "The Possible and the Real" he writes, "We perceive and can conceive only occupied space. One thing disappears only because another replaces it. Suppression thus means substitution. We say 'suppression,' however, when we envisage, in the case of substitution, only one of its two halves, or rather the one of its two sides which interests us; in this way we indicate a desire to turn our attention to the object which is gone, and away from the one replacing it"; see Henri Bergson, *Henri Bergson: Key Writings*, ed. Keith Ansell Pearson and John Ó Maoilearca (New York: Bloomsbury, 2014), 276. Levinas articulates the ethical implications of this Bergsonian insight into "substitution."

2. Emmanuel Levinas, *Otherwise Than Being or Beyond Essence*, trans. Alphonso Lingis (Dordrecht: Kluwer, 1991), vii.

3. William James, *The Principles of Psychology* (Cambridge, MA: Harvard University Press, 1981), 1:221.

4. Nancy Tuana is particularly sensitive to the subtler and often overlooked losses of place in Chapter 11 of this volume, "Climate Change and Place: Delimiting Cosmopolitanism." Tuana reminds us: "the slow onset, gradual transformations of home and place are often ignored. In particular, the psychic impacts of altered physical environments, the distress and anxieties caused by loss of belonging, and the social importance of the intricate interweavings between physical and social environments are often overlooked" (167).

5. This means that a loss of place requires a more nuanced psychological account than Freud provides of either mourning or melancholia, both of which he describes as "pass[ing] off after a certain time has elapsed without leaving traces of any gross changes"; see "Mourning and Melancholia," *The Freud Reader*, ed. Peter Gay (New York: W. W. Norton, 1989), 589.

6. See Chapter 6, page 85 of this volume.

7. Dante Alighieri, *Inferno*, trans. Robert Hollander and Jean Hollander (New York: Anchor, 2002), 3.

8. René Descartes, *Discourse on Method and Meditations on First Philosophy*, trans. David Cress (Indianapolis: Hackett, 1998), 16.

9. Ralph Waldo Emerson, "Experience," in *The Portable Emerson*, ed. C. Bode (New York: Penguin, 1981), 266.

10. Freud explains the uncanny as related to "what arouses dread and horror" and links this with experiences in which doubt and ambivalence play crucial roles, as in Nathaniel's inability to differentiate between the horrific fictional figure of the Sandman and Coppelius, the friend of his father who terrifies him as a child.

11. As Ed Casey notes, "Although there are displaced occasions, there are no *non* placed occasions, i.e., occasions without any form of implacement whatsoever.... To exist at all ... is

to have a place—*to be implaced*"; see Ed Casey, *Getting Back into Place* (Bloomington: Indiana UP, 2009), 13.

12. Gaston Bachelard, *The Poetics of Space*, trans. Maria Jolas (Boston: Beacon, 1994), 26.

13. Emerson, "Experience," 266–67.

14. Ibid., p. 269. John Lysaker explains Emerson's attitude about the death of his son in these terms: "Not that Waldo's loss was incidental, or that it didn't transform Emerson's outlook on life, but I am suggesting that it less introduced Emerson into an entirely new order of thought than intensified concerns already present and potent"; see John Lysaker, *Emerson and Self-Culture* (Bloomington: Indiana University Press, 2008], 91. I am suggesting that the failure of Waldo's death to occasion a radical, permanent rupture, is itself experienced by Emerson as more decisive, more traumatic, than the loss itself.

15. Walt Whitman, *I Ebb'd with the Ocean of Life, Walt Whitman: Selected Poems*, ed. Harold Bloom (New York: Library of America, 2003), 132.

16. Emerson, *The Portable Emerson*, 239.

17. Ibid., 384.

18. Emerson, "Experience," 283.

19. The stress on "conjunctive relations" is a cornerstone of James's radical empiricism, but in the *Principles*, he describes the different "paces" of the stream of consciousness in the following terms (which foreshadow his radical empiricism): "Like a bird's life, [consciousness] seems to be made of an alternation of flights and perchings. . . . *Let us call the resting-places the 'substantive parts,' and the places of flight the 'transitive parts,' of the stream of thought*" (243). He goes on to elaborate how difficult it is to "see the transitive parts for what they really are." Thought tends toward stability, toward nouns, names, and certitude. The difficulty of seeing the "places of flight" is analogous to the challenge of thinking about stairs without reducing them to the floors they connect or the buildings they occupy. A phenomenology of stairs would entail a radically empirical focus on "conjunctive relations."

20. From June to September 2001, I painted the city from the ninety-first floor of 1 World Trade Center as part of the "Worldviews" residency sponsored by the Lower Manhattan Cultural Council.

21. Bergson associates "spontaneous memory" with the life of dreams. He writes, "If almost the whole of our past is hidden from us because it is inhibited by the necessities of present action, it will find strength to cross the thresholds of consciousness in all cases where we renounce the interests of effective action in order to replace ourselves, so to speak, in the life of dreams"; see *Matter and Memory*, trans. N. M. Paul and W. S. Palmer (New York: Zone, 1990), 133. Put otherwise, only by cultivating receptivity to *useless* memories (a receptivity Bergson finds particularly alive in children) can one experience the full breadth of memory, "the infinite multitude of the details of . . . past history" (ibid., 134). To recall the particularities of lost places, recalling the "infinite details," we need to let ourselves dream them.

22. Quoted in Bachelard, *Poetics of Space*, 91.

23. The home provides the space in which the body can curl up and sleep. This is part of Levinas's description of the interiority distinctive to "dwelling," an interiority that provides the self with a basis for waking up and going out. See Jessica Wahman's discussion of this issue in Chapter 12 of this volume. John Stuhr also emphasizes the positive, ethical implications of not being at home in the world, writing, "to succeed [in creating pluralistic democracies] is not to find one's self at home everywhere in the world; it is to feel one's self not quite fully or ever at home any place in the world" (Chapter 17, page 292).

24. Bachelard, *Poetics of Space*, 8.

25. Ibid., 183. In his chapter on corners, Bachelard describes the corner as "the sure place" (137).

26. Home, whatever it may be, provides a point of orientation from which a child can venture forth—and yet there are many degrees and kinds of homelessness. I agree with José Medina's account of our collective responsibility to those who are "eternally homeless, without the possibility of identifying with a place at all"; the responsibility to "figure out what would count as a place in the world that this subject can properly relate to . . . even if it is a place that has never existed and needs to be created" (see Chapter 7, page 117).

27. Nancy Tuana relates this ambiguous, slow loss to the psychic condition of "solastalgia." She writes, "solastagia is a reminder that we can lose our place while still in place. . . . What is lost is a sense of belonging that comes from the interdependence between individuals and the land that they know and are of. While there is some attention to the impacts of disasters on homes and places . . . the slow onset, gradual transformations of home and place are often ignored" (see Chapter 11, page 187).

28. Marcel Proust, *The Guermantes Way: In Search of Lost Time*, trans. Mark Trehane (New York: Penguin, 2005), 3:870.

29. Gilles Deleuze and Felix Guattari, *A Thousand Plateaus*, trans. Brian Massumi (London: Continuum, 1987), 22.

30. Ibid., 348.

31. Ibid., 290.

32. Ibid., 347.

33. Ibid., 531.

34. Ibid.

35. Deleuze and Guattari explain the "smoothing" forces inherent in these terms: "The smooth spaces arising from the city are not only those of worldwide organization, but also of counterattack combining the smooth and the holey and turning back against the town: sprawling, temporary, shifting shantytowns of nomads and cave dwellers, scrap metal and fabric, patchwork, to which the striations of money, work, or housing are no longer relevant" (ibid., 531). For a stunning legal and political elaboration of this aspect of cities, see Michelle Wilde Anderson, "Dissolving Cities," *Yale Law Journal* 121 (2012): 1364.

36. Deleuze and Guattari, *A Thousand Plateaus*, 551.

37. Emerson, "Experience," 239.

38. One of the best ways of gaging the age of an iceberg is to lick it (measuring time by taste): newer ice will still be salty from the sea; older ice will be fresh enough to melt and drink. Elizabeth Kolbert describes this procedure in *Fieldnotes from a Catastrophe* (New York: Bloomsbury, 2007), 25–27, elaborating other scientific attempts to accurately "date" ice.

39. Ibid., 13.

40. Kolbert's most recent book, *The Sixth Extinction: An Unnatural History* (New York, Henry Holt, 2014), 3, continues her work of visiting and reporting from places under siege in an effort to show the irreversible effects of climate change on those species most vulnerable to environmental shifts, but she notes that "such is the scope of the changes now taking place that I could've gone pretty much anywhere, and, with the proper guidance, found signs of them." Her first chapter begins in Panama, and the last chapter looks at extinction taking place in her own backyard.

41. Deleuze and Guattari explain, "The same terms are used to describe ice deserts and sand deserts: there is no line separating earth and sky; there is no intermediate distance, no perspective or contour; visibility is limited, and yet there is an extraordinary fine topology that relies not on points or objects but rather on haeccities, on sets of relations (winds, undulations of snow or sand, the song of the sane or the creaking of ice, the tactile qualities of both). It is tactile space" (*A Thousand Plateaus*, 421).

42. Kolbert, *Fieldnotes*, 17.
43. *Grizzly Man*, written and directed by Werner Herzog (Discovery Channel, 2005).
44. Many thanks to John J. Stuhr and all the participants of the 2011 American Philosophies Forum conference in Madrid for discussion and questions that have enriched and challenged my own thinking. My thanks as well to Ed Casey for his subtle and invaluable comments on an earlier draft of this chapter.

10   The Loss of Confidence in the World

Josep E. Corbí

IN THIS CHAPTER, I focus on the experience of torture and, more specifically, on Jean Améry's account of it in his book *At the Mind's Limits*.[1] There he claims that *the loss of confidence in the world* is the most devastating effect he experienced as a victim of torture. I thus explore what cosmopolitan aspiration may be revealed by this loss and also discuss whether it is to be discredited as an irrational reaction on the victim's side or instead as proportional to the facts and, consequently, as relevant to the conditions under which a certain cosmopolitan aspiration could be achieved or, at least, favored.

More specifically, the structure of this chapter goes as follows. In the first section, I argue that, despite appearances to the contrary, torture has three poles, namely: the victim, the torturer, and third agents. The notion of confidence in the world plays a central function in my line of argument and is expressed in terms of two expectations of protection, namely: (a) "Nobody will illegitimately hurt me" and (b) "If someone illegitimately hurts me (or I am in a state of need), someone else will come to help and protect me." In the second section, I argue that these two expectations manifest a cosmopolitan aspiration insofar as they constitutively involve an appeal to third agents, and, in this respect, they constitutively address the world. Some people might object that these two expectations can hardly express a cosmopolitan aspiration because, even though they address the world, they are only concerned with the particular agent who bears them. In the third section, I motivate the use of "me" to characterize the content of such expectations, but argue that they go beyond the particular person who holds them to embrace everyone. And, yet, this projection onto everyone's expectations departs from the sort of impartiality that a Kantian approach may demand, since our expectations of protection (and the corresponding cosmopolitan aspiration) are anchored to our identity in ways a Kantian approach can hardly allow for. Once the content of our expectations of protection have thus been specified, I take up, in the two last sections, the issue about the rationality of their loss. Thus I argue that the loss of confidence in the world can hardly be regarded as an irrational sequel of a traumatic experience; on the contrary, I defend the rationality of the process by which the victim of serious harm may become deprived of this confidence. I conclude that an attitude of confidence in the world rests on an illusion that third agents (and the torturer) cannot help being trapped by. This brings to light a profound sense in which the unredeemed victim feels exiled from the human world for only her life is being shaped by a most poignant truth: the impossibility of a world where a fundamental cosmopolitan aspiration is fulfilled, that is, a world that could be trusted.

The Three Poles of Torture and the Loss of Confidence in the World

Paradigmatically, torture takes place in an isolated cell.[2] There, the victim suffers the pain inflicted by the torturer. Only two poles are apparently involved in such an act: after all, "every weapon has two ends."[3] Think then of a weapon pointing at you. You will inevitably sense the vulnerability of your flesh in front of the cutting edge, but what about the person who holds the handle? She experiences instead her own capacity to hurt. Some profound asymmetries seem to exist between the holder of the handle and whoever may face the cutting edge. From an epistemic perspective, the victim experiences her pain as the paradigm of the undeniable, whereas the torturer, despite being in the process of inflicting pain, regards it as something that can be doubted and even denied.[4] From a metaphysical perspective, whoever is confronted with the injuring side of a weapon feels weak and powerless: she is someone who can only be hurt. And the mere fact that her life is being threatened by another human being already counts as harm.[5] On the other hand, the torturer, the one who holds the weapon, is someone who has the power to hurt and kill; as when soldiers are displayed holding their guns or driving their tanks: we perceive their power and also the strength they are convinced they possess, while the injured bodies at the other end of their weapons are easily kept out of sight.[6]

Torture seems then to reflect the bipolar structure of a weapon: the torturer holds the handle while the victim feels her flesh torn by the cutting edge. Yet the content itself of the victim's experience, as well as the role that interrogation is supposed to play in that context, suggest that some other people may also be essentially involved. To motivate this point, I argue that an appeal to third agents lies at the core of both the victim's experience and the torturer's action. As a result, I conclude that, despite appearances to the contrary, torture has constitutively three poles: the torturer, the victim, and third agents. Let us look at the victim's experience first.

As a victim of torture, Jean Améry claims that a crucial aspect of the harm experienced is *the loss of confidence in the world*:[7]

> Yet I am certain that with the very first blow that descends on him he loses something we will perhaps temporarily call "trust in the world." Trust in the world includes all sorts of things: the irrational and logically unjustifiable

belief in absolute causality perhaps, or the likewise blind belief in the validity of the inductive inference. But more important as an element of trust in the world, and in our context what is solely relevant, is the certainty that by reason of written or unwritten social contracts the other person will spare me—more precisely stated, that he will respect my physical, and with it my metaphysical being. The boundaries of my body are also the boundaries of my self. My skin surface shields me against the external world. If I am to have trust, I must feel on it only what I *want* to feel.[8]

Améry finds the concept of human dignity to be of no avail to understanding the psychological impact of the first blow, which he finally identifies as the loss of some expectations.[9] He did not expect anyone to touch his skin unless he allowed them to. He trusted his neighbors to this extent, but suddenly his flesh is intentionally injured by another human being and, as a result, his initial expectation is seriously challenged.

Third agents may feel tempted to represent themselves as *mere spectators* of that attack, but this temptation goes against a second component of our confidence in the world. We expect nobody to touch our skin unless we would allow them to, but we also expect that someone would come and help us if that primary expectation failed or we were in a state of need. Whenever a person is injured in a traffic accident, she assumes that passersby will soon take care of her plight and call for an ambulance, which will speedily arrive and provide medical aid. Even in war conditions, the Red Cross is supposed to rescue the wounded and bring them to a hospital. It seems then that a response on the side of third agents is constitutive of the expectations that the victim (or the needy) has insofar as she may still trust the world and, thereby, regard it as a hospitable place to dwell in. The victim does not look upon third agents as mere spectators, but as people from whom she expects a certain response.[10] Only on the assumption that such a response will take place, will the victim retain her confidence in the world once the primary expectation has failed. This suggests that third agents cannot coherently conceive of themselves as mere spectators and also preserve their confidence in the world. For the mere fact that they conceived of their own situation in that way, would undermine the conditions under which the world could reasonably be trusted. In the next section, we will see, however, that some robust motivations impel third agents to distance themselves from the victim and to believe instead what the torturer might say to justify her action.

Interrogation and Third Agents

Third agents are present in the torturer's experience in more than one way. Consider, for instance, those cases where torture involves a process of interrogation. Elaine Scarry analyzes the role of interrogation in such cases as follows:

> Torture ... consists of a primary physical act, the infliction of pain, and a primary verbal act, the interrogation. The verbal act, in turn, consists of two parts, "the question" and "the answer," each with conventional connotations that wholly falsify it. "The question" is mistakenly understood to be "the motive"; "the answer" is mistakenly understood to be "the betrayal." The first mistake credits the torturer, providing him with a justification, his cruelty with an explanation. The second discredits the prisoner, making him rather than the torturer, his voice rather than his pain, the cause of his loss of self and world. These two misinterpretations are neither accidental nor unrelated. The one is an absolution of responsibility; the other is a conferring of responsibility; the two together turn the moral reality of torture upside down.[11]

The interrogation brings about, as we see, a reversal of the moral significance of torture. Such a reversal is fostered by the way the torturer conceives of her action, but also (and most importantly) by how such an action is perceived by third agents and, to some degree, by the victim herself. The question raised by the torturer is stereotypically regarded as providing the motive, the justification, for the infliction of pain; whereas the answer is interpreted as a betrayal and, consequently, as a symptom of the victim's moral degradation. This interpretation easily induces third agents (as well as the torturer) to concluding that the victim actually deserves the pain she is being inflicted. For she is viewed as a threat to the hospitable world they and the torturer herself, are at pains to protect. By this means, torture, which was perceived at the outset as a disgusting and almost unintelligible action, emerges now as an urgent and inescapable maneuver of self-defense. But why is it that third agents are so inclined to endorse the torturer's apology for her act? Why, in the absence of any specific evidence, do they regard the torturer as a defender of the human world and interpret the victim's eventual answer as a betrayal? There are many mechanisms that allow third agents to look away from the victim's suffering and side with the torturer's discourse, but they all seem to be fueled by a fundamental passion: fear and our aversion to it.

Several kinds of fear are, nevertheless, involved. There is, to begin with, fear of being attacked and hurt, no matter whether the assailant is a human being or a tiger. Insofar as the torturer may have *a specific reason* to assault a certain agent, there is no reason why third agents should be afraid of the weapon eventually turning to them. So, they may dispel their initial anxiety at the perception of the torturer's act by coming to think that the agent in question actually deserved it or, in general, that there was a reason for the attack that applies specifically to that agent. In the absence of such a reason, the attack would be regarded as arbitrary and unjustified, so that third agents would no longer feel protected from the torturer's eventual attack.

This fear, as it stands, is entirely unrelated to the humanity of the torturer. Third agents may thus be afraid of the latter in the same sense in which they may fear a tiger that has escaped the zoo or a bull grazing in the meadow. Yet third agents may feel specifically upset at the idea of regarding another human being (that is, the torturer) as an enemy, as someone who, instead of protecting them, may easily attack them. A certain kind of awareness of such a fact would render the primary expectation, "No one will hurt me," untenable. This comes as a second fear, a kind of fear that another human being, but not a tiger or a rock, may arouse. This fear comes together with a third one, though. The fear that an agent may have in virtue of a certain kind of awareness of the following counterfactual: "if I were attacked by another human being, no one would come in my defense because everybody would, like myself at present, be paralyzed by fear and, thereby, strongly inclined to find virtue in the torturer's act." As a result, third agents will not only be terrified by their perception of the torturer's arbitrariness, but by their awareness of the fact that, just by becoming a victim, they will appear as enemies to those who were supposed to protect them. This fear has then to do with the discovery that our confidence in the world is ungrounded and, therefore, that the world is, after all, a rather inhospitable place. Related to this, comes out a fourth fear, namely: the fear of guilt, since third agents may find it difficult to meet the demands that the victim legitimately makes upon them, and awareness of this failure would confirm her own contribution to the inhumanity of the world she dwells in.

Yet these four fears are easily exorcised by assuming that the interrogation was really justified and, consequently, that the victim poses an actual threat to the humanity of our world. By this simple procedure, the torturer's attack, which initially appeared as a challenge to our confidence in the world, is finally perceived as an attempt to preserve this space of confidence. If, on the contrary, third agent dared look at the victim's plight and listen to her claims, they would be haunted by fear. For this will induce them to perceive the torturer's attack as arbitrary and illegitimate, so that the world could no longer be experienced as a hospitable place to dwell in. No wonder, then, that third agents are ready to accept the faintest declaration on the torturer's side as a proper justification for her attack, since, by this means, they can easily identify themselves as inhabitants of a human world that the victim challenges and the torturer is meant to protect.

Identification of these four fears as lying at the bottom of third agents' tendency to side with the torturer's legitimizing discourse presupposes a certain conception of the self and its deliberative abilities. I have so far assumed that, at the outset, third agents tend to perceive the victim as helpless and the torturer, as well as the institutions that back up her actions, as a threat. The role of interrogation is thus designed to cover up that perception without fully canceling it out, so that third agents, at some level of awareness, may still sense the torturer as powerful and the victim as defenseless. For otherwise they wouldn't feel inclined to endorse the torturer's view in the absence of any evidence that might support it.

We may thus distinguish between *what third agents may sincerely declare* ("Torture is justified in order to preserve our human world from the victim's attack"), and what *their behavioral dispositions reveal* ("I am afraid of the torturer. She is so powerful, and the victim so weak"). We may thus say that there is a conflict between their *declarative awareness* of the significance of the torturer's act and the psychological attitudes that their behavior (linguistic and otherwise) may express or manifest, that is, their *expressive awareness* of that act. To be expressively aware of a situation S, involves, as we see, a disposition to act in a certain way, but what does this certain way consist of? To answer this question, I would like to introduce the notion of proportionality, namely, the idea that the agent's response must be proportional to the situation S. It is clear that third agents' expressive awareness of the torturer's arbitrariness leads them to deny that fact and, therefore, we can hardly regard their response as proportional to the situation at stake. This is why the kind of expressive awareness that third agents may have in those circumstances is to be described as biased or slanted.[12] For their response may still be regarded as proportional, although not to the situation S in itself, but to that situation in combination with the agent's fears. Hence, we may say that a *proper* expressive awareness of a situation S by an agent A is such that A feels motivated to respond proportionally to S, whereas expressive awareness of S will come up as slanted or biased insofar as some idiosyncratic feature in the agent's character is to be mentioned in order to make sense of the way she feels motivated to respond. The latter must then be conceived of as a deviation for the kind of proportionality that is present in proper cases of expressive awareness.

Be that as it may, it is clear that some expectations of protection play a central role in the way the three poles of torture relate to each other. We may state those expectations as follows and call "human" a world where they are satisfied:

> (PE) *Primary Expectation*: Nobody will illegitimately hurt me.
> (SE) *Secondary Expectation*: If someone illegitimately hurts me (or I am in a state of need), someone else will come to help and protect me.[13]

The victim certainly appeals to this notion of a human world to describe her plight; after all, it is the loss of the primary and the secondary expectations that Améry claims to have experienced with the first blow.[14] But the torturer and third agents also rely on that notion to justify their respective actions and attitudes. For the most robust warrant for the torturer's act has to do, as we have seen, with the need to protect the humanity of our world from the threat that the victim may represent. Third agents are eager to grant that view, for this way they may still trust the torturer and thereby experience their world as a safe and comfortable place to dwell in. All this requires a certain complexity of mind, as we have seen. We must thus assume the possibility of a mismatch between an agent's declarative awareness of what the torturer is actually doing and her expressive awareness of it. In light of this distinction, we may now examine a certain worry that the primary and secondary expectations will most likely raise.

The Human World: Egocentric vs. Impartial Expectations

Some may object that expectations (PE) and (SE) fall short of apprehending the nature of a world that might coherently be called 'human' and, therefore, that they could express an aspiration that qualifies as cosmopolitan. Inspired by some well-entrenched Kantian assumptions, they may insist that a human world (and the corresponding cosmopolitan aspiration) is to be conceived of as one where certain expectations are satisfied, though not just with regard to *me*, but to *anyone*. After all, a world may deserve to be called "human" only if it is moral, and it seems that the morality of a world is constitutively independent of the situation that any particular individual may occupy within it and, consequently, the expectations whose satisfaction are constitutive of a human (and, thereby, moral) world cannot be intelligibly individuated in egocentric terms.[15] Thus, one might conclude that a world, a society, a culture, can be regarded as human if and only if the following expectations are met:

> (IPE) *Impartial Primary Expectation*: Nobody will illegitimately hurt anyone.
> (ISE) *Impartial Secondary Expectation*: If someone is illegitimately hurt by someone else (or if someone is in a state of need), other people will come to help and protect the hurt (or the needy).

It seems then that (IPE) and (ISE) express expectations that could properly be regarded as cosmopolitan, since to qualify as such an expectation must not only address the world but everyone must be equally entitled to bear it. Hence, a shift from an egocentric to an impartial perspective seems to follow from a conception of "human" and "cosmopolitan" inspired by the demands of morality as they are to be interpreted in virtue of some deeply ingrained Kantian assumptions.

Still, we must beware of projecting some Kantian assumptions onto our description of any particular moral experience we may eventually decide to examine, for, otherwise, we run the risk of distorting the moral significance of any such experience insofar as we may just approve of (or condemn) it in light of how much it fits or clashes with our previous assumptions about morality. To avert such a risk, I am inclined to favor a sort of investigation that heeds the discernment of specific experiences of harm, so that some of our cultural stereotypes could be unearthed and eventually discarded as misleading.[16] Hence we better examine at this stage whether the expectations, as Améry presents them (that is, in egocentric terms), do properly express the victim's experience, so that later on we may discuss the significance of this analysis for our conception of morality. This proposal is indeed inspired by the demands of reflective equilibrium, that is, by the methodological approach that John Rawls vindicates and I gladly underwrite.

In this respect, to determine the content of an agent's expectations, we must again distinguish between what she may sincerely declare and what her behavioral dispositions must actually express or manifest. The latter must, indeed, be individuated in virtue of the conditions under which certain expectations are actually acquired and eventually abandoned or transformed. Thus, we cannot take it at face value what an agent sincerely claims to expect, since her avowals conflict with the kind of attitude that her behavior (linguistic and otherwise) may manifest in a number of different contexts. But, how do impartial expectations (IPE) and (ISE) (and the corresponding cosmopolitan aspiration) fare with regard to this methodological constraint?

Kantian views tend to conceive of these expectations neither as expectations that any particular person sincerely claims to have nor as expectations that are actually manifested in everyone's behavior, but as expectations that any rational agent must have within a world that can legitimately be called "human." Such expectations do thereby concern anyone and, consequently, they can hardly rely on any idiosyncratic feature that a particular agent might possess. It seems then that only rational considerations must figure in our deliberation as to whether such expectations ought to be either adopted or dropped. All this fits nicely with a Kantian approach like Rawls's insofar as he assumes that, in the original position, we must abstract away from our specific traits of character and just rely on our rational capabilities, as they are commonly understood in decision theory (i.e., as merely instrumental), together with a few additional resources like a sense of justice and the idea of a conception of the good.[17] The design itself of the original position is, in any case, assumed to guarantee the reasonableness of the principles that such deliberative process might eventually deliver. What are, however, the conditions under which a deliberator of this nature may actually lose or instead retain her impartial expectations (IPE) and (ISE)? It seems that any changes in this respect ought to track what she may justifiably believe about the world as a result of the evidence she has gathered about it. Hence, it seems that such expectations *ought to be challenged or lost by mere knowledge of the fact* that someone has actually been hurt and then abandoned in their distress.

Yet Améry's experience suggests that an agent's confidence in the world is not ruined by mere knowledge of those facts.[18] For, even though she may access to a significant amount of evidence that manifestly challenges (IPE) and (ISE), her confidence in the world will still remain intact. This experience seems to conflict with the Kantian approach. We must then either revise the conception of reason and the self that this approach vindicates or discard those expectations as irrational inclinations and, consequently, as divested of any normative import to the detriment of the Kantian initial defense of them. They cannot be dismissed as irrational, though, if the experience of harm is to be taken as the starting point of a philosophical reflection on morality. Hence, we must make room for some moral expectations to be anchored to our identity in ways that differ from both those of a mere irrational disposition and those of a sincere explicit endorsement. Our egocentric expectations seem to be ingrained in our lives in this alternative way, since they may easily resist the mere gathering of evidence to the contrary and still we have renounced to discard them as merely irrational. The depth our need to feel protected by our fellow creatures, to feel members of a hospitable world, is corroborated in the last sections by the fact that only quite a direct exposure to some experiences will really challenge her confidence in the world. A certain kind of awareness of some facts, deeper than mere knowledge of them, seems then to be required to account for the conditions under which our confidence in the world may be lost.

The question arises, however, as to whether expectations (PE) and (SE) would suffice to articulate a cosmopolitan aspiration, for they certainly address the world, but they are so focused on the bearer of such expectations that they could hardly express an aspiration that could qualify as cosmopolitan, that is, an aspiration to which everyone is entitled. It is true that these expectations fall short of meeting the Kantian standards of impartiality; this does not imply that they are egocentric to the point of being exclusively concerned with the fate of a particular person. In fact, the loss of such expectations expresses the victim's plight in a way that she must project it beyond her particular case.[19] For it seems constitutive of the sense of protection that (PE) and (SE) provide that they should be granted to her not in virtue of some idiosyncratic feature that she may happen to possess, but simply as a result of her human condition. For this seems to be the sort of the demand that (PE) and (SE) place on third agents: "I expect you not to hurt me, and also to help me in case of need, not in virtue of some specific, attractive traits of mine or some idiosyncrasy feature of yours, but just because I am your fellow creature." So, it seems that there are elements in my confidence in the world that point in the direction of impartiality, but it would be quite misleading to claim that only impartial expectations are involved, at least if impartiality is to be construed as Kantian views understand it.[20] Once the content of our primary and secondary expectations has been specified in terms that surpass the concern for the particular individual, it seems that their demands qualify as cosmopolitan, since they not only address the world but also entitle everyone to make them. Let us now examine whether the loss of such expectations on the victim's side should be construed as an irrational reaction or instead as a proportional to the facts and, ultimately, as having a bearing on how anyone else should face the world. I discard that it could reasonably be interpreted as an irrational reaction, and I vindicate such a loss is an inescapable move within the realm of reasons. A consequence of this will be that the cosmopolitan aspiration cannot be fulfilled. A few suggestions are finally made as to how it could at least be favored.

The Loss of Confidence in the World as an Irrational Reaction

Whenever a victim may lose her confidence in the world, she will lose it forever. This is, at least, what Améry claims at some point:

> Whoever has succumbed to torture can no longer feel at home in the world. The shame of destruction cannot be erased. Trust in the world, which already collapsed in part at the first blow, but in the end, under torture, fully, will not be regained. That one's fellow man was experienced as the anti-man remains in the tortured person as accumulated horror. It blocks the view into a world in which the principle of hope rules. One who was martyred is a defenseless prisoner of fear. It is *fear* that henceforth reigns over him. Fear -and also what is called resentment. They remain, and have scarcely a chance to concentrate into a seething, purifying thirst of revenge.[21]

But is it really so? Is it true that the victim will under no circumstance be able to recover her confidence in the world?[22] The specific way we may answer this question depends on how exactly this loss is to be interpreted. There is, for instance, a rather extended view according to which the victim's loss is simply the sequel of a trauma that some therapeutic procedures will eventually be able to heal. From this perspective, Améry's experience should be interpreted in light of those more ordinary cases where an agent may become extremely anxious as she enters a quiet place where she had been previously assaulted. Such a level of anxiety must thereby be dismissed as *irrational* insofar as it is *disproportionate* to the *actual* risk. The fact that a certain agent may feel that sort of tension will thereby emerge as purely idiosyncratic and, consequently, as providing no reason for us to respond similarly. It is clear that, from this perspective, the loss of confidence in the world could hardly be vindicated as irreversible, since the victim's actual capacity to recover will depend on the efficiency of available therapies, which may significantly vary from one to another individual case. To challenge this therapeutic interpretation of the victim's loss, let me briefly introduce a new case of harm, namely, that of Claude Eatherly, an American pilot directly involved in the dropping of the atomic bomb on Hiroshima. Clearly, we are not dealing here with a victim but with a perpetrator instead. A few years after his action, he was tormented by nightmares where figures of the injured appeared in his dreams and, in general, a deep sense of guilt haunted him. These emotional reactions, together with some outlandish actions that he may have done, were publicly interpreted as symptoms of a severe psychic impairment, badly in need of psychiatric treatment. As a result, he was soon confined to a military asylum, where he ended up regarding his own anxieties as part of an attempt to articulate a more *proportional* response to his deed.

We may now examine some of the metaphysical and epistemic assumptions that lie behind the sort of psychiatric institution to which Eatherly was confined, that is, a kind of institution were the treatments provided were exclusively addressed to release the patient's allegedly irrational anchorage to the past. This sort of institution may apparently find some philosophical ground in a subjectivist view about values, which may, in turn, be regarded as an implication of the disenchanted conception of world that the natural sciences supposedly favor. Hence, insofar as psychiatric institutions may like to inherit the social prestige of the natural sciences,[23] they better adapt to this worldview and articulate their practices on the assumption that there are no moral or evaluative features in the world. Moreover, psychiatric institutions tend to assume that a subjectivist view about value can only be properly honored if their therapeutic practices put aside any moral aspects of the situation at stake, given that they do not exist from an objective point of view. As a result, issues such as whether a victim of torture may legitimately reject any therapeutic procedure before her moral damage had been properly repaired, or whether the torturer should carry the weight of her deed or instead be alleviated as efficiently as possible, will be systematically neglected. They will not even leave it for the patient to decide as a matter of personal choice. The institution simply operates on the assumption that moral matters are irrelevant to its purposes.

It is easy to see however that, even if the subjectivist view proclaims the need to be axiologically blind as we investigate the world as it is in itself, the actual practices and policies of any psychiatric institution that might subscribe to such a view will inexorably involve a number of morally significant commitments. The application of psychiatric treatment guided by the subjectivist view implies, for instance, that Eatherly's guilt and Améry's distrust are to be dispensed with as inappropriate, pathological reactions, that is, as reactions they must get rid of insofar as they may interfere with our natural orientation toward the future.[24] These emotional attitudes are not thereby approached as part of a morally relevant (and rational) response to a certain experience of harm. Yet the choice of this interpretation presupposes a commitment to a certain view about the role that morality must play in our lives. For the fact that such a stance is adopted with regard to certain situations may be significant from a moral perspective. Thus, we may say that those psychiatric institutions that are inspired by the subjectivist view cannot legitimize their practices on the axiological neutrality that the latter view seems to impose. For, by choosing their therapies and practices to be morally blind, they express a particular moral attitude toward those morally significant situations they may actually confront, which as such conflicts with the alleged moral neutrality of that view.

It may be relevant to stress at this point that, in order to regard Eatherly's response as irrational and, thereby, as in need of some medical treatment, we cannot exclusively rely on the fact that his anxiety and fears were not under his control. For there are many psychological states that an agent may not control and, nevertheless, lie at the core of any significant notion of rationality. Think, for instance, of perceptual beliefs. Almost none of our perceptual beliefs are directly under our control, but nobody views this fact as a reason to dismiss them as inappropriate, just the opposite. For the idea itself of an agent that might modify her perceptual beliefs at will is almost unintelligible or, in other words, the mere fact that a certain psychological state could thus be modified counts as a most serious reason to discard it as a perceptual belief at all.[25] But, more to the point, it is clear that a mother's appalling sorrow for her daughter's sudden death can hardly be regarded as irrational. It is instead a sign of the intensity of her motherly love that she may not be able to get rid of her grief at will and, consequently, that the latter may only (and partly) wane after a proper time of mourning. Hence, the concern about Eatherly's guilt (or Améry's distrust or Levi's shame) cannot just be that it escapes his control. The relevant issue should instead be whether his guilt (and the corresponding anxieties and fears) is *proportional* to his deed and, therefore, whether it appropriately contributes to shaping his life.

It follows, however, that, if Eatherly's response turned out to be relevantly proportional to his deed (and, *mutatis mutandis*, Améry's and Levi's, as well), then we would be forced to acknowledge that, contrary to what some therapeutic approaches appear to assume, the most meaningful life he could live is necessarily disfigured or misshaped. Moreover, we may end up acknowledging that the facts by which Eatherly's life has been legitimately disfigured ought to have an impact on the shape of our own lives as well. And, from this perspective, Améry's loss could hardly be perceived as just a disgrace of his but as matter of concern everyone. Not only because it is a situation that calls for our care and consideration or because one might eventually fall into Améry's position, but mainly because his predicament reveals that his loss is grounded on some serious reasons that apply to us all to the effect that, if Améry has reason to lose his confidence, everyone has. To motivate this view, I briefly argue that the question "*Why* does Améry lose his confidence in the world?" may legitimately be raised within the *realm of reasons*, that is, the *why* in that question points to facts that Améry has become (expressively) aware of, such that they make it reasonable for a person of his character to lose her confidence in the world. A further issue to be considered is whether the relevant aspects of his character are to be regarded as merely idiosyncratic or instead as constitutive of an agent's humanity, so that his reasons will become anyone's.[26]

The Realm of Reasons and the Faustian Ideal

As Améry and Bruno Bettelheim repeatedly emphasized, some victims of torture manage to make sense of their experience in such a way that their confidence in the world remains intact.[27] This is the case of *believers* in a *redemption* plan. They try to make sense of the horrendous harm they may have suffered by interpreting every instance of it as a necessary step toward a better future whose particular details are, nevertheless, inscrutable. The believer often delegates to a superior mind, either God or Stalin, the ultimate significance of the facts she is facing and by these means her deepest hurt is averted. From this perspective, no matter how terrible and inhuman a situation might be, there is still the hope that humanity will in the end prevail and this may provide sufficient consolation.[28] Faith in an inscrutable redemption plan may help the victim to make sense of her harm, but it often contributes to the production itself of harm. For massacres and genocides are often legitimized in such terms, that is, as a necessary action for a promising human future. Hence, the kind of representation that may, at some stage, comfort the victim is often the source of her own plight, as well.

Not all victims are able to retain their faith in a redemption plan; as Bettelheim emphasizes, people belonging to the German and Austrian middle class were especially vulnerable to the atrocities of the Nazi extermination camps.[29] Even if they were active members of one or another religion, what deep in their minds made sense of their lives was some sort of Faustian ideal, that is, the conviction that our daily efforts contribute to a better future, that is, to the social, economic, and technological *progress* of our society and the humanity as a whole. From that perspective, their capacity to make sense of their own activities and endeavors was conditional on the assumption that they were contributing not only to their personal progress but to the overall advance of mankind as such. The relevance of keeping such overall progress in view, and not merely the furthering of one's own individual interests, indicates a bond with one's fellow creatures that goes beyond what a fair contract may deliver and may be adequately expressed by the dictum "no man is an island."[30]

It seems, then, that torture has a devastating effect on the victim with a Faustian ideal only if it comes with the recognition that torture (and, in general, harm) is in a relevant sense inexorable. What such a victim may experience in her flesh and soul is not only that scientific and technological development may turn out to be *insufficient* to protect her, but something more significantly disturbing than that. For she will painfully realize that technological development *can be* (and, thereby, *will be*) put to work in the opposite direction, namely: to increase our capacity to produce harm and devastation. One of the most frightening aspects of the Nazi's regime was precisely that it emerged as a *highly innovative and efficient machinery*. Let me examine here just one of the psychological mechanisms that lies behind the efficiency of this machinery.[31] "But then, almost amazingly, it dawns on one that the fellows not only have leather coats and pistols, but also faces: not 'Gestapo faces' with twisted noses, hypertrophied chins, pockmarks, and knife scars, as might appear in a book, but rather faces like anyone else's. Plain, ordinary faces. And the enormous perception at a later stage, one that destroys all abstractive imagination, makes clear to us how the plain, ordinary faces become Gestapo faces after all."[32] As Améry points out, understanding these facts weakens the victim. It extracts from her any hope in a human future.[33] If only so-called Gestapo faces were prepared to torture, then one might reasonably expect torture to take place rather exceptionally insofar as ordinary faces could easily outnumber and counteract them. By contrast, if everyday faces can easily be transformed into Gestapo faces, if anybody could readily torture (or actively cooperate with a torturer) in some circumstances, then the fact that a normal person does not actually torture (or does not actually cooperate with a torturer) turns out to be purely *accidental*. For, in some circumstances, almost anyone might easily be induced to torture. Recognition of this fact alters the victim's perception of normal faces in everyday circumstances. It undercuts her capacity to trust the world. In the punishment cell, she realizes that Gestapo faces are ordinary ones, but, after her liberation, she tends to see Gestapo faces in the ordinary people whom she may daily encounter. The cruelty of the SS transcends the walls of the camp and transforms her view of mankind: the victim feels forced to accept as a basic aspect of our human condition that the elderly women who today so kindly welcomes her, may tomorrow report her presence to the Gestapo.

Some may surely reply that, no matter how moving Améry's experience might be, his reaction is still irrational, given that, from the fact that normal people may torture in some *exceptional* circumstances, nothing follows as to whether a normal person may be prepared to torture in *normal* circumstances. Consequently, it sounds quite unreasonable that anyone might lose her confidence in expectation (PE) by the mere fact that, in some exceptional circumstances, such an expectation will likely fail. I would like to say, to begin with, that this objection neglects a crucial feature of the victim's loss. The content of (PE) is not "In normal circumstances, I will not illegitimately be hurt," but "I will not illegitimately be hurt, period." For only the latter provides us with the need of protection and homeliness that gave rise to them in the first place. Even in normal circumstances, the victim may be incapable of trusting the world just because, in some other circumstances, *the same people* who are now kind to him, or even love him, may rather easily contribute to her destruction.[34] It follows that whenever third agents are needed most, they tend to cooperate with the torturer, and, as a result, there is reason to deny expectation (SE) once expectation (PE) has been infringed. So we may conclude that, even though torturers and third agents can't help trusting the world, one should not trust it; this truth does shape the way in which some victims stand in the world, so that they can't experience it, not even some privileged regions of it, like home.

Conclusion

In this chapter, I have examined Améry's elaboration of his experience of a victim of torture in order to identify a certain cosmopolitan aspiration. The loss of confidence in the world is the way he describes the impact that this experience had upon his life. He regards this confidence as composed of two expectations of protection, namely: (PE) "Nobody will illegitimately hurt me" and (SE) "If someone illegitimately hurts me (or I am in a state of need), someone else will come to help and protect me."

I have argued, to begin with, that (PE) and (SE) constitutively involve the appeal to third agents as seems to be confirmed by the role of interrogation in some standard cases of torture. In general, we can say that third agents feel threatened by the act of torture and are inclined to interpret it in ways that may preserve their confidence in the world. Such a maneuver of self-deception comes to confirm the depth of our need to trust the world and, consequently, of the cosmopolitan aspiration associated with it.

Some people might object, however, to the fact that those expectations of protection as they stand, that is, stated in egocentric terms could properly express a cosmopolitan aspiration or, in other words, the idea of a human world. For to qualify as cosmopolitan an aspiration must not only address the world, as Améry's expectations certainly do, but also entitle everyone to make it. And the fact that expectations (PE) and (SE) are stated in egocentric terms seems to be at odds with this constraint.

I have replied, however, that these two expectations do involve a projection beyond the particular individual to which "me" might refer, for it seems constitutive of the sense of protection that such expectations provide that they should be granted to any particular individual not in virtue of any specific trait but simply because of her human condition. And, yet, this transition from the particular to the universal cannot coherently be construed in light of the Kantian approach, that is, as involving two impartial expectations (IPE) and (ISE). It is clear that an agent's ability to shape her life in light of these impartial expectations could hardly depend on what might actually happen to her, that is, the kind of experience she might actually have faced, since, otherwise, we would have reason to identify her expectations as including an egocentric element. And, yet, I have argued that only the victim of torture, unlike the torturer and third agents, loses her confidence in the world. Hence, it seems that this egocentric element is constitutive of the experience of the victim of harm and the cosmopolitan aspiration that is expressed by her loss of confidence in the world. It is an egocentric way of addressing the world that, nevertheless, includes a projection beyond oneself onto any other human being.

Once the content of the cosmopolitan aspiration involved in the experience of the victim of torture has been elucidated, I have examined the question as to whether her loss of confidence in the world belongs to the realm of reason or should instead be discarded as a disproportionate, irrational reaction. In this respect I have stressed that those therapeutic institutions that favor the latter can hardly rely on any sort of axiological impartiality. And once we accept that values are also involved in therapeutic response to harm, we are in a position to vindicate Claude Eatherly's guilt as rational insofar as it may be proportionate to his deed. In other words, we can make sense of the idea that he could only preserve his humanity (and, in this sense, to honor a certain cosmopolitan aspiration) if he allowed his life to be disfigured by his expressive awareness of the moral significance of his deed. This is, however, a rare achievement. Third agents tend to side with the torturer's view so that they may still trust the world. In some sense, we could say that their need to trust the world stands in the way of a world that could justifiably be trusted and, therefore, of a world where the cosmopolitan aspiration could be fulfilled. And this is precisely the fact the victim of torture becomes poignantly aware of.

The question arises, indeed, as to what could be done in these circumstances or, more specifically, how could the cosmopolitan aspiration be at least cultivated given that it cannot be fulfilled and, perhaps, not even advanced. This is not a question I meant to specifically address in this chapter and, yet, a few ideas have been suggested in this direction.[35] First, it seems that this question will require different answers depending on one's location with regard to the three poles of torture. Second, it has been stressed that, regarding the torturer and third agents, their ability to honor the cosmopolitan aspiration should be more a matter of becoming expressively aware of certain facts by being exposed to them than just becoming declaratively aware of them. Moreover, they should be ready to allow such expressive awareness to disfigure one's life to a certain degree. And, yet, there is no way in which they could legitimately feel satisfied insofar as they are bound to preserve their confidence in the world and leave the victim alone with her loss.[36]

JOSEP E. CORBÍ is Philosophy Professor in the Department of Metaphysics and Theory of Knowledge at the University of Valencia. A specialist in epistemology, philosophy of mind, and meta-ethics, his most recent book is *Morality, Self-Knowledge, and Human Suffering: An Essay on the Loss of the World* (Routledge, 2012).

Notes

1. Jean Améry, *At the Mind's Limit* (Bloomington: Indiana University Press, 1980).
2. This claim is challenged by the fact that US soldiers in Abu Ghraib had not only tortured some Muslim prisoners but taken pictures of themselves in such circumstances in order to distribute them to their friends and relatives. This is certainly a novel and striking situation that seems to call for an explanation, as Susan Sontag has emphasized in "What Have We Done?," Guardian, March 24, 2004. The need itself of an explanation seems to confirm the extent to which it is assumed that torture is to be kept out of sight and often denied.
3. Elaine Scarry, *The Body in Pain: The Making and Unmaking of the World* (Oxford: Oxford University Press, 1987), 39.
4. As Scarry points out: "So, for the person in pain, so incontestably and unnegotiably present is it that 'having pain' may come to be thought of as the most vibrant example of what it is to 'have certainty,' while for the other person it is so elusive that 'hearing about pain' may exist as the primary model of what it is 'to have doubt'" (ibid., 4). Relatedly: "How is it that one person can be in the presence of another person in pain and not know it—not know it to the point where he himself inflicts it, and goes on inflicting it?" (12). This perplexity seems to calls for a distinction between two ways of being aware of the victim's pain. For this purpose, I later on introduce the distinction *a merely declarative awareness* of a certain fact and *an expressive awareness* of it.
5. See Simone Weil, "The Iliad or the Poem of Force," in *Simone Weil: An Anthology*, ed. S. Miles (New York: Weidenfeld and Nicolson, 1986), 165.
6. See Scarry, *The Body in Pain*, 3–11.
7. Some may object that Améry's experience, like any other individual experience, is after all merely idiosyncratic, whereby nothing of significance could be derived from it into the nature of torture. This raises the rather general issue as to how the relevance of any particular experience is to be assessed. The first thing to be noticed is that this line of objection also applies (and, presumably, more severely) to the series of examples and counterexamples that are typically discussed in thought experiments, except, of course, if one is in the business of providing necessary and sufficient conditions for a certain X. Once such a project is dropped, as it seems it should concerning any matters of importance, then examples and counterexamples are to be assessed for their respective *relevance*, and, from this perspective, some reason must be provided to justify why sketchy examples should generally be preferred to full-fledged experiences. In either case, it seems clear that what really matters is whether the examination of any particular example or experience sheds some light on the experience of harm or, in other words, contributes to *making sense* of one or another aspect of it. "Making sense" is, indeed, relative to a certain audience and involves a certain amount of circularity; cf. Bernard Williams, *Truth and Truthfulness* (Princeton, NJ: Princeton University Press, 2002), chap. 10. For the precise boundaries of the "we" whose understanding is supposed to be significantly favored by Améry's experience, must be fixed by an appeal to some common moral intuitions that, in turn, are closely connected to our capacity to perceive some experiences of harm as central or paradigmatic. The study of Améry's experience will then appear as pertinent and justified only insofar as his reflections on torture may eventually shed some light on some other experiences of harm and the ways in which one should relate to them.
8. Améry, *At the Mind's Limit*, 28.
9. Noelle McAfee, in Chapter 2 of this volume, introduces the concept of addressing the world as central to her account of cosmopolitanism. As we shall soon see, Améry's analysis of the experience of torture involves a similar invocation insofar as third agents are expected to

be not mere spectators of the victim's plight, but actively contribute to her recovery and reparation. Améry claims, however, that the notion of dignity can hardly make sense of the victim's experience, and vindicates the loss of confidence in the world as a more suitable concept. As we shall see in the third section of this chapter, this will diminish the capacity of a Kantian view to account for the normative aspects of the expectations of protection that, according to Améry, torture tends to undermine.

10. A normative demand certainly forms a part of the victim's expectations. She assumes that third agents *owe* her a certain response. Someone may think that the legitimacy of this demand is to be grounded on the fact that the expectations at stake are obviously reciprocal. But having reciprocal expectations fall short of imposing mutual demands. Something else must be added.

11. Scarry, *The Body in Pain*, 37. Scarry presents the interrogation as a constitutive aspect of torture, disregarding those cases of torture where the infliction of pain is not accompanied by this specific verbal act. In fact, article 1 of the UN Convention Against Torture enumerates a significant number of modes of torture where interrogation is absent.

12. José Medina, in Chapter 7 of this volume, stresses the role of ignorance in our ability to feel comfortably at home in the world. As he forcefully argues, the denial of some truths is not a peripheral aspect of one's place within it, but lies at the core of it, as happens with white ignorance. An exercise of self-estrangement or disidentification (and therefore being ready to endure the discomfort that comes with it) seems required if such a bias is to be tempered and the cost that the victim has to pay for it partly repaired. This is an idea that not only Medina but Jeff Edmonds (Chapter 8), Jennifer Hansen (Chapter 13), and Jessica Wahman (Chapter 12) stress here as well. The parallel notion of hospitality toward the stranger, the migrant, the other is vindicated by McAfee (Chapter 2).

13. "The expectation of help, the certainty of help, is indeed one of the fundamental experiences of human beings, and probably also of animals. . . . The expectation of help is as much a constitutional psychic element as is the struggle for existence. Just a moment, the mother says to her child who is moaning from pain, a hot-water bottle, a cup of tea is coming right away, we won't let you suffer so! I'll prescribe you a medicine, the doctor assures, it will help you. Even on the battlefield, the Red Cross ambulances find their way to the wounded man. In almost all situations in life where there is bodily injury there is also the expectation of help; the former is compensated by the latter. But with the first blow from a policeman's fist, against which there can be no defense and which no helping hand will ward off, a part of our life ends and it can never again be revived" (Améry, *At the Mind's Limit*, 29).

14. It may be relevant to stress at this point that the loss of confidence in the world is not specific of torture, but may be the outcome of some other experiences of harm, such as war or rape. There is, besides, the more complex issue as to whether it may come in degrees or, perhaps, the more pertinent question as to how transient and deep such a loss may be in each case. A virtue of this question is that it allows us to apply Améry's notion to make sense of some less extreme experiences of harm like school-yard bullying.

15. Both the primary and the secondary expectations comprise a normative demand. So, whenever the primary expectation might fail, the secondary expectation involves a cosmopolitan address that, to put it in McAfee's terms, "is the announcement of the situation that *ought to be* other than the one that is" (see Chapter 2, page 29 of this volume). I argue however that, contrary to what she assumes, a Kantian approach can hardly account for the normative import that is constitutive of this cosmopolitan address.

16. For a more detailed examination of this point, see Josep E. Corbí, *Morality, Self-Knowledge, and Human Suffering* (New York: Routledge, 2012), chap. 1. An exercise of self-estrangement

or disidentification as a result not only of the exercise of one's imagination, which is prey to all sorts of misconceptions, but of one's exposure to some situations that shake one's homely space and highlights how much of it rests on the denial of some deeply upsetting facts. This idea is thoroughly explored in this volume: see Edmonds (Chapter 8), Hansen (Chapter 13), Medina (Chapter 7), and Wahman (Chapter 12).

17. See John Rawls, *A Theory of Justice* (Oxford: Oxford University Press, 1999), 125; John Rawls, *Justice as Fairness* (Cambridge, MA: Harvard University Press, 2001), 18–19; and John Rawls, *Political Liberalism* (New York: Columbia University Press, 2005), 19.

18. Cf. S. Alexievich, *Zinky Boys. Soviet Voices from a Forgotten War* (London: Chatto and Windus, 1992); Primo Levi, *The Drowned and the Saved* (London: Abacus, 1986), chap. 3; and my *Morality, Self-Knowledge, and Human Suffering* (New York: Routledge, 2012), chaps. 1–3.

19. See section 5.3 in my *Morality, Self-Knowledge, and Human Suffering*.

20. Needless to say, the emphasis on impartiality is certainly associated with the normative import that both (PE) and (SE) certainly carry with them and whose legitimacy calls for some justification. Pressure in the direction of the impartial expectations may thus be regarded as part of an attempt to ground such normative import within the framework set by Kantian views. Hence, were we to stick to the egocentric expectations suggested by Améry, an alternative account of their legitimacy ought to be elaborated, although this task must be left for another occasion (cf. *Morality, Self-Knowledge, and Human Suffering*, chaps. 5–6).

21. Améry, *At the Mind's Limit*, 40. Cf. Levi, *The Drowned and the Saved*, 22; Bruno Bettelheim, *Surviving and Other Essays* (New York: Alfred A. Knopf, 1981), 19–37.

22. Megan Craig, in Chapter 9 of this volume, explores Emerson's reflection on the impact that the death of his son had on his life Here, the worry is not that the sense of loss will last forever, but just the opposite, namely, that no loss is serious enough to stay for long and thus be acknowledged as part of one's identity: "Two year on, the loss of his son has proved no more substantial or lasting than any other experience, no more *real*. Sobered by the meaninglessness of loss, Emerson articulates the melancholy realization that the loss of his child fails to become a point of contact with something real, or a lasting sense of something *really having happened*. The experience that should have altered everything, the death that should have meant the end of life, ends everything in some sense, and yet ends nothing" (145). Yet, in the case of a son's death, his father's recovery does not constitutively depend on other people's attitudes, whereas the victim of torture (or so I argue, following up from Améry's view) can only legitimately recover her confidence in the world if third agents are ready to take care of her plight. So, we could conclude that the victim's recovery is anchored to someone else's attitude in a way that a person's attitude toward the death of her son is not.

23. Cf. Marcia Angell, "The Epistemic of Mental Illness: Why?," *New York Review of Books*, June 23, 2011, www.nybooks.com/articles/archives/2011/jun/23/epidemic-mental-illness-why; and "The Illusions of Psychiatry," *New York Review of Books*, July 14, 2011, www.nybooks.com/articles/archives/2011/jul/14/illusions-of-psychiatry.

24. Cf. Améry, *At the Mind's Limit*, 72.

25. This is not to deny, of course, that an agent might intentionally engage in a certain process that could *indirectly* lead to a change in her beliefs on some specific matters.

26. Some may object, however, that after all the victim's loss of confidence is the outcome of a terrible situation and, therefore, her voice will necessarily be distorted by the emotional impact, so that it can hardly guide us in the articulation of a proper response to her plight. This reply sounds, though, just as a further manifestation of the conviction that emotional involvement distorts, whereas distance potentiates our deliberative capabilities. This is not, however, a conviction we could take for granted at this stage. For we are at a point in our search

of reflective equilibrium where our general views about moral deliberation are still to be examined in the light of some particular moral experiences.

27. Améry, *At the Mind's Limit*, chap. 1; Bettelheim, *Surviving*, 19–37; Levi, *The Drowned and the Saved*, chap. 6.

28. The *religious* believer relies on the idea that he will be *personally* compensated for his present suffering and distress. Not so for the *communist* believer, who finds consolation in the idea that her action will contribute to the dawning of a human world, which she is, nevertheless, unlikely to enjoy personally. This second attitude apprehends the specific way in which the confidence in human progress may be consolatory.

29. Bettelheim, *Surviving*, 56–57.

30. Levi, *The Drowned and the Saved*, 65.

31. For further discussion concerning the nature and power of this psychological mechanism, see sections 2.6, 5.4–5.6 in my *Morality, Self-Knowledge, and Human Suffering*.

32. Améry, *At the Mind's Limit*, 25. Cf. Levi, *The Drowned and the Saved*, 52–67; Hannah Arendt, *Eichmann in Jerusalem: A Report on the Banality of Evil* (London: Penguin, 1994).

33. Hansen elaborates on the notion of hope in a very interesting manner. She regards hope as an emotion that includes a cognitive aspect within it. This is why hope is not a mere wish, but involves some sort engagement on the agent's side to promote the state of affairs she hopes for. Moreover, Hansen stresses that our hopes must be anchored to a specific social space: "In this sense, our hopes are reasonable; they emerge out of a specific cultural locatedness. Our hopes emerge in response to specific needs that arise in specific contexts. And, those needs are intelligible to those who share a form of life with us. So too is hope intelligible as a response to those needs" (see Chapter 13, page 228 of this volume). Améry's experience tends to confirm this point. After all, it is his situation as a victim of torture (that is, a very specific position within the social space) that makes him lose his confidence in the world and, thereby, give up a fundamental kind of hope. My line of argument has been that this loss, far from being an irrational reaction on his side, counts as a move within the space of reasons, and, as a result, the cognitive aspects of hope are acknowledged. This move, however, is unavailable to those who have not had their flesh torn by the cutting edge and, in this respect, a pluralistic epistemology (that is, the kind of epistemology that Hansen defends as fundamental for a cosmopolitan hope) may help reduce the deep epistemic asymmetries that are constitutive of the three poles of harm but will hardly cancel them out.

34. Moreover, it is not hard to demonstrate that those circumstances where normal people may easily be induced to torture are not as exceptional as they may seem, and also that they tend to overlap with those where third agents are most inclined to avert their eyes from the victim's plight. See S. Milgram, *Obedience to Authority: An Experimental View* (New York: Harper and Row, 1974); Günther Anders, *Wir Eichmann Söhne* (Munich: C. H. Beck, 1988); Claude Eatherly, *Burning Conscience: The Case of the Hiroshima Pilot* (Saint Paul, MN: Paragon House, 1961); Corbí, *Morality*, 2.6.

35. For further discussion, see my *Morality, Self-Knowledge, and Human Suffering*, chap. 7.

36. This chapter draws on materials published as part of chapter 2 in *Morality, Self-Knowledge, and Human Suffering: An Essay on the Loss of Confidence in the World* (New York: Routledge, 2012). Credit is due to Routledge for authorizing partial reproduction in this volume. I must, finally, acknowledge that research for this chapter has been funded by the Spanish Ministry of Science and Innovation (BFF2003-08335-C03-01, HUM2006-08236, PR2008-0221, CSD2009-00056) and the Valencian Regional Ministry of Culture, Education and Sports (GRUPOS04/48, GV04B-251, ACOMP06/13).

11 Climate Change and Place
Delimiting Cosmopolitanism

Nancy Tuana

> All conduct is interaction between elements of human nature and the environment, natural and social.
> —John Dewey, *Human Nature and Conduct*
>
> In fact, as a woman, I have no country. As a woman I want no country. As a woman my country is the whole world.
> —Virginia Woolf, *Three Guineas*

FEW WOULD CONTEST the claim that climate change raises complex and profound ethical issues including questions of responsibility for climate change related damages, how to act in the face of the deep uncertainties (how much and how fast) regarding the future impacts of climate change, what current generations owe future generations, or how to balance the costs of climate change related mitigation and adaptation with other global problems like poverty and healthcare.

The most significant human impact on the climate results from fossil-fuel burning, which increases the atmospheric concentrations of greenhouse gases. This leads to a warming of the lower atmosphere, and with that warming, various climate-related changes. The Fifth Assessment Report of the Intergovernmental Panel on Climate Change (IPCC) listed under high to very high confidence a series of impacts of climate change that have already been observed, including shifts in terrestrial, freshwater, and marine species migration patterns, ranges, and abundances in response to ongoing climate change; overall negative impact on crop yields; climate extremes (heat waves, droughts, floods, hurricanes) leading to increased risk of both ecosystems and many human systems such as food production and water supply, morbidity and mortality, mental health and human well-being; and climate-related hazards exacerbating other stressors leading to negative impacts on livelihoods for people living in poverty.[1]

The Environmental Justice Foundation provides the following snapshot of the impact of current and future climate change: "Every year climate change is attributable for the deaths of over 300,000 people, seriously affects a further 325 million people, and causes economic losses of US $125 billion. Four billion people are vulnerable to the effects of climate change and 500-600 million people—around 10% of the planet's human population—are at extreme risk. As such, climate change has been recognised as a fundamental threat to human rights."[2] The impacts of climate change are likely to impact all people, but the harms and benefits of climate impacts will not be evenly distributed, thus raising social justice concerns.

While there has been a clear recognition in the philosophical literature of the ethical dimensions of climate change, comparatively little attention has been paid to the ethical aspects of place in the context of a changing climate.[3] My focus for this volume is on approaches to climate change from those who embrace a cosmopolitan lens. By attending to the ways we are in place and recognizing the deep interdependence of humans and environments, we come to appreciate the importance of an enriched conception of inter-relationality that goes beyond the human interdependencies that are the focus of cosmopolitanism. My goal is to argue that attention to place serves as the groundwork in support of a more robust conception of interdependence necessary to any adequate cosmopolitanism.

Climate Change and Cosmopolitanism

Climate change has, for many, become the quintessential "wicked problem" for ethics and for policy formation.[4] In addition, it is well recognized that responses to climate chance cannot be based on the needs or desires of select groups or nations, for all actions, and inactions, will have global impacts. The global nature of the impacts of climate change and the growing efforts to forge an international response have given rise to heightened attention to issues of global justice.[5] The urgency of the problem and the belief that the solutions will require a concerted international effort have led to renewed attention to cosmopolitanism as a political and a moral theory thought to be adequate to the issues raised by climate change. David Held, for example, argues that cosmopolitanism is key to addressing "the paradox of our times: the inconsistency between the global nature of our pressing problems (from climate change to nuclear proliferation and global poverty) and contemporary forms of governance rooted in the nation-state."[6] Defining cosmopolitanism as "an ethical approach to political life, from the global to the local level," Held contends that given human interdependence, "existing institutions which address the global nature of risk are not fit for [that] purpose" and that "the generation of risks, and the costs borne by their realization, are not commensurate with the nature and form of their governance."[7]

Simon Caney advocates what he calls "a distinctive cosmopolitan theory of justice" as the most appropriate response to climate change.[8] Like Caney, many have argued that the global dimensions of the issue constitute a morally relevant difference that requires a distinctive moral and political approach. Pogge's theory of moral and political cosmopolitanism, which he applies to poverty as well as to climate change impacts, begins with the claim that both problems are perpetuated and often made worse by historical and contemporary economic, political, and legal aspects of the global order.[9] Increased vulnerability to climate-related impacts that are interrelated to nonclimatic factors, such as patterns of poverty and the intersecting and multidimensional inequalities that result from uneven development processes, will not be solved without attention to the complex systems of economic exploitation that are an unfortunate yet intractable feature of our global economy. As many have documented, the continent most vulnerable both to poverty and to negative climate impacts—Africa—has been the stage of many waves of economic exploitation. As DuBois proclaimed: "The methods by which this continent has been stolen have been contemptible and dishonest beyond expression. Lying treaties, rivers of rum, murder, assassination, mutilation, rape, and torture have marked the progress of Englishman, German, Frenchman, and Belgian on the dark continent."[10]

Appropriate responses, whether to climate impacts or to poverty, then, cannot be merely a state-based response, for the units of damage and even more the units of responsibility, cross state borders, particularly given the growth of global corporations. Given histories of colonialization and of economic globalization, the underlying causes of global warming are not accurately attributable to the state level, but must rather be measured at level of the global order. Thus the growing conclusion of theorists such as Held, Pogge, and Caney is that the only adequate response whether to climate change or poverty will be a global response aimed at both addressing and reforming the global order, as well as determining a fair way to compensate for damages it has caused. Caney confirms that "an adequate theory of justice in relation to climate change must explain in what ways global climate change affects persons' entitlements and it must do so in a way that (i) is sensitive to the particularities of the environment; (ii) explores the issues that arise from applying principles at the global rather than the domestic level; and (iii) explores the intergenerational dimensions of global climate change."[11] Cosmopolitanism holds promise for becoming such a theory.

As many have noted, cosmopolitanism has multiple meanings. For those like Caney, Held, and Pogge who focus on issues such as global climate change, it is presented as an approach to global justice, rights and obligations, and the institutions that can sustain them. This version of cosmopolitanism involves a critique of the nation-state as the appropriate domain for action, and rather views the unit to which a theory of justice applies to be that of global humanity. This is typically seen as requiring transnational institutions to establish and ensure justice practices. Other deployments of the term *cosmopolitanism* focus more on the cultural dimensions of cosmopolitanism. These accounts typically involve a conception of the self that rejects the view that an individual's well-being, identity, or agency depends on membership within or identification with determinate cultural groups. These different strands of cosmopolitanism are sometimes interconnected as with Kwame Anthony Appiah's *Cosmopolitanism: Ethics in a World of Strangers*, where he argues that "as every human community has gradually been drawn into a single web of trade and a global network of information" philosophy must embrace new ways of thinking not only about rights and responsibilities, but also about how we understand each other.[12] This means finding a way to balance global responsibilities to one another, while at the same time appreciating and respecting our differences.

While there are many concerns with the conception of the cosmopolitan self, one primary concern is the question of priority. In other words, is such a self-practice attainable or even desirable prior to a cosmopolitan practice of justice? Quoting DuBois, Marilyn Fischer answers in the negative: "How can love of humanity appeal as a motive to nations whose love of luxury is built on the inhuman exploitation of human beings?"[13] Fischer translates this question into the challenge: "Can a people become cosmopolitan until these intertwined local, national, and global injustices are eliminated and replaced by just economic, social, and political relations?"[14]

Where I enter this conversation is not with answering this query, but rather by enlarging it through thinking, so to speak, "on the ground." I argue that interdependence is essential to cosmopolitanism, and that any account of cosmopolitanism, whether focused on conceptions of culture or of justice, that ignores the complex interconnections between individuals and their environments is too *thin*. Ignoring our complex interdependencies with the world we are of and in obscures important elements of who we are as individuals and as communities. These are relations that theories and practices of justice, by any definition, must take into account. My concern is that as those who address the ethical dimensions of climate change, including those who embrace a cosmopolitan lens, ignore important *embodied* and *affective* components of the impacts of climate change that can only be appreciated by a *thick* account of interdependency, one that takes into account not just human interdependencies but also human-environment interactions. While I believe this omission to be the result of the overwhelming attention in this literature to principle-based approaches, from human rights to justice-based to consequentialist approaches, my focus is not this thesis, but rather with calling attention to the rich interconnections between people and places. That is, I focus on place and how our connectedness to certain places and ways of being in place are a too-often neglected component of the erosion of human well-being caused by a changing climate.[15]

My position is that those like Pogge, Held, and Caney who argue for cosmopolitanism as the most adequate moral and political response to climate change, argue for it as a rational principle, but do not attend to the affective or embodied components of cosmopolitanism. What they overlook is the affective dimension, a form of "feeling with others" that starts with attention not just to the physical impacts of climate change, but also the affective impacts. Such a practice sets the stage for what Mark Johnson calls "the moral imagination"[16] and what Martha Nussbaum refers to as the compassionate imagination, which can "carry our hearts to humanity—if we live in a society that encourages us to make the imaginative leap into the life of the other."[17]

But I would also caution against a tendency toward a generic understanding of selves, one that is at risk even with some who embrace cosmopolitan conceptions of selves. Here I rely on the work of Walter Mignolo, who calls for a "critical and dialogic cosmopolitanism" that embraces the essential ground of diversity as a universal project and as the wellspring of this practice of cosmopolitanism. Mignolo's approach "presupposes border thinking or border epistemology grounded on the critique of all possible fundamentalism (Western and non-Western, national and religious, neoliberal and neosocialist) and on the faith in accumulation at any cost that sustains capitalist organizations of the economy . . . [and] should be thought out as new forms of projecting and imagining, ethically and politically, from subaltern perspectives." Here cosmopolitanism is an unending practice "in which everyone participates, instead of 'being participated.'"[18]

What follows is, at best, a gesture toward such a practice, with attention to one's place.

The Importance of Place

The media images of the threats of climate change are most frequently those of catastrophic events—flooding and droughts, hurricanes and sea surges, bushfires and heat waves. While the incremental weather changes, the gradual changes in precipitation, in temperature, and in sea level do not as fully captivate the media, I argue that they are an equally poignant reminder of the importance of place in the context of human well-being. Conceptions of cosmopolitanism that lose sight not only of the ontological interweaving of humans and environments, but the particular interconnections between places and ways of being in those places, miss an essential element of human well-being; an element of human flourishing that is at risk as our world warms.

The 2010 Report of the American Psychological Association Task Force on the Interface between Psychology and Global Climate Change details the ways in which climate-related concerns can "affect interpersonal and intergroup behavior and may result in increased stress and anxiety . . . even in the absence of direct impacts, the perception and fear of climate change may threaten mental health."[19] According to this report, "adapting to and coping with climate change is an ongoing and ever-changing process that involves many intrapsychic processes . . . [including] sense making; causal and responsibility attributions for adverse climate change impacts; appraisals of impacts, resources, and possible coping responses; affective responses; and motivational processes related to needs for security, stability, coherence, and control."[20]

While admitting that there will be clear psychosocial effects from extreme weather events, the report underscores that the majority of the psychosocial effects will be the result of gradual and cumulative weather-related changes. The report lists a variety of such impacts: heat-related violence, conflicts over resources, threats to mental health, anxiety and despair.[21]

In this chapter, I focus on the experience of loss, and in particular place-based experiences of loss, to illustrate one of the many, yet often ignored, harms of climate-related environmental degradation. My goal is to explore the relevance of the experience of loss to a conception of ethics and justice that acknowledges the deep interdependence of humans and environments. In this way, I aim to provide part of the groundwork in support of a thicker conception of interdependence necessary to any adequate cosmopolitanism. One obvious lens through which to study the relevance of place-based experiences of loss is population displacement due to climate change–related impacts. However, my initial focus is a different manner in which people suffer psychosocial harm from the loss of place, namely, those who live in the place that is lost.

Living in the Place of Loss

In *Getting Back into Place* Ed Casey refers to *nostalgia* as the pining for lost places. He frames this discussion by recalling the experiences of those who are forcibly displaced, such as the displacement of the Navajo by the Navajo-Hopi Land Settlement of 1974, which led to high rates of suicide, disorientation, and depression. Reminding us that nostalgia is literally being pained (*algia*) at the non-return home (*nostos* = return to home or native land), Casey argues that the contemporary Western condition is one of nostalgia, loss of place due to ecological damage or negligence, "places we have once been in yet can no longer reenter."[22] Casey argues that while many of us in Western culture have not lost our land, we nonetheless have lost our place, and thus experience symptoms of place pathology including nostalgia, disorientation, homelessness, depression, and various modes of estrangement from self and others.[23] Casey urges renewed practices of emplacement through which we experience not only being in place but becoming part of that place.

While not denying the importance of attention to the phenomenology of responses to being displaced from one's home, to nostalgia, Glenn Albrecht, an environmental philosopher at the University of Newcastle, calls attention to a different form of place-based distress, a "homesickness one gets when one is still at 'home.'"[24] This phenomenon, a form of being lost in place, is a rapidly growing but often ignored impact of climate change that is my focus in this section.

Responding to the distress experienced by those living in Australia's Hunter Region of New South Wales from the impacts of open-pit coal mining, Albrecht coined the term *solastalgia* to call attention to a place-based distress experienced, not by being forcibly displaced, but from losing the place one is in. Solastalgia, is a term Albrecht crafted from the combination of *solari* (solace) and *solus* (desolation), with *algia* (pain), and constructed to have a "ghost reference" to nostalgia to imbed place. He defines it as "the pain or sickness caused by the loss or lack of solace and the sense of isolation connected to the present state of one's home and territory."[25]

Solastalgia is a reminder that we can lose our place while still in place. "It is the 'lived experience' of being undermined by forces that destroy the potential for solace to be derived from the present."[26] Albrecht discovered that the environmental degradation caused by the coal mining was producing a form of homesickness inhabitants of the Hunter Region were experiencing while still at home. Through interviews and dialogue, Albrecht came to realize that those living in the Hunter Region were experiencing high levels of place-based distress at the transformation of the land on which they lived, and experienced it as a destruction of their home. "Distress within the community has been expressed in a multitude of ways but constant themes have been disgust at the assault on the quality of life, fear of ill health (risk imposition) and frustration caused by the inability to stop the pollution and have any real say in the way the region is being developed."[27] Albrecht underscores the feelings of powerlessness and despair, as well as the lived experience of injustice as key affective elements of solastalgia.

It is this affective dimension of loss of home that is too often missed in analyses of the harms of climate change. What is lost is a sense of belonging that comes from the interdependence between individuals and the land that they know and are of. While there is attention to the impacts of disasters on homes and places—the earthquake and tsunami in Japan or the impact of Katrina on New Orleans—the slow onset, gradual transformations of home and place are often ignored. In particular, the psychic impacts of altered physical environments, the distress and anxieties caused by loss of a lived sense of belonging and the social importance of the intricate interweavings between physical and social environments are overlooked.

In a study of the impact of deteriorating environments in Ghana, Petra Tschakert, Raymond Tuto, and Anna Alcaro examine what they refer to as "multi-layered emotional impacts of increasingly hollow homes."[28] To study the impact of migration from the north of Ghana to the southern city and capital of Accra due to the scarcity of fertile land, low crop yields, and unreliable harvests in north Ghana, these researchers conducted in-depth interviews with individuals who had migrated as well as those who had remained "at home." Their focus was to compare the lived experience of those who left their homes with that of those who had stayed behind. They found that the degree of distress an individual or community experiences is connected to the loss of an endemic sense of place. Their interviews revealed that a key catalyst for those who decided to migrate was the loss of familiar and valued landscapes and homes. But those who remained in the north expressed acute feelings of sadness arising from changes in the physical landscapes in the north over several decades—disappearance of shade through trees, loss of beauty, and the drying up of wells, ponds, and dams, which often led to "acute feelings of sadness, fear, anger, disappointment, and helplessness."[29] While residents consistently mentioned fear and anxiety over the loss of farmlands and the impacts of deforestation, many also mentioned the loss of places of beauty and of serenity, and expressed sadness and helplessness in reference to these changes. In sum, those who remained home expressed a "loss of connection to their surroundings and increased levels of sadness and depression."[30]

The affective dimension of loss is illustrated in the responses of those interviewed:

> I am disappointed about the cutting of trees without replanting them and I am also sad about the degraded landscape. I am sad about the irregular rain that is making farming unattractive. Whenever I visit the farm and see my crops drying in the field, I feel so sad. (Aliou, 23 years, Sissala East)
>
> The old woman does not go to the farm because she deems it unnecessary because it is not raining. She said she visited the farm last Saturday and said she could not do anything because the place was dry. She felt like crying and was so sad. She was thinking about how they are going to survive for the next year until the next growing season. (Notes describing Samaata, 53 years, Zabzugu-Tatale District)[31]

While the impact of loss of place impacts men and women alike, there are also gendered dimensions of the experience of loss. For example, in a study of the impact of climate related drought in Australia, Margaret Alston and Jenny Kent identified a key difference between women and men regarding the effect (and the affect) of the loss of place, in this case the loss of home gardens, which the women experienced as an aesthetic and spiritual loss:

> I don't have any lawn because it's totally covered by sand. There's one to two feet of sand drift in our yard. The visual aspect of the drought has been very, very devastating. (Farm woman, Australia)
> My garden was dying. The grass was just brown dirt and that was terrible. So every bit of water from the bath, the washing machine, every skerrick was saved and it would go on a plant or a pot plant. (Farm woman, Australia)
> Our place looks a little bit like what I imagine the moon looks like. It's very bare and ripply . . . because the dirt has been blowing for so long and its half-way up the fences. (Farm woman, Australia)[32]

But sense of place is not simply visual. While landscapes are an important feature of being at home, we can lose our place in other ways as well. Deborah Davis Jackson's study of Aamjiwnaang and the First Nation formerly known as the Sarnia Band of Chippewa Indians, reminds us that human-environment interactions engage all of our senses, not only the visual. Jackson's analysis reveals that we can get lost in place from changes in the "smellscape," as well.

The Aamjiwnaang community's displacement from home is a complex one. It began with a series of physical displacements that began in the late nineteenth century, but accelerated during the two world wars, in which more than two-thirds of the land of their reserve was sold or leased by various companies such as Dow Chemical, Suncor Energy, Imperial Oil, and Shell to set up petroleum-related production plants. The original 10,028-acre reserve was decreased by these intrusions to a mere 2,700 acres. But the petrochemical industries not only altered the physical location and landscapes of the Aamjiwnaang community but caused another profound displacement.

The industries that moved into Aamjiwnaang were high polluters and the land and water absorbed the contaminants. Creeks became off-limits to swimming or fishing because of contaminants and the community began to experience higher than normal levels of asthma, arthritis, learning disabilities, skin rashes, and cancer. But the focus of Jackson's study was the impact of the industry transforming the phenomenological experiences not only of the land but of the very air the Aamjiwnaang community breathed. She calls attention to "the very direct and visceral experience of the strange and often noxious odors that band members must confront as they go about their daily lives. It is these experiences that most powerfully evoke the uncanny feeling of being at the same time firmly emplaced and eerily displaced that I term dysplacement."[33] She argues that for all peoples, but especially for a people who have a strong tradition of healing as well as ceremonial practices that involve breathing in certain fragrances, a change in the phenomenological experience of the air they breathe creates a profound experience of dislocation. She reminds us that the ceremonial custom of burning richly scented sacred plants—cedar, sage, sweet grass, and tobacco—"provide means through which individuals and communities can attempt to achieve Anishinaabe bimaadiziwin, a phrase that can be translated as 'to live well in the Indian way.'"[34] But the land we call home has its own scents, fragrances that evoke seasons and practices that interconnect us to the place of our home and to the practices that make us a community. "There's a piece in the center of my land where there's a bit of a gully, and in the fall when it's dry, you can sit there and look in all directions and not see any stacks, or smoke, or any sign of industry. That's very hard to find in Aamjiwnaang. But [even there], what you still can't escape is the smell [Interview, October 3, 2007]."[35] Forced migration due to climate-induced environmental degradation is a mode of losing place that has received widespread attention in both the scholarly and policy realms. Unlike forced migration, the plight of those who are unable or unwilling to migrate away from the place of environmental degradation has been largely ignored. We need to understand the complex ways that people in these communities live in the place of loss, and appreciate the negative impacts on their experiences of place and on their communities. Any account of cosmopolitan selves that focuses on culture at the expense of place and the complex human-environment couplings, will overlook a key aspect of the wellspring of what Mignolo referred to as critical and dialogic cosmopolitanism or "globalization from below." The power relations that are the focus of Mignolo's genealogy of historical stages of "cosmopolitanism"[36] must also include attention to the creation of places and spaces, that is, of our interrelations with environments we shape and are shaped by.[37] We cannot do justice to cosmopolitanism nor to climate justice if we continue to ignore place and the ways in which climate change will result in many living in the place of loss. While not all will be so impacted, as climate impacts slowly change the faces of home—from the gardens in western Australia to the forests of Ponderosa Pines in Montana—solastalgia will become an increasingly global condition, "felt and articulated differently by different people in highly localized geospatial and socio-cultural settings, yet fueled by similar environmental degradation and transformation."[38]

Out of Place

While I chose to focus in this chapter on a less visible experience of loss of home, it is not my intention to ignore the more visible expression of this phenomenon. The First Assessment Report of the Intergovernmental Panel on Climate Change projected human migration as the greatest single impact of climate change. The report estimated that by 2050, 150 million people could be displaced by climate change–related phenomenon such as desertification, increasing water scarcity, floods, and storms.[39] The complexity of weather-induced displacement is well represented in the Fifth Assessment Report as more data have been gathered about people who are leaving homes made uninhabitable as a result of climate-related disasters, such as coastal flooding or storm surges, as well as millions of others who can no longer gain a livelihood in their homelands because of drought, soil erosion, desertification, deforestation, and other environmental problems. While most displaced people attempt to return to their original place of residence and rebuild, the "structural economic causes of social vulnerability may determine whether temporary displacement turns into permanent migration," as was the case in New Orleans after Hurricane Katrina, where the most economically disadvantaged populations have been the least likely to return. There are also significant gender differences in displacement.[40]

The psychosocial impact of displacement is profound. A Harvard University study documented declines in mental health indexes in low income countries due to the high numbers of citizens who had been dislocated from their home places, but found that these negative effects happened *in spite of* both economic as well as political gains.[41] The work of Mindy Thompson Fullilove helps to explain this phenomenon.[42] Her research establishes that a sense of belonging to a place is necessary for psychological well-being. She documents that belonging to a place is dependent upon strong, well-developed relationships with nurturing places. Her research confirmed that displacement, whether due to environmental degradation or other causes, results in a rupture of the psychic components of belonging to a place, namely, familiarity, attachment, and identity, leading to sadness and a longing for home.

The individuals who migrated from deteriorating environments in the north of Ghana to slums in Accra explained that they moved because of changes to the land, in particular irregular rainfall, reduction of vegetation, and serious soil degradation. These were seen as slow changes, where over time the land became less fertile, the rains became irregular, and farm yields became unreliable. Those interviewed spoke of loss of livelihoods, of food security, and of hope. The move brought with it other problems: frequent fire outbreaks, poor sanitation facilities, and malaria and other diseases as a consequence of dense and substandard housing conditions. But at the heart of their narratives was a "longing for the distant home, the lost rural identity, and a place that provides true solace."[43] A common affective response was feeling out of place.

Conclusion: Understanding Loss

Individuals create and sustain a coherent sense of self through their environmental interactions as well as through their social interactions. The disruption of either can cause affective harms. Hence, any cosmopolitanism that overlooks the interdependences between people and their environments misses an essential aspect of selfhood and flourishing. A key component of our embeddedness in the world is a sense of belonging in place, or place belonging. This includes a strong affective tie between people and places. "Places are locations in which people have long memories, reaching back beyond the indefinable impressions of their own childhoods to the common lores of bygone generations."[44] Place is a locus of meaning, emotion, attachment, and experience. Place matters and must come to matter for cosmopolitanism.

To fully understand the impacts of climate change, it is not enough to quantify the physical impacts. It is also important to appreciate the affective and psychological components. In the case of loss of place, whether in place or through displacement, appreciating how loss of place impacts individuals and communities is essential to a robust theory of cosmopolitanism and of any conception of global justice. Indeed such an appreciation may be the wellspring of just actions and institutions, for activism and for policy.

By appreciating who we are in place, the intricate linkages between humans and environments, we better appreciate our shared vulnerabilities. For we are all at risk of losing our place. That the various modes of loss of place are likely to be accelerated in the context of climate change, makes it all the more imperative that it becomes a focus of attention. Climate induced migration and displacement, as well as shifting national borders, and multiple diasporas, complicate the various trajectories of loss. But understanding and acknowledging such loss may be a key element of challenging environmental degradation. Ursula Kelly, who researches issues of cultural loss and loss of identity, and what it means to educate in times and conditions of social and cultural transition, argues that "without an acknowledgement of loss (the first principle of an educational discourse of loss and place), we inadvertently—and perhaps ironically—cultivate a seedbed for retrenchment, conservatism, and fatalism. Unacknowledged loss helps maintain the illusion that loss is neither real nor as severe as it might seem. Such disavowal inhibits forward thinking and new creations, for it dulls apprehension and inhibits our best efforts to respond, to challenge, to sustain, and to change."[45]

Understanding the various ways in which climate change threatens our very being in place might create the foundation for change. It might turn "love of place into an ethic of responsibility and sustainability."[46] By appreciating the experiences of those who have been displaced, we better understand how places matter as well as our deep interconnectivity with the world that we are in and of. It gives hope for sustaining place, for sustainable modes of being in place. "Sustainability should be a centerpiece of an education that attends to a profound form of inhabitation, involving ethics, politics and affect—a complex and compelling call to care in which transience is a feature of life, a way of thinking, a mode of identification, a form of belonging, and a mark of loss as possibility and hope—of reparation, *for people and their places.*"[47]

NANCY TUANA is the DuPont/Class of 1949 Professor of Philosophy and Women's Studies at Penn State University, where she served as the founding director of the Rock Ethics Institute. Her scholarly work includes books and articles in feminist philosophy, epistemologies of ignorance, and in philosophy of science with particular expertise in coupled ethical-epistemic issues in climate change science.

Notes

My thanks to the participants of the American Philosophies Forum 2011 conference on Cosmopolitanism and Place, and particular thanks to José Medina and John Stuhr for their helpful feedback on this chapter. This work was partially supported by the National Science Foundation through the Network for Sustainable Climate Risk Management (SCRiM) under NSF cooperative agreement GEO-1240507.

1. IPCC, "Summary for Policymakers," in *Climate Change 2014: Impacts, Adaptation, and Vulnerability. Part A: Global and Sectoral Aspects. Contribution of Working Group II to the Fifth Assessment Report of the Intergovernmental Panel on Climate Change*, ed. C. B. Field, V. R. Barros, D. J. Dokken, K. J. Mach, M. D. Mastrandrea, T. E. Bilir, M. Chatterjee, K. L. Ebi, Y. O. Estrada, R. C. Genova, B. Girma, E. S. Kissel, A. N. Levy, S. MacCracken, P. R. Mastrandrea, and L. L. White (Cambridge: Cambridge University Press, 2014), 1–32.

2. Ibid., 4.

3. John Broome, *Climate Matters: Ethics in a Warming World* (New York: W. W. Norton, 2012); Donald A. Brown, *Climate Change Ethics: Navigating the Perfect Moral Storm* (New York: Routledge, 2012); S. M. Gardiner, *A Perfect Moral Storm: The Ethical Challenge of Climate Change* (Oxford: Oxford University Press, 2011).

4. The concept of a wicked problem was initially framed by design theorists Horst Rittel and Melvin Webber, "Dilemmas in a General Theory of Planning," *Policy Sciences* 4 (1973): 155–69. The characteristics of a wicked problem include: there is no definitive formulation of a wicked problem; the solution depends on how the problem is framed and vice-versa; there is no definitive solution to the problem, though options are better and worse; the constraints that the problem is subject to and the resources needed to solve it change over time.

5. As just a few representative examples, consider the following: the NAACP's Climate Justice Initiative (www.naacp.org/programs/entry/climate-justice); the Mary Robinson Foundation for Climate Justice (www.mrfcj.org/about?gclid=CKr37d3ppKoCFaQRNAodMgK fmQ); Climate Justice Now! a global coalition of networks and organizations (www.climate-justice-now.org/); and the World Council of Churches, which has been working for climate justice for decades (www.oikoumene.org/en/programmes/justice-diakonia-and-responsibility-for-creation.html).

6. David Held, *Cosmopolitanism: Ideals and Realities* (Cambridge: Polity, 2010), 23.

7. Ibid., 24.

8. Simon Caney, "Cosmopolitan Justice, Responsibility, and Global Climate Change," *Leiden Journal of International Law* 18, no. 4 (2005): 748.

9. Cf. Thomas Pogge, "Cosmopolitanism and Sovereignty," *Ethics* 103, no. 1 (1992): 48–75; Thomas Pogge, *Global Justice* (Oxford: Blackwell, 2001).

10. W. E. B. DuBois, "The African Roots of War," *Atlantic Monthly* 115 (1915): 708.

11. Caney, "Cosmopolitan Justice," 750.

12. Kwame Anthony Appiah, *Cosmopolitanism: Ethics in a World of Strangers* (New York: W. W. Norton, 2006), xii.

13. DuBois, "African Roots of War," 712.

14. Marilyn Fischer, "A Pragmatist Cosmopolitan Moment: Reconfiguring Nussbaum's Cosmopolitan Concentric Circles," *Journal of Speculative Philosophy* 21, no. 3 (2007): 158.

15. Lorraine Code's *Ecological Thinking: The Politics of Epistemic Location* (Oxford: Oxford University Press, 2006) provides a model of an ecological imaginary that could serve as a valuable resource for developing this conception of the importance of place. Code argues that it "carries within it the normative social meanings, customs, expectations, assumptions, values, prohibitions, and permissions—the habitus and ethos—into which human beings are nurtured from childhood and which they internalize, affirm, challenge, or contest as they make sense of their place, options, responsibilities within a world, both social and physical, whose "nature" and meaning are also instituted in these imaginary significations" (30).

16. See Mark Johnson, *The Moral Imagination: The Implications of Cognitive Science for Ethics* (Chicago: University of Chicago Press, 2004).

17. Martha Nussbaum, "Patriotism and Cosmopolitanism," in *For Love of Country: Debating the Limits of Patriotism*, ed. Joshua Cohen (Boston: Beacon, 1996), 132.

18. Walter Mignolo, "The Many Faces of Cosmo-Polis: Border Thinking and Critical Cosmopolitanism," *Public Culture* 12, no. 3 (2000): 743.

19. Janet Swim, Susan Clayton, Thomas Doherty, Robert Gifford, George Howard, Joseph Reser, Paul Stern, and Elke Weber, "Psychology and Global Climate Change," *APA Task Force on the Interface Between Psychology and Global Climate Change* (2010): 7, www.apa.org/science/about/publications/climate-change.aspx.

20. Ibid.

21. See C. A. Anderson, "Heat and Violence," *Current Directions in Psychological Science* 10, no. 1 (2001: 33–38; R. Reuveny, "Ecomigration and Violent Conflict: Case Studies and Public Policy Implications," *Human Ecology* 36 (2008): 1–13; J. G. Fritze, G. A. Blashki, S. Burke, and J. Wiseman, "Hope, Despair and Transformation: Climate Change and the Promotion of Mental Health and Wellbeing," *International Journal of Mental Health Systems* 2, no. 1 (2008): 13; D. Kidner, "Depression and the Natural World: Towards a Critical Ecology of Psychological Distress," *International Journal of Critical Psychology* 19 (2007): 123–46; J. Macy and M. Y. Brown, *Coming Back to Life: Practices to Reconnect Our Lives, Our World* (Gabriola Island, BC: New Society, 1998); and S. W. Nicholsen, *The Love of Nature and the End of the World* (Cambridge: MIT Press, 2002).

22. Edward Casey, *Getting Back into Place: Toward a Renewed Understanding of the Place-World* (Bloomington: Indiana University Press, 2009), 37.

23. Ibid., 38.

24. Glenn Albrecht, "'Solastalgia' A New Concept in Health and Identity," *Philosophy Activism Nature* 3 (2005): 45.

25. Ibid.

26. Ibid.

27. Ibid., 51.

28. Petra Tschakert, Raymond A. Tutu, and Anna Alcaro, "Embodied Experiences of Environmental and Climatic Changes in Landscapes of Everyday Life in Ghana," *Emotion, Space and Society* 7, no. 1 (2013): 24.

29. Ibid.

30. Ibid., 20.

31. Ibid., 22.

32. M. Alston and J. Kent, *The Social Impacts of Drought: A Report to NSW Agriculture* (Wagga Wagga, Australia: Charles Sturt University Centre for Rural Social Research, 2004), 49, 66.

33. Deborah D. Jackson, "Scents of Place: The Dysplacement of a First Nations Community in Canada," *American Anthropologist* 113, no. 4 (2011): 611.

34. Ibid., 613.

35. Ibid., 610.

36. See Mignolo, "Many Faces."

37. See my essay "Viscous Porosity: Witnessing Katrina," in *Material Feminisms*, ed. Susan Hekman and Stacy Alaimo, 188–213 (Bloomington: Indiana University Press, 2008).

38. Tschakert et al., "Embodied Experiences," 2.

39. See W. J. McG. Tegart, G.W. Sheldon, and D. C. Griffiths, *Climate Change: The IPCC Impacts Assessment, Report prepared for Intergovernmental Panel on Climate Change by Working Group II* (Canberra: Australian Government Publishing Service, 1990).

40. W. N. Adger, J. M. Pulhin, J. Barnett, G. D. Dabelko, G. K. Hovelsrud, M. Levy, Ú. Oswald Spring, and C. H. Vogel, "Human Security," in *Climate Change 2014: Impacts, Adaptation, and Vulnerability. Part A: Global and Sectoral Aspects. Contribution of Working Group II to the Fifth Assessment Report of the Intergovernmental Panel on Climate Change*, ed. C. B. Field, V. R. Barros, D. J. Dokken, K. J. Mach, M. D. Mastrandrea, T. E. Bilir, M. Chatterjee, K. L. Ebi, Y. O. Estrada, R. C. Genova, B. Girma, E. S. Kissel, A. N. Levy, S. MacCracken, P. R. Mastrandrea, and L. L. White, 755–91 (Cambridge: Cambridge University Press, 2014).

41. Robert Desjarlais, Leon Eisenberg, Byron Good, and Arthur Kleinman, eds., *World Mental Health: Problems, Priorities, and Responses in Low-Income Countries* (New York: Oxford University Press, 1995).

42. See Mindy Thompson Fullilove, "Psychiatric Implications of Displacement: Contributions from the Psychology of Place," *American Journal of Psychiatry* 153, no. 12 (1995): 1516–23.

43. Tschakert et al., "Embodied Experiences," 8.

44. Yi-Fu Tuan, "Space and Place: Humanistic Perspective," *Progress in Geography* 6 (1974): 245.

45. Ursula A. Kelly, "Learning to Lose: Rurality, Transience, and Belonging (a Companion to Michael Corbett)," *Journal of Research in Rural Education* 24, no. 11 (2009): 2.

46. Ibid.

47. Ibid., 3, my emphasis.

PART III
REIMAGINING HOME AND WORLD

Introduction

John J. Stuhr

To consider seriously cosmopolitan ideals (in Part I of this volume) is to engage universalism of one or more sorts—moral, political, economic, religious, and cultural. It is to take up notions of universal and equal intrinsic worth, the dignity of all persons, and border-blind, history-blind, color-blind, money-blind, gender-blind (and so on) rights and responsibilities. And it is to entertain worldviews in which tribal, local, regional, national, and other differences are mere artifacts of time, inessential contingencies, instances of good luck or bad fortune, and facts that cannot serve as bases for reason-based values and actions.

On the other hand, to take seriously the realities of places (in Part II of this volume) is to focus on particular histories and traditions, experiences of intimate belonging and foreign not belonging, the ways in which homes and homelessness are created and sustained, and wide ranging differences and cultural pluralism. And it is to contemplate giving up the task and, perhaps, the pretension of transcending or overcoming all these passing particulars when we, in so many different ways, value and speak and reason and forge world views, relationships, practices, and institutions.

Both the push of cosmopolitan ideals and the pull of places and their embodied loyalties and narratives, our narratives, are real and undeniable. And most people, I suspect, feel the power of both in differing degrees and in some mixture or other, perhaps in an unstable and changing mixture.

We live in a world of nations and states and borders, a world of people who are citizens, temporary residents, and aliens. This is also and as much a world of emigrants and immigrants, a world of refugees, diasporas, and displaced populations, a world of travel, relocation, and migration, a world of legal and illegal border crossers, a world of people who got someplace earlier and other people who got there, or want to get there, later. We live in a world in which many of the descendants of earlier immigrants, even just a little bit earlier immigrants, think of themselves as natives—though most anthropologists and biologists agree that all modern humans originated in, and migrated from, Africa. This is a world of global capital, global classes, guest workers, and undocumented laborers, staggering inequality of wealth, widespread homelessness, and angry visions of walls. This is a world inhabited by some persons who do not feel at home or find that their lives matter even in the communities in which they grew up and live—and die. This is a world in which identity is frequently articulated in terms of place and history. To the question, "Who are you?" the reply often comes in the language of one state rather than another ("I am American," "I am Palestinian," "I am Russian"); the language of one creed rather than another ("I am a Vaishnavite," "I am Sunni," "I am a member of the United Church of Christ"); the language of family and tribe ("I am Zulu," "I am Miskito," "I am Tom and Susan's daughter"); the language of one ethnicity rather than another ("I am Hispanic," "I am Asian," "I am mixed race"); and in one language rather than another ("Ich bin . . ." "Soy . . ." "Wǒ shì"). This is at the same time a world in which sometimes in some places some people respond: "I am a global citizen, I am a cosmopolitan, I am a citizen of the world."

In this world, how should we identify ourselves and with whom should we identify ourselves? How should we identify and understand different others? What are the consequences of having or taking up some identities rather than others? How should we feel about persons who live in other cultures? Does it matter how we feel? With what attitude and with what hopes and fears should we engage these different others who are not "us?" Beyond the mere recognition of otherness, how should we respond? What, if anything, do we owe these many different others? What ought these others expect from you or me or us? How should we act? What practices and institutions, perhaps new global institutions, are demanded? In response, can local, regional, national, and even international institutions be adequate? Does our reason, if not our emotion, demand that we be cosmopolitans? And what if cosmopolitanism itself is just the view of particular persons in particular places at particular times—a local fashion of seeking to think less locally?

Is it possible to address adequately these questions merely by bouncing back and forth between the push of universal cosmopolitan ideals and the pull of particular places and histories? Bouncing back and forth between these two poles is business as usual for those who would construct or deconstruct cosmopolitanism in most all of its Enlightenment versions as well as Enlightenment-derived contemporary formulations. It is also business as usual for those who theorize within these two poles of commitment but want to hold onto both of them—those who advance a cosmopolitanism that acknowledges situatedness and those who preach a provincialism that is neither narrow nor merely self-congratulatory.

In the face of business as usual, is it possible to address these questions in significantly different ways? Is it possible not simply to imagine new pro-cosmopolitan and anti-cosmopolitan responses to central and inescapable ethical, social and political, and cultural questions today, but to re-imagine these problems themselves, these problems framed by cosmopolitanism and place?

All of the authors of the chapters in this part answer this question in the affirmative. Drawing on feminist theory, phenomenology, pragmatism, and critical theory and Marxism, these authors advance reimagined accounts of our shared world and our different homes and places in it. In doing so, they ask their readers to think differently as they set forth overlapping and original accounts of a different cosmopolitanism. This is not a cosmopolitanism for autonomous rational agents focused on universal morality and principles of justice but, rather, a cosmopolitanism for heteronomous, interdependent, and ultimately homeless persons with irreducible, ineradicable differences and limits and, as well, imaginations and sympathies. This view points toward an orientation or ethical attunement of radical pluralism, radical humility, and radical hope. Moreover, it points toward a demand for melioristic social change in light of real and unequal concentrations of power and force and real social antagonisms (in which the language and commitments of traditional cosmopolitanism itself sometimes has been a weapon).

Several of these themes are set forth clearly by Jessica Wahman in "Citizen or Guest?: Cosmopolitanism as Homelessness," this part's first chapter. Wahman identifies cosmopolitanism as an attitude or state of mind—an embodied ethical orientation and self-identification rather than belief in a set of global propositions. This is not a sense of being autonomous and at home across the universe but, instead, of dependence, estrangement and destabilization, and homelessness: "A cosmopolitan has not made a home in the world but has made herself homeless." Moreover, it is not a sense in which feelings of home and habits are denied or transcended; it lives with, rather than against, inevitable and particular allegiances. Wahman expands this idea by drawing on the philosophies of George Santayana and Emmanuel Levinas and the plays of Tony Kushner: from Santayana and Levinas she stresses our inevitable biases and our irreducible particularity and situatedness, our "dwelling" in our own world that is rendered interior and that, in turn, renders our actions and lives proper and appropriate, the way things are done; in Kushner's plays she locates dramatic capacity to imagine differently and question and destabilize our own perspectives and situations, to enter into alien viewpoints that remain alien to one's own. The result is a cosmopolitanism of sympathetic imagination rather than universalist reason (or internet-delivered information). For Wahman, this sympathetic imagination demands courage—courage to subject from time to time the comfort and safety of the familiar to the demand to grasp the unfamiliar and, in doing so, to render the familiar a less appropriate and less familiar home. In this light, cosmopolitanism is a challenge—and both a transitory and a strenuous one. Wahman concludes by highlighting the differences and ongoing, not-to-be resolved tension between two ways of meeting this challenge born in the dual recognition of the impossibility of escaping one's own perspective and place and the reality of perspectives and places fundamentally different from one's own. She calls the first way of meeting this challenge a "quietist retreat"—solace seeking with those who share one's worldview, a "minimalist cosmopolitanism." The second way of meeting this challenge is a "full cosmopolitanism," imaginative and hopeful engagement permeated by "the humble recognition that one is in the home of others and has something to learn from them." This cosmopolitanism is an ongoing shattering of boundaries and drawing of new lines.

In Chapter 13, Jennifer Hansen develops this notion of cosmopolitan hope, hope in the context of plural peoples and cultures in contact with diverse other peoples and cultures—and contact that is marked by broadmindedness rather than conquest, domination, and oppression. As Hansen explains, her goal is not conceptual analysis but a phenomenological and first-person account of the affective experience of this broadminded hope. As such, her goal is indirectly, rather than directly, political. What is hope and how is it, or might it be, cosmopolitan? How might cosmopolitanism be understood as a kind of hope—or hoped-for ideal? In response to these questions, Hansen sets forth a five point phenomenological account of hope. First, hope is a disposition, mood, or temperament, frequently cultivated, with cognitive content that is both intentional and not fully conceptualized. Second, hope is an anticipation of a genuinely possible better future, improvement, and progress. Third, unlike mere wishful thinking, hope is a matter of will, an active commitment to changing this world on behalf of that better future—a future that is in part constituted by this hope itself. Fourth, hope is not an exercise in irrationality but, instead, always involves practical reason and the normative horizons of some particular form of life or culture or universe. Finally, fifth, the hopefulness that concerns Hansen is pluralistic because it recognizes its own context is a "multiverse" rather than a universe with a single, infallible way of making sense. This account of hope leads Hansen to assert that hope, oriented in a this-worldly way to what is beyond its own horizon and engaged in an effort to see someone else's world from within that other world's horizon, is "implicitly cosmopolitan" and, no longer settled and at home, "a travel to utopias." By "utopia," Hansen explains that she does not mean an ideal place without tragedy but rather a no-place at all: "Seeking utopias means seeking a space—albeit not a place—to begin the work of criticism and thereby transformation of the present. Cosmopolitan conversations open a space of critique into which pours the animating force of hope." As Hansen shows in her concluding section, in seeking precisely this utopian space, her brand of cosmopolitanism (and its irreducibly pluralistic worldview, epistemology, and values) differs crucially from two historically familiar and influential kinds of cosmopolitanism: the insufficiently hopeful cosmopolitanism of ancient Greek and Roman Stoics, and the insufficiently pluralistic cosmopolitanism of the European Enlightenment.

Hansen's view of cosmopolitan hope as oriented beyond its own horizons to the worlds of others finds parallel expression in Cynthia Gayman's opening observation that cosmopolitanism requires "a certain requisite generosity of perception, an openness to the unfamiliar, foreign, or strange." In her "Hospitality or Generosity?: Cosmopolitan Transactions," Gayman asks not whether we should cultivate this generosity of perception and conceptual openness but, rather, how we should respond to persons other than, or different from, or foreign to ourselves—to persons who are not one of "us." Does—or should—generous perception require generous action? Does it inform a duty of hospitality? Does it entail an obligation to compromise one's own commitments and one's own way of life and to reject one's own truths as singular, monistic, universal truth? And, are persons who endorse cosmopolitanism itself simply fundamentalist true believers in their own supposedly universal truth—worshippers in the church of epistemological pluralism? These questions, Gayman shows, are not merely theoretical: from Hurricane Katrina victims to Somali Muslims in Kentucky to waves of Syrian immigrants in Europe, in practice, concern over what may be lost often prevents people from even seeking to hope for anything new and different—or to respond generously or to respond hospitably to those who already seem different. As Gayman puts this point in the context of her analysis of public reason, universal discursive ethics, and universal human rights: "without some underlying perceptual generosity it is difficult to see how discourse, no matter how civil the rules of argument and justification, would accomplish anything substantive" because "'the moral obligation to justify actions with reasons' had already been met" from some particular, provincial, nonuniversal understanding of what counts as rationality and reason giving. Accordingly on this view, moral justification cannot take a universalistic form. Here Gayman moves to consider the pragmatism of John Dewey and its account of communication and the way in which communication leads people to have things in common and to take up cooperative transactions in the world. As Gayman notes, this requires a massive leap of faith that we share a world with those with whom we do not seem to share in other ways. This, Gayman recognizes, is a form of "radical deference" (and similar to Jessica Wahman's claim that the cosmopolitan, a guest, humbly depends on the graciousness of others). And this creates, at least sometimes, an obligation to take up the duties of a host for others who are one's guests.

Many of our transactions today happen on, or through, the internet—making it not simply a site for shoppers or a resource for information seekers but a site of complex socialization, meaning making, and rich, contested political life. The internet also creates a kind of cosmopolitan, or at least global, connectedness across multiple and changing publics. In "On Cosmopolitan Publics and Online

Communities," Erin Tarver begins with these facts and with a feminist and pragmatic commitment to "democratic transformation" of patterns and practices of disadvantage and devaluation and to "trans-national anti-oppressive work"— whether the target is local or global, face-to-face or online. Like Cynthia Gayman, Tarver in part draws on John Dewey's view of political practices as shared practices of meaning while taking a critical approach to the very notion of what it is to "share" practices and an equally critical approach to any insufficiently pluralistic view that is oriented to the "coming-to-consciousness of The Public" rather than "local cosmopolitan publics." In this context, might new technological developments—such as the internet—present new possibilities for advancing or transforming democratic practices? Examining a handful of feminist blogs, Tarver focuses on a few central features: regular publication of material that disputes dominant cultural meanings that nurture and sustain oppression; comments and comment threads and connected comments that constitute an active meeting space rather than a site of one-way oration; a comment policy and active monitoring (rather than liberal free speech) that prohibit speech that might otherwise undermine the blog's goals and are perceived as oppressive or damaging to their communities. These blog participants, as Tarver reminds us, do not inhabit the same physical places, but they inhabit a different kind of place, "an interacting network of cosmopolitan publics." But is this sort of network cosmopolitan? Tarver answers: not in the typical sense of the term. The feminist blogosphere is transnational and attuned to the ways in which people in one place are involved in, and implicated by, social institutions that are oppressive to other people in other places; however, their concerns are not always global and they often are suspicious or dismissive of all claims about supposedly universal ideal, transcendent values, and human rights—hallmarks of both Stoic and Kantian or European Enlightenment cosmopolitanism, as well as much contemporary cosmopolitan theory. As Tarver concludes, the disparate but linked feminist blogosphere publics highlight the importance of fostering critical thought and dissent about what constitutes a problem (and for whom) as much as how best to solve a problem. This is a cosmopolitanism that seeks cooperation by the creation of spaces for differences.

In the name of humanity as a whole or universal morality, the traditional language of cosmopolitanism can erase or ignore—or appear to erase or ignore— differences. Recalling Louis Althusser's rejection of politically harmful claims that after the Nazi death camps and the possibility of shared annihilation from atomic war have made us all and equally "proletarians of the human condition," William Lewis rejects as incorrect and politically harmful the claims of post–Cold War cosmopolitans (such as Nussbaum and Appiah) that after economic globalization and shared environmental and terrorist threats we all and equally have become cosmopolitans of the human condition—only cosmopolitans of decent feelings. Lewis argues that this universalist cosmopolitanism, often rooted in fear and desirous of order, misidentifies concepts such as common humanity, universal morality, and essential solidarity as metaphysical notions rather than ideological constructs with histories and uses on behalf of particular interests. When this happens, Lewis continues, sometimes cosmopolitanism "results in the forgetting of class differences and in the paving over of existing class struggles" while simultaneously erasing "the evidence of the production of these universal ideals insofar as they can be understood as part of the class struggle." In this light, and despite the fact that prima facie it seems difficult to disagree with Appiah's cosmopolitan recommendation to communicate with others and find common ground and avoid conflicts or with Nussbaum's cosmopolitan advice to gain a liberal education and respect others and establish international institutions to promote justice, Lewis asserts that these sentiments "may actually work to justify institutions and practices that prolong" major problems such as environmental devastation, economic inequality, and poverty: "Cosmopolitanism seeks moral and juridical solutions to problems that have their roots in the (historically local) moral and juridical systems that it wishes to universalize." Here the appeal to a supposed common humanity ignores the exploitation (of some people by some other people) that this appeal itself works in practice. In turn, Lewis concludes, this ensures continuation of the contestations and conflicts that any cosmopolitanism of decent feelings charges itself with overcoming.

Is a different kind of cosmopolitanism possible—a humble, homeless, hopeful, pluralistic, difference-attuned, place- and history-situated cosmopolitanism that rejects any metaphysical status and justification of itself by means of some supposed universal humanity, universal God, universal reason, universal speech conditions, universal morality, or universal rights? Would this different kind of cosmopolitanism be just a dream? In "Somewhere, Dreaming of Cosmopolitanism," John Stuhr addresses this question in light of what he takes to be the problems and failures of all the other options. Those other options include all forms of traditional, narrow provincialism and all forms of traditional, universalistic and abstract view-from-everywhere cosmopolitanism. With regard to the latter, Stuhr argues that cosmopolitanism involves a two-part misunderstanding of social life: It misses the fact that all political practices and institutions are exclusionary as well as inclusionary and it fails to grasp the reality of place as a particular way of life such that one simply cannot be at home everywhere. As important, Stuhr continues, cosmopolitanism is a power, a historical force that simultaneously dignifies and immiserates through many forms of violence and oppression—from colonialism and imperialism to slavery and sexism. Drawing on the work of Frantz Fanon, Stuhr agrees that we need to invent new concepts and rethink humanity and ourselves. This means, Stuhr continues, that all forms of wider and wiser provincialism, like that of Josiah Royce, and all forms of more rooted and more difference-attuned cosmopolitanism, like that of Anthony Appiah, ultimately fail. Stuhr concludes not by proposing a solution to the cosmopolitanism/provincialism dispute but, rather, by proposing a dissolution of the problem—by rejecting notions of moral universalism and monistic identities in favor of a democratic pluralism, and by recognizing the practical problems and opportunities that this presents. Stuhr concludes by putting the problem this way: "What social practices would lead the included to *feel* . . . the importance of the concerns and lives of the excluded? And what nonmanipulative social practices might make this possible? And how is it possible to sustain hope that work toward their creation is reasonable and worthwhile?" To succeed, he claims, would be to become a part of a *different* world, a theme that runs through all the chapters in this final part of this volume.

12 Citizen or Guest?
Cosmopolitanism as Homelessness

Jessica Wahman

THE TERM COSMOPOLITAN typically connotes a "citizen of the world." Such citizenship suggests a kind of belonging to or being at home in the entire world and, furthermore, enjoying all the rights and privileges while accepting the responsibilities that citizenship implies. Furthermore, to many it suggests participation in a universal common ground of humanity transcending all particularities and differences. (It is, perhaps, this purported unifying ground that anchors us "at home" in any part of the world.) I am going to argue, however, that cosmopolitanism requires a different sort of relationship to one's sociocultural environment. A cosmopolitan should be thought of more like a guest in the home of another, comporting herself with propriety, sensitivity, and openness to the unfamiliar. My plan for this chapter is to analyze cosmopolitanism as a state of mind rather than a breadth of experience (for the provincially minded can nonetheless be well traveled) and as one that acknowledges and maintains rather than transcends differences. The cosmopolitan attitude implies an at once estranged and dependent state of being, one without a clear point of reference by which to assimilate the unknown and reliant on another for literal and spiritual sustenance. A cosmopolitan has not made a home of the world but has made herself homeless.

The distinction between being at home versus a guest in the world is important to consider, as it can address the very countercosmopolitan tendencies that have arisen in reaction to increasingly global access to one another. While familiarity with a variety of different cultures is important to a worldly perspective, it can hinder as easily as it might foster the broad-mindedness we associate with the cosmopolitan attitude. What characterizes the provincial mind is not merely ignorance of different beliefs, cultures, or lifestyles but the narrow viewpoint through which everything else is interpreted. The ability to travel (literally or virtually) can only aid a cosmopolitan outlook if one is open to the destabilizing aspects of the experience.

Finally, a cosmopolitan attitude is not one we can maintain continuously. A sense of home is a biological and psychological necessity: we require a place to be safe, to settle in, relax, and feel the familiarity of our surroundings. To take on an attitude of homelessness is a strenuous demand; it is a challenge to our own tenacity that requires the bravery to disrupt our habits and beliefs. To be cosmopolitan, in short, is not just to be a certain kind of person or to live a worldly lifestyle, nor ought it to imply a peeling away of particular attachments and values so as to expose some (questionable) human essence. Cosmopolitanism is a kind of ethical orientation we may strive to approximate even as we recognize the inevitability of our allegiances.[1] It is a reminder that all the world is *not* our home, that it owes us no special rights or privileges, and that, at bottom, we depend humbly on the graciousness of our hosts.

Cosmopolitanism as a State of Mind

It seems relatively uncontroversial that the term *cosmopolitan* conveys something more about a person than an aggregation of experiences. It implies, first of all, a form of self-identification. A cosmopolitan, traditionally considered, relates herself to not only her family, community, or even country, but somehow to humanity in general.[2] Even if we reject cosmopolitanism's traditional notion of a common human essence, there remains the belief—considerably developed by John Lysaker—that "each [of us] is bound in a community of mutual concern, that the affairs of another are one's own, and visa-versa."[3] In addition, *cosmopolitan* implies the broad-mindedness characteristic of a person who does not judge the rest of the world by the extent to which it meets her expectations and fulfills her prejudices. Both of these connotations denote ways of perceiving self and world, and it is worthwhile to investigate these attitudes more closely. I am going to claim, in fact, that the second connotation of *cosmopolitan* is, in at least one important sense, at odds with the first in such a way that it problematizes the very possibility of relating oneself to all humankind, even as we feel the psychological and ethical pull of our connections to others. The state of mind required for openness to new and unfamiliar viewpoints precludes, as I will show, a straightforward and simple identification with the persons holding those views.

Furthermore, treating cosmopolitanism primarily as an orientation suggests that breadth and complexity of experience, whether through travel or due to the benefit of living in a culturally rich and diverse environment, is not a sufficient condition for being cosmopolitan. (Whether it is a necessary condition is an interesting question to pursue as well, but for now I choose to focus on insufficiency.) Some people who travel regularly, whether for pleasure or by necessity, retain a narrow-minded preference for familiar ways of doing things and judge other countries and cultures by the extent to which they measure up to their own expectations. The stereotypical tourist who goes to another country and complains about the habits of the "foreigners" or the soldier or executive overseas who refers to members of the local community in pejorative and dismissive terms even as she defends them or he trades with them epitomize our notion of the irremediably provincial world traveler. Despite the fact that these people encounter a variety of cultures and may even experience some of them in depth, enough to gain a pragmatic mastery of the situation (they learn how "those people think" and how one has to act in order to do business with them), they never allow their experiences to introduce them to an alternative—and possibly equally rich and viable—way of confronting life and interpreting its meaning.

If being cosmopolitan invokes a particular state of mind, then a meaningful way of conceptualizing an honestly cosmopolitan attitude is to compare being at home with being a guest in the home of another. When we think of a world citizen, we frequently think of one who is at home anywhere,[4] but I find this to be a problematic interpretation of cosmopolitanism for two reasons. Not only is this outlook in tension with openness to difference, for it implies familiarity with one's surroundings, it also suggests that the strange and different are to be overcome by transforming them into familiar possessions. In short, I am arguing that a perspective so broad as to make all the world familiar is either the grossest act of assimilation (for, all the world cannot be mine) or humanly impossible (I cannot take a perspective so broad so as to include every other).[5]

The connotation of *guest*, on the other hand, provides a useful corrective to the more problematic sense of citizenship that cosmopolitanism can often call to mind, for being a guest implies, on the one hand, amity and perhaps some familiarity or commonality, but at the same time a recognition that one's present surroundings are not one's own and customary practices are established by the host. Even in the case of great and longtime friends, where one may know the other's habits and belongings very well, the guest never claims ownership of the host's home nor does he refuse to accommodate himself to his host's way of doing things. The cosmopolitan, in order to transcend provinciality, must, like the guest, leave the comforts of home and comport himself according to the rules, habits, and practices of others. To extend the metaphor even further, a fully cosmopolitan outlook would actually involve a suspension of reference to home. A guest may temporarily tolerate the "weird" way her hosts choose to do things, knowing the visit is temporary,[6] but to immerse oneself in a different lifestyle and even worldview, as we'd expect of the cosmopolitan, a more radical reorientation of perspective is required. Thus the metaphor of world citizen becomes inverted and the cosmopolitan is effectively (though not literally) homeless.

My concept of a cosmopolitan as both a guest and in some sense homeless was initially inspired by the title of the final segment of George Santayana's autobiography, *My Host, the World*. I have always taken this title to refer both to

Santayana's breadth of travel and, more importantly, to his own sense of homelessness and detachment from that which he observed. Santayana lived in many different places for extended periods of time. He spent his early childhood in Spain, his later childhood and early adulthood in the United States (specifically Boston, Massachusetts), and part of his early adulthood and much of his later life in Europe (Germany, England, and finally Italy). Yet it is often said that Santayana did not find himself at home in any one of these places. His chosen title seems to indicate, by contrast, that not only did Santayana fail to view the world as his home (to say nothing of any particular place in it), but he felt himself to be dependent on the hospitality of other people, civilizations, and, ultimately, nature itself. To be sure, Santayana did not accomplish the kind of ultimately homeless orientation I am suggesting would epitomize the cosmopolitan, for his interpretations of different cultures could be scathing and highly prejudicial. But he would always acknowledge that he was expressing matters as he saw them, and in his more dispassionate moments both acknowledged his partiality and contemplated a broader perspective. His point, one I wish to stress as well, was that we cannot completely escape our own psychic orientation—our own home, as I will explain—but are going to form judgments based on our biases and predilections.

However, if we cannot completely escape ourselves, a more cosmopolitan outlook would require that we think and feel ourselves into an unfamiliar world, even one we might initially find abhorrent, in order to appreciate as best we can the relativity of our home perspective. The second inspiration for my depiction of a cosmopolitan is the playwright Tony Kushner. The characters in Kushner's plays, even those we might consider to be most contemptible, are fully fleshed out individuals whose expressions and actions regularly destabilize our assumptions, deeply held beliefs, and normative schemas about right and wrong or good and evil. As such, Kushner's cosmopolitanism lies both in his own ability to imagine and express what it is like to hold perspectives he does not share and in his challenge to his audiences to do the same.

For my own part, it is hard to attend one of Kushner's productions and not be startled into questioning what I think I know about the world I inhabit and the people in it. One of the most breathtaking examples of this achievement that I personally encountered took place in the initial New York run of *Homebody/Kabul*, only a couple of months after September 11, 2001. In this play, set primarily in Afghanistan, Kushner managed to make a high-ranking member of the Taliban into an at least briefly sympathetic character to an audience undoubtedly raw and scarred by the recent events in lower Manhattan.[7] And even in less extreme cases, Kushner succeeds in calling attention to the lenses we use to color our worlds without knowing we have done so. In *The Intelligent Homosexual's Guide to Capitalism and Socialism with a Key to the Scriptures (Guide)*, Kushner takes on issues of fidelity—to lovers, family, political parties, and ideologies—and challenges the audience's assumptions about the value and costs of both loyalty and rootlessness, all while getting us to think more deeply about our socio-political ideological attachments. Finally, and perhaps most famously, in *Angels in America* Kushner works his way into the mind and soul of an individual one could only imagine to be the negation of everything the liberal, socialist-leaning, openly gay Kushner himself embodies, namely, the closeted House Un-American Activities Committee lawyer Roy Cohn. (Kushner even indirectly, through two of his characters—Louis Ironson and, most notably, Ethel Rosenberg—bestows the prayer of Kaddish on Cohn.) In all these cases, Kushner stretches to embody different perspectives in the complex and paradoxical manner of the cosmopolitan guest, that is, by compassionately entertaining an alien viewpoint while recognizing it as alien and other to his own. The cosmopolitan attitude as represented by Kushner's work, then, is not the act of simply making the unfamiliar familiar—that is, it does not translate the foreign into something "closer to home"—nor does it display itself as the discovery of a common essential nature binding all humanity and rendering differences mere superficialities. As Kushner himself has acknowledged, it is partly the nature of the dramatic medium that facilitates his efforts, which suggests that a cosmopolitanism attitude may be better served by some methods of inquiry than others.[8] Where a simple logic of identity demands full agreement and must reject the incommensurable, the employment of a sympathetic imagination, as I will explain, can explore the relativity of human perspectives in a way that tolerates and maintains the coexistence of competing views. The cosmopolitan guest relates to the strange as "appreciate-able" without necessarily being agreeable, as imaginable without being fully comprehensible or conceptually assimilable, and in doing so, thereby estranges herself from the comforts of her home vistas and values.

Phenomenological Orientation of the Home

Up to this point I have been straightforwardly asserting that "being at home" involves an orientation centered around oneself where unfamiliar experiences are interpretively assimilated and different is made same. As such I have been drawing on existential phenomenology generally, but I have in mind, in particular, the exposition of the dwelling that Emmanuel Levinas provides in *Totality and Infinity*. Levinas proposes the dwelling as a condition for the establishment of interiority, a self-conscious relation to the world as that of a subject to one's possessions, and one that is radically undermined by the face of the other. Levinas's treatment of one's phenomenological world as a home and confrontation with the other as a transcendence and breach of that world—an encounter which, at the same time, makes an ethical demand—serves as a relevant framework through which to articulate the distinction between provinciality and cosmopolitanism. It is not my plan here, for a variety of reasons, to equate Levinas's ethical philosophy with my position on cosmopolitanism.[9] Nevertheless, his construction of the dwelling as the ground of a stable interior life is a productive means of discussing both the temptations of provinciality and the challenges entailed by a cosmopolitan attitude.

The phenomenological orientation of the dwelling involves a good deal more than simple intentionality or a basic awareness of objects, even objects as implements for one's use, though it includes those. For me to fully inhabit my surroundings, not just live from or off them, my environs must become an orderly world and its objects my possessions. In a condition of habitation, "the objective world is situated by relation to my dwelling."[10] In order to make strange and separate entities into safe and familiar objects, experience must be made coherent, objects put into a context in which they make sense to me, and this sense is such that it specifically suits my needs and purposes. In this way, the potentially alien is rendered "same." In the interior life of the dwelling, two important conditions obtain: everything is oriented around me as the focal point, and phenomena exist to be grasped, both literally and figuratively. Tangible objects become possessions to be manipulated at will and are signified so as to fit into my overarching experience. Thus, the "relation that the home establishes [is] with a world to be possessed, to be acquired, to be rendered interior. The first movement of economy is in fact egoist."[11] For me to feel like I belong—have a place—in the world, in some sense that experienced world must belong to me. Furthermore, the familiarity with my surroundings that I require in order to feel at home is not limited to identifying the world as mine; my habits and interpretations are also experienced as right or proper. In other words, if the world is implicitly taken to be as I perceive it, then my thoughts and practices are not obviously *my* way of doing things; rather, they are just the way things are done. In making the world my home, I formulate an environment without surprises where objects and actions are reduced to a reassuring sameness.

The condition of the dwelling can explain why it would be problematic to consider cosmopolitanism as "at-homeness," for claiming the entire world as one's own would amount to a monstrous egotism. Thankfully this is not possible. The face of the other calls into question my comfortable habitation where everything has its place and life is predictable and reliable. Without going into too much detail about Levinas's phenomenology, the face is such that it defies totalization; the other cannot be reduced to another item that exists for me in my constructed existence. Once the other has faced me, it follows that the world can no longer be my possession. My sense of reality therefore must be fundamentally disrupted by this encounter and the other must threaten the security of my home. For this reason, identification with the other (or, rather, identification of the other with me) cannot be a solution to my discomfort, for it amounts to expecting the other to be just another version of me, to see the world as I see it. A cosmopolitan cannot identify with all of humanity because this attempt to assimilate the multiplicity of cultural viewpoints and lifestyles into one coherent worldview is more likely a disguised means of trying to universalize one's own interpretation of reality and to impose it on others who may not share that interpretation.

While strict identification is impossible, I believe one can strive to achieve a cosmopolitan attitude through sympathetic imagination. (At this point I would depart from a strict interpretation of Levinas's ethical condition of the relation of same to other, because the possibility of empathic understanding would likely be too reciprocal to fit the theory.) While it is not possible to completely escape one's own way of seeing the world in order to view it from the point of view of another, there is a profound difference between assuming everyone is like me and thinking my way into a different perspective. In claiming knowledge of the other person's way of viewing the world, I totalize; in imagining what life might be like for someone else, I recognize this act as my own creation and harbor no expectations that my version is identical to their own. Therefore, even though sympathy seeks commonality with others, it differs significantly from a logic that universalizes and essentializes. It makes connections by seeking out moments of mutual recognition and shared understanding, but it does not extend these moments of personal communication to humanity in general (e.g., if Hamid and I learn that we detest being treated as a pawn in some powerful person's game, we cannot assume that everyone feels this way in all cases or at all times), nor does it follow that other differences can thereby be wished away or overlooked (I cannot assume, based on this one shared understanding, that Hamid should think as I do in other in all matters, such as religion or appropriate social roles for women). In imagining a sense of reality different from my own, I both connect to it and at the same time lose the sense of myself as the center of a world over which I have mastery. Instead, I am a stranger groping about in a world I don't know, in a home that is not mine. A cosmopolitan may visit countless "worlds" and thereby achieve an appreciation for the rich and varied possibilities for human life, but she cannot be said to know them all the way she knows her home.[12]

Provinciality in the Face of Difference

The disorientation inherent in the realization that one's own sense of the world is not universal suggests why provinciality is a tempting attitude and cosmopolitanism an ethical demand. If I could ignore the challenge posed to my assumptions about the nature of things, I would not have to face the fact that my world is in some sense an adaptive invention. However, rejecting a challenge with which I am literally *faced* does not negate the fact of it, and disregarding what amounts to a contestation of my egoistic dominion over reality is ethically problematic at best. Kwame Appiah notes as much when he reflects on the cosmopolitan powers of global technology: "the worldwide web of information—radio, television, telephones, the Internet—means not only that we can affect lives everywhere but that we can learn about life anywhere, too. Each person you know about and can affect is someone to whom you have responsibilities: to say this is just to affirm the very idea of morality."[13] Appiah's point about morality lines up nicely with Levinas's claim that the face of the other makes an ethical demand, for both are asserting that to come in contact with another person is to have ethical obligations to them, including obligations to learn about their way of life and their understanding of their own world, problems, and issues. However, we are at risk of making the same mistake with the internet as we did with worldly travelers if we assume, as Appiah seems to, that sheer access to and confrontation with a wider variety of cultures automatically produces a more cosmopolitan mind-set. To the contrary, despite our access to information from all over the globe, the internet can actually increase our provinciality and intolerance. First of all, access to a wider variety of cultures creates the possibility of more and more challenges to one's own worldview, which, as I have already noted, can be threatening to one's sense of self and world. Secondly, the World Wide Web has provided us with unprecedented means to shut out different viewpoints even as we become exposed to more and more varied ways of life. Through social networking sites like Facebook or just our own web-surfing choices, we are increasingly able to self-select for information and people we already agree with and ignore or vilify those we don't. Unlike actual face-to-face relationships, we can literally tune out viewpoints we don't want to expose ourselves to even as we form judgments about ways of the world we might never have encountered without current technology. What emerges is a stronger and therefore more dangerous version of C.S. Peirce's a priori method in that we reinforce our own limited and provincial sense of the world by giving ourselves the illusion of worldwide universal agreement.[14] Of course, it is not the case that that the internet is inherently either good or bad for cosmopolitanism. As with any technology, the merits of twenty-first-century communication devices will depend on how we choose to use them. We can either recognize the ethical demand made by individual and cultural others that we critically reflect on our most deeply held beliefs—that is, we can aspire to a cosmopolitan attitude—or we can be narrow-minded provincials in a global context.

The current coexistence of narrow-mindedness and globalization calls to mind another paradoxical example of provinciality in the face of difference, namely, the temptations of urbanite New Yorkers[15] to use their own sense of worldly superiority as a means of closing themselves off to the perspectives of other—frequently rural or small-town—Americans.[16] As a result of the culturally rich and diverse nature of New York City (and probably to other historical factors I can't examine here), its denizens have a way of taking their own cosmopolitanism for granted and sneering at the limited lifestyles, experiences, and viewpoints of the rest of America. This would, of course, be a standard use of the terms of *cosmopolitan* and *provincial*, where the supposedly worldly city dweller contrasts herself with the attitudes of the "provinces."[17] But insofar as the New Yorker (a) views her home perspective as the viewpoint from the world's center, and (b) refuses to openly consider small-town life (or life in other American cities) as a different but viable orientation, our New York native epitomizes the provincial attitude.[18]

The Challenge of Cosmopolitanism

As we can see from these two examples of "worldly" provinciality, cosmopolitanism as I have conceived it involves more than access to different cultures; it instead requires the courage to undermine one's own sense of comfort, safety, and control. Perhaps this is why "[t]here's a sense in which cosmopolitanism is the name not of the solution but of the challenge."[19] Unless we plan to be hermits, we need to venture out from home, and once we do, a minimal sense of ethics demands that we recognize ways of the world that are not our own. To go beyond acknowledgement and embrace cosmopolitanism is to try to live in an unfamiliar place without clinging to beliefs and habits that feel obviously true to us; a cosmopolitan state of mind is, in a way, that of a homeless guest.

As pleasant as it can be to be a guest in someone else's home, it can also be stressful. Nothing is where one expects it to be—the automatic movements we make for our everyday belongings are fruitless in new surroundings; and our most familiar habits, like eating and sleeping, are inevitably disrupted as we adjust to our host's style of life. Furthermore, to be, not just a guest but homeless is to be vulnerable and exposed. The world traveler is a guest insofar as he respects and abides by his host's cultural perspectives and practices, but a cosmopolitan attitude goes beyond this; it involves a recognition that home is, to some extent, an illusion. It is in this way that cosmopolitanism involves a kind of homelessness. While maintaining a cosmopolitan perspective, one cannot at the same time take refuge in the comforts of home precisely because the orientation undermines the security and predictability that our constructed sense of reality provides.

There are important limits to the metaphor of homelessness that at the same time serve to shed light on the limitations of a cosmopolitan outlook. Because I am focusing on cosmopolitanism as a phenomenological orientation, there is a sense that one can never be completely homeless (unless one was so mentally disordered that integrated self-consciousness was fundamentally compromised), and therefore one cannot be entirely or permanently cosmopolitan. "Man abides in the world as having come to it from a private domain, from being at home with himself, to which at each moment he can retire."[20] To have an integrated consciousness at all is to possess some kind of phenomenological home, a retreat into our own sense of order that we require in order to rest and recuperate, just as we require a physical home to protect ourselves and our possessions from the elements and other people.[21] Cosmopolitanism is a strenuous attitude because it takes effort to venture out into unfamiliar territory; it is also, because of this fact, a temporary perspective, neither automatic nor achieved once and for all. Cosmopolitanism is better measured as a transitory state of mind than a constant way of life. In a sense, it is both like and unlike Santayana's "spiritual life," in which one takes an aesthetic holiday from the everyday burdens of the world. As with the spiritual life, the "cosmopolitan life" is not a life or even a lifestyle, but an orientation one strives to attain but cannot maintain continuously. Unlike an aesthetic holiday, however, cosmopolitanism is an ethical challenge, namely to give up, even for a while, our sense of place in the world and allow ourselves to be governed by others.

Postscript: Aesthetic Retreats and Cosmopolitan Hopes

My reasons for inquiring into provinciality and the challenges of cosmopolitanism grow out of a felt sense of despair at the possibility of building anything resembling shared meanings in ways broad enough to sustain a legitimate public. When I consider the emergence of the World Wide Web, social networks like Facebook, and the blogosphere, I see a possibility for shared meanings that more frequently drives the gulfs among our various positions farther and farther apart. Yes, within subsets we refine and clarify our opinions and build communities of like-minded fellows, but we find ourselves speaking less to those with whom we are inclined to substantively disagree, thereby reinforcing the illusion of consensus that our mini-communities of discourse provide. This is how the a priori method can develop monstrous power: we speak to increasingly broad networks of those with whom we already agree and reassure ourselves of the obviousness and indubitability of our beliefs.[22]

What this despair gives rise to, then, is a desire to more fully appreciate the complexity of the cosmopolitan outlook, as I see it, and the psychological roadblocks to its attainment. By considering a worldview as a kind of home we carry with us, I better understand the appeal of provincialism and the hidden and misguided motivations of universalism. If we recognize the cognitive and emotional needs met by a home vantage point, provincialism and universalism can be viewed as not opposed but equally provincial temptations insofar as they protect one's own sense of the world by rendering anyone who thinks differently either evil or confused. Furthermore, in characterizing as homelessness an orientation to the world sufficiently open to difference that it can truly learn from very distant others (in both the literal and metaphorical senses of the word "distant"), I not only conceive of the difficulties in attaining a cosmopolitan attitude but also begin to imagine the outlines of possibilities for its achievement. Cosmopolitanism's hope to overcome provincialism lies neither in universalizing nor in merely tolerating differences but by engaging and appreciating these deep and sometimes incommensurate pluralities of opinion even as we try to forge connections among them.

My two inspirations for this chapter, George Santayana and Tony Kushner, further illuminate the competing pulls of home and abroad in their quite different responses to the relativism that can inspire a cosmopolitan outlook, thus giving me a better understanding of and respect for my own allegiances and attachments even as I sustain hopes for the amelioration of personal and cultural misunderstandings, hostilities, and enmities. Both writers display elements of cosmopolitanism in their work, but their responses to the recognition of the cosmopolitan challenge are quite different: one is a kind of quietist retreat, the other a hopeful striving. In accepting the reality of a plurality of worldviews and the impossibility of fully escaping one's particular perspective, one can seek solace with those who share one's vision—I will call these aesthetic friends—or one can embark on the adventurous challenges to build shared meanings that a cosmopolitan attitude invites. The quietist move is a kind of minimal cosmopolitanism, in that, unlike a wholesale provincialism, it does not stigmatize different views but embraces the inevitability that we are not all going to think alike and even appreciates the fact that our lives can offer up a wealth of perspectives. But to the extent that it retreats from a wholly compassionate inquiry into the lives of very different others, it cannot be positively cosmopolitan in the manner of the homeless guest I have envisioned.

George Santayana's notion of himself as guest and the world as host contributes the sense of the rootlessness, epistemic humility, and even gratitude involved in my concept of a cosmopolitan. In this way, Santayana represents the sort of baseline conditions for the possibility of an exploration into what life might be like for another person, especially one who views matters in fundamentally different ways. And yet Santayana is very uncosmopolitan in an important sense in which I am trying use the term. Though he claims no *geographical* location for his home—he carries his worldview with him wherever he goes, like a philosophical turtle, and benefits from its reassurances and protections. But his attitude toward the world is that of an observer rather than a fully invested participant, and his interactions with others are more akin to the salon than the agora.[23] In the preface to his perhaps most well-known work, *Scepticism and Animal Faith*, Santayana announces that he is speaking to those who already recognize the world he envisions and that others may clean "the windows of [their] soul" differently if they see fit.[24] Santayana therefore is not interested in building shared meanings across differences but in finding aesthetic friends, those who picture reality in generally the manner that he does. He is a guest everywhere he goes, but in another sense, he is a spiritual hermit; his home is his own reflective consciousness, and he does not venture far from its threshold.

My hope for a full cosmopolitanism, then, lies not so much with Santayana (though I think his detachment provides an important element) but with Tony Kushner. In his work, Kushner repeatedly demonstrates the ability to crawl into the skin of very different others, imagine their perspectives, and present them compellingly to his audience. Kushner more often than not exhibits both the empathy and creativity required to exert oneself in this regard. I use the word *hope* in speaking of Kushner as a deliberate reference to Jennifer Hansen's concept that she articulates in Chapter 13 of this volume.[25] In Kushner's work I see the cognitive possibilities of an open orientation to plurality and a steadfast commitment, in the face of despair (*Guide*, I think, is in some ways the most despairing of his plays to date), to making and building connections without essentializing or totalizing, to exploring new horizons with the humble recognition that one is in the home of others and has something to learn from them.

These parallel inspirations, Kushner and Santayana, reflect in me a tension between optimistic hope for building connections and a more pessimistic quietism that accepts the status quo, seeks out like-minded companions, and—contrary to the cosmopolitan attitude—minds my own business. On the one hand, I consider myself one of Santayana's aesthetic friends. I take pleasure in hearing already familiar thoughts expressed back to me in so eloquent a form, and I find myself believing he and I must be *right* to see the world as we do. This leads me to turn my analysis back on myself and acknowledge my own provincial tendencies as an understandable and somewhat inevitable psychological reality even as I understand their limitations and flaws. As a New Yorker, I reliably and unreflectively find myself thinking of New York City as the center of the universe, and I sometimes will admit it outright and with pride (though, I hope, with a sense of humor about the absurdity of my attitude). I love the famous *New Yorker* cover (see note 11) in which the rest of the planet is dwarfed in comparison to Manhattan's west side, and I am guilty of an urban provincialism in that I cannot seem to stretch myself to fully appreciate the town of Carlisle where I lived for ten years and where I nonetheless felt like an exile from my beloved New York home. I admit that there are times where I do not want to appreciate life in a town where I can't get a meal at midnight, see cutting-edge theater or a film not involving a comic book hero whenever I want to, listen to people speaking at least four different languages I don't understand on a subway platform while the subway itself sings the melody from *West Side Story*'s "Somewhere,"[26] or be surrounded by people of liberal opinion who don't feel they have to justify or explain their liberalism. On the other hand, I feel the limitations of my own pessimistic avoidance of the unfamiliar. I admire those who eagerly seek out other viewpoints and ways of living and confront disagreements head-on with the hope of expanding one another's horizons. And in the cases in which my own bravery and compassion allow me to stay with difficult conversations and conflicts, I find myself rewarded with new camaraderies and greater friendships that broaden the vistas of my own experience, expand my world, and occasionally even shatter its boundaries.

In the end, I find myself in fundamental tension between my aspirations for building shared meanings across boundaries and my desire to find repose and shelter in a home where meanings are already shared and where familiarity and resonance with friendly others prevails. I imagine this may be a common tension for many of us. We need that sense of home, and perhaps we cannot begin to build shared meanings without acknowledging our personal allegiances. Even though the security of a home worldview can present itself as an obstacle to building shared understandings (and perhaps the challenges to that worldview a threat to one's sense of security), the self-aware recognition of its presence and power may be what enables us to resist the temptation to universalize away the great diversity of human experience. I want a cosmopolitanism that acknowledges the significance and attraction of a shared worldview and also affirms the ethical importance of accepting the relativity of our most deeply held beliefs as we explore unfamiliar landscapes and benefit from the offerings of our various hosts. In this vein, the two writers who have served as my inspiration together embody my vision of the possibilities of cosmopolitanism. George Santayana represents those aesthetic friends who seem to me a kind of home. Tony Kushner is my ethically adventurous hope.

A co-editor of this volume, **JESSICA WAHMAN** is a Senior Lecturer in philosophy at Emory University. Her interests include philosophical psychology, philosophy of mind, modern European philosophy, American pragmatism, and philosophy and drama, and her many publications include *Narrative Naturalism: An Alternative Framework for Philosophy of Mind* (Lexington Books, 2015).

Notes

1. Cf. Chapter 1 in this volume, where John Lysaker stresses that attention to a certain kind of character is essential to any contemporary discussion of cosmopolitanism. Furthermore, his point underscores the notion that the ethical orientation I am describing is not a superficial attitude one can put on or take off at will but depends on the cultivation of practices and habits.

2. For this connotation of the term, see Kwame Anthony Appiah's introduction to *Cosmopolitanism: Ethics in a World of Strangers* (New York: W. W. Norton, 2006). While this is not

the view of cosmopolitanism held by Appiah (in fact, the position I am taking in this chapter is greatly indebted to Appiah's own characterizations of cosmopolitanism), he nonetheless identifies enlightenment humanism as a kind of cosmopolitanism.

3. See Chapter 1, page 13 of this volume.

4. Citizenship certainly implies a good deal more than this, and, in fact, a rich discussion of citizenship could challenge the association of "citizen" with "being at home." But the fact remains that when we think of a cosmopolitan person, we frequently think of a jet-setter who is at home anywhere; in other words, she belongs to (is a citizen of) any place she inhabits.

5. This claim contains an epistemological presumption, one that Cynthia Gayman in her chapter in this volume, points out is not universally shared and is rejected by those whose ethical and religious commitments entail a concomitant adherence to the absolute truth of their beliefs. My argument relies on the assumption that knowledge is both existential in origin and irremediably perspectival in scope. One's perspective may be comparatively narrow or broad, but it cannot be escaped. A full justification of this belief is (obviously, I hope) beyond the parameters of this chapter. I mean here only to call attention to the epistemological position I am taking and to note its influence on my criticism of universalist interpretations of cosmopolitanism.

6. The notion of a guest also assumes that there is a home to return to (think of the recent proposals regarding "guest worker" status for noncitizen workers in the United States, the implication being that one can work in the United States but will belong to—call "home"—some other country and will not try to be eligible for or attain US citizenship). We may not so easily assume that everyone who confronts unfamiliar ways of living is doing so from the secure vantage point of possessing a place to call home. See Chapters 7, 8, and 9, by José Medina, Jeff Edmonds, and Megan Craig, in this volume for discussion of displacement and loss of place, whether cultural, geographical, political, or phenomenological.

7. I further develop this case as an example of pluralistic empathy in "Drama as Philosophical Genre," *Journal of Speculative Philosophy* 28, no. 4 (2014): 454–71.

8. In a recent video interview, Kushner explains that his ability to explore the internal contradictions in his characters and the limitations of all ideological perspectives has to do with the fact that "drama is essentially about exploring questions much more than, I think, providing answers" (www.youtube.com/watch?v=XPhRhxhxXr4&feature=BFa&list=PL949658CDE 629431D). As I understand him, participation in a dramatic medium (whether as a writer or an observer) gives us an opportunity to experience multiple, even contradictory, viewpoints (sometimes even from within a single character) without the pressure to determine whether one, in the end, is correct. I suggest that a sympathetic imagination, the kind that might be involved in both artistic creation and appreciation, can allow us to maintain and consider the legitimacy of these competing perspectives in a way that logical argumentation does not so easily tolerate.

9. In particular, I want to avoid incorporating here the controversial aspect of the welcoming feminine other that Levinas introduces in this section of *Totality and Infinity*. An exposition and consideration of the conditions that give rise to habitation, while possibly fruitful to the discussion, are beyond the present limits of the chapter, and analysis and exposition of the possible interpretations of femininity in Levinas's work would, at this point, detract from my focus. See Emmanuel Levinas, *Totality and Infinity*, trans. Alphonso Lingis (Pittsburgh: Duquesne University Press, 1969).

10. Ibid., 153.

11. Ibid., 157.

12. This statement may seem to contradict my thesis that cosmopolitanism is a kind of homelessness, for I here assert that a cosmopolitan in fact has a home. But I do not take

cosmopolitanism to be a permanent way of life so much as an attitude one strives to take on. In other moments, it is important (indeed, it is unavoidable) that even the most cosmopolitan individual have recourse to a home orientation.

13. Appiah, *Cosmopolitanism*, xiii.

14. In "The Fixation of Belief," Peirce characterizes the a priori method as the practice of believing what is most "agreeable to reason." This method, which appears rational and grounded in universals, is actually governed by personal taste and cultural preferences and reinforced by agreement among people who happen to already think the same way, so "while [the method] is a process which eliminates the effect of some casual circumstances, [it] only magnifies that of others"; see C. S. Peirce, "The Fixation of Belief," in *The Essential Peirce: Vol. I (1867–1893)*, ed. Nathan Houser and Christian Kloesel (Bloomington: Indiana University Press, 1992), 119.

15. Of course, it may well be the case that denizens of other "worldly" cities can formulate a similar provincial attitude toward rural dwellers, but, as a native New Yorker, I am in a better position to speak from this particular position.

16. I would like to thank John Stuhr for pointing this out to me about my hometown.

17. Or rather, this may illuminate the need for a three-way distinction among urbanity, provinciality, and cosmopolitanism. The apparently opposed urbanite and provincial are actually quite similar in their narrow-minded preference for their particular ways of life, while the cosmopolitan would focus on the limitations and biases of either localized preference.

18. The famous *New Yorker* magazine cover (see http://bigthink.com/ideas/21121) in which the entire world is dwarfed in comparison to the west side of Manhattan captures perfectly the way in which the New Yorker's provinciality amounts to a "home-based" orientation to the world in which everything else exists only in reference to one's own perspective. As Frank Jacobs notes beneath this illustration on his "Strange Maps" blog, "Many New Yorkers feel their city is more than just the (self-proclaimed) capital of the world. They think it actually is most of the world, the rest of the planet merely being the unavoidable orchard in which their Big Apple grows."

19. Appiah, *Cosmopolitanism*, xv.

20. Levinas, *Totality and Infinity*, 152.

21. I should note another significant distinction, which is that the literally homeless person cannot suspend or alter her condition at will in the way that I am suggesting a cosmopolitan-minded person can and must. Furthermore, one who is in a condition of forced displacement experiences challenges to a sense of home that are not of her choosing. The active choice to disorient oneself from the comforts of home may presuppose a place of privilege, namely, of possessing a secure home in the first place.

22. This concern may well, of course, have to do as much with my particular experiences and temperamental outlook as with inherent challenges facing internet communication. For more hopeful interpretations of the democratic and cosmopolitan possibilities of the World Wide Web, see Chapter 15 by Erin Tarver and Chapter 2 by Noëlle McAfee in this volume.

23. Thanks to my colleague Peter Grahame for pointing this out to me.

24. George Santayana, *Scepticism and Animal Faith* (New York: Dover, 1955), vi–vii.

25. Chapter 13, pp. 216–223.

26. Jim Dwyer, "Under Broadway, the Subway Hums Bernstein," *New York Times*, February 20, 2009, www.nytimes.com/2009/02/21/nyregion/21about.html?_r=0.

13 Cosmopolitan Hope

Jennifer L. Hansen

> Hope is thus ultimately a practical, militant emotion, it unfurls banners.
> —Ernst Bloch
>
> Where hope is lacking the soul dries up and withers.
> —Gabriel Marcel

PRESUMABLY, THERE ARE many cosmopolitans: the well-traveled, sophisticated, polyglot; the stoic serenely navigating heterogeneous (and fractious) cultural spaces; the migrant following new capital flows; the hospitable host; the religious seeker; or, the peace builder appealing to our shared earth. Cosmopolitans—whatever motive—are mapmakers redrawing the boundaries of the familiar in order to seek what is better.[1] And, it is this broadly shared goal—seeking what is better—that occupies me here because it is often motivated by hope. To seek what is better might be a way to describe what Gabriel Marcel calls "the fundamental situation to which it is hope's mission to reply as a signal of distress."[2]

Some disclaimers are necessary before proceeding with my analysis of cosmopolitan hope. First of all, the emphasis of this argument is on the nature of hope and not on grounding cosmopolitanism for the twenty-first century. The tradition of cosmopolitanism is a tradition of attempting to articulate a political or moral ideal; it "implies the broadmindedness," as Jessica Wahman aptly explains, "characteristic of a person who does not judge the rest of the world by the extent to which it meets her expectations and fulfills her prejudices."[3] Those who advocate such an ideal, such as Martha Nussbaum or Kwame Anthony Appiah,[4] intend to prescribe how each of us should comport ourselves to others, particularly those perceived to be wholly different from us. However, my invocation of cosmopolitanism here is not in order to contribute to the prescriptive moral project, nor toward clarifying what is required for a global politics, but rather to describe a feature of the experience of hope. *Cosmopolitan* here is intended in two senses: as an adjective to denote pluralism or plural frames of intelligibility, and to characterize individuals who come into contact with diverse peoples.

I recognize, however, a discussion of the "cosmopolitan" may evoke for some readers a specific, Western intellectual tradition. And, to make matters trickier, many critics of this tradition, such as William Lewis and John Stuhr in Chapters 16 and 17 of this volume, point out how this ideal rationalizes a bloody history of colonialism and domination of various lands by white Europeans. Given this association, I could be persuaded to give up the use of the word *cosmopolitan* if it cannot be reconstructed. What John Dewey says about philosophy could apply equally well here for cosmopolitan: "There is a kind of intellectual work to be done which it is of utmost importance to mankind to have done, but which from the general human point of view does not need to be done in the name of philosophy provided only that it be done."[5] I suspect, however, that here the situation is reversed. From the general human point of view, *cosmopolitan* is not likely to evoke images of conquest and domination, but vaguely some sort of broadminded "citizen of the world." And yet, given that part of my readership is philosophers, I would rather give up "cosmopolitan" if it proved to be a stumbling block to what I see be a more important endeavor, namely, describing the experience of hope.[6]

Second, in analyzing "cosmopolitan hope," I am not purporting a conceptual analysis, wherein I clarify either the extension or intension of this concept. Rather, I am proposing a phenomenological account of cosmopolitan hope, which attempts to describe, from a first-person point of view, the affective experience of hope as well as background epistemological and metaphysical commitments assumed by those who hope. Given the everydayness of expressions of hope, and the widely different contexts, for example, "I hope it won't rain," "hope for the best, expect the worse," or President Obama's 2008 campaign slogan, "Hope," my aim is to attempt to trace a root, affective experience in common to seemingly incompatible expressions of hope. And, like all good phenomenological work, my account is intended as a dialogue, not an authoritative monologue.

Last, while my aim is to describe a root of experience of hope, I do so primarily with an eye to the role hope plays in political engagement and activism. Without hope, few of us are likely to devote energy toward political causes or building international institutions. Hope is inspirational, motivational, and as I stress in the following, may lead to action. Hence, while this project does not directly consider what is necessary for a (cosmopolitan) politics intended to address global political issues explored in this volume, such as climate change (Nancy Tuana Chapter 11), profound economic inequality due to globalization (John Lysaker Chapter 1; William S. Lewis Chapter 16; and John J. Stuhr Chapter 17), human rights (Noelle McAfee Chapter 2), or what is required to build responsive global institutions (Jeff Edmonds Chapter 8; Cynthia Gayman Chapter 14; Erin C. Tarver Chapter 15; and Stuhr, Chapter 17), it does attempt to do so indirectly by making explicit what motivates us to act.

In this chapter, I argue that hope is cosmopolitan, which means it is grounded in a pluralistic epistemology/metaphysics. In the main, what I have to say about cosmopolitans may be compatible with cosmopolitanisms intended as ethical or political ideals. I end, however, with a brief consideration of why some cosmopolitanisms are insufficiently hopeful, that is, insufficiently pluralistic.

Toward a Definition of Cosmopolitan Hope

Hope

Hope is an emotion with a cognitive aspect.[7] To be hopeful is to anticipate something better that has not-yet come into existence.[8] To be hopeful is to be committed to changing *this* world. To be hopeful is to be reasonable. To be hopeful is to be pluralistic. I now expand on each of these claims before I clarify why hope is implicitly cosmopolitan.

Hope Is an Emotion with a Cognitive Aspect

When we find ourselves mired in bad situations, we are likely to experience a variety of emotional responses: anxiety, fear, despair, or hope. Hope stands out as a possible, but not (likely) reflexive response to tragedy. Hope is not an "occurrent passion" but rather an "entrenched dispositional state."[9] Hope does not *occur* unless one has a hopeful disposition. Hope is, therefore, a mood (à la Ernst Bloch), a *Grundstimmung* (à la Martin Heidegger) or a temperament (à la William James). In each of these formulations—mood, *Grundstimmung*, temperament—the philosophers mentioned have sought to describe perception as inescapably a valuing activity. Perception never occurs without some accompanying feeling, whether it be a cold remoteness from events or a passionate attachment to what is unfolding. And, because perception is always affectively attuned, what we perceived is colored by our mood, and this coloration is what I mean by valuing. Thus, perception is always already affective and thereby always already evaluative. The sort of evaluation present in hopeful perception is discussed below.

Certainly, some "sky-blue tint" souls are born, that is, reflexive hopeful types, but for the majority, to be hopeful in dire circumstances requires cultivation (and sometimes luck). I put "luck" in parentheses to indicate that undoubtedly there will be those who, no matter how strenuously they try to cultivate a hopeful disposition, will be unsuccessful. In those cases, perhaps, only a religious experience such as sudden conversion, wherein a wholesale rearrangement of one's personality takes place (as described by James in *The Varieties of Religious Experience*) will do.[10] Interestingly, what needs to be cultivated in order to become more hopeful is relaxation or patience. To hope is akin to being creative, and being creative often depends on a sort of fluidity or flexibility of character, a willingness to bend or flow with a new inspiration without yet knowing precisely where it will lead.

The tone of hope is vitality: James describes hope as an atmosphere that if one breathes in: "his days pass by with zest; they stir with prospects, they thrill with remoter values."[11] Hope is also courageous; it requires a leap of faith. Bloch asserts, "Danger and faith are the truth of hope, in such a way that both are gathered in it, and danger contains no fear, faith no lazy quietism."[12] Hope thus invigorates and ennobles.

The cognitive aspect of hope is both intentional and nondiscursive. By "nondiscursive," I mean an experience that cannot be conceptualized. Conceptualization requires a prosaic, scientific language that communicates ideas universally. But such language communicates what already exists, what is already marked out and hope intends toward—is directed toward—that which does not yet exist. The intentional "object" cannot *yet* be conceptualized. The cognitive dimension of hope is therefore tacit. Hence, hope trades in images, in daydreams, poetry, and orients itself by felt affinities on the fringes experience.[13] Marcel suggests that hope "transcends the imagination" insofar as in its purest form it cannot be represented to oneself.[14] One who is hopeful reaches out toward a future that she feels will lift her out of a present misery.

To Be Hopeful Is to Anticipate Something Better That Has Not Yet Come into Existence

Hope rests on a habit of belief that what it anticipates will be better for humankind. By "habit of belief," I mean an implicit belief (although capable of being made explicit). One does not hope for pain, suffering, or misery. One hopes for an improvement of one's situation; one hopes for progress. And progress for hopeful types is the coming into existence of something novel, undreamed of, or unbidden.

To hope for progress is to intend toward a "real future." Bloch clarifies that the difference between a "real" and "unreal" future is that the former does not *yet* objectively exist, while the latter is a continuation of the same old, same old, that is, status quo.[15] Another way to clarify this distinction between a "real" and "unreal" future is to consider Marcel's point that true hope is expressed as "I hope" rather than "I hope that . . ."[16] To "hope that . . ." is to attempt to specify in advance, to imagine, to pin down the workings of something that is essentially mysterious. But "to hope" is to take an orientation toward the future as bringing forward something better without a determinate concept of what it is.

This distinction between a real and unreal future is crucial in the arena in politics. Because hope is inspirational, it is vital that citizens be discerning of those who seek to inspire hope in others for ends that essentially maintain the status quo. For example, in a campaign stump speech in Iowa in 2011, presidential candidate Rick Santorum attempted to inspire his audience not by claiming that black lives matter but rather by claiming that he doesn't "want to make black people's lives better by giving them somebody else's money." Not only does such a promise maintain the very status quo that many feel captive to, but it also promotes an egoism that tends to stifle hope. To hope is to reach beyond oneself, one's self-interested desires, toward something beyond myself. Hope liberates itself from possession, which is the expression of anxiety, fear, or despair, not hope.

To Be Hopeful Is to Be Committed to Changing This World

To hope is *not* to wish. One wishes for irrational things or things that one has no power to realize.[17] Obviously, a variety of colloquial expressions seem to blur the line between hope and wish, that is, "I hope it won't rain." And yet to hope it won't rain is not quite the same thing as wishing it won't rain. In the former case, it is still possible that the day will clear up: the event isn't already determined and out of our hands.[18] Even in expression of "I hope that . . ." is a sense that something else is possible. Wishing it wasn't raining is irrational, because it is already raining. However, while in this mundane example, hope is not intimately tied to our agency, the experience of hope vital to political action is, the "I hope."

When one feels hopeful that a better future is possible, one's energy is boundless. Because the world is a hospitable place again, one who is hopeful can spare more generosity, more patience for others and oneself. One who is hopeful walks with more purpose, holds oneself more openly, looks sincerely into the eyes of another. One's mind is calmer, one feels relaxed, graceful and yet energetic. Being hopeful is not wholly free from stress: knowing a new possibility may be on the horizon given the right timing, the right effort, the right confluence of events can provoke profound anxiety. But it is the sort of anxiety that precedes the first kiss of a new lover, the jitters before a wedding, or the labor pains signaling a new birth.

Agitation or distraction, on the other hand, often accompanies wishing. To say, "I wish today had been less brutal," is to absentmindedly cast off a thought because the day has been so brutal. Expressions of wishes are tinged with pessimism or despair, with an acknowledgment that we are trapped by circumstances outside of our control. Moreover, to wish is to hand over one's agency; to wish for change is like wishing for Superman. That is, what one wants seems so unlikely, so implausible, that only a miracle (which isn't likely) will bring it to pass.

Hope, on the contrary, engages with the possible. And, insofar as hope is engaged with the possible, it is instrumental to willing (voluntary action) in circumstances where human agency is causal, that is, capable of bringing something new into the world.

Hope not only anticipates what is better, but also participates in its realization.[19] To have hope is to feel that acting in service of what is better is worthwhile.

The sphere of our actions is *this* world. So when we hope for what is better, we are favorably predisposed to act in some way in this world. This does not rule out the possibility that what is better is found beyond this world. But it does mean that we act in ways in *this* world that puts us in a good position to enjoy what is better beyond this world. Hope, as Bloch says, is not a quietist faith.

To Be Hopeful Is to Be Reasonable

Because hope aspires for what is better, it is also attendant to practical reason (*phronesis*). Practical reasoning is, most generally, a tool for problem solving; it is a process of deliberation over certain desired goals. In other words, practical reason is intimately tied to action *and* is inherently normative. We deliberate when are irritated by doubt, or find our usual ways of doing things no longer satisfy, or when we are on the cusp of change.

Practical reason, moreover, is not procedural, but substantive.[20] Reasoning requires a context. I mean this in two senses: (a) we deliberate in the event of some irritation, obstruction, or loss of faith, that is, we have occasion to deliberate; (b) we deliberate in light of several background commitments that we inherit from the community, social tradition, culture—"form of life"—to which we belong. A form of life includes not only shared practices but also shared norms. This shared form of life serves as a framework of intelligibility: what we "see" depends to a large degree on what we already "believe." Another way to understand a form of life is as a cultural horizon. By "cultural horizon," I wish to emphasize not only that our framework for making sense derives from a cultural tradition we inherit but also that this tradition is historical and dynamic. The metaphor of horizon is pervasive in phenomenological examinations of experience because it aptly conveys the sense that in the background of all our activity—what we are doing or paying attention to—is a blurry fringe that indicates we are located somewhere. We are always in the middle of the field of experience that is marked out by the horizon.[21] Our experience within this penumbral fringe (horizon) is historical, not eternal. That is, we do not have "a view from nowhere,"[22] but a view situated in a certain culturally and historically shaped perception. A horizon is also that which we will never approach and thereby have completely in our grasp because as we move toward it, it moves too; our horizons expand (they can also contract).

Kwame Appiah illustrates well historically and culturally shaped reasoning in *Cosmopolitanism* when he demonstrates how difficult it would be to persuade his Asante kinfolk that witchcraft is factually untrue. Witchcraft serves all the purposes for the Asante that the germ theory serves for those of us raised in Western scientific cultures: it explains illness, it prescribes treatments, and it predicts recovery from illness. It uses a different "theoretical language" to do so, and it might not do so as well as our germ theory language does (at least for certain purposes), but it, for the most part, satisfies the needs of the Asante. If you try to explain illness to an Asante kinswoman using a scientific language of "tiny, invisible atoms, strung together to make viruses, particles so small you cannot see them with the most powerful magnifying lens, yet so potent they can kill a healthy adult," your explanation will be as unintelligible to her as witchcraft is to you.[23] A feature of intelligibility, therefore, is that it belongs to a larger framework, to background concepts, or exists within a cultural horizon.

In this sense, our hopes are reasonable; they emerge out of a specific cultural locatedness. Our hopes emerge in response to specific needs that arise in specific contexts. And those needs are intelligible to those who share a form of life with us. So too is hope intelligible as a response to those needs. What hope aims at (a not-yet future) will further expand our horizon of intelligibility, but it will do so in a way that makes it possible for others in my community to understand the reasons given. After all, we begin with a stock of beliefs to which we are deeply loyal. We do not abandon those beliefs all at once, but alter, reconsider, augment, or abandon some when we are frustrated in achieving our goals.[24]

To Be Hopeful Is to Be Pluralistic

Because being hopeful is pragmatic, both in the sense of useful and good, pluralism is a constitutive feature. Pluralism is an epistemological position: there are plural frames or horizons for making sense of the world. "Making sense" here always implies that meaning is communal, rather than private. Furthermore, "making sense" encompasses inert facts, norms, and artistic inventiveness. In other words, what makes sense, what is intelligible, is not reducible to what is conceptual or discursive. Emotions, artistic expressions, daily habits, rituals, and body language all play a role in knowing. And last, knowing takes place, as explained above, within a shared frame of intelligibility.

A concomitant pluralistic metaphysics, moreover, posits (a) that the nature of reality is turbid, abundant, and in its pulsations, vibrations, and emanations excessive to any of our attempts to capture it tidily with concepts; and, (b) that we do not have a "view from nowhere" of this "primordial chaos of sensations."[25] We are in *media res* of this endless pulsation. By necessity, we extricate out from this murky thickness some concepts with which to make useful predictions—a framework of intelligibility—to give us a foothold. The work of framing is communal because in part it emerges out of our need to coordinate activities with each other.

The pluralist metaphysical description of nature makes possible a pluralist epistemology: the universe is open to many ways of making sense, many conceptual schemes, many rationalities, assuming that each serves well its purpose of solving problems. The universe is more aptly understood as a "multiverse."[26] In the *Principles of Psychology*, James offers a helpful metaphor to further clarify the relationship between "sense-making" and "reality": "The mind . . . works on the data it receives very much as a sculptor works on his block of stone."[27] Hence, as there are many sculptors, there are many statutes, all wrought from the same stone. This metaphor, however, might be misleading because the "same stone" is not inert, but dynamic.

Pluralism is a constitutive feature of hope precisely because hope is not yet conceptualized. If we could unambiguously describe what a "better" future would look like, then it would not be a "real future." What we conceptualize is what we already know, what has been (the past). To assert that the future is a continuation of the past is a hallmark of what William James calls monistic thinking: that ultimately the world is reducible to *one* essential structure.[28] To put it another way, to claim that the future is of one cloth with the past is to claim that we can have a god's-eye view or second sight, namely, that we can have an eternal point of view on the universe. Such an epistemological assumption would hollow out any sense of the future, that is, what is not-yet known, experienced, or contemplated. If the future were already known, then hope would be inappropriate. An unflappable, content, certainty that the world is as it should be is a more appropriate disposition for a monist.

Hope, because it rests upon a pluralist epistemology, is also fallible. A particular path taken by a hopeful creature may lead to more suffering, to worse conditions, or to no change whatsoever. Hope is risky; it carries no guarantees that it will arrive at what is better. Hope's work is to embolden us enough to take the risk. Risk-taking makes no sense if the world is what the monist presupposes and defends.

Cosmopolitan Hope

Now that I have sketched out the important features of hope—cognitive, anticipatory, practical, reasonable, and pluralist—I now clarify how hope is implicitly cosmopolitan. There are as many hopes as there are dreamers: hope is not singular in its orientation but reflects the specific context in which it emerges. Hope looks ahead, beyond one's horizon, for what is better. In the sense that hope extends beyond one's horizon, it is cosmopolitan. Hope crosses familiar boundaries and landscapes; hope travels to a no place, namely, utopia. But, in keeping with the pluralist nature of hope, there are many utopias. I now bear down on the following claim: hope is cosmopolitan because it travels to utopias.

Hope Is Cosmopolitan

Cosmopolitans are in search for what is better, for example, economic stability, spiritual fulfillment, virtuous character, or perpetual peace. Insofar as cosmopolitans anticipate and seek out what is better, they are hopeful. Moreover, because cosmopolitans are *worldly*, rather than otherworldly, they are hopeful. But of particular interest here, the cosmopolitans are hopeful because they are pluralists.

Cosmopolitans are practical, but in such a way that enables them to widen their perspectives. In "On a Certain Blindness in Human Beings," James asserts that as practical beings going about things in the usual way, we seem to be so constituted that we cannot appreciate differences of perspective on the world.[29] We are too engrossed in our own projects to have the interest (or energy) to see the world from another's point of view.[30] James suggests that only the "pitiful dreamer, some philosopher, poet, or romancer" is in a position to get a "gleam of insight" into the inner lives of worth of others.[31] Whether James here is being ironic is beyond the focus of this essay, but in any case, James' list seems incomplete. For, as practical men and women, we are in a position to widen our perspective—become cosmopolitan—when what we usually do no longer satisfies. Our typical myopia, that James details, abates when the familiar begins to alienate us. When we find ourselves no-longer-at-home, we become curious.

Cosmopolitan curiosity is not idle, but vital. While Heidegger in *Being and Time* viewed curiosity as superficial, distracting, and inauthentic, cosmopolitans are suspicious of authenticity, especially if to be *authentic* means to mine the depths of one's own tradition (frame of intelligibility) for "new" possibilities. Heidegger suggests that we build our future out of a forgotten past—what is always already there—but overlooked as we chase trivialities. For Heidegger, curiosity is a sort of superficial, rootless wandering. The cosmopolitan, on the other hand, believes that possible futures are in the making, and that a healthy curiosity of the unfamiliar is good preparation for it. As curious we are open to the strange, the novel, or the alien. Curiosity then is not dilettantism, but receptivity to otherness. And out of this receptivity, we loosen ourselves from certain substantive commitments that no longer serve us, that is, that the dinner meal is interruption to our work, rather than an occasion to reconnect with our family and friends, through the shared experience of a delicious meal.

Another way to conceive of cosmopolitan curiosity is in terms of playfulness. Maria Lugones describes playfulness as openness to surprise.[32] To be open to surprise means I am *not* wedded to my way of doing things, my way of seeing the world. I can only feel surprise if something unusual happens, something new. Cosmopolitan playfulness, in other words, is a disposition of flexibility, a willingness to try a new way.

Cosmopolitan habits—curiosity, playfulness, and flexibility—pattern themselves after a pluralist view of the world. Cosmopolitans believe there is something new to experience, something to be gained from moving toward the unfamiliar. Cosmopolitans, in other words, in their very actions, acknowledge that there are many worlds, that is, many horizons.

Cosmopolitan Hope Seeks Utopias

Cosmopolitans, furthermore, are committed to a sort of conversation with others that puts them in a position to imagine other worlds of worth. As Appiah rightly notes, not all conversation—or perhaps most conversation—is about reaching agreement.[33] Conversation with those from different cultural horizons draws upon different skills than persuasion: imagination and, perhaps, empathy. Appiah writes, "Conversations across boundaries of identity—whether national, religious, or something else—begin with the sort of imaginative engagement you get when you read a novel or watch a movie or attend to a work of art."[34] Cross-cultural conversations—in other words—require a hermeneutical rationality: that is, an effort to see another's world from within their own horizon.

The practical result of such cross-cultural exchanges need not be a wholesale adoption of another's form of life, that is, "going native." Moreover, such conversations are not so superficial as to breed a shallow exoticism—a fascination in what is totally other without any sense that there is a rationality undergirding it to which I can find some point of connection. While we all operate from within a frame of intelligibility, and while there are indeed multiples frames, this need not imply that there are no points of contact between them. At the very least, as Immanuel Kant points out, all of us strangers share "the surface of the earth."[35] We also share certain fundamental biological experiences. From those points of contact, we gain entrance into the stranger's world.

What conversations across familiar boundaries *should* yield are "utopias." Here, I am not invoking a notion of utopia as ideal place: a place without tragedy. Rather, for the purposes of my argument, a utopia is quite literally a no-place. A utopia is, rather, a practice of criticizing the present moment; certainly this is what the literary genre of utopia accomplishes. So, it is in this sense of utopia that I am claiming cosmopolitan hope seeks utopias. Cosmopolitan hope is a habit of belief that beyond our familiar horizons is something better than our present situation. Seeking utopias means seeking a space—albeit not a place—to begin the work of criticism and thereby transformation of the present. Cosmopolitan conversations open a space of critique into which pours the animating force of hope.

Insufficiently Hopeful Cosmopolitanisms

Above I claimed that my account of cosmopolitanism would differ from some others because pluralism is a constitutive feature. I now briefly clarify the differences.

The Stoic

The Stoics practice a sharpening of reason. However, their account of reason is closer to what above I call procedural, rather than substantive. The Stoic philosophers argue that the critical function of reason enables us to criticize conventional beliefs. In the process, we are to hold only on to those beliefs for which we can offer sufficient justification. Reasoning transcends cultural commitments and from an ideal place evaluates their worth. The pluralist, however, denies that reason is transcendent to cultural frames of intelligibility. Hence Stoic cosmopolitanism does not anticipate something new or surprising; its hope rests on a belief that reason will help us pick out the true from the merely parochial beliefs we already hold.

Furthermore, hope is likely to be a foreign experience to a stoic. After all, stoics teach us to distinguish what is in our control and what isn't so that we will reduce suffering. In other words, stoics advocate a sort of resignation rather than revolt in the face of certain realities. Stoicism often presupposes a deterministic universe (obviously with exceptions such as Epicurus's swerving atoms). And as I attempted to sketch out above, such a metaphysical assumption forecloses the possibility of hope, that is, of something new and better. Hope is possible for pluralists.

The Kantian (Including Appiah)

Kant's cosmopolitanism differs from the account I have offered here for similar reasons to the Stoic's. Kant posits the procedures of reasoning to be subjectively universal; reason is a feature of subjective consciousness, but we all have the same basic categories with which we synthesize the world of experience. Kant acknowledges plural frames of intelligibility, especially on matters of political organization. However, his pluralism belies an underlying monism: a view that the most basic structures we use to make sense of the world are the same.

Appiah's position is quite similar to Kant's. While Appiah champions pluralism throughout *Cosmopolitanism*, he restricts it to practical matters. Appiah writes, for example, "Cosmopolitans think that there are many values worth living by and that you cannot live by all of them."[36] Our theoretical view (read: scientific view) of the world, however, is not pluralistic. Returning to his discussion of Asante witchcraft, Appiah concludes, "What's wrong with the theory of witchcraft is not that it doesn't make sense but that it isn't true."[37] Witchcraft isn't true, on Appiah's view, because it is not a theory supported by the superior institutions that refine and test scientific theories. These passages suggests that pluralism is good for practical affairs of life, but *not* for "carving up the world." Hence, he is not a thoroughgoing pluralist.

Conclusion

The preceding is a provisional attempt to sketch out a phenomenology of cosmopolitan hope that in turn deepens our understanding of a crucial feature of cosmopolitanism: a commitment to pluralist epistemology. I have argued that pluralism is presupposed in a robust account of hope. Pluralism entails that something new, surprising, or "not-yet" is possible. Pluralism thereby also entails a "real future." A constitutive aspect of pluralism, however, is *not* that what is new is "something better." The anticipation of something better follows from a hopeful disposition facing tragedy. Pluralism, however, is the condition for the possibility of something better may emerge.

JENNIFER L. HANSEN is Professor of Philosophy and Associate Dean of the First Year at St. Lawrence University. Specializing in feminist philosophy, phenomenology, philosophical issues in psychiatry, and the philosophy of William James, she is the author of "Continental Feminism," in the *Stanford Encyclopedia of Philosophy*.

Notes

1. In "'A Colored Man Hasn't Got Any Country': Roots, Routes, and the Practice of Diaspora," his unpublished presentation at the 2011 American Philosophies Forum conference in Madrid, Spain, Paul Taylor makes a strong case that those following capital flows, such as the Filipino nurse who sends remittances home, are not cosmopolitans. Taylor takes this position because he believes cosmopolitanism is an essentially *optimistic* way of thinking about transnationality and global mobility. I have no quarrel with Taylor insofar as I agree that the effects of globalization on many workers from developing nations are not positive developments to be celebrated. However, my invocation of cosmopolitanism for the purposes of this chapter should not be read as an endorsement or romanticization of globalization.

2. Gabriel Marcel, *Homo Viator: Introduction to a Metaphysic of Hope*, trans. Emma Craufurd (New York: Harper and Brothers, 1962), 31.

3. Chapter 12, 208.

4. See Martha Nussbaum, "Kant and Stoic Cosmopolitanism," *Journal of Political Philosophy* 5, no. 1 (1997): 1–25; Martha Nussbaum, "Duties of Justice, Duties of Material Aid: Cicero's Problematic Legacy," *Journal of Political Philosophy* 8, no. 2 (2000): 176–206; and Kwame Anthony Appiah, *Cosmopolitanism: Ethics in a World of Strangers* (New York: W. W. Norton, 2006).

5. Quoted in John J. Stuhr, ed., *Pragmatism and Classical American Philosophy*, 2nd ed. (New York: Oxford University Press, 2000), 434.

6. Appiah is keener to reconstruct cosmopolitanism despite this history because his project is to articulate a moral ideal. I am more interested in the epistemological aspects of this ideal, namely, the fact of difference and how this fact is crucial to the possibility of hope.

7. By "cognitive aspect," I do not mean "propositional content" nor, necessarily, discursive content. I am roughly agreeing with Lakoff and Johnson's definition of *cognitive*: "to describe any mental operations and structures that are involved in language, meaning, perception, conceptual systems, and reason. Because our conceptual systems and our reason arise from our bodies, we will also use the term *cognitive* for aspects of our sensorimotor system that contribute to our abilities to conceptualize and reason"; see *Philosophy in the Flesh: The Embodied Mind and Its Challenge to Western Thought* (New York: Basic Books, 1999), 12.

8. See Ernst Bloch, *The Principle of Hope*, trans. Neville Place, Stephen Plaice, and Paul Knight, 3 vols. (Cambridge: MIT Press, 1986).

9. For discussion of this distinction, see Martha Nussbaum, *The Therapy of Desire: Theory and Practice in Hellenistic Ethics* (Princeton, NJ: Princeton University Press, 1994), 371; cf. Bloch, *Principle of Hope*, 70.

10. See Lecture IX in William James, *The Varieties of Religious Experience, Writings 1902–1910* (New York: Library of America, 1987), 79; cf. Marcel, *Homo Viator*.

11. James, *Varieties*, 133.

12. Bloch, *Principle of Hope*, 112.

13. See William James, *The Principles of Psychology* (Cambridge, MA: Harvard University Press, 1981), 1:251.

14. Marcel, *Homo Viator*, 45.

15. Bloch, *Principle of Hope*, 75

16. See Marcel, *Homo Viator*, 29–30, 32–35, and 45.

17. See Aristotle, *The Complete Works of Aristotle*, ed. Jonathan Barnes (Princeton, NJ: Princeton UP), vol. 2, 1111B: 20–25; cf. Bloch, *Principle of Hope*, 46; and Anthony Steinbock, "Hoping Against Hope," in *Essays in Celebration of the Founding of Organization of Phenomenological Organizations*, ed. Chan-Fai Cheung, Ivan Chvatik, Ion Cooperu, Lester Embree, Julia Iribarne, and Hans Rainer Sepp (www.o-p-o.net, 2003).

18. Steinbock, "Hoping Against Hope," 3.

19. See Bloch, *Principle of Hope*, 4; cf. Ernst Bloch, "Dialectics and Hope," *New German Critique* 9 (1976): 8.

20. See Linda Alcoff, *Visible Identities: Race, Gender, and the Self* (Oxford: Oxford University Press, 2007), 49–54.

21. See Hans Georg Gadamer, *Truth and Method*, trans. Sheed and Ward (New York: Seabury, 1975), 269–74.

22. See Thomas Nagel, *The View from Nowhere* (New York: Oxford University Press, 1986).

23. Appiah, *Cosmopolitanism*, 37.

24. And, of course, some of our goals are inherited from the cultures we grow up in. Our goals too may change as our horizons expand or contract.

25. James, *Principles of Psychology*, 277.

26. See William James, *A Pluralistic Universe* (New York: Longmans, Green, 1977), 325.

27. James, *Principles of Psychology*, 277.

28. Cf. Marcel, *Homo Viator*.

29. William James, "On a Certain Blindness in Human Beings," *Talks to Teachers on Psychology: And to Students on Some of Life's Ideals* (New York: Henry Holt, 1906), 241.

30. Cf. Martin Heidegger, *Being and Time*, trans. John Macquarrie and Edward Robinson (New York: Harper and Row, 1962), 216.

31. James, *Principles of Psychology*, 241.

32. Maria Lugones, "Playfulness, 'World'-Travelling, and Loving Perception," *Hypatia* 2, no. 2 (1987): 3–19.

33. Appiah, *Cosmopolitanism*, 78, 85.

34. Ibid., 84–5.

35. Immanuel Kant, *Perpetual Peace*, trans. Lewis White Beck (New York: Library of Liberal Arts, 1957), 21.

36. Appiah, *Cosmopolitanism*, 144.

37. Ibid., 43.

14 Hospitality or Generosity?
Cosmopolitan Transactions

Cynthia Gayman

WHILE "there are many cosmopolitanisms," as Jennifer Hansen notes in Chapter 13, "Cosmopolitan Hope," a feature linking them in their various contemporary instantiations is a certain requisite generosity of perception, an openness to the unfamiliar, foreign, or strange.[1] Perceptual generosity puts no additional demand on the function of eyesight, although it is a refusal of blindness; what is required is a capacious moral purview. This is a shift in relational comportment, something like what Noëlle McAfee in Chapter 2, "Home, Hospitality, and the Cosmopolitan Address," terms "cosmopolitan imaginary," by which we think about "how and where we and others are situated" and the relationships we have—and might have—to each other.[2] Perceptual generosity exacts a moral demand that seems to me to be eminently practical: recognizing that others have ways of doing things different from our own, but that because we share common contexts we must risk taking imaginative and moral leaps toward sympathetic understanding. Yet there are some who would make the argument (even if it is never uttered aloud) that it is not necessary to think about how we are situated in relation to those with whom we have nothing in common, despite even geographic proximity, because differences in beliefs, habits, ways of being are intractable, necessitating clear and distinct social separations.

Setting aside, for a moment, consideration of cosmopolitan generosity, what welcome is due those whose perspectives do not align with what is considered "normal" or "right" or "good" or "true"? This question of welcome, not even to mention inclusion, is a highly contested and politically polarizing issue in the United States today, as well as elsewhere, perhaps everywhere. The refusal of welcome, the rejection of social multiplicity, informs other actions: deportation, border patrols/walls, confinement, ghettoization, unemployment, imprisonment, isolation, marginalization, historical revisionism, economic stratification, hate crimes. These refusals fuel injustices that are self-perpetuating and can ignite in violence, even war. Kant's hope for perpetual peace makes hospitality an imperative directed towards the visitor, the transient, whose right it is to be protected from harm. But what is owed those who move in next door?

Perceptual generosity is different than the duty to be hospitable in that it directs a way of seeing, which would undoubtedly inform subsequent action. Seeing and perceiving generously compels us first to *see* without violence, that is, without condemnation or hate, without a hardened heart or closed mind. Perhaps required is something like "the broad-mindedness characteristic of a person who does not judge the rest of the world" on his or her own terms, as Jessica Wahman puts it in Chapter 11, "Citizen or Guest?: Cosmopolitanism as Homelessness."[3]

But how are we to adjudicate differences if not on our own terms? What is entailed in this broad-mindedness? What does cosmopolitan generosity presuppose, and does it presuppose too much? I raise these questions in order to give due deference to a counterperspective: that too generous a welcome—and concomitant toleration, respect, and inclusion—of those who do not share our views demands from us not generosity but compromise, of religious commitment and way of life; and at the heart of this compromise lies a violation of our relationship to truth (in the singular), which is unacceptable. This view is deeply entrenched in American life and politics today, and extends across too vast a landscape to be dismissed as provincial. And so I ask: Is cosmopolitan generosity fundamentally at odds with univocal belief and singularity of truth? Is this even the right question?

The impasse today between those who hold out for objective truth and cosmopolitan broadmindedness seems irremediable. John J. Stuhr, in Chapter 17, "Somewhere, Dreaming of Cosmopolitanism," adroitly describes the dichotomy it presents as "the longstanding philosophical problem of the one and the many in that problem's only real—that is, political—form."[4] Today the form this problem takes is quite literally political—to wit, 2012 and 2016 candidates for the Republican nomination in presidential campaigns bearing witness to the fact that, "the notion of America as a 'Christian nation' has emerged as a theme,"[5] although this seems hardly to have united the Republican party. Nevertheless, as Murphy writes, "When President Obama, in 2009, maintained in a speech that what united America was not a specific religious tradition but 'ideals and a set of values,' he was attacked by a wide range of public figures."[6] There is a strong strain among Christians today, particularly adherents to a conservative and/or evangelical view, that the only resolution to the problem of the many is indeed one: one faith, and maybe one instantiation of it. There is nothing insincere in this view, which does not preclude Kantian hospitality, even as it lacks sufficient generosity.

If religious belief is grounded by adherence to one truth, some strains of cosmopolitanism are haunted by a fantasy of unity, too, informed by hope in the subjunctive mode that differences might be transcended, overcome, if only all people would recognize themselves as citizens of the world, and so be conjoined as one. But if "cosmopolitanism invites us to see ourselves as citizens of the world," in the words of David Miller, what does this mean, "if we are not to take that in a political sense—[since] we do not aspire to share in political authority at a global level—what does it mean?"[7] Lacking a core dogmatic alliance, not to mention a common situation, cosmopolitanism in this ideal sense lacks coherency. Although its "seductive powers are large and real" as Stuhr points out in Chapter 17 of this volume, this visionary cosmopolitanism offers only illusory and abstract hope—albeit feel-good "membership in the Kingdom of Ends" (280–81).

In Chapter 13, "Cosmopolitan Hope," Jennifer Hansen rejects fantasy resolution of the problem of the many into one and instead gives a thoroughgoing pluralist account of cosmopolitanism—an approach compelling on its own merit, but of particular interest here in considering the strong resistance to perceptual generosity. Hansen views cosmopolitans as "mapmakers redrawing the boundaries of the familiar in order to seek what is better." She argues that it is hope that orients these mapmakers and that, if it be "*genuine*, [this hope] . . . is grounded in a pluralistic epistemology." She offers no anodyne for the problem of the many into one; multiplicity and diversity will not be unified: "the universe is open to many ways of making sense, many conceptual schemes, many rationalities, assuming that each serves well its purpose of solving problems."[8] If the universe is open to these many ways of making sense, inhabitants within particular worlds are not so inclined to believe that some ways of making sense may be as good as others. But perhaps they should be.

Hansen's epistemological pluralism necessitates a healthy dose of perceptual generosity, that is, "receptivity to otherness," because it is "out of this receptivity [that] we loosen ourselves from certain substantive commitments that no longer serve us."[9] For Hansen, the kinds of commitments that no longer serve seem to be those that stand in the way of more vital engagement with others. Instead, we can look at how we stand in relation to each other, how we are "situated," to recall McAfee's term, and learn from one another. Hansen's example of a substantive commitment that no longer serves is mundane but captures the impact of even a simple change of habit. The typical American attitude about dinnertime is, as Hansen describes, "an interruption to our work," which, when relinquished after influence from a different—perhaps more European—model, comes to be viewed as "an occasion to reconnect with our family and friends."

Discovering new meaning in ordinary activities is no a small thing, and the perceptual openness underlying Hansen's epistemological pluralism creates opportunities for redrawing the borders of shared community life. But epistemological pluralism is precisely what epistemological monists reject. The possibility of being "loosened from" certain "substantive commitments" looks less like an opportunity for growth than it does temptation to real danger. Concern over what might be lost as an effect of openness and inclusion begins to justify a lack of receptivity to other beliefs and habits of being. Fear arises, but not fear of or related to difference per se, but due to corruption of influence. The possibility of redrawing the community map and erasing or extending borders begins to look more like a conspiracy of destruction. An example of what I am describing is illustrated by a situation that took place in the next county over from my own. This situation is neither unique nor unfamiliar, since it has been enacted in countless small towns and cities throughout the United States today, and so is not exclusive to the region where I now live: the Bible Belt.

A conditional-use application to utilize an empty storefront building as a prayer center was recently turned down by the Mayfield City zoning board. Case closed. Due process had been followed and, in fact, not one but two public meetings were held—the second so packed that the Mayfield City fire marshal had to bar entrance to the building a good ten minutes before the meeting even began. Since this was prior to the arrival of the permit applicant, no time was wasted in discussion before the final vote. Officially, the reason given for the unprecedented rejection of a conditional-use application was that insufficient parking space outside the storefront made its use as a prayer center impracticable, never mind the city zoning ordinance code: "whenever there is a change of use of change of business in an exiting building no additional parking is required."[10] Rejection of the application only briefly interrupted the normal flow of city business because there had been nothing much to talk about, no controversy. The proposed house of prayer was not a church, but a mosque—and in western Kentucky not all roads lead to Mecca.

Some people call this part of Kentucky the buckle of the Bible Belt. The rural landscape is dotted with churches of every denomination and in more densely populated areas there may be something as exotic as a Mormon temple, or even a Catholic church. Farther out in the county, there is an Amish community. Here, that counts as diversity. Dogmatic differences are matters of serious contention; not many think that these differences don't matter and fewer still believe that that all these churches are what they purport to be: Christian. In other words, even on what may appear to be a vast and relentlessly homogeneous landscape, from the point of view of the resident, heterogeneity abounds: My neighbor is not like me because he goes to a different church. These differences are not much discussed, but I have as of yet to see one church close so that its members may be conjoined as a larger body in another. Even variational monism cuts too close; epistemological pluralism cannot be considered.

Packing the Mayfield City public meeting before it began was an intentional ploy by the local citizenry to prevent public address by the Somali Muslims requesting a prayer center. But it was also a means to forestall broader public discussion on the matter. That perceptual generosity was lacking in this situation is obvious. Also lacking was hospitality, maybe even in a Kantian sense, except for the fact that these "foreigners" are not visitors, but residents: no doubt those who did not want a Muslim prayer center in their community would view the barring of Christian worship as harm to their person, body and soul.

In the Third Article of "Perpetual Peace," Kant introduces the term *Weltbuergerrecht*, translated as "cosmopolitan right" with respect to "the duty of hospitality."[11] The duty of hospitality is not directed according to attitude or inclination, as Seyla Benhabib emphasizes, for hospitality "cannot be refused, if such refusal would involve the destruction—Kant's word here is *Untergang*—of the stranger."[12] The Kantian cosmopolitan right to hospitality affirms not much more than basic protection, that is, as Benhabib explains, it makes no claim for supererogatory obligation toward the stranger as a person or even make a "moral claim pertaining to the *rights of humanity in the person of the other*," which is what she wants to establish.[13] Her enhancement of the Kantian schema dislocates the circumstances under which the Kantian "duty of hospitality . . . [is extended toward] an individual coming into contact with an organized and bounded political community."[14] Before addressing the ramifications of Benhabib's view, it must at least be acknowledged that Kant's limited view of hospitality is not without practical application today, given that political exigencies and natural crises present the kind of need that refusal to meet would result in the destruction of the stranger.

In the wake of Hurricane Katrina, several hundred Louisianans arrived in my small western Kentucky city and were set up in a private camp, indeed "at the boundaries of the polity," where they received shelter and food and other basic necessities. But there are limits to southern hospitality, as there are of the Kantian kind. Alcoholic beverages were strictly prohibited in the camp and use of tobacco strongly discouraged. Church services were provided. That very few of the hurricane refugees decided to relocate permanently illustrates what Benhabib identifies as "the juridical and moral ambivalence that affects discussions of the right to asylum and refuge to this day."[15]

If the Somali Muslims living in Mayfield had been just "passing through" and needed food or shelter, the county natives would have been first on the scene with assistance and a covered dish. But consideration of usage rights for an empty building as a prayer center or inclusion in public debate—while arguably de facto rights of American citizenship—seems to lie outside the perimeters of warm welcome. If the duty to respect the right to be protected from harm is too minimal a view of hospitality, does Benhabib's claim for the right of personhood evoke a sense of duty to others at a more fundamental level?

Benhabib broadens the Kantian view of hospitality by shifting the context of its borders from a geographical space to an interpersonal one, "that space between human rights and civil and political rights."[16] This space is "discursive" and its context is public conversation, where the "rights' claims of human beings" can be justified through the assertion of norms that arise from a "universalist moral standpoint."[17]

Benhabib's view of the discursive process, or "conversation of justification," assumes neither a common point of departure for discussion nor a universal end, that is, a point at which all reasonable persons would agree. She is less concerned with a kingdom of ends than that of means, since hers is a "philosophical project of mediations, not of reduction or totalization."[18] Each of these "mediations" becomes, ideally, a new assertion in a series of "democratic iterations," through which a process of justification leads to further explanation, renegotiation and reiteration of the universal principles generated by "discourse ethics."[19] These universal norms are not conceived as presuppositions in Benhabib's account, for they are generated through the iteration of values that express what they serve to uphold. This grounds the universal moral standpoint for talking across differences in the first place. Evoked in this process are the ideals of democratic engagement, at least in the sense that each participant must be respected by right to participate in the conversation. Further, this process becomes what Benhabib terms "jurisgenerative," as generated norms of engagement become institutionalized in practice and by law through the "creative interventions that mediate between universal norms and the will of democratic majorities."[20] But without some underlying perceptual generosity, it is difficult to see how discourse, no matter how civil the rules of argument and justification, would accomplish anything substantive, especially absent the specific contexts that require a loosening of the sorts of "substantive commitments" (see Chapter 13 of this volume) that prevent understanding.

Benhabib's form of cosmopolitanism as "a normative philosophy for carrying the universalistic norms of discourse ethics beyond the confines of the nation-state," appeals to the universality of human rights reinforced by an ever-expanding discursive scope.[21] This idealization of democratic process, where everyone gets a voice is echoed by what Amartya Sen describes "as no longer seen just in terms of the demands for public balloting, but much more capaciously, in terms of . . . the exercise of public reason."[22] The exercise of public reason founded upon equal access of participation may welcome a multiplicity of participants, but it presupposes that the fundamental respect for this shared process—discursive ethics—will itself transcend the differences the participants share.

Public reason, universal discursive ethics, universal human rights, and the injunction of hospitality towards the universally human in Everyman take us far astray from the concrete situation that arose in Western Kentucky. And if Benhabib's hospitable conversation requires a different sort of cosmopolitan commitment than does Hansen's epistemological pluralism, it would be no more compelling to the citizens of Mayfield than the view that beliefs of others are as significant as their own. Those who packed the meeting in Mayfield cut off what Benhabib calls the "discursive scope" of conversation—the entire range of perspectives that might have been expressed, "potentially including all of humanity"—but from the point of view of some of the Mayfield citizens, "the moral obligation to *justify actions with reasons*" had already been met.[23] Benhabib's "positive hospitality" of discursive inclusion, as opposed to a strictly Kantian "negative hospitality" to not harm the stranger, may be of universal import but is not, in this case, locally recognized as a duty, nor is it enforceable.

By what right does the cosmopolitan right of hospitality or the obligation of justification make a claim on us in the first place? While Benhabib sees this as a right that transcends "the specific positive laws of any legal order," she admits that "the obligation to show hospitality to foreigners and strangers cannot be enforced."[24] The enforceability of the right to hospitality is not the only issue; again, the question arises as to why we should be obligated to respect principles of discursive justification in the first place—especially when, in our opinion, we stand on the side of right. But Miller suggests that, although unenforceable, "the special duties" necessitated in a "strong version of cosmopolitanism" are also irrelevant unless need for them arises "only from relationships that are intrinsically valuable."[25]

The right to hospitality in Benhabib's account may not suffice as incentive for discursive interaction—not because the concept "moral agent" is an abstraction that presumes too much but because it leaves out too much—the very reason that we would be motivated to interact with those with whom we presume to have nothing in the common in the first place. This must be something that is transcendent to ourselves, for instance, a problematic situation, a controversy—even the sort of controversy constituted by the unwillingness to listen to the point of view of someone we are sure not to agree with.

My neighbors in the next county no doubt recognize that they share with their Muslim neighbors a common humanity, but this alone is not a sufficient criterion to engage in the ethics of discourse. It would be a mistake to see this merely as prejudice. Many of those who rejected the presence of a prayer center in Mayfield (with or without public discussion on the matter) believed they were acting in accordance with their Christian faith, according to a duty owed *not* to their fellow discursive agents, but to what Miguel de Unamuno calls "the transcendental economy" of religious belief.[26] There is painful irony in the fact that an essential principle of Christianity—that of loving the neighbor as oneself—was ignored.

But maybe there is greater irony in the fact that the "universal moral standpoint" assumed in Benhabib's discursive framework for hospitality makes moral agency stand in for what it cannot in reality replace.[27] As Joseph Margolis argues, the "moral justifications" asserted as reasons for actions are "the historically entrenched practices and convictions of reasonably demarcated peoples."[28]

Justifications, as well as actions, vary among cultures and nations, and so "it is effectively impossible to suppose that legitimation must take a universalistic form or that it can actually do so in most seriously contested cases."[29]

Anthony Appiah makes this point more concretely, "What it's reasonable for you to think, faced with a particular experience, depends on what ideas you already have."[30] He makes this statement in the context of the Sudanese Asante tribal belief in witchcraft. Thus, "if what's reasonable to believe depends on what you believe already... then you can't check the reasonableness of all your beliefs."[31]

What is the point of justification if reasonable people believe theirs is the side of truth? Why enter a discussion when there is no possibility of agreement? Packing the meeting illustrated what might be referred to under less objectionable circumstances as unified civic engagement or majority rule, but mostly it conveyed the tensions between the ideals of discursive process and the operative norms of community life. On the other hand, as the situation in Mayfield shows, community is no longer a guarantor of even relative commonality, if it ever was, and increasing diversity in the social realm raises questions about what kind of society people want to live in, not in an abstract sense, but with respect to proximity and relationships.

John Dewey writes, "Democracy must begin at home, and its home is the neighborly community."[32] These words challenge the contemporary propensity for gates and subdivisions, not to mention legal and extralegal constraints on status and inclusion. Who is this new neighbor? Why should his values and beliefs be accommodated, especially if they are so very different from our own? Why should we talk to him—or listen to what he has to say? John Calvin provides an answer to this question:

> It is the common habit of mankind that the more closely men are bound together by the ties of kinship, of acquaintanceship, or of neighborhood, the more responsibilities for one another they share.... But I say: we ought to embrace the whole human race without exception in a single feeling of love; here there is no distinction between barbarian and Greek, worthy and unworthy, friend and enemy, since all should be contemplated in God, not in themselves. When we turn aside from such contemplation, it is no wonder we become entangled in many errors.[33]

The moral claim of cosmopolitanism that we have obligations to others beyond the boundaries of our local communities, cultures and nations, vies for an appeal to universality in John Calvin, as well Benhabib, but Calvin's appeal is grounded by an engagement not based on equality but obligation. And obligation is owed always in the particular situation, to a particular person or persons who make a claim on us. Noëlle McAfee describes this in Chapter 2 of this volume as the "cosmopolitan address," which is "the announcement of the situation that ought to be other than the one that is. Rather than announce a fact, it announces an aspiration and opens up the possibility that this aspiration might come to be."[34] This is an ethical claim, and the call to transform a situation—"cosmopolitan hope," in Hansen's rubric—"is the call to make things otherwise than they are."

Hansen's pragmatist pluralism enjoins us to see that the possibility (the hope) of interaction and participation make a better community than one cordoned off according to like minds and shared views. Her outline for hopeful engagement is grounded neither by religious faith nor faith in human reason vis-à-vis discourse, but in something like Merleau-Ponty's notion of perceptual faith in the existence of the real world, which is not an abstraction but constitutes the context and extant situations that bind us together. It is the reality of our situatedness in a particular place that holds us together and accountable to each other, and this common world is shared. This is a real locus of conversation, if not agreement.

How our differences are adjudicated necessitates thinking about what sort of framework would serve to uphold, in Benhabib's phrase, "cosmopolitan norms of justice"—surely worth thinking about with respect to the "religious war" in my neighboring county.[35] Is eventual agreement possible? Does accommodation demand the kind of compromise that violates a deeply held belief? These are important questions. Underlying them is Appiah's compelling observation: "What makes conversation across boundaries worthwhile isn't that we're likely to come to a reasoned agreement about values."[36] What, then, is required of us in order that we might engage in what John Dewey calls "the responsive art of communication" fundamental to democratic process and cosmopolitan pluralism?[37]

Dewey writes, "Communication is the way in which men come to possess things in common."[38] Surely curtailing discussion diminishes the chance of seeing that some interests and values might already be shared, but Dewey's emphasis on possessing *things* in common rather than finding interests and values in common differs from Benhabib's compelling account of discourse ethic. For Dewey, conversation is more than an exchange of ideas and disagreement; it is a transactional expression of meaning and perception in context of a shared world.

Language is the means for making sense of and bringing new meanings to experience, continuously rethreaded through new experience, and this complex interface between "experience" and "experiencing" is what Dewey named the "transactional"—the core concept of his philosophy.[39] For Dewey, all experience is transactional, but what grounds communication is the shared world, the world that is held in common. It is what Sidney Hook describes as "the objective situation, not the form of the sentence, that determines whether words are primarily an expression of opinion, used to induce a change of opinion or an incitement to action."[40]

Communication is generative of the ways meanings are formed and problems are described, interpreted, reflected on, and critically evaluated with respect to a world that is constituted by and constitutive of our interactions, and "language is a tool"—"the tool of tools"—for this process.[41] Communication may be jurisgenerative, too, that is, create new norms of interaction, but it is the given situation that is the focus.

Bonds of association forged in relation to a shared reality are not unified through a commitment to reasoned justifications, but likely multiplied by attention to a diversity of accounts of a given situation. What makes these conversations across boundaries worthwhile is somehow linked to the fact that more viewpoints necessitate more inquiry and maybe more insight into the complexity of a given situation. As Appiah notes, "There's a sense in which cosmopolitanism is the name not of the solution but of the challenge."[42] The hospitable inclusion of many points of view broadens discursive scope, and perhaps deepens acceptance of pluralism as inherently diverse. Dewey's account of discourse requires self-reflective intelligence and a generosity of spirit: a "faith" in the possibilities of cooperation in solving problems and creating a better world.[43] Dewey writes: "The failure of the controversy to arrive at a solution through agreement is an important ground of the idea that is worth while to take these constituents of controversy out of an ontological context, and note how they look when they are placed in the context of the use they perform and the service they render in the context of inquiry."[44] What a leap of faith this requires! A leap into the world we share with those with whom we seem to have nothing in common orients attention on what is beyond ourselves. That we would recognize that the lack of communication is itself a serious problem portends the possibility of communication, and is even perhaps revelatory of "a new dimension of personhood," to use Paul Ricoeur's phrase: our own, as well as another's.[45]

The epistemological pluralism that grounds what Hansen call "*genuine* cosmopolitan hope," to be distinguished from abstract or decontextualized hope, necessitates not only a willingness to listen to others' views but an openness to them that allows for a degree of "flexibility" with respect to our own. This does not mean that all perspectives are of equal merit, but that sincere consideration of other views gives us a space in which to look at, critique, and maybe reconsider our own. This should not be threatening to those who are secure in their metaphysical and epistemological commitments. However, the view that all epistemological commitments that work are of equal epistemological merit is harder to swallow, not only for those who are epistemological monists but perhaps for those who seek truth in the eventual long run.

Hansen notes, "While Appiah champions pluralism . . . he restricts it to practical matters." She refers to his discussion of the beliefs underlying practices in Asante witchcraft, about which Appiah writes, "What's wrong with the theory of witchcraft is not that it doesn't make sense but that it isn't true." Hansen states, "These passages [from Appiah] suggest that pluralism is good for practical affairs of life, but not for 'carving up the world'... hence, he is not a thoroughgoing pluralist."[46] If Hansen's position is problematic for those whose pluralism does not reach all the way down, I wonder if it is necessary. At issue for both epistemological pluralism and epistemological monism seems to be a conflation of knowledge and belief commitments with ethical responsibility and relational orientation. Perhaps a distinction would allow for a more generous perception of persons, if not their ideas. In saying this I realize that persons and what they believe in and stand for is not radically (or even practically) separable from who they are (or conceive of themselves to be). But maybe there are degrees of separation that sufficiently open a space through which an invitation might be extended: a welcome that is more generous than hospitality.

An assumption underlying cosmopolitan sensibility is that it is good. Freed from constrictions imposed by local norms and provincial views, the cosmopolitan awakens to the rich diversity of the wider world and is open, respectful, interested. Travel is not a necessary requirement for the cosmopolitan; openness to the unfamiliar might begin with a welcome of the stranger at home. Or maybe welcome presupposes too much, as if where we are is home, leaving others always (and only) a guest. I would say that the good underlying cosmopolitan welcome demands more than equal regard of others; it requires a more radical deference.

In Chapter 12 of this volume, Jessica Wahman goes so far as to argue that the typical connotation of the cosmopolitan as "citizen of the world" should be amended to mean, "guest in the home of another."[47] "A true cosmopolitan," she writes, "has not made a home of the world but has made herself homeless." This is an ethical orientation, she says, that serves as a "reminder that... at bottom, we depend humbly on the graciousness of our hosts."[48]

I am drawn to this position of radical humility, because after my first few years of living in western Kentucky it began to dawn on me that my own prejudicial biases against those who reside in this part of the country signified a provincialism on my part not much different than I impugned in them. Wahman describes this by way of "the temptation of New Yorkers to use their own worldly superiority as a means of closing themselves off to the perspectives of other—frequently rural or small-town—Americans."[49] I am not from New York City, but as a former urban dweller and present faculty member at a midsize university in a rural state, I guiltily attest to succumbing to the same temptation. At some point my perspective changed, however. I began venturing beyond the boundaries of university life and social circles and soon noticed that if the new people I met—conservative and rural—seemed strange to me, *I* seemed even stranger to them. When I recognized myself as a stranger, I realized I was a *guest*. And then a whole new world opened up, one more multitudinous than I had perceived at first face.

It is certainly true that taking on an attitude of homelessness is a strenuous demand, as Wahman writes. Yet it directs "a kind of ethical orientation we may strive to approximate, though we recognize our inevitable allegiances," she offers.⁵⁰ This last point is crucial. Deference to the other as host requires that I be a good guest, but a guest is not a prisoner, and a host can be a rube. I can imagine for a moment the possibility that everyone in the community where I live—residents, newcomers, strangers alike—is in this radical sense, homeless, dependent on the hospitality of others, for I hope—and believe—that this sense of homelessness shared might engender a sense of mutual belonging and deeper kindness. But I have lived here too long as a guest not to recognize that sometimes it is necessary to assume the duties of host.

Addendum: The Mayfield Zoning Board reconsidered its decision the following fall after a complaint from the American Civil Liberties Union. Fewer people attended the subsequent third public meeting, and those who did supported by a large majority Khadar Ahmed's permit application for a Muslim prayer center in Mayfield. According to the executive directory of the ACLU of Kentucky, this is the first case of its kind in the Commonwealth of Kentucky and will be "important in helping communities understand tolerance for new residents and different beliefs."⁵¹ Michael Aldridge, ACLU of Kentucky executive director, said, "It's important not to let situations like this go unchecked, because that is how our rights can get eroded very quickly."⁵²

CYNTHIA GAYMAN is Professor of Philosophy in the Department of English and Philosophy at Murray State University. Her primary philosophical interests in both her teaching and her published work are in ethical theory and the nature of the good life, political philosophy and feminist theory, pragmatism, and the thought of Simone Weil.

Notes

1. Chapter 13, 223.
2. Chapter 2, pp. 22, 25.
3. Chapter 12, 237.
4. Chapter 17, 280.
5. Cullen Murphy, "Torturer's Apprentice," *Atlantic*, January–February 2012, 77.
6. Ibid.
7. David Miller, "Cosmopolitanism," in *The Cosmopolitan Reader*, eds. Garrett Wallace Brown and David Held (Cambridge: Polity, 2012), 378.
8. Chapter 13, 228.
9. Chapter 13, 230.
10. Murray State University News, vol. 86, no. 14.

11. Quoted in Seyla Benhabib, *Another Cosmopolitanism: Hospitality, Sovereignty, and Democratic Iteration* (Oxford: Oxford University Press, 2006), 21.
12. Ibid., 22.
13. Ibid.
14. Ibid., 21.
15. Ibid.
16. Ibid., 22.
17. Ibid., 19, 20.
18. Ibid., 20.
19. Ibid., 18.
20. Ibid., 49.
21. Ibid., 18.
22. Amartya Sen, *The Idea of Justice* (Cambridge, MA: Belknap, 2009), 324.
23. Benhabib, *Another Cosmopolitanism*, 18.
24. Ibid., 25, 26.
25. Miller, "Cosmopolitanism," 383.
26. Miguel de Unamuno, *The Tragic Sense of Life* (New York: Dover, 2012), 318.
27. Benhabib, *Another Cosmopolitanism*, 47.
28. Joseph Margolis, *Moral Philosophy After 9/11* (University Park: Penn State University Press, 2004), xi.
29. Ibid.
30. Kwame Anthony Appiah, *Cosmopolitanism: Ethics in a World of Strangers* (New York: W. W. Norton, 2006), 39.
31. Ibid., 31.
32. John Dewey, *The Public and Its Problems, John Dewey: The Later Works, 1925–1953*, ed. Jo Ann Boydston (Carbondale: Southern Illinois University Press, 2008), 2:368.
33. Quoted in Marilynne Robinson, *The Death of Adam: Essays on Modern Thought* (New York: Picador, 2014), 172.
34. Chapter 2, 29.
35. Benhabib, *Another Cosmopolitanism*, 16.
36. Appiah, *Cosmopolitanism*, 72.
37. Dewey, *The Public and Its Problems*, 172.
38. John Dewey, *Democracy and Education: An Introduction to the Philosophy of Education* (New York: Free Press, 1944), 4.
39. Quoted in John Stuhr, *Genealogical Pragmatism: Philosophy, Experience, and Community* (Albany: SUNY Press, 1997), 61.
40. Sidney Hook, *Pragmatism and the Tragic Sense of Life* (New York: Basic Books, 1974), 92.
41. John Dewey, *Experience and Nature, The Later Works: 1925–1953*, ed. Jo Ann Boydston (Carbondale: Southern Illinois University Press, 1988), 1:146.
42. Appiah, *Cosmopolitanism*, xv.
43. John Dewey, "Creative Democracy," in *The Later Works of John Dewey*, ed. Jo Ann Boydston (Carbondale: Southern Illinois University Press, 1991), 14:228.
44. John Dewey, "Knowing and the Known," in *John Dewey: The Later Works*, ed. Jo Ann Boydston (Carbondale: Southern Illinois University Press, 2008), 16:284.
45. Paul Ricoeur, *The Course of Recognition*, trans. David Pellauer (Cambridge, MA: Harvard University Press, 2005), 209.
46. Chapter 13, 232.
47. See Chapter 12 of this volume.

48. Chapter 12, 208.
49. Chapter 12, 214.
50. Chapter 12, 208; see also 217–219.
51. Murray State University News.
52. Ibid.

15 On Cosmopolitan Publics and Online Communities

Erin C. Tarver

IT IS NO SECRET that life in the twenty-first century happens, for many of us, in a "place" that defies traditional conceptions of place, community, and communication—namely, in the nebulous and Heraclitean world of the internet. Not only information but socialization and political life exist online; for many people, in fact, those relationships and conversations accessed via electronic mediums constitute the majority of all such interactions. And despite the hand-wringing that this fact might inspire in those nostalgic for pre-internet days, these interactions are *real*: they are lived by flesh-and-blood people who not only inhabit traditionally physical communities but also communicate and interact (cognitively, physically, affectively) with other flesh-and-blood people—even those they have never met face-to-face—whether through writing, reading, or listening, or even sometimes through loving or arguing. Just about everything that happens in the offline world also takes place in an online version—and perhaps surprisingly, not always as a disappointing approximation.[1] Indeed, as I suggest, particular versions of online engagement make for better and more productive communications and interactions than were previously possible, particularly if we are concerned with the democratization of our lives together. Voices that could not be heard and problems that simply were not understood *as problems* can both find expression and struggle for solutions in newly created corners of the online world. And if it is true, as Carlos Thiebaut suggests, that the agency of an individual is determined, at least in part, "by her relations to those things that she comes to define as salient and relevant,"[2] then these creations and interactions are far from inconsequential for democratic practice. Our relations to communities of meaning, whether these are inhabited offline or online, not only help us to make sense of the world and our place in it, they change what is possible for us—what that place might be.

My concern in this chapter is precisely with the democratic transformation of communities, as they exist both offline and online. Although it is not always conceived in this way, I understand the process of "democratic transformation" as necessarily requiring the alteration of entrenched patterns of oppression. That is, I take as a starting point the notion that a community cannot and will not be truly democratic insofar is it remains a community in which some of its members are systematically disadvantaged and devalued, while others systematically benefit from their disadvantage and devaluation. Thus, I suggest throughout that our political practices, whether they be "local" in a traditional, town-hall sense, or wildly cosmopolitan, ought—if we truly seek to live democratically—to work actively against oppression. This is a common enough sentiment, of course, but its practical application is too often unclear. In his work most directly concerned with democratic practice, *The Public and Its Problems*, John Dewey argues that political life in the United States is hampered by not only by sweeping injustices but also populations too diffuse and media too concerned with the status quo to enable the formation of the genuine public that would be necessary for addressing the concerns of a truly democratic nation. Dewey suggests that new developments in technology could facilitate the formation of a genuine public—and by extension, the reconstruction of American democracy—but cautions that neither the telegraph nor the steam engine is a silver bullet.

Today, the proliferation of web-based communication through globally connected online communities enables a cosmopolitan connectedness of localities that parallels the shifts in mass-communication technologies in Dewey's era. And it is just as assuredly true that the communications they foster do not guarantee more effective democracy, or sweeping changes in our habits of discourse. But, the current transformation of global communication makes clear that the notion of *the* public as a unified set of interests is neither possible nor desirable. Instead, the complex and shifting spaces of internet communities (as, for example, we find in a collection of places I'll call "the feminist blogosphere") give reason to question whether it might be more effectively democratic—and indeed, more consistently Deweyan—to insist on the importance of maintaining multiplicitous *publics*, which may or may not share common knowledges, goals, interests or methodologies.

This claim is not a small one, and it is in marked tension with traditional approaches to cosmopolitanism—such as the one nicely examined by Cynthia Gayman in Chapter 14, "Hospitality or Generosity?: Cosmopolitan Transactions"—in which the obligation is to greater conversational inclusion, since our problems are fundamentally the result of lives *in common*. Indeed, in this chapter, I argue not that what is missing from our democratic practices (offline or on) is a more unifying discourse, but that the simultaneously local and cosmopolitan spaces of online communities—particularly those whose desideratum is the fight against oppression—make salient the extent to which a consistently Deweyan approach to democracy and social reform would not call for the formation of The Public, but instead recognize the value of plural *publics*, which might by turns be coalitional, contentious, or overlapping. My argument proceeds through attention to two lines of thought: first, I suggest that the account of meaning Dewey develops in *Experience and Nature* and elsewhere is inconsistent with the consensus-driven account of shared public meaning and the management of consequences he articulates toward the end of *The Public and Its Problems*; second, I problematize this tension with reference to the political spaces of online feminist communities. My working hypothesis, then—which is both feminist and Deweyan—is that political relationships (including patterns of domination and democratic practice) may be understood, for some purposes, as shared practices of meaning. But, as I suggest, feminist considerations reveal that these practices are "shared" in a rather different sense than we typically imagine. My conclusion, thus, is that while he does not correctly follow out the implications of this claim about meaning, Dewey's thought could in fact be valuable for those interested in theorizing and participating in transnational anti-oppressive work, particularly within these new globally connected web-based spaces—if only we work with an understanding of democratic practice that insists on local cosmopolitan publics, rather than the coming-to-consciousness of The Public.

Problems of "The Public"

Dewey's version of a democratic approach to public life has not been immune to criticism, even from fellow pragmatists. Most notably, Rob Talisse has argued that the Deweyan account of democracy is inconsistent because it imposes an odd sort of pluralism—that is in fact a comprehensive political program—on its would-be participants.[3] More recently, Colin Koopman has suggested that Talisse misreads Dewey, who understands pluralism in a non-Rawlsian way, and whose outlook implies skepticism about the possibility of unified self-government and so emphasizes "the need for a reinvigoration of participatory democracy in the context not of singular overarching forms seeking political consolidation but, rather, in multiple contexts of pluralities of publics."[4] My claim in what follows suggests that both Talisse and Koopman are correct in their characterizations of Dewey—though not in the ways they suggest. Koopman rightly identifies what Dewey's pragmatism *ought to* imply for democratic practice, but the normative program of *The Public and Its Problems* actually entails the sort of comprehensive political requirements Talisse warns against—but this does not necessarily follow from the requirements of Dewey's theoretical outlook. On the contrary, I argue that if Dewey consistently followed the implications of his interactional account of meanings in his political writing, he would emerge with a rather different picture, one that more closely resembles what Koopman describes.

As Dewey reminds us, meanings—whether we are talking about the meaning of "democracy" or the meaning of the concept "two"—are not formed merely ideally, but through embodied inter-actions which are themselves inter-active with a particular surrounding environment: "Language, signs and significance, come into existence not by intent and mind but by overflow, by-products, in gestures and sound. The story of language is the story of the *use* made of these occurrences; a use that is eventual, as well as eventful."[5] Elsewhere, Dewey explains that by "eventual" he has in mind the status of being "an outcome of directed experimental operations, instead of something in sufficient existence before the act of knowing."[6] This is not to say that meanings are directly imposed by their users (since significance exceeds the intentions of individual speakers as a sort of "overflow" beyond their objects). Rather, the point is that signification is produced in a milieu of interactions that have as their aims a multiplicity of purposes and use-functions. Or, as José Medina puts it, "the meaning of words and sentences becomes contextually determinate through the *tacit agreement in action* of the participants in communicative practices."[7] Thus, for Dewey, meanings are produced and transmitted by virtue of their effectiveness for achieving a particular purpose or enabling a particular action—although this purpose or action is of necessity *not* located in the mind or initiative of an isolated self. Meanings thus produced are, moreover, necessarily localized, since they are dependent on some set of shared actions, which are contingent and potentially revisable by virtue of that dependence.

In *The Public and Its Problems*, Dewey offers an account of the formation of political affiliations that grows directly out of his model of experience and nature as interactional. Rejecting the idea that an account of The State as such is possible or desirable, Dewey suggests that political associations are the situated products of increasingly complex patterns of interaction, which tend to emerge when the consequences of those interactions "involve others beyond those directly engaged in them. When these consequences are in turn realized in thought and sentiment, recognition of them reacts to remake the conditions out of which they arose. Consequences have to be taken care of, looked out for."[8] When consequences are extensive enough to warrant an organized effort to manage them, Dewey suggests that a "public" has emerged, which "consists of all those who are affected by the indirect consequences of transactions to such an extent that it is deemed necessary to have those consequences systematically cared for."[9] So while states may be formed to manage the transactions of a public, the state is not the public, and not all publics give rise to states. Central to the emergence of a public, however, is the perception of the consequences (both direct and indirect) of localized patterns of interaction, and the concomitant possibility of "project[ing] agencies which order their occurrence."[10] That is to say: a public only becomes a public in virtue of its consciousness or apprehension of shared meanings—which are, as Dewey notes both here and in *Experience and Nature*, meaning-full to the extent that they result in "the establishment of cooperation in an *activity* in which there are partners, and in which the activity of each is modified and regulated by the partnership."[11] The point here is not that publics must be cooperative in the strong sense of a harmonious endeavor for an agreed-on telos; instead, it is to stress the extent to which both publics and the shared meanings on which they depend are fundamentally matters of situated—yet alterable—interaction. As Medina puts it, "they emerge from our concerted interactions and pragmatic engagements with the environment,"[12] such that signification may be conceived as at once active or use-driven *and* contextually (socially, environmentally, politically) dependent.

And yet, Dewey's descriptions of publics—or, more often, *the* public—at times forget the heterogeneity by which such shared meanings are constituted. That is, given that public meanings result from complex and indirect consequences of inter-action that are not reducible to a singular set of concerns, it is curious that Dewey suggests that a true public (or perhaps a truly effective public) requires not merely interactionally shared meanings, but unified concerns. Lamenting the state of political discourse in the United States at the time of his writing, he claims:

> It is not that there is no public, no large body of persons having a common interest in the consequences of social transactions. There is too much public, a public too diffused and scattered and too intricate in composition. And there are too many publics, for conjoint actions which have indirect, serious and enduring consequences are multitudinous beyond comparison, and each one of them crosses the others and generates its own group of persons especially affected with little to hold these different publics together in an integrated whole.[13]

Moreover, in a move that appears to pre-figure a Habermasian faith in the potential for adequately communicative deliberation to produce democratic justice, Dewey goes on to suggest that the fundamental task of such an "integrated whole" is "the improvement of the methods and conditions of debate, discussion and persuasion. That is *the* problem of the public."[14] Such improved communicative conditions are crucial, Dewey suggests, for the transmission of the knowledge necessary to make informed democratic decisions: "what is required is that they have the ability to judge of the bearing of knowledge supplied by others *upon common concerns*."[15]

While improved communication and wider democratic participation are certainly worthwhile goals, Dewey's shift to emphasizing unified rather than diffuse publics, and concerns held in common rather than shared by virtue of their indirect effects is worrisome, even if, as Vincent Colapietro puts it, Dewey's public "is ever a problem unto itself."[16] The implications of such a common-denominator approach to identifying *the* public are expressed in John Covaleskie's discussion of publics, which suggests that while the divergent concerns of various advocacy groups (for LGBTQ people, people of color, women, and so on) may constitute "something like Deweyan publics in search of common solutions to shared problems, these groups are *defined as much by who is not included as who is*, which is quite different from what Dewey had in mind."[17] Such an observation depends, of course, on a covered-over privileging of dominant groups (such that "common solutions" and "shared problems" are understood as transparently universal, while concerns felt directly by marginalized groups are deemed exclusive or specific to them), and also highlights the extent to which this particular way of conceiving a public is inconsistent with Dewey's foregoing account of meaning as interactional.

Conceiving the concerns of the majority as transparently shared while dismissing the concerns of groups motivated by "identity politics" as exclusionary ignores *both* the practical exclusions of oppression and privilege (that result in some voices being rendered silent or unintelligible, our theoretical efforts to provide for idealized democratic deliberation notwithstanding) *and* the constitutive rhetorical exclusion of this framing of the concept of the "public." This latter exclusion, moreover, makes clear the difficulty of conceiving a "shared problem" or "shared meaning" as such. If by "shared problem" we have in mind strictly a set of circumstances whose non-address would negatively affect everyone involved, then it seems clear that our shared problems will be quite few (though they might *possibly* include "taking care of children" and "taking care of elderly people," as Covaleskie suggests). Other (non-shared) problems, on this view, would be conceivable as a set of circumstances whose non-address would only affect a select group negatively, and thus, while perhaps unfortunate, do not constitute shared problems. But the problem with such a strict conception of "shared" problems is that it is insufficiently attentive to the relationality—or, indeed, the interactional character—of such problems. That is, "special" concerns such as those of the NAACP or GLAAD are not merely a matter of the negative effects suffered by particular individuals but of the constitutively privileging effects of those same circumstances for many other populations (who may or may not recognize their direct or indirect implication in or benefit from them). While it might thus appear on this conception of a "public" that the effects of globalization on Latin America or the classification of transgender identity as a pathology by the DSM-IV are necessarily non-shared problems, and that groups existing for the purpose of advocating for changes in these arenas are necessarily non-publics, or fail to function as part of a larger unified "public," this is misguided—and it is misguided precisely because, as Dewey points out, concerns and actions are relational.[18]

Indeed, because Dewey has suggested that publics are formed by the indirect consequences of interactions, which *necessarily* exceed the individuals who appear to be directly involved, it is odd to suggest that the "shared concerns" or shared meanings that constitute publics should be uniform. Yet this seems to be precisely Dewey's suggestion: the public, he claims, will not find itself in the way necessary for true democratic practice until "the Great Society is converted into a Great Community."[19] And becoming such a community requires nothing less than "conjoint activity whose consequences are appreciated as good by all singular persons who take part in it . . . such as to effect an energetic desire and effort to sustain it in being just because it is a good shared by all."[20] But given that Dewey has previously understood the apprehension of meanings as enabling coordinated action, which is, importantly, always interactive (meaning that it is of necessity not unidirectional), it is dubious that the meanings and concomitant concerns that give rise to publics could *ever be* isolated bodies with homogeneous concerns. Or, to put it in a different way, "we" have never been the public, nor could the public exist—apart from the undemocratic exclusion of populations whose concerns are deemed noncommon—if by this we mean a sort of transparently unified and autonomous body. On the contrary, insofar as we can conceive publics as existing political relations or entities, they must be exactly this: publics, plural—which is to say that Dewey's lament about "too much" and "too diffuse" publics is misguided on his own terms, since every public's multiplicitous and divergent concerns and meanings are necessarily involved with various overlapping and nebulous publics, both within and "outside" of them. That is, because the interactional character of meanings is dependent *not* on the unity of thought or intent, but on the further enabling of coordinated interaction, neither the concerns resulting from such interactions *nor* the subsequent management of those concerns will be univocal or reducible to a single set of localized actions.

It is curious, then, that the suggestions Dewey offers near the conclusion of *The Public and Its Problems* include exhortation to search for more effective means of communication that would bring everyone to the table of communal deliberation, so as to achieve real consensus. Of course, Dewey does not claim that "the flow of social intelligence . . . by word of mouth from one to another in the communications of the local community"[21] is sufficient for the establishment of a democratic public, but he does claim that it is a necessary one—and this is worrisome both for its apparent nostalgia for hyperlocal community life built on face-to-face interactions, and for the veiled exclusions that such an emphasis on strictly shared meanings, concerns and intelligence requires. Nevertheless, Dewey's (quasi-ambivalent) suggestion that new technological developments might present new possibilities for reinvigorating transformative democratic practices among far-flung populations is worth taking seriously. Not primarily because, as he suggests, such publication and transportation technologies could make our local neighborhoods and communities more efficient in their deliberations,[22] but because his description of such technologies is interestingly prescient of recent developments of our current situation, which make space for a proliferation of anti-oppressive democratic practices that are much more in line with that for which (I have argued) Dewey ought to have hoped.

Feminist Blogging, Online Communities, and Cosmopolitan Publics

From those concerned with national and transnational political commentary, to the idiosyncrasies of academic philosophy, blogs have become such an important and ubiquitous feature of contemporary life that offering a blanket explanation of the phenomena involved with them would be as difficult (and as useless) as a general statement about "the media." Rather than focusing my analysis in this section on blogging qua blogging, then, my interest here will be in discussing a few blog spaces that are situated within a larger web of online communities often known as "the feminist blogosphere." What sort of "space" these sorts of online communities take up is a complicated question I address below. Throughout, I suggest that these blogs function not merely as sites for the electronic publication of texts but as locales, meeting places, and virtual communities. The blogs I discuss here have an established readership and presence in the feminist blogging world,[23] though they are certainly less familiar to populations who do not make a point to investigate them. *Feministe, Tiger Beatdown, Muslimah Media Watch, Angry Black Bitch,* and *Feminist Philosophers* may not be household names to many people, but they do form a representative sample of English-language feminist blogging.[24] Each, in various ways, takes itself to be involved in anti-oppressive discourse. Each discusses the gendered (and often racial and sexual) facets of the details of everyday life—some, like *Feministe* and *Tiger Beatdown*, tend to be more interested in popular culture, while others, like *Feminist Philosophers*, spend a great deal of time addressing sexism in the academic world. Some are more specialized in their focus: *Muslimah Media Watch* is particularly interested in popular portrayals of Muslim women, and in pointing out how radically unhelpful Western views of Muslim women as helpless victims of supposedly cultural misogyny are. *Angry Black Bitch* focuses mostly on American politics and policy.

There are a few central features of these blogs that make them unique, and of particular interest for a discussion of the possibility of democratic publics. The first is simply the bare fact of their publication of material on a daily basis that disputes the dominant meanings—of femininity, of whiteness, of citizenship, and so on—that enable and support oppression. They are talking back. And because there are so many of them, these blogs are, in a small way, producing a counterdiscourse, a set of countermeanings, simply by repeating the refusal to accept the ones that govern our lives. Those dominant meanings, as Dewey might say, depend on habits of interaction that form a sort of worn groove of sexist (and more broadly oppressive) practices—the same way that trails through the forest get tramped down and, over time, impressed in a seemingly permanent way.

We can think of these blogs, on the contrary, as efforts to wear new grooves, or to blaze new trails; they do this not just because they want to be innovative, but because it's only by making a new trail that we can get off the old one.

Additionally, looking at the structure of these blogs, it is crucial to notice that while their most obvious feature is the centrality of posts or essays written by the blogger or team of bloggers, in almost every case, the comments section is nearly as prominent (if not more so, when we see posts with comment threads producing hundreds of responses). If you spend time following these blogs, you begin to notice from their screen names that the commenters on individual posts are regulars, and that they seem to know one another: they appeal back to previous conversations, they link to one another's blogs, they even talk about one another's lives (often on "Open Threads" dedicated to this more general social purpose). You will often, moreover, see major posts on one blog linking to or commenting on posts on another blog, with bloggers and commenters going back and forth between blogs in conversation. You might also encounter comments from people apologizing that they don't have time to respond in greater detail at the moment, but indicating that they'll be back later, after their work or meeting or lunch. What we begin to see in the blogosphere, then, is not so much analogous to the old days of magazines and newspapers as it is to a meeting space: a coffee shop, a salon, the water cooler.

But it's also something more than this. Another crucial feature of these blogs is that while they are meeting spaces, or social spaces, or conversation spaces—they aren't strictly open spaces. Many of the blogs I've mentioned here have both a strict comments policy and comment moderators, whose job is to monitor the comments to prevent sexist, racist, or homophobic language—and to disallow those comments containing it, and if necessary, to ban (block the IP address) of repeat offenders. The individual blogs often explain their comments policy and practices by claiming something like the following: the outside world is a hostile place, the sort of place in which our voices cannot be heard (or minimally, can't be heard without the threat of harassment); thus, it is necessary for us to cultivate a safe online space to have the kinds of conversations we have here, and part of that cultivation means prohibiting speech that undermines its goals.[25] These blogs are thus not only *not* apologetic about their restrictive comments policies; their claim is that these policies are absolutely necessary for them to do the work they need to do, given the social realities in which they exist. Their position is thus quite similar to the one advanced by Nancy Fraser, in her own articulation of the importance of multiplicitous democratic publics. Because the world as it currently exists features clear power disparities between groups (even groups within ostensibly democratic communities), Fraser argues, the liberal ideal of open speech is counterproductive: "Insofar as the bracketing of social inequalities in deliberation means proceeding as if they don't exist when they do, this does not foster participatory parity. On the contrary, such bracketing usually works to the advantage of dominant groups in society and to the disadvantage of subordinates. In most cases it would be more appropriate to *unbracket* inequalities in the sense of explicitly thematizing them."[26] Contrary to liberal ideals of free speech, then, it would be more democratic to approach questions of policy and governance from a feminist outlook that draws attention to, and seeks to mitigate, power differentials (such as those fostered by oppressive speech) rather than ignoring them.

One might object at this point, of course, that there is something prima facie antidemocratic about the refusal to engage with some group or viewpoint. How different, really, is the sentiment of feminist blogs' comment policies from that expressed by those western Kentuckians, described by Cynthia Gayman, attempting to block public hearing of a mosque's zoning application: "Why enter a discussion with someone with whom you know you are never going to agree?" If it is true that "more viewpoints necessitate more inquiry and maybe more insight into the complexity of a given situation,"[27] then surely the answer is to allow open forums to all comers, no matter how reprehensible we find their views. The difficulty, however, is that although our problems do exist in the context of a shared world, as Gayman suggests, sometimes those problems exist precisely because of the exploitation of that sharing by those in positions of greater power. That is, in relationships characterized by oppression, the imperative toward inclusion and hospitality to all comers is exactly *antidemocratic*, insofar as it requires disadvantaged people to continue interactions that sustain their disadvantage. The notion that participants in the feminist blogosphere have an obligation to engage in open conversation with purveyors of misogynist speech is problematic, then, because that sort of discursive interaction requires the admission that these communities' problems may not actually be problems at all, and a fortiori, that they may not be agents or citizens worthy of respect or attention. More viewpoints in a democratic conversation may, sometimes, lead to further inquiry and more complex insight—but they may also, in cases of actually existing disparities in power, lead to further entrenchment of antidemocratic patterns of interaction. It is crucial, then, that when we consider the value of further conversation and the establishment of a big-tent public, we take into account the realities of life on the ground. Democracy, after all, isn't most fundamentally an abstracted philosophical ideal, but something we actually try to do and to live *in this world*—the one we currently have. These blogs, then, suggest that what they are doing is not merely writing; they are forming communities within particular sorts of spaces, which aim to make participation in a democratic public possible in a way that many communities in the offline world simply do not.

And yet these communities are not entirely like offline ones: their members do not bump into one another at the market or at work; often, they have never seen one another, and know one another only through their words. Most of the reason for this, of course, is that the members of these communities are dispersed around the world. The bloggers from *Tiger Beatdown* and *Angry Black Bitch* are American but live in cities across the country from one another; *Feminist Philosophers*'s contributors are from the United Kingdom and the United States and Canada; *Feministe* features bloggers from the United Kingdom, the United States, and Australia; *Muslimah Media Watch*'s contributors come from Iran, France, Saudi Arabia, Malaysia, Egypt, the United States, and the United Kingdom. Commenters on these blogs identify themselves as being American, Canadian, British, Russian, Australian, Indian, and Saudi. The spaces that these blogs thus create are not strictly local in the typical sense of the term: they foster communities that are not restricted by national boundaries. The individuals who make them up are at once localized, via participation in a single space of discussion, and disparate in their regional, national, cultural, ethnic, racial and religious identities. I want to suggest that they form an interacting network of cosmopolitan publics that we can understand as Deweyan in spirit—though in a way that reaches beyond the constrained conception of "the public" featured in *The Public and Its Problems*.

Of course, what one means by "cosmopolitan" is often an open question. When contemporary political philosophers talk about cosmopolitanism, they, like Dewey,[28] often have in mind a sort of universalism of the human family: when we're thinking about making the right choices in ethics and politics, the story goes, the truly cosmopolitan thing to do is to notice that everyone, no matter their national identity, is a citizen of the global human race, and to treat them accordingly. That is, even while respecting radical cultural and national differences, a person committed to cosmopolitanism will often maintain, as Anthony Appiah does, that "there are some values that are, and should be, universal, just as there are some values that are, and should be, local."[29] Now, there's a way in which the feminist blogs I am addressing here appear to be cosmopolitan in this common sense: they seem to be committed to the universal ideal of ending women's oppression, for example. But there's an important sense in which they don't foster this particular kind of cosmopolitanism: there is frequently large-scale disagreement internal to each blog on everything from who counts as a woman, to whether "women" as such can be said to be oppressed in the same way; there is, moreover, an overarching suspicion of attempts to make claims about universal ideals, or even about which of their concerns are definitely "shared" in the strict sense advanced by Covaleskie or (sometimes) Dewey. Finally, when looking at the "feminist blogosphere" as a whole, it's not obvious that the concerns of each individual blog are global ones. While the communities they foster are transnational, and thus cosmopolitan in some weak sense, they are not explicitly concerned with the kind of universal values that Appiah—or Dewey—argues are important for philosophical cosmopolitanism.

So, I am not claiming that the publics feminist blogging fosters are *cosmopolitan* in the typical sense of the term. I am suggesting, on the contrary, that the communities of the feminist blogosphere have a way of confronting us with what Dewey might understand as the transnationally interactional character of our meanings and problems. They suggest, in other words, something *similar* to what Thomas Pogge calls the "institutional cosmopolitan" position—the position that claims we ought to be concerned with the problems of others around the globe "insofar as they are produced by coercive social institutions in whose imposition we are involved."[30] This notion of the cosmopolitan nature of the world forces us to acknowledge that many of the institutions we participate in (whether they're nations or corporations, gender or cultural practices) have indirect consequences for others, even if our intended meanings or actions aren't directly or concerned with them. Pogge's position, of course, involves a larger claim about what sorts of universal human rights cause us our obligations to accrue, which doesn't interest me here. Instead, I am concerned with how Pogge's articulation of this version of the cosmopolitan position forces us to confront our responsibility for others' situations via the global connections between our institutions. Feminist blogs—and to a greater extent, the feminist blogosphere as a whole—do just this sort of thing on a regular basis. The diverse communities that they make possible, in their sometimes-conflicting and divergent concerns, ask both their members and the outside world to come to grips with the many ways in which the institutions in which they/we participate have meaningful negative consequences for all sorts of people beyond ourselves, even when these consequences exceed the scope of our intentions. In 2011, for example, *Muslimah Media Watch* discussed the oppressive effects of France's recent decision to ban the niqab for Muslim women throughout the world—despite some previous discussions on *Feministe* (2010) and *Feminist Philosophers* (2010) that were more ambivalent about such bans. Other ongoing discussions at *Tiger Beatdown* (2011) and *Angry Black Bitch* (2011) suggested that ongoing public discourse about public funding and policy for access to reproductive healthcare has both violently oppressive consequences for women (particularly poor women and women of color) *and* simultaneously privileging effects for many men not obviously connected to them. Moreover, when bloggers fail to notice particular implications, when they fail to see how their view of anti-oppressive action further alienates others, commenters often show up to register their disagreement. Such disagreement can range from friendly dissent to the dreaded, heated "call-out," and may or may not be resolved in consensus.

Whether it does or not, however, the interactions that bring these various sorts of concerns into contact with one another—or that, just as often, make salient their preexisting relations and contacts, even if these are contentious—are precisely in line with the theory of meaning and change that Dewey articulates in his work prior to *The Public and Its Problems*. That is, while it is certainly not the case that feminist blogging fosters the kind of big-tent communication that prevents the supposedly un-democratic division "of human beings into sets and cliques, into antagonistic sets and factions,"[31] it does help make clear how the meanings and interactions that constitute these groups are related, across concerns and national boundaries. And concomitantly, the feminist blogosphere thus suggests that democratic publics worthy of the name cannot be (at least in our present moment of globalization) strictly localized within national borders; nor can they be clearly unified under a banner of strictly shared problems. Such disparate and interacting cosmopolitan publics as those formed in and by the feminist blogosphere demonstrate the need for consistently democratic practice to foster dissent—not only about how to deal with "our" common problems, but about what *constitutes* a problem, and what it means for those problems to be shared relationally. The problems that consistently democratic, anti-oppressive practice must address are not, as feminist blogs show, strictly shared in the sense of affecting all involved in the same way; neither will they be most effectively addressed by attempting to bring conversation about all such problems into the open forum of some (future?) unified public. The *inter*actional character of our meanings and practices suggests, as feminist blogging illustrates and as Dewey agrees in his better moments, that what is important for democratic life is not a localized consensus of concerns, but the fostering of communities that make visible and vocal the underside of "our" shared problems, that make the cosmopolitan and relational character of those problems clear. This would not entail a better, more inclusive, more *really* public version of The Public, but instead, a recognition of the value of multiplicitous (perhaps even fractured), cosmopolitan, interacting *publics*. This version of democratic life is thus, I submit, not only feminist but Deweyan. Though it is not the democracy of many of his political writings, it is democracy that would take seriously his radical claims about what it is to share meanings, or to interact. It is a democratic practice that would seek, as Dewey says, to "cooperate by giving differences a chance to show themselves."[32]

ERIN C. TARVER is Assistant Professor of Philosophy at Oxford College of Emory University. Her areas of specialization include feminist philosophy, American pragmatism, continental philosophy, and the philosophy of sport, and her publications include *The I in Team: Sports Fandom and the Reproduction of Identity* (Chicago, 2017) and (coedited with Shannon Sullivan) *Feminist Interpretations of William James* (Penn State University Press, 2015).

Notes

1. Throughout, I will refer to the world of non-internet-based interactions as "the offline world." I deliberately avoid phrases like "in real life," or "in the real world," as these give the mistaken impression that life as we live it online is radically distinct from life as we live it offline. Likewise, I will resist the notion that online interactions are somehow nonphysical, as this too seems to invoke a dualism that I find untenable.
2. Carlos Thiebaut, "Cosmopolitanism, Identity, and Belonging," paper presented at the American Philosophies Forum: Cosmopolitanism and Place, Círculo de Bellas Artes, Madrid, June 2–4, 2011.
3. See Robert Talisse, *A Pragmatist Philosophy of Democracy* (New York: Routledge, 2007).
4. Colin Koopman, "Good Questions and Bad Answers in Talisse's *A Pragmatist Philosophy of Democracy*," *Transactions of the Charles Peirce Society* 45, no. 1 (2009): 170.
5. John Dewey, *Experience and Nature. In the Later Works of John Dewey: Experience and Nature*, ed. Jo Ann Boydston (Carbondale: Southern Illinois University Press, 1981), 1:139.
6. John Dewey, *The Quest for Certainty. The Later Works of John Dewey (1929): The Quest for Certainty*, 2nd ed., ed. Jo Ann Boydston (Carbondale: Southern Illinois University Press, 2008), 4:136.
7. José Medina, "In Defense of Pragmatic Contextualism: Wittgenstein and Dewey on Meaning and Agreement," *Philosophical Forum* 35, no. 3 (Fall 2004): 344.
8. John Dewey, *The Public and Its Problems. In the Later Works of John Dewey (1925–1927): Essays, Reviews, Miscellany, and the Public and Its Problems*, ed. Jo Ann Boydston (Carbondale: Southern Illinois University Press, 1984), 2:252.
9. Ibid., 245–46.
10. Ibid., 306.
11. Dewey, *Experience and Nature*, 1:141, emphasis mine.
12. Medina, "In Defense of Pragmatic Contextualism," 350.
13. Dewey, *The Public and Its Problems*, 2:320.
14. Ibid., 365.
15. Ibid., emphasis mine.
16. Vincent Colapietro, "American Evasions of Foucault," *Southern Journal of Philosophy* 36 (1998): 347.
17. John Covaleskie, "What Public? Whose Schools?," *Educational Studies* 42, no. 1 (2007): 30, emphasis mine.
18. American Psychiatric Association, "Gender Identity Disorders," *DSM IV-TR* (2000): 302.xx–302.6.
19. Dewey, *The Public and Its Problems*, 2:324.
20. Ibid., 328.
21. Ibid., 371–72.
22. See Ibid., 377ff.
23. By "presence" I mean a certain popularity that results in these blogs being or having been frequently cited and linked to by other blogs and websites. (*Tiger Beatdown* remains online but is not longer an active blog.) This does not mean that these blogs are intrinsically more valuable than others; as Leow points out, the practice of reciprocal linking and citation is often both reflective and reproductive of the same sorts of cultural hierarchies of offline life (and indeed, of the Academy); see Rachel Leow, "Reflections on Feminism, Blogging and the Historical Profession," *Journal of Women's History* 22, no. 4 (2010): 241.
24. See www.feministe.us/blog, http://tigerbeatdown.com/, http://muslimahmediawatch.org/, http://angryblackbitch.blogspot.com/, http://feministphilosophers.wordpress.com/.

There is, of course, non-English-language feminist blogging, though it is rather infrequently linked to or interacted with by the English-language feminist blogosphere (even though not all participants .on the English-language feminist blogs are native English speakers). This is a serious limitation—one that is both important and extremely difficult to rectify, given the present dominance of English worldwide. Rather than highlighting additional non-English-language blogs, however, I am focusing on this group of English-language blogs specifically for two reasons: first, my suggestion is precisely that fractured and multiplicitous publics (plural) are useful for democratic practice, even when they fail to provide big-tent unity; second, my interest here is in articulating how an actually existing set of interactions might be useful in some key ways, *not* in claiming that it does or will, on its own, give rise to a perfect dawn of cosmopolitan democracy.

25. See, for example, *Tiger Beatdown*, "#Dearjohn: On Rape Culture and a Culture of Reproductive Violence," blog comment, February 4, 2011, http://tigerbeatdown.com/2011/02/04/dearjohn-on-rape-culture-and-a-culture-of-reproductive-violence/.

26. Nancy Fraser, "Rethinking the Public Sphere: A Contribution to the Critique of Actually Existing Democracy," *Habermas and the Public Sphere*, ed. Craig Calhoun (Cambridge: MIT Press, 1992), 120.

27. Chapter 14, pp. 242, 244.

28. Ignas Skrupskelis persuasively argues that Dewey's suspicion of nationalism is both a feature of his commitment to this sort of human-family cosmopolitanism *and* evidence of his own problematic assumptions about the universalizable character of large-nation nationalism. See his article, "Some Oversights in Dewey's Cosmopolitanism," *Transactions of the Charles Peirce Society* 45, no. 3 (2009): 308–47. Ironically, then, Dewey's understanding of cosmopolitanism is too inflected with unquestioned American view of nationalism to be cosmopolitan in the way I suggest.

29. Kwame Anthony Appiah, *Cosmopolitanism: Ethics in a World of Strangers* (New York: W. W. Norton, 2006), xxi.

30. Thomas Pogge, *World Poverty and Human Rights*, 2nd ed. (Malden, MA: Polity, 2008), 178.

31. John Dewey, *Creative Democracy. In the Later Works of John Dewey (1939–1941): Essays, Reviews, and Miscellany*, ed. Jo Ann Boydston (Carbondale: Southern Illinois University Press, 1991), 14:230.

32. Ibid., 231.

16 A New "International of Decent Feelings"?
Cosmopolitanism and the Erasure of Class

William S. Lewis

> We are confronted with a phenomenon that is international in scope, and with a diffuse ideology, which, though it has not yet been precisely defined, is capable of assuming a certain organizational form.... One senses, in these attempts, a mentality in search of itself... an ideology seeking to define itself, entrench itself, and also furnish itself with means of action. If this mentality is international, and in the process of taking institutional form, then a new "International" is in the making. There is perhaps something to be gained from trying to discover what it conceals.
>
> —Louis Althusser

FIFTEEN YEARS BEFORE he renewed philosophical Marxism with his re-readings of Marx and Lenin, Louis Althusser authored a polemic titled "The International of Decent Feelings." The student philosopher who wrote this piece had yet to renounce his Christianity and was heavily influenced by Catholic theology as well as by Hegelian interpretations of Marx. Though these interests do not distinguish him from many of his philosophical peers who were also looking to Hegel to make Marxism more philosophically sophisticated or were trying to reconcile Marxism with progressive theology, the scope of his critique of postwar Internationalism is startlingly original.

In "The International of Decent Feelings," Althusser argues that the postwar claim made by Existentialists, Socialists, and progressive Christians that—after the death camps and under the threat of mass annihilation from the Atom Bomb—we have all become "proletarians of the human condition" is a fallacious one and, further, that its adoption has pernicious political consequences. Against the contention of Malraux, Mauriac, Jaspers, Camus, and other public intellectuals that fear of death is what we now all experience and that this sentiment may form the basis for universal solidarity and universal peace, Althusser points to the existence of a real, existing, proletariat. These persons are a class distinguishable from "humanity as a whole." Real social antagonisms exist for them and they are mostly aware that their interests are not those of capitalist states, be these national or universal. Universalizing myths of fear, Althusser argues, have the "effect of tearing these [people] from the very reality of their existence, from their daily political and social struggles."[1]

In this chapter, I suggest that the major arguments for cosmopolitanism advanced by philosophers after the end of the Cold War and whose major impetuses have been post–Cold War political realignments, globalization, resurgent nationalist and ethnic struggle, environmental crises, and the rise of global terrorism are analogous to those of certain post–World II French philosophers and their calls for universal solidarity in the face of atomic destruction. The two are analogous in their universalizing tendency and in their shared intention to provide moral and political order to a world historical situation that has undergone rapid change and where political and moral hegemony is ambiguous. Though the universalizing tendency of the affect of fear is not always a constant (the sentiment of common suffering or the judgment of universal justice sometimes supplementing it and sometimes taking its place), I suggest that it still plays a role in these arguments. Further, I show how the cosmopolitan appeal to common ideals, to what we can learn from each other, to our universal humanity, or to our deep attachments to others, often but not necessarily results in the forgetting of class differences and in the paving over of existing class struggles. It also erases the evidence of the production of these universal ideals insofar as they can be understood as part of the class struggle. This is true of the moral theory of cosmopolitanism, as well as the political theory that follows from it, and it can also be seen in cultural cosmopolitanism.

Clearly, Althusser is not a common reference point for contributors to this volume, Appiah, Bohman, Nussbaum, McKinnon, or other contemporary cosmopolitan theorists mentioned in this volume. However, in the second half of the twentieth century, he was a perspicacious critic of the position that human values are universal or that they can be universalized. In addition, he developed a philosophical method by which the origin of a call for universal values could be identified and the effects of these values' adoption understood. Though he has obviously not been a participant in the last twenty plus years of debates on ethical and political cosmopolitanism, the critical framework that Althusser's developed provide us with insights into the origin and effects of contemporary theories that rely on notions of universal human values or characteristics and it is for this reason that I wish to bring his heterodox ideas about value theoretical universals into this ongoing debate.

To make the point that Cold War internationalism and contemporary cosmopolitanism are analogous in their universalizing tendency and in their shared intention to provide moral and political order to a world historical situation that has undergone rapid change, I first lay out Althusser's argument against a "cosmopolitanism of fear." I then update this argument by generalizing it and by making it consistent with Althusser's mature understanding of "humanity" and of the role that class struggle and the working class in particular play in human history. The critical framework that this updated argument provides will then be applied to two variants of cosmopolitan value theory, moral and cultural, as these are represented in the works of Nussbaum and Appiah. Insofar as their arguments are subject to the same criticisms, I similarly reference and examine the companion chapters in this volume. With this accomplished, I conclude this chapter with the assertion that both moral and cultural cosmopolitans not only fail to sufficiently recognize the global class struggles that are the responses of the masses to globalization (and to the cosmopolitanism institutions and practices that provide it with its juridical and political apparatuses), but that this forgetting makes the ethical or political projects which are to follow from these theories unrealizable.

The International of Decent Feelings, Althusser explains, is a growing but still somewhat inchoate political movement that has formed in response to the horrors of the war and by a vision of a future for humanity that now includes the immanent possibility of such horrors as show trials, death camps, and atomic bombs.[2] This movement is based on the recognition that "humanity is threatened," that we are all equal under this fear, and that we have therefore have become "a proletariat of terror."[3] The leaders of this movement, Camus, Koestler, Mauriac, Malraux, and Jaspers are a diverse group of individuals; they are novelists, Christian theologians, journalists, politicians, and philosophers and they come from many sides of the political spectrum. These men find themselves united rhetorically, sentimentally, and politically by a shared consciousness of man's destiny. This consciousness motivates them to make speeches and films, to write plays and novels, to analyze the human condition in academic journals, and to begin the organization of international moral campaigns for peace and for human rights. They do these things because they abhor the "peace" and the possibilities for violent and horrible ends with which the end of the war has left them. For these diverse thinkers, Althusser observes, it is the "growing awareness that humanity is threatened," that motivates the "'International' of humane protest" for which they call.[4]

A protest movement, but also only a cosmopolitanism of good sentiments. It remains merely this, argues Althusser, because the unity that humans are encouraged to see themselves under and to act from—that of fear of our fate—is a psychological one. As he writes, "This is a *de facto* equality, which governs all our acts in which we live and move."[5] The universal consciousness of this equality is that which motivates a good conscience and good political action: if we are all united by fears of the end of humanity then, conscientiously, we should all engage in a struggle to regain and secure our common humanity.

However, as Althusser points out, this is not a struggle for a new order, this is too risky, but for the preservation and securing of what we have. The war has taught us that we are mortal, that we all can die, and that experiments with new social forms can lead to horrible consequences. For this movement, "there can no longer be any question of inventing new customs; what is at stake for us today is maintaining the life which . . . is the only one we have." Further, there is no need to invent new ways of life because the phenomenon is psychological; all that we have to do is "convert the content of our fear into the tranquility of our soul."[6] That is, according to those who champion this new International, all that we need do is to imagine the possibility of our nonexistence and we will be motivated to do those things that will ensure the continuity of ourselves as human beings.

The motivation for these sentiments, the fact that all of us will cease to exist at some point is, as Althusser points out, a banality and no more defines us than does the fact that it will rain.[7] In addition, because "the content of [this] fear is something imaginary, non-existent" those who are anxious cannot emancipate themselves from the object that they fear through any type of definite action.[8]

If this fear is indeed irrational and its origin insurmountable, then why are so many people making these arguments for a New International and what interests do they serve? Althusser's answer to this question is that the International of Decent Sentiments is an ideology,[9] a viewpoint that serves certain functions in the postwar social, economic, political, and psychical landscape. First, it absolves the bad consciences of those who were the aggressors in the war and also of those who killed in defense. "'We are all murderers!' cries Camus. Our crimes make us equal because we have all killed."[10] Those who gain from this acknowledgment, Althusser argues, are those who want to "conceal real reason and present [contemporary] realities," who want to show all humanity as, once again, morally equal, and who want to "buy mercenaries for the next war."[11] Second, it serves the interests of those who want to "conjure away social antagonisms" by invoking the immanent death of humanity and to achieve European unity and peace not through action, but by "a verbal, moralizing socialism" that maintains "the essential positions of capitalism."[12] In short, the International of Decent Feelings is an ideology, one which serves those who desire a "Western" socialism and are dismayed by the possibility for Europe of domination by American industry or by Soviet totalitarianism.[13]

Not only are the fear that motivates this International irrational and the political effects that it engenders conservative, forgetful, and, at base, immoral; Althusser argues that the phenomenon is un-Christian as well. In these postwar analyses of the human condition, the Christian recognition of our equality before God is replaced by our equality before the fear of death.[14] In addition to the sin of idolatry, where death becomes identical with God and the promise of an afterlife is forgotten, the International of Decent Feelings homogenizes humanity.

It misses the existence of proletarians, a particular class that does not have to suffer in anguish and who is actually capable of delivering the emancipation from fear by re-appropriating the products of human production, including the atomic bomb.[15] Unlike the universal "proletariat of terror," this class does not have as its object something outside itself. As Althusser points out, "poverty for the proletariat is not the fear of poverty, it is an actual present that never disappears, it is on the walls, on the table, [etc.]."[16] Because the oppression of the proletariat is real, concrete oppression, the proletariat has the possibility of transforming its condition, of "converting concrete servitude into concrete freedom." It can do so by harnessing and directing technology, by re-appropriating the products of its labors, and by instantiating a true fraternity of men. Thereby, it will lead "the whole of humanity towards its emancipation."[17] At this point in Althusser's intellectual development, his Catholic theology is better developed than his Marxism (which is largely of the type to be gained from party pamphlets). Further, as Roland Boer has pointed out, Althusser's Hegelian-Marxist eschatology goes not sit easily with his theology. If the International of Decent Feelings can be critiqued for the idolatry of mistaking universal fear of death for the universal human condition under God, then Althusser himself can be critiqued for his faith in the proletariat as the agent that will bring human beings to their universal destiny.[18]

In his mature philosophy, Althusser abandoned the idea of the proletariat as a universal subject and the telic view of history that came with it. However, he kept something resembling the notion of the "ontological reserve," that there always exists something in the universe that exceeds any conception that we may have of it, from his theological argument.[19] This concept appears in his later works as the notion of the "void," or that background condition in which any and all historical events may occur.[20] This concept has some affinities with what Robert Innis labels the "non-object" or, quoting François Jullien, the "great Process of the world, which exceeds human beings to the point of being 'unfathomable' and encompasses all human activity."[21] Though to do so is to embrace anachronism in intellectual history in order to make a philosophical argument, this essay's argument starts with this metaphysical notion of the void and maintains that the principal features of Althusser's developed Historical Materialism: contradiction, ateleology, structural causality, uneven development, anti-humanism, overdetermination, and so on, are consistent with the notion of the void and with his critique of the International of Decent Feelings. Accordingly, my argument makes use of these concepts in its critique, even if they are not mentioned by name. However, one can only make use of these concepts if one abandons this early work's Hegelian-Marxist teleology and acknowledges that its theological argument is consistent with his mature work. This done, one no longer understands the proletariat or "workers" as the universal subject which is in the process of coming to be. Instead, one acknowledges that capitalism is a social formation that tends toward the production of social antagonisms between those who largely control capital and those who are controlled by those who control it.

If one discards the idea of history as the progressive realization of humanity in its full freedom through the overcoming of its alienation and adopts Althusser's later position that history is a series of socioeconomic-political-ideological orders that coalesce or "take" and that have their own analyzable regularities, then his critique of the International of Decent Feelings still holds and the contradiction between this early essay's critique of idolatry and his idolization of the proletariat can be avoided. From this perspective, the two essential aspects of his critique can be distilled. The first is that an internationalism or cosmopolitanism based on a universal feature that all human beings share is philosophically and politically suspect. Such cosmopolitanisms are suspect because they identify one or more features as essential to our common humanity and suggest solidarity based on these features even though the concept of "humanity" is an ideological rather than a metaphysical concept. To say that it is ideological is to note that the concept has a history, that it has been defined differently, at different times, by different peoples, for different uses, and that the reasons for these definitions can be understood by looking at how they function politically and at what motivates them. Second, when the concept of humanity is used universally, it tends to occlude and forget the fact of real, existing, concrete antagonisms among people that are the result not of their common humanity but of their respective roles in the production, ownership, and distribution of capital. In short, it is used to erase the reality of class and class struggle.

With the critical framework distilled from Althusser's critique of post–World War II Internationalism I now engage with two contemporary variants of cosmopolitan value theory: moral and cultural. After a brief summary of the two variants, I argue that each not only fails to sufficiently recognize the global class struggles that are the responses of the masses to globalization (and to the cosmopolitanism institutions and practices that provide it with its juridical and political apparatuses), but that this forgetting makes the ethical or political projects which are to follow from these theories unrealizable. However, before beginning this critique it may be of interest to note that the contemporary resurgence of cosmopolitan philosophizing since 1990 has its analogue not only in the period of Internationalist discussion immediately following World War II, but also that following the Great War. In each of these periods, the temporary stability of global political relations was disturbed by crisis. After a state of sudden change, political theorists started to think about cosmopolitanism. When order was restored (such as when the Cold War took the place of World War II's peace), thinking about cosmopolitanism died down. That we are now, twenty years after the end of the Cold War and ten years after September 11, still talking about cosmopolitanism suggests that we are still in a state of global political crisis. Cosmopolitanism may well be one of those things that allow us to emerge from the present crisis. However, we may also wish to interrogate its limits lest we think that it can provide the whole solution to our current socio-economic-environmental problems.

In the past twenty years, it sometimes seems like there have been as many cosmopolitanisms proposed as there are adjectives designating value theoretical positions capable of modifying the term.[22] The two variants of cosmopolitanism examined here are among the most prominent and have each been widely disseminated and discussed. With the exception of economic and political cosmopolitanism, these two also represent the main areas in contemporary cosmopolitan thought.[23]

Beginning in the early 1990s and continuing with a series of popular and academic articles that blended scholarship in the history of philosophy with contemporary moral philosophy, Martha Nussbaum formulated her moral cosmopolitanism in response to philosophical appeals for a reconstructed patriotism and to her own engagement with "international quality-of-life issues."[24] In these articles, cosmopolitanism is presented as a possible solution to humanity's problems inasmuch as these are caused, at least in part, by loyalties to family, tribe, nation, class, ethnicity, or race.[25] Examples of the problems that Nussbaum believes cosmopolitanism can address include the unequal distribution of the world's resources, war, racism, sexism, international cooperation, and environmental justice.[26] In addition, she argues that this principle can provide guidance as to the proper political form for human society.[27]

Nussbaum presents the solution to these problems in the guise of a reconstructed cosmopolitanism that borrows arguments from Greek and Roman philosophers about the loyalties humans owe to one another and about the virtues inherent in self and civic cultivation. Added to this classical mix are Kantian ideas about human nature and the obligations that this nature entails. In this hybrid cosmopolitanism, Nussbaum starts with Diogenes's radical idea that he was not loyal to any particular group, be it family, local origin, or class, but to the world.[28] Approvingly, she recognizes Diogenes still heterodox position as a choice to be "an exile from the comfort of patriotism and its easy sentiments, to see our own ways of life from the point of view of justice and the good."[29]

However, in order to see our own lives in this way, it is necessary to posit that there is: (a) some ontological unity that binds all humans together in some morally significant way; (b) that there is some recognizable good or goods that we all share; and (c) that we have the capacity to discern and deliberate about these goods. In support of these positions, Nussbaum basically reiterates Kant's political philosophy as it is presented in "Idea for a Universal History with a Cosmopolitan Intent" and the "Perpetual Peace" essays, minus his historiography. The larger unity we all share is our common humanity, she maintains. This common humanity fulfills each of these three conditions because its contents include the fact that we are all created equal, that we are endowed with reason, that we have the capacity for moral choice, and that we share certain fundamental moral norms.[30] It is these qualities and capacities that Nussbaum argues allows us to see ourselves as "citizens of the world," to feel that we owe duties to one another, and to deliberate with one another rationally about ways to achieve human goods globally.[31] Thus can we be motivated to deliver material aid to those who are not part of our immediate community[32] or to engage in discussion with one other about whether it is right to cause environmental devastation in areas of the globe that are not where we presently live.

Though the moral and political framework that Nussbaum embraces is that of Kantian cosmopolitanism, she does not believe that we are endowed with an innate universal moral sense that allows us to know immediately what is right and wrong for human beings. Instead, she presents her ideal cosmopolitan individual as one who comes to this position through a rich process of stoic self-cultivation and study of other cultures. She therefore proposes as salutary for all a passionate and cognitive education whereby individuals and particular groups come to know themselves in relation to the common humanity that they share with others "as similarly human, as bearers of an equal moral dignity, as members of a single body and a set of purposes."[33] Because she emphasizes exposure to and learning about others as well at the active transformation of our own reactions to otherness and to differences in human beings, Nussbaum's moral cosmopolitanism could equally embrace Jeff Edmonds's "nomadology" (Chapter 8) and Noëlle C. McAfee's philosophy of address and audition (Chapter 2). Through these and other similar experiences which she outlines in her work, Nussbaum argues that we can transform our evaluative capacities such that we become capable of thinking first about what we owe to others, about that which we share with them, and about what is best for us all as human beings.

In his 2006 book, *Cosmopolitanism: Ethics in a World of Strangers*, Kwame Anthony Appiah shares Nussbaum's appreciation for diverse cultures and also notes the morally beneficial effects that may result from exposure to them. However, he does not fully endorse her argument that there are universal moral principles, which result from our common humanity, and that brook no exceptions.[34] Instead, Appiah outlines a cosmopolitanism that incorporates aspects of both moral cosmopolitanism and cultural parochialism but which modifies both from their strong forms.[35] Thus, in regard to moral cosmopolitanism, Appiah strongly tempers the moral universalism found in such philosophers as Singer, Unger, or Nussbaum and replaces it with the argument that, though universal human values exist, they are not sufficient on their own for overcoming disagreements about values and practices between individuals and groups. Similarly, in regard to cultural parochialism, Appiah challenges the argument that ethnic or national cultures have a right to exist and to preserve their culture, while still endorsing the claim that cultural differences can be useful for discovering best how to live.

Appiah's endorsement of parochialism is a limited endorsement. It is based, fundamentally on a respect for cultural difference both for its own sake and for the sake of the human good. Though he does not provide a strictly functionalist definition of norms, Appiah notes that a culture's particular system of value is the result of its own unique experience in the world. As these values reflect on and mediate this experience, they are good for the specific culture that developed them.[36] This is Appiah's intrinsic justification of the preservation of difference. Further, because specific values are human responses to their lived environments and, as such, represent solutions to general human problems, then it is reasonable to believe that we can learn about what to value and how to value from other cultures.[37] This is Appiah's extrinsic justification for the preservation and respect of difference. It is also one of the factors that limit his cosmopolitanism: one cannot simultaneously respect difference and expect everyone to become a cosmopolitan.

Though learning about other cultures may be salutary and teach us more about what we should or might value, it is not the case for Appiah that learning about or even experiencing diverse cultures will make one a good person concerned with the welfare of humanity. In this regard, he cites the example of Sir Richard Burton who, though he traveled extensively and modified his language, appearance, and gesture such that he could pass as a native in many places, retained many of the prejudices of Victorian culture.[38] Therefore, Appiah concludes, familiarity with and learning about diverse human cultures is insufficient to generate tolerance of human difference, an understanding of the common qualities that unite us all, and compassion for humanity. If any progress is to be made in this regard, it must be done by other means, and the principal methods that Appiah cites are living with and engaging in conversation with people who hold different values from us.

But why is learning about other cultures insufficient to generate tolerance, understanding, and compassion? Appiah argues that this insufficiency is due to the nature of moral value and to our moral psychology. In terms of the metaphysics of morals, he rejects the "positivist" argument, which holds that values are merely beliefs or opinions about states of things and that these values cannot, therefore, be subjected to rational scrutiny or empirical demonstration as to their veracity.[39] On the contrary, moral concepts are understood psychologically by Appiah as primarily action guiding. They are thus subject to empirical scrutiny.[40] Further, inasmuch as values are shared among individuals, they are objective and represent a social consensus.[41] The meanings and import of values are communicated, he believes, in conversations and stories. In the latter, values are shown "at work," guiding specific actions and leading to specific consequences. In the former, they convey content about what the holder of that value thinks is the appropriate response to a situation or situations.

That moral values have an objective status within a culture does not mean that someone outside the culture from which they originate can understand them immediately. However, it is also not the case that we cannot communicate our values to others. By virtue of being human, we share certain experiences and certain features of the mind and these provide a basis for communication and understanding between different cultures.[42] In addition, we share many "thin" values, such as politeness, good parenting, or piety, in which there is a shared notion of a certain obligation, but which becomes fleshed out or "thick" when embedded in a particular culture. Though we might disagree strenuously with what a certain culture (or the representative culture) says it means to be a good parent, the thin value of good parenting is shared. We can move from these thin concepts to discussions of the thicker, culturally embedded values.[43]

Despite the possibility of this conversation, there are still many hurdles to a discussion that can result in a shared understanding and to having a dialogue that can help guide us to a shared approach to the decisions that face us all.[44] Just because we have had a discussion with someone with whom our values conflict and understand what value is at stake for both of us, does not mean that we come to any agreement about what is to be done.[45] In addition, people do not change their actions or beliefs because of discussion and agreement.[46] They do so, Appiah maintains, because, after prolonged exposure to different ways of life, they gradually come to a new way of seeing things.[47] Women, he argues, increased their status and freedom in the developed West in the last generation not because of argument but because we got used to them exercising a different status and making different choices.[48]

This then, is Appiah's strongest endorsement of cultural cosmopolitanism: we should take interest in what other people do because exposure to them makes us accept them and therefore makes us less likely to have conflicts with them.[49] Starting with those thin values and obligations we hold in common as humans, we need to have conversations across borders and to engage with the experience and ideas of others.[50] However, because there is no possibility of a final casuistry of values, where we might be able to decide which values are the best and which should take precedence for all,[51] Appiah argues that we need to be fallibility in regard to morals. In addition, if it is the case that there is no way to adjudicate between values and potentially useful values can emerge from any culture, then we must also be value pluralists.[52]

Nussbaum's and Appiah's cosmopolitanisms are tough to argue with. Who, except for fundamentalists could disagree with Appiah's conclusion and who but jingoists would reject Nussbaum's? Prima facie, the political and moral program that each endorses as the outcome of the adoption of their version of cosmopolitanism is similarly unobjectionable. Live with others, talk to them, find common ground, avoid conflicts, come to a shared approach to how we will face our common problems, live morally, and think about helping those beyond your immediate community says Appiah. Cultivate yourself, respect one another, do not discriminate, apply the same values globally that you do locally, establish internationalist institutions that promote justice, says Nussbaum. It seems intuitively obvious that, if we did any of these things, we would be making the world, a healthier, saner, less violent, and, yes, more humane place.

Undoubtedly, if we adopted all or some of the practices that Nussbaum and Appiah suggest, there would be, for some people, for some amount of time, less suffering in the world and more happiness. However, these practices cannot be a total solution to the problems that motivate them and, further, the philosophies that support these actions may actually work to justify institutions and practices that prolong these problems' existence. These problems include globalization, and its associated environmental devastation, the exploitation of nonhuman animals, population displacement, increased global poverty and inequity as well as resurgent nationalist and ethnic struggle, xenophobia, human rights violations, religious fundamentalism, and the associated rise of global and local terrorism.[53]

Using the critical framework distilled from Althusser's work on the International of Decent Feelings, one may question the initial intuition that, by adopting Nussbaum's moral cosmopolitanism or Appiah's cultural cosmopolitanism, we could make the world a healthier, saner, less violent, and more humane place. Directed by Althusser's hermeneutic of suspicion, the first place that we should look is at these philosophies' idea of what is humane or "human" and what values or possibilities for valuing this definition entails. Second, we should look at what is insufficiently recognized when that which all humans share is the primary (Nussbaum) or secondary (Appiah) justification for our global and local actions, rather than some other force or loyalty.

As detailed above, the common humanity that Nussbaum's cosmopolitanism appeals to are the facts that we are all created equal, that we are endowed with reason, that we have the capacity for moral choice, and that we share certain fundamental moral norms. These qualities, she argues, allows us to see ourselves as "citizens of the world," to feel that we owe duties to one another, and to deliberate with one another rationally about ways to achieve human goods globally. Motivated by these duties, we should feel compelled to, for instance, feed those who are hungry, work to end persistent discrimination, and to work against environmental devastation. Further, we should set up and support institutions that take care of these needs or who work to prevent these wrongs, or to undo the damage that has been done.

What is missed in this discussion, however, is that many of these problems and wrongs cannot be traced to a lack of compassion for or duty toward our fellow man or insufficient institutions to realize these common ideals. Nor can they be permanently repaired by the adoption of this duty. They can, however, be traced back directly to the impacts of the expansion of global capital and its interest in exploiting labor and land in support of increased profits. Focused on what all humanity shares and needs—equality, rationality, respect, the fulfillment of basic human needs—Nussbaum's cosmopolitanism misses that which divides people from one another most consequentially: whether or not and how they have power to direct their lives by virtue of the role that they play in the economic system. By addressing what we may all share but forgetting that which we do not all share, a common class, Nussbaum's cosmopolitanism can address the symptoms of discrimination but not its causes. Appealing to moral cosmopolitanism, an NGO can recognize and seek to repair the harm done to the environment or the immiseration of a local economy that is caused by the actions of a multinational agricultural company. However, it cannot, by the same appeal, argue that the multinational has no right to buy up land, plant a monoculture, displace persons, employ some at below a living wage, and benefit in this regard from the mass of unemployed these actions have left in these actions' wake. Cosmopolitanism seeks moral and juridical solutions to problems that have their roots in the (historically local) moral and juridical systems that it wishes to universalize and it ignores these systems' relations to the economic systems whose functioning they assure.

A priori, we may not be able to establish that capitalism tends to violate our common humanity. On the contrary and as John J. Stuhr wryly notes in Chapter 17 of this volume, cosmopolitanism, with its emphasis on the exchangeability of every person and place,[54] allows some aspects of liberalism to be well expressed, at least for a certain class of people. However, for another class of people, those negatively affected by the role they play in the capitalist system, the appeal to our common humanity and the institutions that may safeguard the "humanity" we share in common is insufficient to address the ills that they suffer by it. Recognizing that "there but for the grace of God go I," as moral cosmopolitanism encourages us to do cannot by itself put an end to the reality that we inhabit a social and economic system which requires one part of the population to exploit another of its parts. Neither is the Golden Rule sufficient, which, formulated in a Kantian way, could equally be one of moral cosmopolitan's maxims.

In his argument, Appiah notices this fact, at least insofar as it involves the impossibility of putting oneself into an "other's" shoes so that the Golden Rule might be put into effect. Given the difference between the norms that different cultures (and individual human beings embrace), it is impossible to know what an other would have done unto here. Appiah points out that, even in what to most people would be clearly defined situations in which the rule should be applied, it is impossible to know that when you are doing for others what you would have done for yourself is going to be accepted as the right thing to do. One example that he gives is of a person who desperately needs a blood transfusion if he is not going to die and of a doctor who believes that, if she were in the situation, she would want to have that transfusion. However, the patient in this example is a Jehovah's Witness and believes that he will go to hell if the transfusion is performed.[55] In this situation, the particularity of each culture's norms makes applying this seemingly anodyne universal moral criterion impossible.

Looked at as a whole, one of the main themes of Appiah's book is that there are no universal moral values that have sufficient content to guide every action. However, he notes well and gives copious examples of particular moral values that allow individuals, in a particular group, in a particular situation and time, to act well. In short, like many of the contributors to this volume—and most particularly Kegley (Chapter 4), Colapietro (Chapter 6), Edmonds (Chapter 8), Tarver (Chapter 15), and Stuhr (Chapter 17)—Appiah understands particularity, whether it be religious, artistic, political, historical, or ethnic. He also notes well that it is the particular moral norms that a specific culture evolved over time to guide relations among its members that precipitate conflicts when we try to live together with people from different cultures. These situations are the motivation for his cultural cosmopolitanism: it is designed to provide us with a means to become comfortable with the diverse practices of others so that these conflicts do not lead to oppression and violence.

Appiah's emphasis on particularity also allows him to diagnose with acuity why and when it is that values clash such that oppression and violence occurs. This happens, he maintains, when the moral principles that were evolved in order to support a particular way of life are stripped of the forms of life to which they gave support and then believed to be applicable to all humanity. In other words, they are thought to be universal moral cosmopolitan principles, even if they are recognizably particular in origin. He gives examples of religious fundamentalisms in this regard, but also of certain Marxisms.[56] Certainly, in the figure of Pol Pot that he cites and Pol's combination of dialectical materialist laws with certain tenets of Theravada Buddhism, this type of transformation is recognizable.[57]

But does this critique hold for all Marxisms? Is there just something that is particularly dangerous about taking a set of normative assumptions that originated from a mid-nineteenth-century intellectual and worker's movement and taking them to be universal? Appiah would probably argue that there is. However, to see the claims of the working class as merely normative claims generated by a particular culture to serve its needs is to misdiagnose these claims' status and origin. It is not a clash of beliefs between capitalist and worker that motivates the worker's animus to the capitalist.[58] Capitalist and worker are often, after all, from the same culture, and the antagonism between worker and capitalist is global. What motivates this antagonism is that, daily, the worker's form of life is ordered, controlled, and threatened with extinction by the capitalists' actions in pursuit of profits. The values that the worker expresses: that she would want more control over her own life and the freedom and power to experience different modes of life, just as the capitalist enjoys, are therefore not merely particular judgments but are universal sentiments expressed from a particular viewpoint.

Appiah would probably not see in this explanation how the values expressed by workers differ in their origins from other sorts of particular values. After all, these values originate from a particular form of life and come in conflict with the values of the capitalist, which themselves may be thought to originate from another form of life. However, one point of this chapter is that both values originate from the same form of life—capitalism—in which we are all enmeshed. As such, they enjoy a different status. In addition, the emphasis that Appiah places on the particularity of cultural morals and how they must be respected does not equip his philosophy to deal well with demands made from those who are impoverished by capitalist expansion, whose environment is compromised, and certainly not from those who would argue that capitalism is a system of economics, values, policies, and institutions that must be overthrown or otherwise surpassed.

We can see this when Appiah tries to deal with what should be done for the terribly impoverished, for those who do not have enough to eat. Rightly, he says that we should not follow Singer and Unger in their directions to give away our fortunes and save the poor for a day when, the next day, the same structural problems that led to their impoverishment would still exists.[59] One would expect, at this point, for Appiah to endorse working to end or transform the socioeconomic system that contributes to this impoverishment. However, he instead suggests that we should contribute to modest institutional reform.[60] This comes close, but it is the limit of what he can argue for if he takes the claims of those who are affected negatively by global capitalism as having the same status as the claims of those who, say, are offended by polygamous relationships. The conflicts that cultural cosmopolitanism is designed to overcome will keep occurring unless this difference is acknowledged

With this survey of contemporary cosmopolitanism, I have attempted to show how the appeal to common ideals, to what we can learn from each other, to our universal humanity, or to our deep attachments to others, often results in the forgetting of class differences and in the paving over of existing class struggles. This is true of the moral theory of cosmopolitanism as well as for cultural cosmopolitanism. Both variants, if adopted, would surely make the world a better place, for some people, and for some time. However, each variant not only fails to sufficiently recognize the global class struggles that are the responses of the masses to globalization (and to the cosmopolitanism institutions and practices that provide it with its juridical and political apparatuses), but this forgetting makes the ethical or political projects that are to follow from these theories unrealizable.

WILLIAM S. LEWIS is Professor and Chair of the Department of Philosophy at Skidmore College. His teaching and research interests include social and political philosophy, American pragmatism, Marxism, philosophy of the social sciences, and philosophy of race and gender. He is the author of *Louis Althusser and the Traditions of French Marxism* (Lexington Books, 2005).

Notes

1. Ibid., 31.
2. Ibid., 22.
3. Ibid., 23.
4. Ibid.
5. Ibid.
6. Ibid., 33.
7. Ibid., 24.
8. Ibid., 26.
9. Ibid., 28.
10. Ibid., 29.
11. Ibid., 30.
12. Ibid., 23.
13. Ibid., 30.
14. Ibid., 27.
15. This synopsis follows my account in "Louis Althusser," *The Stanford Encyclopedia of Philosophy (Winter 2009 Edition)*, ed. Edward N. Zalta, http://plato.stanford.edu/archives/win2009/entries/althusser/.
16. Althusser, "International of Decent Feelings," 25.
17. Ibid., 26, 31, 26.
18. Roland Boer, "Althusser's Catholic Marxism," *Rethinking Marxism* 19, no. 4 (October 2007): 471–72.
19. Ibid., 471.
20. François Matheron, "The Recurrence of the Void in Louis Althusser," *Rethinking Marxism* 10, no. 3 (Fall 1998): 22–27.
21. See Chapter 5 of this volume.
22. David A. Hollinger, "Not Universalists, Not Pluralists: The New Cosmopolitans Find Their Own Way," *Constellations* 8, no. 2 (2001): 237.
23. Pauline Kleingeld and Eric Brown, "Cosmopolitanism," *The Stanford Encyclopedia of Philosophy (Spring 2011 Edition)*, ed. Edward N. Zalta, http://plato.stanford.edu/archives/spr2011/entries/cosmopolitanism/.
24. Martha C. Nussbaum, "Patriotism and Cosmopolitanism," in *For Love of Country: Debating the Limits of Patriotism*, ed. Joshua Cohen, 3–20 (Boston: Beacon, 1996).
25. Ibid.
26. Martha C. Nussbaum, "Duties of Justice, Duties of Material Aid: Cicero's Problematic Legacy," *Journal of Political Philosophy* 8, no. 2 (2000): 176–206; Martha C. Nussbaum, "Kant and Stoic Cosmopolitanism," *Journal of Political Philosophy* 5, no. 1 (1997): 22;Nussbaum, "Patriotism and Cosmopolitanism."
27. Nussbaum, "Duties of Material Aid," 205.

28. Nussbaum, "Patriotism and Cosmopolitanism."
29. Ibid.
30. Ibid.
31. Ibid.
32. Nussbaum, "Duties of Material Aid," 178
33. Nussbaum, "Kant and Stoic Cosmopolitanism," 22.
34. Kwame A. Appiah, *Cosmopolitanism: Ethics in a World of Strangers* (New York: W. W. Norton, 2006), 162.
35. Ibid., xvii.
36. Ibid., 4.
37. Ibid., 41, 43.
38. Ibid., 8.
39. Ibid., 25.
40. Ibid., 26.
41. Ibid., 28.
42. Ibid., 94–96.
43. Ibid., 47.
44. Ibid., 66, 43.
45. Ibid., 59–60.
46. Ibid., 73.
47. Ibid., 78.
48. Ibid., 76.
49. Ibid., 78.
50. Ibid., 95, 134.
51. Ibid., xxi.
52. Ibid., 144.
53. See Chapter 1 of this volume.
54. See Chapter 17 of this volume.
55. Ibid.
56. Ibid.
57. Robert Short, *Pol Pot: Anatomy of a Nightmare* (New York: Henry Holt, 2004), 149–50.
58. This chapter employs these terms to roughly designate the distinction between those who benefit from global capitalism and those whose labor, for the most part, benefits the accumulators of global capital. It also employs them because they have a rich and resonant history. It does with the awareness that, some workers, in some ways, benefit economically from capitalism, for instance, by holding stocks in their retirement funds. It also recognizes the tenuousness of these benefits and others (such as rising home values) from which workers are sometimes said to benefit.
59. Appiah, *Cosmopolitanism*, 168.
60. Ibid., 170.

17 Somewhere, Dreaming of Cosmopolitanism

John J. Stuhr

> Have you seen the flags of freedom?
> What color are they now?
> Do you think that you believe in yours
> More than they do theirs somehow?
>   —Neil Young[1]

The Political Problem of the One and the Many

The problem of cosmopolitanism and provincialism is the longstanding philosophical problem of the one and the many in that problem's only real—that is, political—form. In its traditional meanings and forms, provincialism is no solution to this problem. Just as Winston Churchill once observed that the best argument against democracy is a brief conversation with the average voter, so the best argument against tribalism, parochialism, provincialism, partisanship, patriotism, protectionism, nationalism, jingoism, and all forms of self-congratulatory exceptionalism is a brief account of the record of their accompanying narrowness, ignorance, failures of imagination, fear, smugness, opportunity costs, and their sad and desperate efforts to police supposed purity and unity—for selves who in reality are nevertheless always mixed and connected multiplicities. History shows that any embrace of unqualified parochialism and provincialism is irresponsible and insane.

Accordingly, cosmopolitanism—the one rather than the many, the universal, the rational, enlightenment itself—beckons. Cosmopolitanism's seductive powers are large and real, and so it has been and still is genuinely tempting to many. To be a cosmopolitan is (literally) to be a citizen of the cosmos, an itinerant, a citizen of the world. Understood negatively, a cosmopolitan is free from, or simply without, merely local, merely provincial, or merely national feelings, values, beliefs, biases, customs, entitlements, obligations, and attachments. Understood positively, a cosmopolitan belongs to, and is at home in, all the world, a world of universal human liberties and benevolence.[2]

This gives cosmopolitanism a real (though not complete) marketing edge over provincialism for shoppers in the marketplace for identities, ethics, and social loyalties and revolutions. In effect, cosmopolitanism asks: Why be at home only one place when you could be at home, well, everywhere? It asks: Aren't you tired of being so particular, so situated, so temporal, so blinkered by the accidents of time and place, so without the rights of all humankind simply in virtue of being human, so irreducibly contingent? It suggests place and history, borders and privileges, are so last season, so pre-Enlightenment; wouldn't you like to trade in your particular place and particular history for universal Space and Time—you can even get it with a veil of ignorance or a dash of objective moral foundation or what Seyla Benhabib has characterized as a transition since the 1948 UN Declaration of Human Rights "from *international* to *cosmopolitan* norms of justice," from norms that arise through treaties and agreements among states to norms that apply to all persons as members of a worldwide society?[3] Cosmopolitanism hits at the heart of the contemporary thinking commuter, stuck in the conceptual traffic of today's problems and looking up at a gleaming new apartment building or conceptual scheme with one of those developer's signs that reads "If you lived here, you'd already be home." It prods this commuter to realize, "Yes, but if I were a cosmopolitan, I would always already everywhere be home!" Cosmopolitanism thus sponsors an ongoing kind of conceptual Miss Universe contest (usually without swimsuits) for which it grooms goodwill ambassadors and hospitality industry spokespersons who just want to bring perpetual peace to all the peoples of the world. I picture Kant with a tiara—and complicit would-be cosmopolitan philosophers giving reasons to one another about why this is, and should be, and must be so. More seriously, to the otherwise displaced and homeless, to the otherwise marginalized and disenfranchised, to the otherwise oppressed and wretched, to travelers and agents of globalization, to hosts and guests alike it offers membership in the Kingdom of Ends here and now. It offers entitlements determined without reference to nationality and national citizenship or any other particulars of a person's life.[4] These persons and everyone else must only abide by the kingdom's rules: reason, dignity, universality, necessity, and hospitality. Cosmopolitanism offers, in effect, a new religion—within the limits of reason alone.[5]

Cosmopolitanism's Shortcomings

Despite the relentless marketing and resulting familiarity of the product, this notion of cosmopolitanism is largely incoherent, almost incredible, and perhaps impossible in practice. Stop and think about this notion. Try to picture such a cosmopolitan, a person unmarked in any self-constitutive way by place and history. To be a cosmopolitan would require even more than this. A person free from local attachments (and from lack of attachments to other places)—equally free and at home everywhere in the world—would be a person whose very being as just that person is free of the particulars of a language (including multiple languages) and free of a particular embodiment, free of social practices and customs, free of the challenges of experience of the foreign that is not home (but may become home) and the experience of interrogation or interruption of the familiar that is home (but may become foreign). Such a person would be free of the acquaintance knowledges and qualities of experience that constitute particular ways of life—ways of living just here and now rather than there and then. Such a life is an abstraction rather than a live option—that is, an option for actual living persons like you or me.

The most telling evidence of cosmopolitanism's abstraction are the facts that it is focused on space and time while it ignores place and history, and that it demands a form of moral and cultural universalism that fails to recognize the situatedness in time and place of this demand itself. This is what William S. Lewis rightly refers to in Chapter 16 in this volume as cosmopolitanism's erasure of the evidence of the particular interests and struggles and times and places that produced its supposedly universal ideals. Because cosmopolitanism in its traditional meanings and forms says otherwise, it is important to add the following. Believing that one is unattached to place and history, or desiring to be unattached to place and history, or hoping that one is or may become unattached to place and history are themselves activities—believings, desirings, and hopings—marked by, and characteristic of, particular places and particular histories even if one ignores or remains ignorant of them. The dream of cosmopolitanism is always dreamed somewhere at some time. It is always a dream of some place and some history.

In part, my goal in this chapter is to suggest a different dream. In its traditional form, cosmopolitanism is not merely an abstraction. It is an abstraction that is constructed on, and advances, a two-part misunderstanding about the nature of political practices and social relations. In the first place, the notion that one may be a citizen of the world misses the fact that all political practices and institutions, like all moral practices and institutions, are exclusionary as well as inclusionary. The complexes of practices and subjects that make some persons (or rational agents or sentient beings, etc.), for example, citizens of Spain or Mexico or the Seneca Nation, or representatives of Hamas or the Green Party or the Nazi Party, at once exclude others from these political groups. These complex relationships do not all or fully reduce to friend-enemy relations, but, even when they are fluid and changing, at any given time they all do mark exclusions (if only in principle) in the very act of marking inclusion. They differentiate; they instantiate differences in the very act of establishing identities; it is not possible to be an X politically unless it is possible (again, at least in principle) to be a not-X politically. The very notion of being a citizen here is at once the notion of not being a citizen somewhere else; the very notion that some are citizens here is at once the notion that some others are not citizens here; any group of citizens is, at least potentially, a subset of one's political ontology. To note this fact is not, by itself, to endorse or to reject harsh policies with respect to asylum seekers, refugees, immigrants, or "illegal aliens."[6] It is simply to note that membership always has both inclusive and exclusive dimensions.

As it does for political citizenship and politics, this point holds true for moral citizenship and morals. Even the most universal and seemingly exclusion-free moral principles extend only, if universally, to some beings rather than others—for example, to human beings or rational beings or beings that have dignity rather than price or beings who are the people of God—that is, to moral beings. A moral principle may be universally inclusive in scope, but the class of beings to which this principle applies—the being that it includes—establishes at once a class of being to which this principle does not apply—the beings that it excludes. The task of marking the conditions for membership in the moral community is at once the task of marking the conditions for exclusion from the moral community.

In the second place, the cosmopolitan notion that one is, or may be, at home everywhere rests on a misunderstanding of what a home is—in the sense in which homes are places. In calling one's home (or homes) a place (or places), I do not simply mean that places: (a) have locations (objective coordinates); (b) are locales (material settings like skyscrapers or sandy islands or a rural village or neighborhood corner); or (c) are objects of emotional or other subjective attachment (a feeling of being just there).[7] Nor do I only mean that places are ways of understanding or seeing or knowing—that place is primarily a matter of epistemology.[8] They are ways of knowing, of course, but places and people are more than ways of knowing and being knowers. Places are ways of living, ways of being, worlds of experience, worlds of relations. As John Dewey wrote that organisms do not live *in* an environment but, rather, *through* an environment, so persons do not live in places but, rather, by means of places or *through* places.[9] As Vincent Colapietro and Megan Craig note in this volume, places are verbs, active, malleable and fluid.[10] A place is a process and a transaction in the pragmatic meaning of this term. In our living, places come in and out of existence; in places, lives come in and out of being. Some (but not all) of these places are homes for some folks sometimes, but the would-be cosmopolitan who would be always at home everywhere and every place is an impossibility: to be at home some place (or places, including places of hypermobility[11] and virtual communities[12]) is to be not at home in—and through—other places. To be part of a particular tribe and to live a particular life—even the life of a multilingual, multi-border-crossing, multi-locale-visiting and globetrotting, frequent host or guest—is to feel (and not just think) and value and live through some particular places and to live apart from other places.

Moreover, to view your particular places as simply morally fuller, conceptually wider, and more in line with some mythological free-floating rationality than those of earlier generations is to lack, to an astonishing degree, attunement to places, worlds, histories, meanings, values, and knowledges that are lost to us. In supposing themselves at home everywhere, would-be cosmopolitan ideologues of the universal fail to know their place as members of particular groups. As political scientists Christopher Achen and Larry Bartels argue in their "*group theory* of democracy," political partisanship "is not a carrier of ideology but a reflection of judgments about where 'people like me' belong": "We conclude that group and partisan loyalties, not policy preferences or ideologies, are fundamental in democratic politics. Thus a realistic theory of democracy must be built, not on the French Enlightenment, on British liberalism, or on American Progressivism, with their devotion to human rationality and monadic individualism, but instead on the insights of the critics of these traditions, who recognized that human life is group life."[13]

Sadly, living in a place does not guarantee knowledge or understanding of that place any more than it guarantees knowledge of one's self. As José Medina critically argues, cosmopolitan ignorance that leads to lives insensitive to other persons and their differences globally is linked to local ignorance that fosters irresponsibility toward the persons with whom we live locally.[14] Because cosmopolitanism in its traditional meanings and forms says otherwise, it is important once again to add the following. Believing that one is, or can be, at home in all places because one has access to transportation and communication technologies and capital more far-reaching than ever before in human history, desiring thus to transcend the particulars of place and history, and hoping that reason and imagination are powerful enough to do this are themselves activities—believings, thinkings, and hopings—marked by, and characteristic of, particular places and particular histories even if one ignores or remains ignorant of them. The dream of being a citizen of the world, someone at home in every place, is always dreamed somewhere. It is always a dream of some citizens and some places.

To repeat, I would like to evoke a different place.

Cosmopolitanism's Violent Universalism

In its traditional understanding, I have argued, cosmopolitanism is an abstraction and a misunderstanding of the politics and morality of citizenship and the experience of place. But it is something more as well. To understand this, it is crucial to understand cosmopolitanism as a force and as a relation of power. And it is also crucial to understand cosmopolitanism as a preference and a hope (or class of hopes).

The notion of cosmopolitanism has roots in ancient Greek thought of the stoics and cynics, but its articulation today is inseparable from the European Enlightenment and its lineages, places, and histories. The Enlightenment, as it markets itself today, speaks the language of reason and proclaims a message of universality, a message of cosmopolitan right and dignity, a message of a principle of hospitality for all rational beings, a message that, as Kant claimed, could finally bring the human race ever closer to a mature and cosmopolitan composition and to a perpetual peace (that does not come only after death).

The facts, however, seem to paint a different picture. In reality, the Enlightenment spoke the language of violence and power rather than pure reason alone, and it proclaimed a message of particularity and exclusion rather than universality. And in fact, cosmopolitanism, Enlightenment cosmopolitanism, spoke the language of invasion and colonialism and domination (in the name of universalism) of many oppressed or supposedly primitive peoples rather than hospitality toward all, proclaiming a message of slavery and occupation and conversion rather than citizenship and home and harmonic difference.

Is the fact that Locke's understanding of toleration stopped short of including atheists and many non-Christians just personal shortsightedness or weakness of his will or too little cosmopolitanism? Is the fact that Jefferson's view of equality stopped short of including slaves just a personal compromise or economic necessity or too little cosmopolitanism? Is the fact that Kant's application of rationality, dignity, and hospitality stopped short of including many non-European "races" (about whom he wrote in blatantly racist terms) just armchair anthropology or bad biology or too little cosmopolitanism? In the context of cosmopolitanism, what, for example, are we to make of Kant's words in *Observations on the Beautiful and Sublime* that follow an extended discussion and comparison of European nationalities to many non-European races and to women? Kant wrote:

> The Negroes of Africa have by nature no feeling that rises above the trifling. Mr. Hume challenges anyone to cite a single example in which a Negro has shown talents, and asserts that among hundreds of thousands of blacks who are transported elsewhere from their countries, although many of them have been set free, still not a single one was ever found who presented anything great in art or science or any other praiseworthy quality, even though among the whites some continually rise aloft from the lowest rabble, and through superior gifts earn the respect of the world. So fundamental is the difference between these two races of man, and it appears to be as great in mental capacities as in color.... The blacks are very vain but in the Negro's way, and so talkative that they must be driven apart from each other with thrashings.... And it might be thought there was something in this [observations by a Negro

carpenter] which perhaps deserved to be considered; but in short, this fellow was quite black from head to foot, a clear proof that what he said was stupid.[15]

These sorts of claims are made with such frequency by so many Enlightenment theorists and proponents of universalism, reason, and rights that it is simply is not credible to attempt to explain them away by labeling them as merely individual shortcomings that have no intrinsic connection to cosmopolitanism and its core commitments. Is this mere coincidence, or is cosmopolitanism not simply what it has claimed to be? Is it mere coincidence that the Enlightenment was an age of cosmopolitan concepts of owner and guests (even guests of races that lack reason) and an age of colonialism, imperialism, empire, an age of domination, disenfranchisement, and inequality, an age in which there is anything but "common possession of the surface of the earth," indeed an age that formulated cosmopolitan right as the right of visitation rather than a right of residence, use, and ownership?[16] Is that mere coincidence? Would-be cosmopolitan philosophers, philosophers of universal human rights and dignity and hospitality, do not like thinking about Locke and Hume and Kant, about their canon, in this way. But how long can this thought be avoided and evaded? Is the alternative to cosmopolitanism simply violence, disorder, privilege and selfishness, inequality, and unreason? Or are violence, disorder, inequality, selfish privilege, and unreason embedded in the heart, the masked heart, of cosmopolitanism?

When the church of cosmopolitanism preaches universal hospitality, is the message that natives have become visitors or guests, and that it is possible simultaneously to dignify and immiserate? Here I recall Sartre's claim in his preface to Fanon's *The Wretched of the Earth*:

> We saw in the human species an abstract premise of universality that served as a pretext for concealing more concrete practices: there was a race of subhumans overseas who, thanks to us, might in a thousand years perhaps, attain our status. In short, we took the human race to mean elite. Today the 'native' unmasks his truth; as a result, our exclusive club reveals its weakness: it was nothing more than a minority. There is worse news: since the others are turning into men against us, apparently we are the enemy of the human race; the elite is revealing its true nature—a gang. Our beloved values are losing their feathers; if you take a closer look there is not one that isn't tainted with blood.

Fanon insightfully stated:

> Challenging the colonial world is not a rational confrontation of viewpoints. It is not a discourse on the universal, but the impassioned claim by the colonized that their world is fundamentally different. . . . The Church in the colonies is the white man's Church, a foreigner's Church. It does not call the colonized to the ways of God, but to the ways of the white man, to the ways of the master, the ways of the oppressor. And as we know, in this story, many

are called but few are chosen. . . . During the period of decolonization, the colonized are called upon to be reasonable. They are offered rock solid values, they are told in great detail that they must rely on values which have proved to be reliable and worthwhile. . . . the colonist only stops undermining the colonized once the latter have proclaimed loud and clear that white values reign supreme.[17]

In its traditional, Enlightenment and Enlightenment-inspired form, cosmopolitanism universalism often, if not always, has been the Atlantic white people's cosmopolitanism, the cosmopolitanism of owners and residents rather than employees and guests.[18] It has been a tool of exclusion, a public relations arm of colonialism, imperialism, and empire. It has served, as Will Kymlicka observed, to "tame not transcend liberal nationhood:" cosmopolitan European institutions "help diffuse the model of a (tamed) liberal nationhood to countries where it does not yet exist" and thus spread (rather than transcend) ideologies of liberal nationhood.[19] Will the homeless, the refugees, the impoverished, the guest workers, the you-should-feel-lucky-to-have-a-job, the manipulated, and the oppressed now, maybe finally, proclaim that cosmopolitan values reign supreme? If so, would this mean that cosmopolitanism has become "an increasingly obnoxious narcissism" and "permanent dialogue" of the European Enlightenment spirit with itself? If this is even partially true, it is hardly surprising that Fanon concluded: "For Europe, for ourselves and for humanity, comrades, we must turn over a new leaf, we must work out new concepts, and try to set afoot a new man."[20]

This new leaf would involve developing a new cosmopolitanism, a different cosmopolitanism, or, perhaps, not cosmopolitanism at all.

Problems with Hybrid Cosmopolitanism and Hybrid Provincialism

Recognizing the immense problems of provincialism and also cosmopolitanism, some theorists have sought to combine or meld them, to supplement each with the strengths of the other, to produce an efficient new hybrid. (There is nothing new or controversial in this: Stoic philosophers—Cicero's metaphor of concentric circles is probably the most familiar—long ago stressed that world citizens have local, provincial identities and associations as well.[21]) Accordingly, in response to the political question of the one and the many, they respond: both. Their efforts constitute a spectrum in which language and emphasis differ but main points are largely shared.

At one pole—the much less populated pole—are those who would shore up provincialism by making it more humble, more fallible, more pluralistic, and more cosmopolitan. Josiah Royce's "wise provincialism" is perhaps this traditions best and philosophically strongest example.[22] Royce understood that provincialism, unlike worthless abstraction, has a central affective dimension, a full-bodied experience of love and pride in one's own customs, traditions, beliefs, and hopes. And he proposed that a "wise provincialism" that has respect for, openness to, and familiarity with the ways of life, the histories and places, of other provinces may serve as an antidote to modern rootlessness, conformity, and often manipulated mob spirit.

Royce observed: "We love the world better when we cherish our own friends more faithfully. We do not grow in grace by forgetting individual duties in behalf of remote social enterprises. Precisely so, the province will not serve the nation best by forgetting itself, but by loyally emphasizing its own duty to the nation and therefore its right to attain and to cultivate its own unique wisdom."[23] There is much to recommend here—Jacquelyn Kegley does this well in Chapter 4 of this volume—but there is also much that demands critical interrogation and reconstruction. Who are our "friends" as Royce employs that term? Are one's friends only members—some members (which?)—of one's own province? What makes a social enterprise "remote"? Simply feeling it to be remote? It's simply being an enterprise of, or in, another province? In what "remote" social enterprises are members of a given province implicated, even if they are ignorant of such implication? Are provinces simply subsets of nations? Don't regions sometimes contain many provinces—many customs, traditions, beliefs, values, languages, and loves? Don't provinces sometimes span many countries—provincial diasporas of migrants, refugees, exiles, guest workers, nomads, racialized groups, and both the wretched of the earth and global capitalists and corporate cultures—and maybe academics and intellectuals too? Is the goal of provincialism the service of "the nation"? Why? In a province or in a nation, who is authorized or empowered to determine what counts as "service" to the nation? Might resistance or revolution or reordering constitute service?

These questions suggest, I believe, provincialism's path to wisdom does not lead through cosmopolitanism. Rather, it leads through greater pluralism and attunement to difference. I do not think a provincialism can be wise unless it recognizes that individuals and provinces are multiplicities rather than unities, and until it untethers provincial self-love and self-pride from the campaigns of nations and their enlightened colonization of the surface of the earth and the limits of moral imagination.

At the other, today more populous, pole of the "provincialism and cosmopolitanism both, please" spectrum are those who would make cosmopolitanism more tied to history and place, more attuned to concrete experience, and more provincial. Anthony Appiah's "rooted cosmopolitanism" is one well-known version of this approach.[24] In many respects, Appiah is attuned to the multiplicities of identity and to "legitimate differences" among peoples and cultures, among different cultures. The moral of his warm message is that in a world of strangers whose poor suffer in ways others may or may not feel, rich countries have duties and can and should do better. Why? Appiah concluded: "Because we are responsive to what Adam Smith called 'reason, principle, conscience, the inhabitant of the breast.'"[25]

The slogan for this cosmopolitanism, Appiah wrote, is "universality plus difference," but it is clear that universality is primary: Appiah noted:

> I want to hold on to at least one important aspect of the objectivity of values: that there are some values that are, and should be, universal, just as there are lots of values that are, and must be local. . . . fortified with a shared language of value, we can often guide one another, in the cosmopolitan spirit, to shared responses. . . if relativism about ethics and morality were true, then, at the end of many discussions, we would each have to end up saying 'From where I stand, I am right. From where you stand, you are right.' And there would be nothing further to say. . . . Relativism of that sort isn't a way to encourage conversation; it's just a reason to fall silent.[26]

Encouraging conversation and recognizing the locality, the history and place, of many values are activities all to the good from the perspective of pluralism and fallibilism and different cultures. But are values objective or universal, as the Enlightenment dreamed and as Appiah asserted he wants to hold?

For the "rooted cosmopolitan," this question can be put this way: Are values necessarily rooted everywhere, rooted universally, rooted as universals? Appiah claimed that persons responsive to reason and conscience and principle and heart—that is, cosmopolitan persons—will find this to be the case. But this seems entirely unpersuasive, merely circular, and also counterfactual as Appiah himself gave example after example of noncosmopolitan thinking, valuing, and living. It is fine to ask for reasons, but what does it mean to give a reason? Who is authorized or empowered to determine what counts as a reason, or a good reason, or a good argument? If the activity of giving reasons is normative—as pragmatists like James recognized so well—then reasons presuppose rather than merely justify values. If the activity of giving reasons is normative, then rationality, like Fanon's example of the church, can be, for example, white people's rationality or capitalist rationality or male rationality or World Bank rationality, and so on. Appiah does not show, I think, that values are universal; rather he illustrates the fact that the belief that values are universal is itself history bound and place bound, that it is particular rather than universal.

Now, if values are not objective and universal, as cosmopolitan reason claims, Appiah worried that we are left with conversation-ending relativism. Ahh, once again, always the menace of relativism; so much worry about truth, so little worry about hope.[27] But the absence of universal values, even "rooted universals" does not mean that values cannot be, or cannot become, shared or jointly taken up. And the absence of an epistemological grounding for any such shared (merely shared, not universal) values does not mean that there cannot be a political basis for them. Appiah, like universalists more generally, converted a genuinely difficult political task that lies always incomplete and ahead of us into a finished epistemological advance justification for undertaking that task in some particular way—despite the fact that every particular way is always marked by provincial differences, by particular histories and places, by exclusions as well as inclusions. Thus the cosmopolitan always says: "Listen to me" and "Here is what it means to give reasons for one's views."[28]

Beyond Cosmopolitanism and Provincialism: Reframing Democratic Pluralism

Provincialism is not a solution to the political problem of the one and the many, the universal and the particular, of space and place, of time and history, of shared identity and individual difference, of unity and multiplicity, of human right and positive law, of hospitality or partisanship.

Cosmopolitanism is not a solution.

Hybrid combinations and supplements of both provincialism and cosmopolitanism—from "wise provincialism" to "rooted cosmopolitanism"—are not solutions.

Is there another option? Is there a solution? No, I think not.

It is important to realize that while provincialism and cosmopolitanism—and hybrid versions of each—differ in crucial ways, they share presuppositions that give rise to their shared problem. We would do well, I think, to reject these presuppositions and, thereby, to reject or dissolve the problem which both provincialism and cosmopolitanism seek to resolve. In any event, progress is possible: The problem of provincialism and/or cosmopolitanism can be dissolved by rejecting the faulty assumptions on which it depends; this problem can be transformed by changing the practices and institutions which frame it. Part of this work of dissolution/transformation is conceptual and part of it is political.

First, the one, the universal, and the identical are only abstractions or class names for some many, some particulars, some differences. The political problem of the one and the many, the problem of provincialism or cosmopolitanism, is a problem of one many and some other many, the problem of one provincialism and other, often competing, provincialisms. Except as abstractions, the cosmos is not one, and the province is not one either. They are many—many places, many histories, unstable and changing, permeable and absorbing, perching and flying. Except as abstractions, morality and reason are not universal. They are particular—particular in meaning and scope, particular in origin and consequence, particular in empowering and constraining. Except as abstractions, self and others are not identities, not self-identical. They are multiplicities and differences, self-differentiating, meaning more than they say, experiencing more than they know, changed and changing, relational conjunctively and disjunctively all the way through.

Citizenship and home are also many, particular, and different. As such (and as noted above) they are modes of exclusion as well as inclusion. In our political lives, we do not face alternatives of one or many, of inclusion or exclusion, of inclusive cosmopolitanism or exclusive provincialism. Instead, the alternative we face to some form of inclusion/exclusion is some other form of inclusion/exclusion. There is no live, nonabstract politics that does not involve practices of exclusion. To realize this is to take a step toward knowing—and changing—one's place.

Second, if this renders cosmopolitanism and its dream of universal inclusion impossible, it poses special problems—or, perhaps, special opportunities—for democratic pluralists. What are the practical consequences for a pluralistic democracy of the fact of exclusion at the very heart of its institutions, practices, and values? It is tempting to answer this question from an individualistic perspective. Here we might stress that we should be falliblilists. Or study many histories and cultures. Or learn many languages. Or travel much. Or expand imagination through novels and poetry and art. Or relentlessly self-interrogate and lead an examined life. In short it is tempting, at least for humanities educators, to argue that people should lead humanistic and liberal arts lives. I firmly believe this and I view it as very important. This sort of life constitutes the connection that John Dewey stressed so tirelessly between democracy and education.

However, this is not enough. It is not enough because it pays too little attention to the limits of any place of critical self-examination, and it is not sufficiently concerned with social institutions and practices. It is not enough, for example, for colonizers—perhaps seeking to engage in critical philosophy, another dream, like cosmopolitanism, of the Enlightenment—to interrogate themselves about the exclusions of their colonialism. Their answer, no matter how thoughtful and earnest—for example, "All Lives Matter"—will be an answer from, and of, their history and their place. It will not be the answer of the colonized, of the wretched of the earth; it will not be the answer of other colonizers; it will not be the answer of people with different histories and different places. It will not be the answer of persons in the making, constantly disrupting and being disrupted, constantly refashioning themselves in, and from, their places.[29]

This raises institutional issues: What social practices would lead the included to *feel*—I want to stress affect rather than cognition—the importance of the concerns and lives of the excluded? And what social practices might make this possible? And how is it possible to sustain hope that work toward their creation is reasonable and worthwhile?[30] These questions point to political, not simply theoretical work. To some extent this work is broadly educational. But in other respects this work is explicitly political, economic, military, environmental, technological, and religious. To recognize that the political practices cherished because they are inclusive establish and police exclusions; to recognize that these exclusions are not fully recognized by those included, by citizens and persons at home; to institutionalize opportunities for those excluded not to be silenced and not to have to speak the language of those included and not to have to give reasons that those included count as reasons; to institutionalize agencies and resources for social change that would result from these opportunities: I take these and the love they require and foster—and not cosmopolitanism—to be the challenge facing pluralistic democracies today.

To succeed, even a little, on this front is not to achieve perpetual peace; it is to engage in perpetual peacemaking and remaking. To succeed is not to find one's self at home everywhere in the world; it is to feel one's self not quite fully or ever at home any place in the world, to feel one's self always at least a little vulnerable and always somewhat lost between multiple places. To succeed is to respond to this finding and this feeling without the aim (impossible to realize) of wholly eliminating them and without fear or attempted conceptual cover-up of this fact. It is to recognize our self-estrangement and our reliance on others.[31] And to succeed is not to become a citizen of the whole world; it is to become a more loving member and hopeful citizen of a different world, a different world of different places.

A coeditor of this volume, **JOHN J. STUHR** is Arts and Sciences Distinguished Professor of Philosophy and American Studies at Emory University, where for many years he served as department chair. Interested in ethics, social and political thought, and the resources that nineteenth- and twentieth-century American and European philosophies provide for critical and practical approaches to contemporary cultural issues, his recent books include *Pragmatism, Postmodernism, and the Future of Philosophy* (Routledge, 2002), *100 Years of Pragmatism: William James's Revolutionary Philosophy* (Indiana University Press, 2009), and *Pragmatic Fashions: Pluralism, Democracy, Relativism, and the Absurd* (Indiana University Press, 2016). He is the editor of the *Journal of Speculative Philosophy*, the director of the American Philosophies Forum, and the editor of the *American Philosophy* series at Indiana University Press.

Notes

1. Neil Young, "Flags of Freedom," *Living With War* (Reprise, 2006), track 6.
2. In *Revolutions Without Borders: The Call to Liberty in the Atlantic World* (New Haven, CT: Yale University Press, 2015), Janet Polasky traces in detail the rise and the demise (at the

hands of nationalism) of the "universal cry for liberty," the "struggle for universal human rights," and the dream of a world "without borders that obstruct the travel of restless itinerants and their ideals" that spanned the Americas, the Caribbean, Europe, and Africa in the last quarter of the eighteenth century.

3. Seyla Benhabib, *Another Cosmopolitanism* (New York: Oxford University Press, 2006), 15–16. Benhabib asks centrally how the will of democratic majorities and legislatures can be reconciled with cosmopolitan norms that originate and are justified outside or independent of democratic states (that cosmopolitanism thus may "trump" as it "disintegrates" state citizenship). In the end, however, Benhabib concludes that we should not see the spread of cosmopolitan norms as the undermining of democratic sovereignty but, rather, as the emergence of new political configurations and agencies in which the local, the national, and the global are mutually implicated (ibid., 74). In contrast, Jürgen Habermas proposed a new international legal order to be effected by a "cosmopolitan transformation of the state of nature among states." Jürgen Habermas, "Kant's Idea of Perpetual Peace, with Benefit of Two Hundred Years' Hindsight," in *Perpetual Peace: Essays on Kant's Ideal*, ed. James Bonham and Matthias Lutz-Bachmann (Cambridge, MA: MIT Press, 1997), 149.

4. All the very different theories of cosmopolitanism, Simon Caney concludes in "International Distributive Justice," hold that entitlements should not be determined by nationality. See *The Cosmopolitan Reader*, ed. Garrett Wallace Brown and David Held (Cambridge: Polity, 2010), 146. In another chapter, "Global Distributive Justice and the State," Caney notes that the state *might* have moral significance simply as an instrument of cosmopolitan (and not nation state) justice (ibid., 210).

5. In "The Myth of Cosmopolitanism," columnist Ross Douthat has called this "basically liberal Christianity without Christ" while arguing that most persons who think of themselves as cosmopolitans are simply members of an elite tribe—Western, educated, industrialized, rich, and democratic. Douthat concludes that most often cosmopolitanism is "a powerful caste's self-serving explanation for why it alone deserves to rue the world" (*New York Times*, July 2, 2016).

6. In "Liberal, Harsh Denmark," Hugh Eakin argues that in Denmark liberalism, toleration and openness, concern with equality, and social democracy are viewed as incompatible with large-scale Muslim immigration—and thus that these liberal values extend "no farther than the Danish frontier" (*New York Review of Books*, February 10, 2016, 36).

7. This three-part distinction is set forth by political geographer John Agnew, *The United States in the World Economy* (Cambridge: Cambridge University Press, 1987).

8. Tim Cresswell, *Place: A Short Introduction* (Oxford: Blackwell, 2004), 11–12.

9. I note that J. E. Malpas stresses that the social exists in and through place and, so, is not simply or fully socially constructed, but he then frames an alternative in terms of a transcendental realism about place that holds "it is within the structure of place that the very possibility of the social arises." The point, however, should not be to see place as a product of social construction or to see social construction as made possible by place, but rather to view nondualistically the social and place as intrinsically and irreducibly connected—a kind of radical empiricism about place. See J. E. Malpas, *Place and Experience: A Philosophical Topography* (Cambridge: Cambridge University Press, 1999), 36.

10. See Chapters 6 and 9 of this volume.

11. I think that geographer David Harvey is wrong to view hypermobility as a threat to place rather than, at most, a threat to particular kind of place. See his excellent *Justice, Nature and the Geography of Difference* (Cambridge, MA: Blackwell, 1986). Other geographers engage in even stronger "end of place" claims, finding mobility and instability as undermining

place and creating "inauthentic" relations to place. See, for example, Edward Relph, *Place and Placelessness* (London: Pion, 1976); and even the pathbreaking Yi-Fu Tuan, *Space and Place: The Perspective of Experience* (Minneapolis: University of Minnesota Press, 1977). More promising, I think, is Nigel Thrift's recognition of the ways in which technological changes and hypermobility constitute new forms of place. He writes: "Places are 'stages of intensity.' Traces of movement, speed and circulation. . . . strategic installations, fixed addresses that capture traffic. . . . frames for varying practices of space, time and speed"; see Nigel Thrift, "Inhuman Geographies: Landscapes of Speed, Light, and Power" in *Writing the Rural: Five Cultural Geographies*, ed. P. Cloke (London: Routledge, 1994), 212–13.

12. See Chapter 15 of this volume.

13. Christopher H. Achen and Larry M. Bartels, *Democracy for Realists: Why Elections Do Not Produce Responsive Governments* (Princeton, NJ: Princeton University Press, 2016), 16–18. In his very positive review of this book, Michael Tomasky, citing these same passages and distinguishing between "values" and "policy positions," notes, "It's values and emotional intuitions that matter. We divide up into tribes and we vote as tribes" (*New York Review of Books*, July 14, 2016, 43).

14. See Chapter 7 of this volume.

15. Immanuel Kant, *Observations on the Beautiful and Sublime*, trans. John Goldthwait (Berkeley: University of California Press, 1960), 180–81.

16. See Jacques Derrida's discussion of Kant on this point in *Cosmopolitanism and Forgiveness*, trans. Mark Dooley (London: Routledge, 2001), 20–22.

17. Frantz Fanon, *The Wretched of the Earth*, trans. Richard Wilcox (New York: Grove, 2004), lix, 6, 7.

18. In this context, see Derrida's distinction (regarding Kant's philosophy) between "a right of residence" and "a right of visitation" in *Cosmopolitanism and Forgiveness*, 21.

19. Will Kymlicka, "Liberal Nationalism and Cosmopolitan Justice," in Benhabib, *Another Cosmopolitanism*, 131.

20. Ibid., 8, 237.

21. Cicero, *Cicero: On Duties*, ed. M. Griffin and E. Atkins (Cambridge: Cambridge University Press, 1991).

22. Josiah Royce, *Race Questions, Provincialism, and Other American Problems* (Freeport, NY: Books for Libraries Press, 1967).

23. Ibid., 99. On nationalism and cosmopolitanism in the context of American identity, see also Jonathan M. Hansen, *The Lost Promise of Patriotism: Debating American Identity, 1890–1920* (Chicago: University of Chicago Press, 2003).

24. See, for example, his *The Ethics of Identity* (Princeton, NJ: Princeton University Press, 2005); and *Cosmopolitanism: Ethics in a World of Strangers* (New York: W. W. Norton, 2006).

25. Appiah, *Cosmopolitanism*, 174.

26. Ibid., xxi, 30–31.

27. See "It's All Relative," in my *Pragmatic Fashions: Pluralism, Democracy, Relativism, and the Absurd* (Bloomington: Indiana University Press, 2016).

28. See Chapter 3 of this volume.

29. In Chapter 8 of this volume, Jeff Edmonds refers to Anzaldúa's views as cosmopolitan "not in the Kantian sense of rising out of a place toward a universal, but in using the very notion of place to uproot settled conceptions of place. . . . This is very different from the way in which philosophy tends to cosmopolitanize from without." I think this is right on the mark, though I am not sure why it is useful to call such a view, one attuned to borderlands and "territory of becoming," a kind of "cosmopolitanism" (132–133).

30. Jennifer Hansen, in Chapter 13 of this volume, discusses this crucial practical question in detail. Hansen writes that this hope "seeks utopias," a "no-place" and practice of criticizing the present moment." This seems more dream than hope and more criticism than reconstruction to me, and so I would prefer to think of hope as melioristic and reconstructive, as seeking something better (rather than wholly best). In practice or action, however, I am not sure that this theoretical difference—or perhaps just the feel of some connotations of language—makes a difference, and I second Hansen's account of pluralism as a condition for the possibility of something better emerging.

31. In Chapter 12 of this volume, Jessica Wahman suggests we think of cosmopolitanism primarily as a state of mind of a homeless and dependent guest, a person oriented both to the familiar and the unfamiliar.

Bibliography

Addams, Jane. *Democracy and Social Ethics.* Urbana: University of Illinois Press, 2002.
Adorno, Theodor W. *Minima moralia.* Madrid: Akal, 2004.
Agamben, Giorgio. *Medios sin fin.* Valencia: Pre-textos, 2001.
Agnew, John. *The United States in the World Economy.* Cambridge: Cambridge University Press, 1987.
Albrecht, G. "'Solastalgia': A New Concept in Health and Identity." *Philosophy Activism Nature* 3 (2005): 41–44.
Alcoff, Linda M. *Visible Identities: Race, Gender, and the Self.* Oxford: Oxford University Press, 2007.
Alexievich, S. *Zinky Boys. Soviet Voices from a Forgotten War.* London: Chatto and Windus, 1992.
Aligerhi, Dante. *De vulgari eloquentia.* Translated by M. Rovira and M. Gil. Madrid: Universidad Complutense, 1982.
———. *Inferno.* Translated by Robert Hollander and Jean Hollander. New York: Anchor, 2002.
Alston, Margaret, and Jenny Kent. *Dirt, Drought and Drudge: Australian Women's Experience of Drought.* In Wellbeing of Women Conference Proceedings. Wagga Wagga, Australia: Charles Sturt University, 2004. www.ruralwomen.org.au/events/health/pfk_drought.doc.
———. *The Social Impacts of Drought: A Report to NSW Agriculture.* Wagga Wagga, Australia: Charles Sturt University Centre for Rural Social Research, 2004.
Althusser, Louis. *The International of Decent Feelings. The Spectre of Hegel: Early Writings.* Translated by G. M. Goshgarian. London: Verso, 1997.
American Psychiatric Association. *Diagnostic and Statistical Manual of Mental Disorders*, 4th ed. Washington, DC: American Psychiatric Association, 2000.
Améry Jean. *At the Mind's Limit.* Bloomington: Indiana University Press, 1980.
Anders Günther. *Wir Eichmann Söhne.* Munich: C. H. Beck, 1988.
Anderson, C. A. "Heat and Violence." *Current Directions in Psychological Science* 10, no. 1 (2001): 33–38.
Angell, Marcia. "The Epistemic of Mental Illness: Why?" *New York Review of Books*, 58, no. 11 (2011). www.nybooks.com/articles/archives/2011/jun/23/epidemic-mental-illnesswhy/.
———. "The Illusions of Psychiatry." *New York Review of Books* 58, no. 12 (2011). www.nybooks.com/articles/archives/2011/jul/14/illusions-of-psychiatry/.
Angry Black Bitch. "The Battle Hymn of a Dangerous Black Woman." Blog comment, March 30, 2011. http://angryblackbitch.blogspot.com/2011/03/battle-hymn-of-dangerous-black-woman.html#comments.
Anzaldúa, Gloria. *Borderlands/La Frontera*, 2nd ed. San Francisco: Aunt Lute Press, 1999.

Appiah, Kwame Anthony. *Cosmopolitan Patriots. Cosmopolitics: Thinking and Feeling beyond the Nation*. Edited by Pheng Cheah and Bruce Robbins. Minneapolis: University of Minnesota Press, 1997.
———. *Cosmopolitanism: Ethics in a World of Strangers*. New York: W. W. Norton, 2006.
———. *The Ethics of Identity*. Princeton, NJ: Princeton University Press, 2005.
Arendt, Hannah. *Escritos judíos*. Edited by Jerome Kohn and Ron H. Feldman. Translated by Miguel Cancel and Eduardo Cañas. Barcelona: Paidos, 2009.
Aristotle. *The Complete Works of Aristotle*. Vol. 2. Edited by Jonathan Barnes. Princeton, NJ: Princeton University Press, 1984.
Arnauld, A., and C. Lancelot. *Grammaire générale et raisonnée contenant les fondements de l'art de parler, expliqués d'une manière claire et naturelle* [General and Rational Grammar: The Port-Royal Grammar]. Translated by J. Rieux and B. E. Rollin. The Hague: Mouton, 1975.
Bachelard, Gaston. *The Poetics of Space*. Translated by Maria Jolas. Boston: Beacon, 1995.
Barry, B. *Culture and Equality*. Cambridge: Polity, 2001.
Barvosa, Edwina. *Wealth of Selves: Multiple Identities, Mestiza Consciousness, and the Subject of Politics*. College Station: Texas A&M University Press, 2008.
Beauzee, N. "Langue." in *L'Encyclopédie: "grammaire" et "language" au XVIIIè siècle*, edited by S. Auroux. Paris: Mame, 1975.
Benhabib, Seyla. *Another Cosmopolitanism: Hospitality, Sovereignty, and Democratic Iteration*. Tanner Lectures. Oxford: Oxford University Press, 2006.
Bergson, Henri. *Matter and Memory*. Translated by N. M. Paul and W. S. Palmer. New York: Zone, 1990.
———. *Creative Evolution*. Translated by Arthur Mitchell. New York: Dover, 1998.
———. *Henri Bergson: Key Writings*. Edited by Keith Ansell Pearson and John Ó Maoilearca. New York: Bloomsbury, 2014.
Bloch, Ernst. "Dialectics and Hope." *New German Critique* 9 (1976): 3–10.
———. *The Principle of Hope*. Vols. 1–3. Translated by Neville Place, Stephen Place, and Paul Knight. Cambridge: MIT Press, 1986.
Boer, Roland. "Althusser's Catholic Marxism." *Rethinking Marxism* 19, no. 4 (October 2007): 469–86.
Bok, Sissela. *From Part to Whole. Cosmopolitics: Thinking and Feeling Beyond the Nation*. Edited by Pheng Cheah and Bruce Robbins. Minneapolis: University of Minnesota Press, 1998.
Brent, Joseph. *Charles Sanders Peirce: A Life*. Rev. ed. Bloomington: Indiana University Press, 1998.
Broome, John. *Climate Matters: Ethics in a Warming World*. New York: W. W. Norton, 2012.
Brown, Donald A. *Climate Change Ethics: Navigating the Perfect Moral Storm*. New York: Routledge, 2012.
Brown, Patricia L. "Itinerant Life Weighs on Farmworkers' Children." *New York Times*, March 12, 2011. www.nytimes.com/2011/03/13/us/13salinas.html.
Brown, Stuart Gerry. From Provincialism to the Great Community: The Social Philosophy of Josiah Royce. *Ethics*, 59(1), (October 1948). 14–34
Buchanan, A. *Justice, Legitimacy, and Self-Determination*. Oxford: Oxford University Press, 2004.

Butler, Judith. *Precarious Life: The Powers of Mourning and Violence*. London: Verso, 2006.
Calhoun, C. *Nations Matter: Culture, History, and the Cosmopolitan Dream*. London: Routledge, 2007.
Calvino, Italo. *Invisible Cities*. New York: Harcourt, Brace, 1974.
Caney, Simon. "Cosmopolitan Justice, Responsibility, and Global Climate Change." *Leiden Journal of International Law* 18, no. 4 (2005): 747–75.
———. *Global Distributive Justice and the State. The Cosmopolitan Reader*. Edited by Garrett Wallace Brown and David Held. Cambridge: Polity, 2010.
———. *International Distributive Justice. The Cosmopolitan Reader*. Edited by Garrett Wallace Brown and David Held. Cambridge: Polity, 2010.
———. *Justice Beyond Borders: A Global Political Theory*. Oxford: Oxford University Press, 2006.
Casey, Edward. "Edges and the In-Between." *PhaenEx: Journal for Existential and Phenomenological Theory and Culture* 3, no. 2 (2008): 1–13.
———. *The Fate of Place: A Philosophical History*. Berkeley: University of California Press, 1998.
———. *Getting Back into Place: Toward a Renewed Understanding of the Place-World*. 2nd ed. Bloomington: Indiana University Press, 2009.
Cash, W. J. *The Mind of the South*. New York: Alfred Knopf, 1941.
Castoriadis, Cornelius. *World in Fragments: Writings on Politics, Society, Psychoanalysis, and the Imagination*. Stanford, CA: Stanford University Press, 1997.
Cavell, Stanley. *Pursuits of Happiness*. Cambridge, MA: Harvard University Press, 1981.
Certeau, M. de, et al. *Une politique de la langue: La Révolution française et les patois*. Paris: Gallimard, 1975.
Churchland, Patricia. *Neurophilosophy*. Cambridge: MIT Press, 1986.
Cicero. *Cicero: On Duties*. Edited by M. Griffin and E. Atkins. Cambridge: Cambridge University Press, 1991.
Code, Lorraine. *Ecological Thinking: The Politics of Epistemic Location*. Oxford: Oxford University Press, 2006.
———. "The Power of Ignorance." In *Race and Epistemologies of Ignorance*, edited by S. Sullivan and N. Tuana, 213–29. Albany: SUNY Press, 2007.
Colapietro, Vincent. "American Evasions of Foucault." *Southern Journal of Philosophy* 36, no. 3 (1998): 329–51.
———. *Fateful Shapes of Human Freedom: John William Miller and the Crises of Modernity*. Nashville: Vanderbilt University Press, 2003.
———. "Fragments from the Log of a Wayfarer: Additional Reflections on Ambulatory Processes." Paper Presented at American Philosophies Forum: Cosmopolitanism and Place, Círculo de Bellas Artes, Madrid, June 2–4, 2011.
———. "A Lantern for the Feet of Inquirers." *Semiotica* 136, nos. 1–4 (2001): 201–16.
———. "Steps Toward an Ecological Consciousness: Loyalty to the Inherited Matrix of Experimental Intelligence." In *Education for a Democratic Society*, edited by Ryder and Gert-Rüdiger Wegmarshuas, 155–64. New York: Rodopi, 2007.
———. "Toward a Pragmatic Conception of Practical Identity." *Transactions of the Charles S. Peirce Society* 42, no. 2 (2006): 173–205.
Coleman, Earle L. *Philosophy of Painting by Shih Ta'o*. The Hague: Mouton, 1978.

Condillac, E. *Essai sur les origin des connaissences humaines*. Paris: Ch. Houel, imprimeur, 1746.

———. *Language des calculs*. Paris: Ch. Houel, imprimeur, 1789.

Corbí, Josep E. *Morality, Self-Knowledge, and Human Suffering*. New York: Routledge, 2012.

Courtine-Denamy, Slvie. *Le souci du monde: dialogue entre Hannah Arendt et quelques-uns de ses contemporains*. Paris: Vrin, 1999.

Covaleskie, John. "What Public? Whose Schools?" *Educational Studies* 42, no. 1 (2007): 28–43.

Cresswell, Tim. *Place: A Short Introduction*. Oxford: Blackwell, 2004.

Dalgarno, George. *Ars signorum*. London: Edimburgo, 1661.

De Certeau, Michel. *The Practice of Everyday Life*. Translated by Steven Rendall. Berkeley: University of California Press, 1988.

Deleuze, Gilles, and Felix Guattari. *A Thousand Plateaus*. Translated by Brian Massumi. London: Continuum, 1987.

Derrida, Jacques. *Cosmopolitanism and Forgiveness*. Translated by Mark Dooley and Michael Hughes. London: Routledge, 2001.

Descartes, René. *Discourse on Method and Meditations on First Philosophy*. Translated by David Cress. Indianapolis: Hackett, 1998.

Desjarlais, Robert, Leon Eisenberg, Byron Good, and Arthur Kleinman, eds. *World Mental Health: Problems, Priorities, and Responses in Low-Income Countries*. New York: Oxford University Press, 1995.

Dewey, John. *Art as Experience*. New York: Perigee, 2005.

———. *Creative Democracy*. In the Later Works of John Dewey (1939–1941): Essays, Reviews, and Miscellany. Vol. 14. Edited by Jo Ann Boydston. Carbondale: Southern Illinois University Press, 1991.

———. *Democracy and Education: An Introduction to the Philosophy of Education*. New York: Free Press, 1944.

———. *The Early Works (1889–1892): Essays and Outlines of a Critical Theory of Ethics*. Vol. 3. Edited by Jo Ann Boydston. Carbondale: Southern Illinois University Press, 1969.

———. *The Early Works (1895–1898): Early Essays*. Vol. 5. Edited by Jo Ann Boydston, Ed. Carbondale: Southern Illinois University Press, 1972.

———. *Experience and Nature*. In the Later Works of John Dewey: Experience and Nature. Vol. 1. Edited by Jo Ann Boydston. Carbondale: Southern Illinois University Press, 1981.

———. *Human Nature and Conduct: An Introduction to Social Psychology*. Amherst: Prometheus, 2002.

———. *Human Nature and Conduct*. In the Middle Works of John Dewey (1922). Vol. 14. Edited by Jo Ann Boydston. Carbondale: Southern Illinois University Press, 1983.

———. *Individualism Old and New*. In the Later Works of John Dewey (1929–1930): Essays, the Sources of a Science of Education, Individualism, Old and New, and Construction and Criticism. Vol. 5. Edited by Jo Ann Boydston. Carbondale: Southern Illinois University Press, 1984.

———. *Knowing and the Known*. In the Later Works of John Dewey (1949–1952): Essays, Typescripts, and Knowing and the Known. Vol. 16. 2nd ed. Edited by Jo Ann Boydston. Carbondale: Southern Illinois University Press, 2008.

———. *The Need for a Recovery of Philosophy*. In *The Middle Works of John Dewey (1916–1917): Journal Articles, Essays, and Miscellany Published in the 1916–1917 Period*. Vol. 10. Edited by Jo Ann Boydston. Carbondale: Southern Illinois University Press, 1980.

———. *The Public and Its Problems*. In *the Later Works of John Dewey (1925–1927): Essays, Reviews, Miscellany, and the Public and Its Problems*. Vol. 2. Edited by Jo Ann Boydston. Carbondale: Southern Illinois University Press, 1984.

———. *The Quest for Certainty*. *The Later Works of John Dewey (1929): The Quest for Certainty*. Vol. 4. 2nd ed. Edited by Jo Ann Boydston. Carbondale: Southern Illinois University Press, 2008.

———. *Reconstruction in Philosophy*. In *the Middle Works of John Dewey (1920): Essays, Miscellany, and Reconstruction in Philosophy Published During 1920*. Vol. 12. Edited by Jo Ann Boydston. Carbondale: Southern Illinois University Press, 1982.

———. *The School and Society*. In *The Middle Works of John Dewey (1899–1901): Journal Articles, Books Reviews, and Miscellany Published in the 1899–1901 Period, and the School and Society, and the Educational Situation*. Vol. 1. Edited by Jo Ann Boydston. Carbondale: Southern Illinois University Press, 1976.

Diderot, D. *Lettre sur les sourds et les muets*. Paris, 1751.

Douthat, Russ, "The Myth of Cosmopolitanism," *New York Times*, July 2, 2016.

DuBois, W. E. B. "The African Roots of War." *Atlantic Monthly* 115 (May 1915). 707–14.

Dwyer, Jim. "Under Broadway, the Subway Hums Bernstein." *New York Times*, February 20, 2009. www.nytimes.com/2009/02/21/nyregion/21about.html?_r=0.

Eakin, Hugh, "Liberal, Harsh Denmark," *New York Review of Books*, February 10, 2016, 34–36.

Emerson, R. W. *Emerson in His Journals*. Edited by Joel Porte. Cambridge, MA: Harvard University Press, 1982.

———. *The Portable Emerson*. Edited by C. Bode. New York: Penguin, 1981.

———. *Ralph Waldo Emerson: Selected Essays*. Edited by Larzer Ziff. New York: Penguin, 1982.

———. *Selected Writings of Ralph Waldo Emerson*. Edited by William Gilman. New York: Penguin, 1965.

———. *Self-Reliance and Other Essays*. New York: Dover, 1993.

Environmental Justice Foundation. (2009) *No Place Like Home—Where Next for Climate Refugees?* London: Environmental Justice Foundation, 2009. www.ejfoundation.org/reports.

Fahim, Kareem. "Slap to a Man's Pride Sets off Tumult in Tunisia." *New York Times*, January 21, 2001. http://nyti.ms/1BGHvV7.

Falk, William W., Larry L. Hunt, and Matthew O. Hunt. "Return Migrations of African-Americans to the South: Reclaiming a Land or Promise, Going Home, or Both?" *Rural Sociology* 69 (2004): 490–509.

———. "Who Is Headed South? Return Migration in Black and White." *Social Forces* 85 (2008): 95–119.

Fanon, Frantz. *The Wretched of the Earth*. Translated by Richard Wilcox. New York: Grove Press, 2004.

Feller, Avi, and Chad Stone. "Top 1 Percent of Americans Reaped Two-Thirds of Income Gains in Last Economic Expansion." *Center on Budget and Policy Priorities*, September 9, 2009. www.cbpp.org/cms/index.cfm?fa=view&id=2908.

Feministe. "Outlaw Clothing: Burqas, Islamophobia and Women's Rights." Blog comment, July 14, 2010. www.feministe.us/blog/archives/2010/07/14/outlaw-clothing-burqas-islamophobia-and-womens-rights/.
Feminist Philosophers. "Our Policies." Blog comment, December 12, 2008. http://feministphilosophers.wordpress.com/our-policies/.
———. "Why Ban the Niqab?" Blog comment, September 17, 2010. http://feministphilosophers.wordpress.com/2010/09/17/why-ban-the-niqab-2/.
Fischer, Marilyn. "A Pragmatist Cosmopolitan Moment: Reconfiguring Nussbaum's Cosmopolitan Concentric Circles." *Journal of Speculative Philosophy* 21, no. 3 (2007): 151–65.
Fisch, Max H. *Peirce, Semeiotic, and Pragmatism*. Bloomington: Indiana University Press, 1986.
Foucault. Michel. *Foucault Live*. Edited by John Johnson and Sylvère Lotringer. New York: Semiotext(e), 1989.
———. *The Foucault Reader*. Edited by Paul Rabinow. New York: Pantheon, 1984.
Fraser, Nancy. "Clintonism, Welfare, and the Antisocial Wage: The Emergence of a Neoliberal Political Imaginary." In *Marxism in the Postmodern Age: Confronting the New World Order*, edited by Antonio Callari, Stephen Cullenberg, and Carole Biewener, 493–505. New York: Guilford, 1994.
———. "Rethinking the Public Sphere: A Contribution to the Critique of Actually Existing Democracy." In *Habermas and the Public Sphere*, edited by Craig Calhoun, 109–42. Cambridge: MIT Press, 1992.
———. "Transnationalizing the Public Sphere: On the Legitimacy and Efficacy of Public Opinion in a Post-Westphalian World." *Theory, Culture & Society* 24, no. 4 (2007): 7–30.
Freud, Sigmund. "Mourning and Melancholia." In *The Freud Reader*, edited by Peter Gay, 584–88. New York: W. W. Norton, 1989.
Friedman, Marilyn. "The Social Self and the Partiality Debates." In *Feminist Ethics*, edited by Claudia Card, 161–79. Lawrence: University of Kansas Press, 1991.
Fritze, J. G., G. A. Blashki, S. Burke, and J. Wiseman. "Hope, Despair and Transformation: Climate Change and the Promotion of Mental Health and Wellbeing." *International Journal of Mental Health Systems* 2, no. 1 (2008): 13.
Fullilove, M. T. "Psychiatric Implications of Displacement: Contributions from the Psychology of Place." *American Journal of Psychiatry* 153, no. 12 (1996): 1516–23.
Gadamer, Hans-Georg. *Truth and Method*. Translated by Sheed and Ward. New York: Seabury, 1975.
Gans, C. *The Limits of Nationalism*. Cambridge: Cambridge University Press, 2003.
Gardiner, S. M. *A Perfect Moral Storm: The Ethical Challenge of Climate Change*. Oxford: Oxford University Press, 2011.
Gardiner, S. M., et al., eds. *Climate Ethics: Essential Readings*. Oxford, UK: Oxford University Press, 2010.
Gatens, Moira. *Imaginary Bodies: Ethics, Power and Corporeality*. New York: Routledge, 1995.
Gellner, E. *Nations and Nationalism*. Oxford: Blackwell, 1983.
Goldfarb, Jeffrey. *The Politics of Small Things: The Power of the Powerless in Dark Times*. Chicago: University of Chicago Press, 2006.
Gomila, Antoni. "De Babel a Pentecostés. Actitudes ilustradas ante la diversidad lingüística." *Laguna* 5 (1997): 29–38.

Gomila, Antoni, and Miqel Comas. "Enlightened Attitudes Toward Linguistic Diversity: Multilinguistic Cosmopolitanism." Paper delivered at the Conference of the American Philosophies Forum, Madrid, Spain, 2011.
Greenfield, L. *Nationalism and the Mind*. Oxford, UK: Oneworld, 2006.
———. *The Spirit of Capitalism: Nationalism and Economic Growth*. Cambridge, MA: Harvard University Press, 2001.
Griffin, Larry J., Renae J. Evenson, and Ashley B. Thompson. "Southerners All." *Southern Cultures* 16, no. 1 (Spring 2012): 6–25.
Grimm, D. "Does Europe Need a Constitution?" In *The Question of Europe*, edited by P. Gowan and P. Anderson, 239–58. New York: Verso, 1997.
Habermas, Jürgen. "Citizenship and National Identity: Some Reflection on the Future of Europe." *Praxis International* 12, no. 1 (1992): 1–19.
———. *Die Einbeziehung des Anderen: Studien zur politischen Theorie*. Frankfurt: Suhrkamp, 1996.
———. *Die postnationale Knostellation*. Frankfurt: Suhrkamp, 1998.
———. *The Divided West*. Cambridge: Polity, 2008.
———. *Kant's Idea of Perpetual Peace, with Benefit of Two Hundred Years' Hindsight. Perpetual Peace: Essays on Kant's Ideal*. Edited byJames Bonham and Matthias Lutz-Bachmann. Cambridge: MIT Press, 1997.
———. *Reply to Grimm. The Question of Europe*. Edited by P. Gowan and P. Anderson. New York: Verso, 1997.
———. "Struggles for Recognition in Constitutional States." *European Journal of Philosophy* 1, no. 2 (1993): 128–55.
Hansen, Jonathan M. *The Lost Promise of Patriotism: Debating American Identity, 1890–1920*. Chicago: University of Chicago Press, 2003.
Harris, J. *Hermes, or philosophical investigations in universal grammar*. London: Author, 1751.
Hartsock, Nancy. "The Feminist Standpoint: Developing the Ground for a Specifically Feminist Historical Materialism." In *Discovering Reality*, edited by Sandra Harding and Merrill B. Hintikka, 283–310. Boston: D. Reidel, 1983.
Harvey, David. *Justice, Nature and the Geography of Difference*. Cambridge, MA: Blackwell, 1986.
Heidegger, Martin. *Being and Time*. Translated by John Macquarrie and Edward Robinson. New York: Harper and Row, 1962.
———. *The Fundamental Concepts of Metaphysics*. Translated by William McNeil and Nicholas Walker. Bloomington: Indiana University Press, 1995.
———. *Poetry, Language, Thought*. Translated by Albert Hofstadter. New York: Harper and Row, 1975.
Held, David. *Cosmopolitanism: Ideals and Realities*. Cambridge: Polity, 2010.
———. *Principles of Cosmopolitan Order. The Cosmopolitan Reader*. Edited by Garrett Wallace Brown and David Held. Cambridge: Polity, 2010.
Hinchliffe, Steve. "'Inhabiting': Landscapes and Natures." In *Handbook of Cultural Geography*, edited by K. Anderson et al., 207–25. London: Sage, 2003.
Hollinger, D. A. "Not Universalists, Not Pluralists: The New Cosmopolitans Find Their Own Way." *Constellations* 8, no. 2 (2001): 236–48.
Honig, Bonnie. *Democracy and the Foreigner*. Princeton, NJ: Princeton University Press, 2001.

Honneth, A., and N. Fraser. *Umverteilung oder Anerkennung? Eine politisch-philosophische Kontroverse.* Frankfurt: Suhrkamp, 2003.

Hook, Sidney. *Pragmatism and the Tragic Sense of Life.* New York: Basic, 1974.

Ingold, Tim. "Bindings Against Boundaries: Entanglements of Life in an Open World." *Environment and Planning A* 40 (2008): 1796–1810.

———. "Earth, Sky, Wind, and Weather." *Journal of the Royal Anthropological Institute* 13 (2007): S19–S38.

———. "Epilogue: Towards a Politics of Dwelling." *Conservation and Society* 3, no. 2 (2005): 501–8.

———. "The Eye of the Storm: Visual Perception and the Weather." *Visual Studies* 20, no. 2 (2005): 97–104.

———. "Footprints Through the Weather-World: Walking, Breathing, Knowing." *Journal of the Royal Anthropological Institute* 16 (2010): S121–S139.

———. *Lines: A Brief History.* London: Routledge, 2007.

———. "Materials Against Materiality." *Archaeological Dialogues* 14, no. 1 (2007): 1–16.

———. "Rethinking the Animate, Re-Animating Thought." *Ethnos* 7, no. 1 (2006): 9–20.

Innis, Robert E. *Consciousness and the Play of Signs.* Bloomington: Indiana University Press, 1994.

———. "Dimensions of an Aesthetic Encounter: Perception, Interpretation, and the Signs of Art." In *Semiotic Rotations: Modes of Meaning in Cultural Worlds*, edited by Jaan Valsiner, Sun-Hee Geertz, and Jean-Paul Breaux, 113–34. Charlotte: Information Age, 2007.

———. *Pragmatism and the Forms of Sense: Language, Perception, Technics.* University Park: Penn State University Press, 2002.

———. "The 'Quality of Philosophy': On the Aesthetic Matrix of Dewey's Pragmatism." In *The Continuing Relevance of John Dewey: Reflections on Aesthetics, Morality, Science, and Society*, edited by Larry Hickman, Matthew Caleb Flamm, Krzysztof Piotr Skowroński, and Jennifer A. Rea, 43–60. Amsterdam: Rodopi, 2011.

———. *Susanne Langer in Focus: The Symbolic Mind.* Bloomington: Indiana University Press, 2009.

IPCC. "Summary for Policymakers." In *Climate Change 2014: Impacts, Adaptation, and Vulnerability. Part A: Global and Sectoral Aspects. Contribution of Working Group II to the Fifth Assessment Report of the Intergovernmental Panel on Climate Change*, edited by C. G. Field, V. R. Barros, D. J. Dokken, K. J. Mach, M. D. Mastrandrea, T. E. Bilir, M. Chatterjee, K. L. Ebi, Y. O. Estrada, R. C. Genova, B. Girma, E. S. Kissel, A. N. Levy, S. MacCracken, P. R. Mastrandrea, and L. L. White, 1–32. Cambridge: Cambridge University Press, 2014.

Jackson, D. D. "Scents of Place: The Dysplacement of a First Nations Community in Canada." *American Anthropologist* 113, no. 4 (2011): 606–18.

Jacobs, Frank. "Strange Maps 72—The World as Seen from NY's 9th Avenue." *Big Think*, February 7, 2007. http://bigthink.com/ideas/21121.

James, William. *Essays in Radical Empiricism.* Edited by Ralph B. Perry. New York: Dutton, 1971.

———. *The Letters of William James.* 2 vols. Edited by Henry James. Boston: Atlantic Monthly, 1920.

———. *On a Certain Blindness in Human Beings.* In *Talks to Teachers on Psychology: And to Students on Some of Life's Ideals.* New York: Henry Holt, 1906.

———. "Philosophical Conceptions and Practical Results." *University Chronicle* 1, no. 4 (1898): 287–310.
———. *A Pluralistic Universe*. New York: Longmans, Green, 1977.
———. *Pragmatism & the Meaning of Truth*. Cambridge, MA: Harvard University Press, 1975.
———. *The Principles of Psychology*. 2 vols. Cambridge, MA: Harvard University Press, 1981.
———. *The Varieties of Religious Experience*. In *Writings: 1902–1910*. Edited by Bruce Kuklick. New York: Library of America, 1987.
Janz, Bruce. "Walls and Border: The Range of Place." *City and Community* 4, no. 1 (2005): 87–94.
Jay, Martin. *Permanent Exiles*. New York: Columbia University Press, 1986.
Johnson, Mark. *The Moral Imagination: The Implications of Cognitive Science for Ethics*. Chicago: University of Chicago Press, 1994.
Jullien, François. *Detour and Access: Strategies of Meaning in China and Greece*. Translated by Sophie Hawkes. New York: Zone, 2000.
———. *The Great Image Has No Form, or On the Nonobject Through Painting*. Translated by Jane Marie Todd. Chicago: University of Chicago Press, 2009.
———. *The Impossible Nude*. Translated by Maev de la Guardia. Chicago: University of Chicago Press, 2007.
———. *In Praise of Blandness: Proceeding from Chinese Thought and Aesthetics*. Translated by Paula M. Varsano. New York: Zone, 2004.
———. *Vital Nourishment: Departing from Happiness*. Translated by Arthur Goldhammer. New York: Zone, 2007.
Kant, Immanuel. *Observations on the Beautiful and Sublime*. Translated by John Goldthwait. Berkeley: University of California Press, 1960.
———. *Perpetual Peace*. Translated by Lewis White Beck. New York: Library of Liberal Arts, 1957.
Keillor, Garrison. "Appreciation for a Great Appreciator." *A Prairie Home Companion*, February 3, 2009. www.publicradio.org/columns/prairiehome/the_old_scout/archives/2009/02/03/appreciation_for_a_great_appreciator.shtml.
Kelly, Ursula A. "Learning to Lose: Rurality, Transience, and Belonging (a Companion to Michael Corbett)." *Journal of Research in Rural Education* 24, no. 11 (2009): 4.
Kidner, D. "Depression and the Natural World: Towards a Critical Ecology of Psychological Distress." *International Journal of Critical Psychology* 19 (2007): 123–46.
Kim, David, and Ronald Sundstrom. "Xenophobia and Racism." *Critical Philosophy of Race* 2, no. 1 (2014): 20–45.
Kleingeld, Pauline, and Eric Brown. *Cosmopolitanism*. The Stanford Encyclopedia of Philosophy. Edited by Edward N. Zalta. 2011. http://plato.stanford.edu/archives/spr2011/entries/cosmopolitanism/
Kolbert, Elizabeth. *Fieldnotes from a Catastrophe: Man, Nature and Climate Change*. New York: Bloomsbury, 2007.
———. *The Sixth Extinction: An Unnatural History*. New York: Henry Holt, 2014.
König, M. "Cultural Diversity and Language Policy." *International Social Science Journal* 51 (1999): 401–8.

Koopman, Colin. "Good Questions and Bad Answers in Talisse's *A Pragmatist Philosophy of Democracy*." *Transactions of the Charles Peirce Society* 45, no. 1 (2009): 60–64.
Kracauer, Siegfried. *History, the Last Things Before the Last*. New York: Oxford University Press, 1969.
Krayem, Hassan. *The Arab Spring and the Process of Democratic Transition. The Arab Spring: Revolutions for Deliverance from Authoritarianism: Case Studies*. Edited by Hassan Krayem. Translated by Jeffrey D. Reger. Beirut: Al Sharq, 2014.
Kushner, Tony. "Additional Footage: Tony Kushner on *The Intelligent Homosexual's Guide*." YouTube. March 4, 2011. www.youtube.com/watch?v=XPhRhxhxXr4&feature=BFa&list=PL949658CDE629431D.
Kymlicka, W. *Liberal Nationalism and Cosmopolitan Justice. Another Cosmopolitanism: Hospitality, Sovereignty, and Democratic Iteration. (By Seyla Benhabib)*. Oxford: Oxford University Press, 2006.
———. *Multicultural Citizenship: A Liberal Theory of Minority Rights*. London: Oxford University Press, 1995.
———. *Politics in the Vernacular*. London: Oxford University Press, 2001.
———, ed. *The Rights of Minority Cultures*. London: Oxford University Press, 1995.
Lakoff, George, and Mark Johnson. *Philosophy in the Flesh: The Embodied Mind and Its Challenge to Western Thought*. New York: Basic, 1999.
Latour, Bruno. *Politics of Nature*. Cambridge, MA: Harvard University Press, 1999.
Leibniz, G. W. *Dissertatio de arte combinatoria*. Paris: Hachette Livre, 2012.
Leow, Rachel. "Reflections on Feminism, Blogging and the Historical Profession." *Journal of Women's History* 22, no. 4 (2010): 235–43.
Levinas, Emmanuel. *Otherwise Than Being or Beyond Essence*. Translated by Alphonso Lingis. Dordrecht: Kluwer, 1991.
———. *Totality and Infinity*. Translated by Alphonso Lingis. Pittsburgh: Duquesne University Press, 1969.
Lewis, William S. *Louis Althusser. The Stanford Encyclopedia of Philosophy*. Edited by Edward N. Zalta. 2014. http://plato.stanford.edu/archives/spr2014/entries/althusser/.
———. "The New International of Decent Feelings: Fear, Cosmopolitanism, and the Erasure of Class." Paper presented at American Philosophies Forum: Cosmopolitanism and Place, Círculo de Bellas Artes, Madrid, June 2–4, 2011.
Long, A. A. "The Concept of the Cosmopolitan in Greek & Roman Thought." *Daedalus* 137, no. 3 (Summer): 50–58.
Lugones, Maria. "Playfulness, 'World'-Travelling, and Loving Perception." *Hypatia* 2, no. 2 (1987): 3–19.
Lukes, S. *El viaje del professor Caritat*. Barcelona: Tusquets, 1997.
Lyon, Richard C. "Introduction." In *George Santayana. Persons and Places*, xv–xl. Cambridge: MIT Press, 1986.
Lysaker, John T. "Cosmopolitanism: A Kind of Philosophical Praxis." Paper Presented at American Philosophies Forum: Cosmopolitanism and Place, Círculo de Bellas Artes, Madrid, June 2–4, 2011.
———. *Emerson and Self-Culture*. Bloomington: Indiana University Press, 2008.
———. "Praxis as Form: Thirty Notes for an Ethics of the Future." *Journal of Speculative Philosophy* 25, no. 2 (2011): 213–38.

Macy, J., and M. Y. Brown. *Coming Back to Life: Practices to Reconnect Our Lives, Our World*. Gabriola Island, BC: New Society, 1998.
Malpas, J. E. *Place and Experience*. 2nd ed. Cambridge: Cambridge University Press, 2007.
Marcel, Gabriel. *Homo Viator: Introduction to a Metaphysic of Hope*. Translated by Emma Crauford. New York: Harper and Brothers, 1962.
Margalit, Avishai. *The Moral Psychology of Nationalism. The Morality of Nationalism*. Edited by R. McKim and J. McMahan. Oxford: Oxford University Press, 1997.
Margolis, Joseph. *Moral Philosophy after 9/11*. University Park: Penn State University Press, 2004.
Mason, A. "Political Community, Liberal-Nationalism and the Ethics of Assimilation." *Ethics* 109 (1999): 261–86.
Matheron, François. "The Recurrence of the Void in Louis Althusser." *Rethinking Marxism* 10, no. 3 (Fall 1998): 22–37.
McLuhan, Marshall. *Understanding Media: The Extensions of Man*. New York: McGraw-Hill, 1965.
McLuhan, Marshall, and Quentin Fiore. *The Medium Is the Massage: An Inventory of Effects*. New York: Bantam, 1967.
McWhorter, L. *Racism and Sexual Oppression in Anglo-America: A Genealogy*. Bloomington: Indiana University Press, 2009.
Medina, Jose. *The Epistemology of Resistance: Gender and Racial Oppression, Epistemic Injustice, and the Social Imagination*. New York: Oxford University Press, 2012.
———. "Identity Trouble: Disidentification and the Problem of Difference." *Philosophy and Social Criticism* 29 (2004): 655–80.
———. "In Defense of Pragmatic Contextualism: Wittgenstein and Dewey on Meaning and Agreement." *Philosophical Forum* 35, no. 3 (Fall 2004): 341–69.
———. *Speaking from Elsewhere: A New Contextualist Perspective on Meaning, Identity, and Discursive Agency*. Albany: SUNY Press, 2006.
———. "Toward a Foucaultian Epistemology of Resistance: Counter-Memory, Epistemic Friction, and Guerrilla Pluralism." *Foucaultian Studies* 12 (October 2011): 9–35.
Merleau-Ponty, Maurice. *The Phenomenology of Perception*. Translated by Colin Smith. London: Routledge, 1995.
Mignolo, W. *The Idea of Latin America*. London: Blackwell, 2005.
———. "The Many Faces of Cosmo-polis: Border Thinking and Critical Cosmopolitanism." *Public Culture* 12, no. 3 (2000): 721–48.
Milgram, S. *Obedience to Authority: An Experimental View*. New York: Harper and Row, 1974.
Mill, J. S. *On Representative Government*. Liberty Library of Constitutional Classics. 1861. www.constitution.org/jsm/rep_gov.htm.
Miller, David. *Cosmopolitanism. The Cosmopolitan Reader*. Edited by Garrett Wallace Brown and David Held. Cambridge: Polity, 2010.
Miller, John William. "Afterword." In *History as System & Other Essays*, edited by José Ortega y Gasset, 237–69. New York: W. W. Norton, 1961.
———. *The Midworld of Symbols*. New York: W. W. Norton, 1982
———. *The Philosophy of History*. New York: W. W. Norton, 1981.
Mills, Charles. *The Racial Contract*. Ithaca, NY: Cornell University Press, 1997.

———. "White Ignorance." In *Race and Epistemologies of Ignorance*, edited by Shannon Sullivan and Nancy Tuana, 11–38. Albany: SUNY Press, 2007.
Misak, Cheryl J. "Making Disagreement Matter: Pragmatism and Deliberative Democracy." *Journal of Speculative Philosophy* 18, no. 1 (2004): 9–22.
Moles, John. "Cynic Cosmopolitanism." In *The Cynics: The Cynic Movement in Antiquity and Its Legacy*, edited by R. B. Branham and M-O. Goulet-Cazé, 105–20. Berkeley: University of California Press, 2006.
Moore, M., ed. *National Self-Determination and Succession*. Oxford: Oxford University Press, 1998.
Moreno Cabrara, J. C. *De Babel a Pentecostés: Manifiesto Plurilingüista*. Barcelona: Horsori, 2006.
Moreno, I. *La Antigua Hermandad de los Negros de Sevilla. Etnicidad, Poder y Sociedad en 600 Años de Historia*. Seville: Universidad de Sevilla Press, 1997.
Morrison, Toni. *Unspeakable Things Unspoken*. Tanner Lecture. Ann Arbor: University of Michigan, 1988.
Murphy, Cullen. "Torturer's Apprentice." *Atlantic*, January–February 2012, 72–77.
Muslimah Media Watch. *The Republic Lives Its Islamophobia Openly: France's Newest Anti-Niqab Campaign*. March 21, 2011. http://muslimahmediawatch.org/2011/03/the-republic-lives-its-islamophobia-openly-frances-newest-anti-niqab-campaign/.
Myers, Fred R. *Pinpui Country, Pinpui Self*. Canberra: Australian Institute of Aboriginal Studies, 1986.
Nagel, Thomas. *The View from Nowhere*. New York: Oxford University Press, 1986.
Neville, Robert. *Boston Confucianism: Portable Tradition in the Late-Modern World*. Albany: SUNY Press, 2000.
Nicholsen, S. W. *The Love of Nature and the End of the World*. Cambridge: MIT Press, 2002.
Nietzsche, Friedrich. *The Gay Science*. Translated by Walter Kaufmann. New York: Random House, 1974.
Noë, Alva. *Action in Perception*. Cambridge: MIT Press, 2004.
Nussbaum, Martha. *Cultivating Humanity: A Classical Defense of Reform in Liberal Education*. Cambridge, MA: Harvard University Press, 1997.
———. "Duties of Justice, Duties of Material Aid: Cicero's Problematic Legacy." *Journal of Political Philosophy* 8, no. 2 (2000): 176–206.
———. "Kant and Stoic Cosmopolitanism." *Journal of Political Philosophy* 5, no. 1 (1997): 1–25.
———. "Patriotism and Cosmopolitanism." In *For Love of Country: Debating the Limits of Patriotism*, edited by Joshua Cohen, 3–20. Boston: Beacon, 1996.
———. *The Therapy of Desire: Theory and Practice in Hellenistic Ethics*. Princeton, NJ: Princeton University Press, 1994.
———. "Toward a Globally Sensitive Patriotism." *Daedalus* 137, no. 3 (Summer 2008): 78–93.
Orosco, José-Antonio. "Cosmopolitan Loyalty and the Great Global Community: Royce's Globalization." *Journal of Speculative Philosophy* 19, no. 3 (2003): 204–15.
Ortega, José y Gasset. *Some Lessons in Metaphysics*. Translated by Mildred Adams. New York: W. W. Norton, 1969.
———. *What Is Philosophy?* Translated by Mildred Adams. New York: W. W. Norton, 1960.

Pakovi, A., and P. Radan, eds. *Creating New States: Theory and Practice of Succession.* London: Ashgate, 2007.
Parker, Kelly. *The Continuity of Peirce's Thought.* Nashville: Vanderbilt University Press, 1998.
Parry, M. L., O. F. Canziani, J. P. Palutikof, P. J. van der Linden, and C. E. Hanson, eds. *Climate Change 2007: Impacts, Adaptation and Vulnerability. Contribution of Working Group II to the Fourth Assessment Report of the Intergovernmental Panel on Climate Change.* Cambridge: Cambridge University Press, 2007.
Peirce, C. S. *The Essential Peirce.* 2 vols. Edited by Peirce Edition Projects. Bloomington: Indiana University Press, 1992.
———. "The Fixation of Belief." In *The Essential Peirce: Vol I (1867–1893),* edited by Nathan Houser and Christian Kloesel 109–23. Bloomington: Indiana University Press, 1992.
———. MS 598. *Reason's Rule.* Houghton Library, Harvard University.
Pereda, Carlos. "Local Traditions and Cosmopolitan Rules." Paper presented at American Philosophies Forum: Cosmopolitanism and Place, Círculo de Bellas Artes, Madrid, June 2–4, 2011.
Perry, Ralph Barton. *The Thought and Character of William James.* Boston: Little, Brown, 1935.
Pogge, Thomas. "Cosmopolitanism and Sovereignty." *Ethics* 103, no. 1 (1992): 48–75.
———. *Global Justice.* Oxford: Blackwell, 2001.
———. *World Poverty and Human Rights.* 2nd ed. Malden, MA: Polity, 2008.
Polasky, Janet. *Revolutions Without Borders: The Call to Liberty in the Atlantic World.* New Haven, CT: Yale University Press, 2015.
Potter, Vincent. *Peirce's Philosophical Perspectives.* Edited by Vincent Colapietro. New York: Fordham University Press, 1996.
Proust, Marcel. *The Guermantes Way: In Search of Lost Time.* Vol. 3. Translated by Mark Trehane. New York: Penguin, 2005.
Putnam, Hilary. *Must We Choose Between Patriotism and Universal Reason? Cosmopolitics: Thinking and Feeling Beyond the Nation.* Edited by Pheng Cheah and Bruce Robbins. Minneapolis: University of Minnesota Press, 1998.
Rawls, John. *Justice as Fairness.* Cambridge, MA: Harvard University Press, 2001.
———. *Political Liberalism.* New York: Columbia University Press, 2005.
———. *A Theory of Justice.* Oxford: Oxford University Press, 1999.
Read, Peter. *Returning to Nothing: The Meaning of Lost Place.* Cambridge: Cambridge University Press, 1996.
Reed, J. S. "The Cardinal Test of a Southerner: Not Race but Geography." *Public Opinion Quarterly* (1973): 232–40.
Relph, Edward. *Place and Placelessness.* London: Pion, 1976.
Reuveny, R. "Ecomigration and Violent Conflict: Case Studies and Public Policy Implications." *Human Ecology* 36 (2008): 1–13.
Ricoeur, Paul. *The Course of Recognition.* Translated by David Pellauer. Cambridge, MA: Harvard University Press, 2005.
Rittel, Horst, and Melvin Webber. "Dilemmas in a General Theory of Planning." *Policy Sciences* 4 (1973): 155–69.
Riverrol, A. *Discours sur l'universalité de la lange française.* Berlin: Author, 1784.

Robinson, Marilynne. *The Death of Adam: Essays on Modern Thought*. New York: Picador, 2014.
Rorty, Richard. "Justice as a Larger Loyalty." In *For Love of Country: Debating the Limits of Patriotism*, edited by Joshua Cohen, 45–58. Boston: Beacon, 2002.
Rousseau, J. J. *Essai sur l'origine des langues. Oeuvres XIII*. Paris: Chez Dalibon, Imp. de G. Doyen, 1826.
Royce, Josiah. *The Hope of the Great Community*. New York: Macmillan, 1916.
———. *Provincialism. Race Questions, Provincialism, and Other American Problems*. Freeport, NY: Books for Libraries, 1967.
Ruiz, Alicia Garcia. "The Displacement of the Gaze: Becoming a Conscious Cosmopolitan." Paper presented at American Philosophies Forum: Cosmopolitanism and Place, Círculo de Bellas Artes, Madrid, June 2–4, 2011.
Said, Edward. *Reflexiones sobre el exilio*. Madrid: Debate, 2005.
Santayana, George. *The Birth of Reason & Other Essays*. Edited by Daniel Corey. New York: Columbia University Press, 1968.
———. *Persons and Places*. Cambridge: MIT Press, 1986.
———. *The Realms of Being*. New York: Charles Scribner's Sons, 1942.
———. *Scepticism and Animal Faith*. New York: Dover, 1955.
Sartwell, Crispin. *Six Names of Beauty*. New York: Routledge, 2006.
Scarry, Elaine. *The Body in Pain: The Making and Unmaking of the World*. Oxford: Oxford University Press, 1987.
———. "The Difficulty of Imagining Other People." In *For Love of Country: Debating the Limits of Patriotism*, edited by Joshua Cohen, 98–110. Boston: Beacon, 1997.
Scharfstein, Ben-Ami. *Art Without Borders: A Philosophical Exploration of Art and Humanity*. Chicago: University of Chicago Press, 2009.
Scott, Charles E. *The Lives of Things*. Bloomington: Indiana University Press, 2002.
Seel, Martin. *Aesthetics of Appearing*. Stanford: Stanford University Press, 2005.
Sen, Amartya. *The Idea of Justice*. Cambridge, MA: The Belknap Press, 2009.
Sheets-Johnstone, Maxine. *The Primacy of Movement*. Amsterdam: John Benjamins, 1999.
Short, Robert. *Pol Pot: Anatomy of a Nightmare*. New York: Henry Holt, 2004.
Skrupskelis, Ignas. "Some Oversights in Dewey's Cosmopolitanism." *Transactions of the Charles Peirce Society* 45, no. 3 (2009): 308–47.
Slaughter, Matthew J. *How US Multinational Companies Strengthen the US Economy: Data Update*. Washington, DC: United States Council for International Business, 2010. www.uscib.org/docs/foundation_multinationals_update.pdf.
Smith, John E. *Experience and God*. New York: Fordham University Press, 1995.
Stegner, Wallace. *Where the Bluebird Sings in the Lemonade Springs*. New York: Random House, 1992.
Steinbock, Anthony. "Hoping Against Hope." In *Essays in Celebration of the Founding of Organization of Phenomenological Organizations*, edited by Chan-Fai Cheung, Ivan Chvatik, Ion Cooperu, Lester Embree, Julia Iribarne, and Hans Rainer Sepp. 2003. www.o-p-o.net.
Stevens, Wallace. *To an Old Philosopher in Rome*. In *The Collected Poems of Wallace Stevens*. New York: Vintage, 1990.
Striffler, S. "Neither Here nor There: Mexican Immigrant Workers and the Search for Home." *American Ethnologist* 34, no. 4 (2007): 674–88.

Stuhr, John. *Genealogical Pragmatism: Philosophy, Experience, and Community.* Albany: SUNY Press, 1997.
———. *Pragmatic Fashions: Pluralism, Democracy, Relativism, and the Absurd.* Bloomington: Indiana University Press, 2016.
———. *Pragmatism and Classical American Philosophy.* 2nd ed. New York: Oxford University Press, 2000.
———. *Pragmatism, Post-Modernism, and the Future of Philosophy.* New York: Routledge, 2003.
Sullivan, Shannon. *Revealing Whiteness: The Unconscious Habits of Racial Privilege.* Bloomington: Indiana University Press, 2006.
———. "White Ignorance and Colonial Oppression: Or, Why I Know So Little About Puerto Rico." In *Race and Epistemologies of Ignorance*, edited by Shannon Sullivan and Nancy Tuana, 153–72. Albany: SUNY Press, 2007.
Sullivan, Shannon, and Nancy Tuana, eds. *Race and Epistemologies of Ignorance.* Albany: SUNY Press, 2007.
Swain, Tony. *A Place of Strangers.* Cambridge: Cambridge University Press, 1986.
Swim, Janet, Susan Clayton, Thomas Doherty, Robert Gifford, George Howard, Joseph Reser, Paul Stern, and Elke Weber. *Psychology and Global Climate Change: Addressing a Multifaceted Phenomenon and Set of Challenges. Report of the American Psychological Association Task Force on the Interface Between Psychology and Global Climate Change.* 2010. www.apa.org/science/about/publications/climate-change.aspx.
Talisse, Robert. *A Pragmatist Philosophy of Democracy.* New York: Routledge, 2007.
Taylor, Charles. *Modern Social Imaginaries.* Durham, NC: Duke University Press, 2004.
———. *Reconciling the Solitudes.* Montreal: McGill University Press, 1993.
———. *Sources of the Self: The Making of Modern Identity.* Cambridge, MA: Harvard University Press, 1989.
Taylor, Paul. "'A Colored Man Hasn't Got Any Country': Roots, Routes, and the Practice of Diaspora." Paper presented at American Philosophies Forum: Cosmopolitanism and Place, Círculo de Bellas Artes, Madrid, June 2–4, 2011.
Tegart, W. J., G. W. Sheldon, and D. C. Griffiths. *Climate Change: The IPCC Impacts Assessment, Working Group Two.* 1990.
Telhami, Shibley. *Of Power and Compassion. The Philosophical Challenge of September 11.* Edited by Tom Rockmore, Joseph Margolis, and Armen Marsobian. London: Blackwell, 2004.
———. *The Stakes: America and the Middle East.* Boulder, CO: Westview, 2002.
Terence. *Heautontimorumenos; The Self-Tormentor.* Project Gutenberg, 2015. www.gutenberg.org/files/22188/22188-h/files/terence3_4.html.
Thiebaut, Carlos. Cosmopolitanism, Identity, and Belonging. Paper Presented at American Philosophies Forum: Cosmopolitanism and Place, Círculo de Bellas Artes, Madrid, June 2–4, 2011.
Thrift, Nigel. "Inhuman Geographies: Landscapes of Speed, Light, and Power." In *Writing the Rural: Five Cultural Geographies*, edited by P. Cloke, 191–248. London: Routledge, 1994.
Tiger Beatdown. "#Dearjohn: On Rape Culture and a Culture of Reproductive Violence." Blog comment, February 4, 2011. http://tigerbeatdown.com/2011/02/04/dearjohn-on-rape-culture-and-a-culture-of-reproductive-violence/.

———. "FAQ: Commenting." 2011. http://tigerbeatdown.com/faq-commenting/.
Toscano, M. "El desafío de Mill: diversidad lingüística y democracia en Europa." In *Ciudadanos de Europa*, edited by M. T. López de la Vieja, 123–46. Madrid: Ed. Biblioteca Nueva, 2005.
Traverso, E. *Cosmópolis: figuras del exilio judeo-alemán*. Mexico City: UNAM, 2004.
———. "Interview with Enzo Traverso: History can be an 'Arm of Power.'" Alicia García Ruiz. 2010. http://w2.bcn.cat/bcnmetropolis/arxiu/en/page1517.html?id=21.
———. *La historia desgarrada. Ensayo sobre Auschwitz y los intelectuales*. Barcelona: Herder, 2001.
———. *Sigfried Krakauer: itinerario de un intelectual nómada*. Valencia: Alfons el Magnánim, 1998.
Trilling, Lionel. *That Smile of Parmenides Made Me Think*. In *A Gathering of Fugitives*. New York: Harcourt Brace Jovanovich, 1977.
Trotter, Griffin. "Royce, Community, and Ethnicity." *Transactions of the Charles S. Pierce Society* 30, no. 3 (1994): 231–69.
Tschakert, P., R. Tutu, and A. Alcaro. "Embodied Experiences of Environmental and Climatic Changes in Landscapes of Everyday Life in Ghana." *Emotion, Space and Society* 7, no. 1 (2013): 13–25.
Tuan, Yi-Fu. "Space and Place: Humanistic Perspective." *Progress in Geography* 6 (1974): 211–52.
———. *Space and Place: The Perspective of Experience*. Minneapolis: University of Minnesota Press, 1977.
Tuana, Nancy. "Viscous Porosity: Witnessing Katrina." In *Material Feminisms*, edited by Susan Hekman and Stacy Alaimo, 188–213. Bloomington: Indiana University Press, 2008.
Tully, James. *Strange Multiplicity: Constitutionalism in an Age of Diversity*. Cambridge: Cambridge University Press, 1995.
Unamuno, Miquel de. *The Tragic Sense of Life*. New York: Dover, 2012.
United Nations. *World Summit Outcome Document (for the Right to Protect)*. New York: United Nations, 2005.
Van Parijs, P. "Linguistic Justice." *Politics, Philosophy and Economics* 1, no. 1 (2011): 59–74.
Vico, Giambattista. *The New Science*. Translated by Thomas Goddard Bergin and Max Harold Fisch. Ithaca, NY: Cornell University Press, 1984.
Wahman, Jessica. "Drama as Philosophical Genre." *Journal of Speculative Philosophy* 28, no. 4 (2014): 454–71.
Waldron, Jeremy. *What Is Cosmopolitanism? The Cosmopolitan Reader*. Edited by Garrett Wallace Brown and David Held. Cambridge: Polity, 2010.
Walker, Margaret. *Moral Understandings*. New York: Routledge, 1998.
Waltzer, M. *What It Means to Be an American*. New York: Marsilio, 1992.
Weil, S. "The Iliad or the Poem of Force." In *Simone Weil: An Anthology*, edited by S. Miles, 162–95. New York: Weidenfeld and Nicolson, 1986.
Whitman, Walt. *Walt Whitman: Selected Poems*. Edited by Harold Bloom. New York: Library of America, 2003.
Wilkins, J. *An Essay Towards a Real Character and a Philosophical Language*. Oxford: Author, 1668.

Willett, Cynthia. "Eros in the Biosphere: Political Ethics for Cosmopolitan Animals." Paper presented at American Philosophies Forum: Cosmopolitanism and Place, Círculo de Bellas Artes, Madrid, June 2–4, 2011.
Williams Bernard. *Truth and Truthfulness*. Princeton, NJ: Princeton University Press, 2002.
Wilson, Edmund. "Santayana: A Boyhood Between Spain and Boston." *New Yorker*, January 8, 1944, 56–58.
Wittgenstein, Ludwig. *Philosophical Investigations*. Translated by G. E. M. Anscombe. New York: Macmillan, 1958.
Woodbridge, Frederick J. E. *An Essay on Nature*. New York: Columbia University Press, 1940.
Woolf, Virginia. *Three Guineas*. London: Hogarth, 1952.
Young, Neil. "Flags of Freedom. Living with War (Reprise)." Track 6. 2006.

Index

Achen, Christopher, 284, 294n13
Addams, Jane, 79, 81, 115, 121n22
Agnew, John, 293n7
Ahmed, Khadar, 246
Albrecht, Glenn, 187, 194n24
Alcaro, Anna, 188, 194n28
Alcoff, Linda, 234n20
Aldridge, Michael, 246
Alexievich, S., 179n18
Alighieri, Dante, 53, 141, 146, 157n7
Alston, Margaret, 188, 195n32
Althusser, Louis, 204, 264–269, 274, 278
Améry, Jean, 79, 83, 161–163, 166–168, 170–175, 177n1, n7–9, 178n13, n14
Ames, Roger, 74n32
Anders, Günther, 180n34
Angell, Marcia, 179n23
Anzaldúa, Gloria, 82, 127, 129–136, 138n21, n27
Appiah, Kwame Anthony, 12, 14, 15, 20n9, n11, 25, 46, 47, 51, 56n2, n6, 57n35, n37, n38, 100n11, 184, 194n12, 204, 205, 214, 219n2, 221n13, n19, 227, 230–232, 233n4, n6, 234n23, 242–244, 247n30, n36, n42, 259, 273n29, 265, 266, 271–277, 289n34, 288–300, 294n25
Arendt, Hannah, 16, 23, 25, 28, 32, 180n32
Aristotle, 23, 60, 67, 98, 23, 28, 4n17
Art, 4, 8, 42, 43, 53, 59–62, 65–67, 69–73, 73n1, n4, n7, 74n13, n14, n28, n29, 75n44, n51, n54, 126, 142, 157, 231, 243, 276, 291, 292
Augustine, 72
Aurelius, Marcus, 13

Bachelard, Gaston, 49, 56n23, 83, 140, 142, 148–151, 158n12, n22, n24, n25
Bacon, Francis, 152
Barry, Brian, 48, 56n17
Bartels, Larry M., 284, 294n13
Barvosa, Edwina, 122n28
Beauty, 7, 8, 60–63, 73n10, 104n48, 106n60, 188
Beitz, Charles, 12, 21n15
Benhabib, Seyla, 18, 21n21, 239–243, 247n11, n23, n27, n35, 281, 293n3
Bergson, Henri, 157n1
Bettelheim, Bruno, 173, 180n27, n29

Bloch, Ernst, 222, 224, 225, 227, 233n8, 234n9, n12, n15, n17, n19
Boer, Roland, 278n18
Bohman, James, 265
Bok, Sissela, 47, 56n10
Borders, vii, 7, 22, 26, 34, 57n30, 59, 73n1, 125–128, 133, 140, 149, 155, 183, 192, 199, 237–239, 261, 273, 281, 292n2
Bouazizi, Mohamed, 26–28, 34n7
Boundaries, vii, 61, 63, 66, 99n1, 102n24, 104n49, 105n52, 123, 125, 133, 163, 177n7, 202, 219, 222, 229, 231, 237, 239, 242–245, 249, 261
Broome, John, 193n3
Brown, Donald A., 193n3
Brown, Eric, 278n23
Brown, Garrett Wallace, 19, 20n7, 21n20, 246n7, 293n4
Brown, Michael, 29
Brown, Stuart Gerry, 54, 57n49
Buchanan, Allen, 56n13
Burton, Richard, 272
Butler, Judith, 12, 18, 21n24

Calhoun, Craig, 48, 56n15, 263n26
Calvin, John, 242
Camus, Albert, 264, 266, 267
Caney, Simon, 12, 84, 183, 185, 193n8, n11, 303n4
Casey, Ed, 96, 104n49, 157n11, 160n44, 186, 194n22
Castoriadis, Carlos, 22, 23, 25, 34n4
Chinese painting, 63–72
Cicero, 233n4, 278n26, 287, 294n21
Citizen, vii, 13–19, 27–29, 32, 33, 48, 51–53, 120n4, 125, 134, 191, 199, 201, 220n4, 223, 225, 236, 238–241, 256, 258, 285, 291, 292, 293n3; of the world, 4, 5, 12, 19, 20n8, 21, 25, 53, 54, 81, 98, 200, 207, 209, 245, 259, 271, 274, 280–284, 287
Class, 32, 49, 50, 52, 119, 122n27, 126, 173, 199, 205, 264–270, 275–277
Climate, vii, 55n1, 80, 83, 84, 126, 138n27, 140, 151, 157n4, 159n40, 181–195, 223
Code, Lorraine, 25, 34n5, 112, 121n12, 194n15
Cohn, Roy, 211

315

Colapietro, Vincent, 56n3, 73n3, 79–81, 107, 128, 137n9, 141, 148, 253, 262n16, 276, 283
Coleman, Earle L., 75n47
Colonialism, 32, 111, 112, 118, 120, 121n7, n12, 127–131, 135, 183, 205, 223, 285–288, 291
Communication, 243, 244, 249, 252, 253; and power, 3, 4, 8, 102n28, 104n48, 106n60, 219, 252
Communities, 4, 7, 26, 36, 46–48, 50, 53, 54, 71, 80, 81, 82, 108, 125, 129, 134, 136, 184, 190, 200, 204, 216, 242, 246, 249–261, 283
Corbí, Josep, 79, 84, 84
Cosmopolitan: address, 6, 8, 22, 26–30, 177n9, 227, 235, 242, 254, 271; aesthetics, 3, 4, 7, 8, 59, 61–64, 66–68, 72; as homeless, 207–219; aspiration and confidence, 161–176, 260; character, 5, 13–14, 16–19, 20n7, 21n21; culture, vii, 19, 31, 184; generosity, 235–237, 240, 245; hope, 133, 180n33, 202, 203, 205, 206, 216–219, 222–237, 243, 285, 291, 292; ignorance, 107–120, 125; imaginary, 5–7, 22–27, 29–34, 53, 235; morality, vii, 4, 51–55, 108, 124, 125, 127, 205, 208, 222, 245, 259; nature, 13, 15, 182, 185; pluralism, 222, 228, 229, 232, 233, 237, 238, 240, 244, 245, 290–292; politics, vii, 107–120, 124, 184, 205, 222, 223, 236, 237, 243, 259, 260, 282; totality, 4, 5, 8, 16, 17, 63, 64, 98, 99n5, 105n55
Cosmopolitanism: as an orientation, 3, 207, 208–211, 216, 260; as homelessness, 209, 207–219, 245; rooted and situated, 3–5, 7, 8, 36, 46–49, 51–55, 59, 72, 88, 93, 94, 182, 185, 205, 206, 243, 244, 260, 280, 288–290; traditional, 4, 6, 14, 15, 19, 31, 200, 201, 240, 250, 270–275, 280, 282
Covaleskie, John, 253, 254, 259, 262n17
Craig, Megan, 57, 73n3, 79, 83, 98, 107, 108, 126, 179n22, 220n6, 283
Cresswell, Tim, 293n8Cynics, 12, 13, 20n5, 285
Culture, vii, 3–7, 9, 10–15, 19, 20n7, 24, 28, 31, 45–52, 57n5, n8, 72, 73n7, 79, 82, 102n27, 110, 116, 118, 119, 125n25, n27, 127–135, 158n14, 167, 180n33, 184, 186, 190, 192, 194n18, 199, 200, 202, 204, 207–210, 213–217, 220n6, 221n14, 222, 227, 228, 231–234, 242, 256, 259, 262, 263n25, 269, 271–277, 288, 289, 291, 292, 294n11; and cultural heritages, 6, 36–44; global, 20, 59–62, 125, 265, 266, 282

Deleuze, Gilles, 83, 138n31, 140, 151–153, 159n29, n35, n41
Democracy, 5, 7, 10–12, 18, 22–24, 27, 28, 33, 44, 46, 48, 52, 54, 109, 115, 121n22, 124, 128, 129, 134, 136, 137n4, 158n23, 204, 206, 221n22, 240, 242, 243, 247n11, 249–251, 253–258, 261, 262n3, n4, 263n24, n26, 280, 284, 290–292, 293n3, n5, n6, 294n13, n27
Denes, Agnes, 147
Derrida, Jacques, 12, 30, 31, 35n17
Descartes, René, 141, 146, 157n8
Dewey, John, 8, 60, 61, 63–71, 79, 97, 98, 99n1, n4, 100n7, n9, n14, 101n19, n20, n23, 102n25, n26, 113n33, n34, n39, n40, 104n46, 115n56, 116n61, 125, 129, 134–136, 137n5, n11, 181, 223, 247n37, n38, n43, n44, 250, 262n6, 263n28; on the public, 204, 247n32, n37, 250–256, 259–261, 262n8, n13, n19, 263n31; on democracy and education, 125, 134–136, 137n4, 138n28, 291; view of experience, 8, 60, 61, 63–71, 73n7, 74n13, n15, n25, n28, 75n44, n46, n51, n54, 87, 90, 247n41, 262n5, n11, 283; view of community and communication, 82, 203, 242–244
Diogenes, 12, 13, 270
Diotima, 152
Diversity, 46, 52, 54, 121n23, 128, 185, 219, 227, 238, 242–245
Douthat, Ross, 293n5
DuBois, W. E. B., 183, 184, 193n10, 194n13
Dussel, Enrique, 129
Dwyer, Jim, 221n26
Dylan, Bob, 123

Eakin, Hugh, 293n6
Earth, 26, 30, 81, 83–86, 89, 92–98, 99n1, 102n24, 106n59, 139, 140, 144, 145, 150–156, 222, 231, 286, 288, 291, 294n17
Eatherly, Claude, 170–172, 176, 180n34
Edmonds, Jeff, 79, 82, 178n12, 179n16, 220n6, 223, 271, 276, 294n29
Emerson, Ralph Waldo, 20, 61, 69, 79, 82, 83, 94, 101n17, 103n31, 104n44, 106n60, 126, 129, 132, 133, 135, 137n6, n11, 138n25, 140–146, 148, 149, 153, 157n9, 158n13–18, 159n37, 179n22
Empathy, 3, 52, 201, 230n7, 231
Enlightenment, 129, 130, 200, 203, 204, 220n2, 280, 281, 284–287, 291
Epistemic comfort and discomfort, 38, 81, 109–117, 120, 121n6, n16, 162, 171, 180n33, 193, 217
Eriugena, John Scotus, 72
Evenson, Renae J., 56n5, 57n29
Exclusions, 82, 108, 112, 117, 205, 254, 255, 282, 285, 287, 290–292

Falk, William W., 57n27
Fanon, Frantz, 205, 286, 287, 289, 294n17

Faulkner, William, 59
Feminism, 25, 34, 120, 193, 201, 214, 251; and feminist blogs, 250, 256-261, 262n24
Fischer, Marilyn, 184, 194n14
Foucault, Michel, 23, 111, 112, 129, 138n17, 262n16
Fraser, Nancy, 24, 25, 34n3, 257, 263n26
Freedom, 5, 10, 24, 28, 29, 32, 44, 48, 52, 54, 116, 129, 268, 269, 273, 277, 280
Freud, Sigmund, 23, 142, 157n5, 157n10
Fullilove, Mindy Thompson, 191, 195n42

Gadamer, Hans-Georg, 60, 73n6, 74n35, 234n21
Galeano, Eduardo, 129
Gans, Christopher, 56n13
Gardiner, S. M., 193, n3
Gatens, Moira, 113, 121n19, n20
Gayman, Cynthia, 44n1, 125, 131, 203, 220n5, 223, 258
Globalization, vii, 3-7, 10-13, 19, 20n3, n5, 22, 25, 26, 30, 31, 48, 50-55, 57n50, 79, 81, 82, 108, 109, 120, 126, 135, 140, 155, 156, 181-185, 190, 192, 193n1, n5, n8, n9, 194n19, 195n40, 199-204, 207, 214, 222, 223, 233n1, 237, 250, 251, 254, 260, 261, 265, 266, 269, 276, 277, 279n58, 281, 284, 288, 293n3, n4
Goethe, Johann Wolfgang von, 67
Goffman, Erving, 28
Goldfarb, Jeffrey, 23, 28, 34n11
Greenfield, Liah, 48, 56n16d
Griffin, Larry J., 56n5, 57n29
Guattari, Felix, 83, 140, 151-153, 159n29, n35

Habermas, Jürgen, 10, 12, 16, 20n1, 253, 263n26, 293n3
Hall, David, 74n32
Hansen, Jennifer, 21n25, 133, 178n12, 179n16, 180n33, 202, 203, 218, 235, 237, 240, 243-245
Hansen, Jonathan, 294n23
Harvey, David, 293n11
Heidegger, Martin, 74n32, 89, 102n24, 139, 224, 230, 234n30
Hegel, G. W. F., 45, 60, 264, 268
Held, David, 19, 20n7, 21n20, 84, 182, 183, 185, 193n6, 246n7, 293n4
Herzog, Werner, 155, 160n43
Hollinger, David, 278n22
Home, vii, 5, 6, 10, 11, 19, 22, 31-34, 37, 50, 51, 71, 79-83, 88, 89, 103n30, 107-111, 113, 114, 116-120, 126, 127, 134, 136, 140, 142, 145-149, 155, 156, 157n4, 158n23, 159n26, n27, 174, 178n12, 179n16, 186-191, 207-219, 220n4, n6, 221n12, 221n18, 233n1, 242, 245, 281-285, 291, 292

Homelessness, vii, 24, 29, 72, 73n3, 79, 100n12, 139, 152, 170, 175, 199-202, 205, 207-219, 230, 245, 246, 287, 292, 295n31
Homer, 30
Hook, Sidney, 243, 247n40
Hope, vii, 24, 55, 62, 84, 123, 126, 133, 145, 153, 170, 173, 174, 180n33, 191, 192, 194n21, 200-202, 206, 288, 289, 291, 292
Hospitality, 5, 12, 22-24, 30-32, 34, 178n12, 203, 210, 235, 236, 238-241, 245, 246, 247n11, 250, 258, 281, 285, 286, 290
Hugo, Victor, 148, 151
Hume, David, 60, 285, 286
Hunt, Larry L., 57n27
Hunt, Matthew O., 57n27

Imagination, viii, 11, 22-25, 34n4, 52, 53, 65, 81, 82, 86, 95, 101n20, 113, 115-117, 120, 121n6, 126, 148, 153, 174, 179n16, 185, 194n16, 201, 210, 211, 213, 220n8, 225, 231, 280, 284, 288, 291
Immigration, vii, 51, 119, 124, 125, 136, 138n30, 199, 203, 283, 293n6
Innis, Robert, 3, 4, 7, 8, 268
Interdependence, 55n1, 83, 84, 109, 115, 159n27, 182, 184, 186, 187, 191
Internationalism, 6, 26, 31, 54, 55, 182, 200, 205, 223, 259; and international law, 30, 33, 193n8; and international rights, 10-12, 281
International of decent feelings, 204, 205, 264-277, 278n16

Jackson, Deborah Davis, 189, 195n33
James, William, 64-68, 71, 79, 83, 88, 90, 95, 96, 99n1, 100n10, n12, n15, 101n8, 112n30, 114n47, n51, 115n53, 116n63, 129, 139, 140, 146, 147, 158n19, 224, 225, 228-230, 233, 234n10, n11, n13, n25-27, n29, n31, 261, 289, 292
Janz, Bruce, 47, 50, 51, 56n5, 57n30
Jaspers, Karl, 264, 266
Johnson, Mark, 185, 194n16, 233n7
Jullien, François, 8, 62-72, 73n3, 74n20, n26, n30, n31, n32, n33, 75n36, n38, n39, n41, n48, n53, n56

Kant, Immanuel, 23, 25, 29-31, 74n35, 83, 84, 102n24, 104n45, 129, 131, 132, 161, 167-169, 175, 178n9, 179n20, 204, 231, 232, 233n4, 236, 238, 241, 270, 271, 275, 278n26, 279n33, 286, 293n3; and perpetual peace, 12, 30, 35n16, 229, 234n35, 235, 239, 270, 281, 285, 302
Kegley, Jacquelyn, 4, 7, 8, 20n8, 276, 288

Kent, Jenny, 188, 195n32
Kim, David, 122n28
King, Steve, 125
Kleingeld, Pauline, 278n23
Koestler, Arthur, 266
Kolbert, Elizabeth, 154, 159n38, 160n42
Koopman, Colin, 251, 262n4
Korsgaard, Christine, 29
Kushner, Tony, 201, 10, 211, 217–219, 220n8
Kymlicka, Will, 56n8, 287, 294n19

Langer, Susanne, 73
Lenin, Vladimir, 32, 264
Leow, Rachel, 262n23
Levi, Primo, 179n18, 180n27, n30
Levinas, Emmanuel, 19, 29, 83, 149, 157, 157n1, n2, 158n23, 201, 211–214, 220n9, 221n20
Lewis, William, 204, 205, 223, 282
Liberalism, 9, 22, 34n3, 48, 56n15, 130, 179n17, 185, 204, 205, 211, 218, 219, 257, 258, 275, 284, 287, 293n5, n6
Locke, John, 50, 285, 286
Lopes, Iñigo, 118
Lysaker, John, 3, 4, 5, 29, 73, 158n14, 208, 219, 223

Machado, Antonio, 123
Malpas, J. E., 57n24, 293n9
Malraux, André, 264, 266
Marcel, Gabriel, 222, 225, 233n2, 234n10, n14, n16, n28
Margalit, Avishai, 48, 56n12
Margolis, Joseph, 58n53, 241, 247n28
Marx, Karl, 23, 32, 129, 131, 264, 276
Marxism, 34n3, 129, 201, 264, 268, 276, 278, 278n18–20
Mauriac, François, 264, 266
McAfee, Noëlle, 4, 5, 6, 7, 8, 21n25, 53, 177n9, 221n22, 223, 235, 237, 242, 271
McKinnon, Catherine, 265
McLuhan, Marshall, 22, 26, 34n1
Medina, José, 56, 81, 82, 98, 126, 178n2, 179n6, 193, 220n6, 252, 253, 262n7, 284
Merleau-Ponty, Maurice, 104n47, 243
Michnik, Adam, 28
Mignolo, Walter, 82, 127–135, 137n10, n13, 185, 190, 194n18, 195n36
Milgram, Stanley, 180n34
Miller, David, 236, 241, 246n7, 247n25
Mills, Charles, 112, 113, 121n13–17
Moore, M., 56n8
Moreno, Isidoro, 118n26

Morrison, Toni, 49, 103n40
Multinationalism, 11, 20n4, 131, 275
Myers, Fred R., 56n20

Nagel, Thomas, 234n22
Nation, 5, 11–13, 30, 31, 33, 34, 45–48, 52, 54–55, 57n35, 127, 184, 189, 200, 240, 242, 250, 260, 288; and national differences, 26, 125, 133, 192, 199, 231, 259, 265; and nationalism, 5, 45–49, 51, 52, 236, 263n28, 274, 280, 287, 292n2, 293n4, 294n23; and nationalist theories, 4, 113, 136, 183
Neville, Robert, 74n32
Nietzsche, Friedrich, 15, 20n12, 138n17
Nussbaum, Martha, 12, 14, 20n5, 42, 43, 47n41, 185, 194n14, 204, 205, 222, 233n4, 234n9, 265, 268, 270–275, 278n24, n26, n27, 279n28, n32, n33

Obama, Barack, 223, 236
Oliver, Kelly, 19
Orosco, Antonio-José, 57n50

Pakovi, A., 56n13
Pascal, Blaise, 139
Peirce, Charles, 65, 66, 69, 70, 75n46, 79, 90–92, 100n16, 102n8, n9, 103n31, n32, n35–37, n39, 214, 221n4
Pereda, Carlos, 3, 4, 6, 7, 8, 21
Petit, Phillipe, 146
Place, vii, 3–8, 20n8, 41, 46–54, 56n3, 49–51, 59, 62, 72, 73n3, 79–93, 95–98, 103n32, 105n55, 107–120, 127–137, 138n27, 139–156, 158n19, 163, 166, 178n12, 191, 194n4, n22, 195n33, n42, n44, 199–202, 204, 205, 208, 210, 212, 215, 216, 226, 262n2, 272, 275, 281–285, 288–292; and climate change, 181–193; and cosmopolitan ignorance, 107–20; and online communities, 156, 214, 216, 249–261; and power, 7, 12, 16, 24, 29–32, 111–120, 145, 152, 170, 187, 189; loss of, 139–156, 157n4, n11, 159n26, n27, 165, 186–190, 220n6, 221n21, 229–232, 274, 275, 281–285
Plato, 72, 278n5
Plotinus, 72
Pluralism, vii, 6, 36, 37, 44, 54, 59, 61, 71, 107, 128, 129, 201, 203, 206, 222, 228, 229, 231–233, 237, 238, 240, 243–245, 251, 288–290, 292, 294n27, 295n30
Pogge, Thomas, 84, 183, 185, 193n9, 260, 263n30
Polasky, Janet, 292n2
Power, vii, 3, 9, 17, 23, 24, 26–28, 32–34, 55, 58n53, 59, 67–69, 80, 112, 121n10, 162, 166, 180n31,

190, 201, 205, 216, 226, 257, 258, 275, 277, 285, 288–300
Pragmatism, 7, 69, 72, 73, 90, 96, 98, 100n12, 105n55, 107, 201, 219, 233n5, 246, 247n40, 278, 292; and John Dewey, 60, 63–71, 203, 251, 261; and William James, 66–71, 104n47, 105, n53, n58; and Charles Peirce, 65, 66, 69, 70, 79, 90–92, 214
Proust, Marcel, 49, 151, 159n28
Provincialism, 54, 57n49, 60, 82, 127, 200, 205–207, 209, 213–218, 280, 281, 287, 288, 290, 291, 294n22
Puryear, Martin, 142
Putnam, Hilary, 47, 48, 56n9

Qaddafi, Muammer, 33

Radan, P., 56n13
Rawls, John, 12, 13, 16–19, 21n15, n18, n21, n23, 168, 179n17, 251
Read, Peter, 56n22
Reed, John Shelton, 49, 57n25
Reid, Alec, 55
Relph, Edward, 294n11
Rittel, Horst, 193n4
Rorty, Richard, 47, 52, 56n9
Royce, Josiah, 7, 46, 47, 53–55, 57n48, 58n51, 95, 100n16, 205, 287, 288, 294n22
Rushdie, Salman, 59

Santayana, George, 60, 87, 91, 94, 97, 98, 100n8, 104n43, 106n64, 201, 209, 210, 216–219, 221n24
Santorum, Rick, 226
Sartre, Jean Paul, 285
Sartwell, Crispin, 18, 62–63, 73n10
Scarry, Elaine, 52, 53, 57n43, 163, 177n3, n4, n6, 178n11
Schapiro, Meyer, 68, 69
Scharfstein, Ben-Ami, 7, 59–61, 71, 72, 73n1
Schelling, Friedrich Wilhelm Joseph, 60
Seel, Martin, 73n11
Shih Ta'o, 69, 75n47
Short, Robert, 279n59
Skrupskelis, Ignas, 263n28
Socrates, 38, 142, 143
Sontag, Susan, 177n1
Stalin, Joseph, 173
Stein, Gertrude, 51, 57n37

Steinbock, Anthony, 234n17, n18
Stendhal (Marie-Henri Beyle), 62, 73n8
Stoics, 12, 13, 203, 204, 222, 231, 232, 233n4, 271, 278n26, 279n33, 285, 287
Striffler, Steve, 136, 138n30
Stuhr, John, 57n50, 73n2, 98, 107–109, 120n4, 158n23, 160n44, 193, 205, 206, 221n16, 223, 233n5, 236, 237, 247n39, 275, 276
Sullivan, Shannon, 111, 112, 121n7, n10, n12, n18, n20, 261
Sundstrom, Ronald, 122n28
Swain, Tony, 56n7

Talisse, Robert, 251, 262n3
Tarver, Erin, 44n1, 204, 221n22, 223, 276
Taylor, Charles, 47, 48, 56n11, n18, 93
Taylor, Paul, 233n1
Telhami, Shibley, 55, 58n53
Terence, 12, 13, 15, 17
Thiebaut, Carlos, 249, 262n2
Thompson, Ashley B., 56n5, 57n29
Thrift, Nigel, 294n11
Torture, 80, 83, 161–166, 170–176, 177n2, n7, n9, 178n11, n14, 179n22, 180n33, 183, 246n5
Tschakert, Petra, 188, 194n28, 195n43
Tuan, Yi-Fu, 195n44, 294n11
Tuana, Nancy, 55n1, 79, 83, 84, 98, 121n7, 128n27, 157n4, 159n27, 223
Tully, James, 128n23
Tuto, Raymond, 188, 194n28

Unamuno, Miguel de, 241, 247n26
Unger, Roberto, 271
Universalism, vii, 3, 133, 199, 203, 206, 216, 240, 259, 271, 282, 286, 287
Universality, 5, 6, 21n13, 28, 39–44, 51, 60, 133, 240–242, 281, 285, 286, 289

Wahman, Jessica, 21n25, 73n3, 158n23, 178n12, 179n16, 201, 203, 217, 222, 236, 245, 295n31
Waldron, Jeremy, 12, 20n7
Webber, Melvin, 193n4
Weil, Simone, 177n5
Whitehead, Alfred North, 22
Whitman, Walt, 133, 145, 158n15
Wittgenstein, Ludwig, 92, 103n38, 111, 141, 262n7
Woolf, Virginia, 181

Young, Neil, 280, 292n1

www.ingramcontent.com/pod-product-compliance
Lightning Source LLC
Chambersburg PA
CBHW021344300426
44114CB00012B/1066